Affective Circuits

Affective Circuits

African Migrations to Europe and the
Pursuit of Social Regeneration

EDITED BY JENNIFER COLE
AND CHRISTIAN GROES

The University of Chicago Press   Chicago and London

JENNIFER COLE is an anthropologist and professor in the
Department of Comparative Human Development at the University of
Chicago. She is the author of *Forget Colonialism* and *Sex and Salvation*
and coeditor of *Love in Africa*, the latter two published by the University
of Chicago Press. **CHRISTIAN GROES** is an anthropologist and
associate professor in the Department of Culture and Identity at
Roskilde University in Denmark. He is the author of *Transgressive
Sexualities* and coeditor of *Studying Intimate Matters*.

The University of Chicago Press, Chicago 60637
The University of Chicago Press, Ltd., London
© 2016 by The University of Chicago
All rights reserved. Published 2016.
Printed in the United States of America

25 24 23 22 21 20 19 18 17 16   1 2 3 4 5

ISBN-13: 978-0-226-40501-8 (cloth)
ISBN-13: 978-0-226-40515-5 (paper)
ISBN-13: 978-0-226-40529-2 (e-book)
DOI: 10.7208/chicago/9780226405292.001.0001

Library of Congress Cataloging-in-Publication Data
Names: Cole, Jennifer, [date] editor. | Groes, Christian, editor.
Title: Affective circuits: African migrations to Europe and the pursuit of
    social regeneration / edited by Jennifer Cole and Christian Groes.
Description: Chicago: The University of Chicago Press, 2016. | Includes
    bibliographical references and index.
Identifiers: LCCN 2016009802 | ISBN 9780226405018 (cloth: alk.
    paper) | ISBN 9780226405155 (pbk.: alk. paper) | ISBN 9780226405292
    (e-book)
Subjects: LCSH: Africans—Kinship—Europe. | Africans—Social
    networks—Europe. | Africans—Europe—Social life and customs.
    | Africans—Europe—Social conditions. | Africa—Emigration and
    immigration—Social aspects.
Classification: LCC DT16.5 .A29 2016 | DDC 305.896/04—dc23 LC
    record available at http://lccn.loc.gov/2016009802

♾ This paper meets the requirements of ANSI/NISO Z39.48-1992
(Permanence of Paper).

Contents

Illustrations

Acknowledgments

Words, Mikhail Bakhtin reminds us, gather history around them, and each word tastes of the contexts in which it has lived. The same can be said of collaborative projects such as this edited collection. The idea for this volume emerged from the conference "Intimate Migrations: Marriage, Sex Work and Kinship in Transnational Migration" that Christian Groes organized at Roskilde University and the Danish Institute for International Studies in the spring of 2013. The book took on its Africanist focus and metamorphosed into its present form in conversation with Jennifer Cole. Together we developed the *affective circuits* framework and asked scholars working on African migration to Europe to engage with the concept in relation to their own research. The collection of essays presented here is the product of that many-sided collaboration.

Much as migrants' journeys are made possible by the support of kin and friends, so too we have depended on the support of many institutions and individuals in bringing *Affective Circuits* to fruition. We had time to research, think, and write together thanks to a generous fellowship from the John Simon Guggenheim Foundation awarded to Jennifer Cole, to a Young Elite Researcher Grant from the Danish Council for Independent Research awarded to Christian Groes. We were able to further develop and elaborate the ideas for this volume in a workshop entitled "Of Love and Family, States and Borders: Comparative Perspectives on Afro-European Couples and Families" that Jennifer Cole and Violaine Tisseau held at the University of Chicago's Paris center in the fall of 2014, which several of this volume's contributors attended. For their help, inspiration, and support along the way, we thank Signe Arnfred, Caroline Bledsoe, Maurice Bloch, Cati Coe, John and Jean Comaroff, Debbie Durham, Nicole Constable, Laura Oso Casas, Nadine Fernandez, Pamela Feldman-Savelsberg, Bolette Frydendahl Larsen, Sasha Newell, Mikkel Rytter, and Ninna Nyberg Sørensen. We are especially grateful for the constructive feedback of Julie Chu, Deborah Durham, Costas Nakassis, Erin Moore, Cati Coe, Pamela Feldman-Savelsberg, and Lynn Thomas on our introductory essay. We also thank the anonymous reviewers for the University of Chicago Press who provided comments on the introduction, the individual chapters, and the book as a whole. Once again, David Brent has proved an excellent editorial guide as well as a tireless champion of African Studies at the University of Chicago Press; working with David and with Ellen Kladky has been a pleasure. Thanks also to Erin Moore for her painstaking work in preparing the volume for publication, to Steve Larue for help with the bibliography, to Linda Forman for her excellent copyediting, and to Kelsey Robbins for her careful reading of the proofs. Our respective families generously allowed us time away from home to work on the project. Last but not least, we wish to acknowledge our tremendous debt to our Malagasy and Mozambican interlocutors who shared their lives and their migration experiences with us. Their ways of thinking about and interacting with the world deeply inform the ideas developed in these pages. Without their kindness, generosity, and insight, this book would not exist.

Introduction: Affective Circuits and Social Regeneration in African Migration

JENNIFER COLE AND CHRISTIAN GROES

In recent years, migration from Africa to Europe has increasingly made headlines. Boats packed with migrants sinking in the Mediterranean, women trafficked as sex workers, and unrest in squatter settlements like the so-called Calais Jungle—these are just some of the ways African migrants have figured in the news of late. In many European countries, the visibility of immigrants and refugees from Africa and, more recently, the Middle East, has been accompanied by the growth of right-wing parties—the National Front in France, the UK Independence Party in Great Britain, and the Alternative for Germany are examples—which often blame immigration for the many problems facing the continent.

In response to these developments, scholars have analyzed the way European immigration laws and bureaucratic practices contribute to many of the problems associated with migration. Some have pointed to the ways various bureaucratic practices aimed at regulating immigration increase state power at the expense of democratic ideals, institutionalize racism, and facilitate the exploitation of migrant labor (Balibar 2004; Carling 2006; Fassin 2005; Rodier 2007; Spire 2008; Ticktin 2011). Others have demonstrated the ways that right-wing parties deploy immigration as a hot-button issue to promote nationalist and xenophobic agendas (De Genova 2013; Gingrich and Banks 2006; Hervik 2004). And still others have illuminated the important role of political movements such as those launched by the *sans papiers* (e.g., undocumented workers, literally "without papers") in France (Balibar et al. 1999; Raissiguier 2010) and by the Danish group Marriage without Borders (Ægteskab uden Grænser; see Olwig 2014), which fight for migrants' rights to residence or family reunification. These kinds of legal and institution-based analyses raise important issues regarding the political and economic stakes of contemporary immigration. But when paired with the public focus on humanitarian disasters and the social tensions associated with migration, they often inadvertently obscure African perspectives. They also pay scant attention to the effects of migration on intimate relations and family life.

This book examines the intimate dimensions of African migration to Europe. We focus especially on the myriad exchanges of goods, people, ideas, and money through which migrants negotiate their social relationships, drawing particular attention to the deeply held sentiments that ride alongside and become a part of these exchanges. We also attend to the ways various actors, including migrants, state officials, and kin seek to facilitate, block, or otherwise control mobility through the resulting social networks. We call the social formations that emerge from the sending, withholding, and receiving of goods, ideas, bodies, and emotions *affective circuits*. Examining practices that range from child fosterage to binational marriage, from coming-of-age to religion and healing, this book's chapters focus on the social processes that shape these circuits and their role in families, social networks, and broader social and cultural formations.

Both historical and contemporary factors make African migration to Europe a particularly salient place to interrogate these processes. Europe's colonization of Africa during the nineteenth and much of the twentieth century means that Africans and Europeans share a long history of entanglement. They were brought together through practices ranging from forced labor and tax collection to concubinage, domestic employment, and conscription into colonial armies, and their relationships sometimes brought Africans to Europe. Africans continued to travel to Europe as students and labor migrants and to build transnational family ties long after decolonization. Although today Africans migrate within Africa and all over the globe, the connections forged with Europeans during the colonial period, and that have continued in new guises since decolonization, make Europe a popular destination.

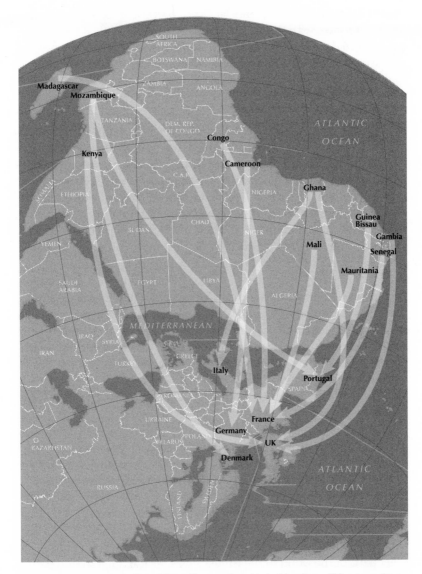

I.I   The migratory streams from Africa to Europe referred to in this volume. This map portrays
       the various migration streams as viewed from the Southern Hemisphere, offering a visual
       representation of what it means to think about African migration to Europe from the
       perspective of Africa. Map by Chicago Cartographics.

In the past twenty years, however, new political and economic arrange-ments associated with the growing pervasiveness of neoliberal capitalism have shifted the terms of interaction. In many parts of Africa, these trans-formations have increased economic hardship. Combined with political instability in some countries, these circumstances have placed enormous strain on families, prompting growing numbers of people to emigrate to seek a better life for themselves and ensure the well-being of their kin. In Europe, by contrast, these same economic and political conditions have led many states to feverishly seek to control their national borders and selectively limit immigration (Brown 2010; Comaroff and Comaroff 2011; De Genova 2013; Geschiere 2009). Whereas in the 1960s and 1970s immigration regulations allowed—and even deliberately encouraged—labor migration, implicitly recognizing the economic needs of both sides, today most European countries have less need for unskilled labor. Instead, most primarily consider family reunification rather than migrants' eco-nomic needs or country quotas (as is partly the case in the United States) in granting visas. Consequently, joining a European spouse or kin who have already obtained citizenship in a European country offers migrants one of the few remaining legal paths to migration and the potential up-ward mobility it brings (Beck and Beck-Gernsheim 2010; Beck-Gernsheim 2007; Charsley 2012; Fernandez 2013). In other words, family ties do not just motivate African migration to Europe. They are also crucial for gaining entry at a time when most European countries have put an end to work visas for unskilled migrants from non-Western nations. This regulatory shift draws particular attention to the nexus of migration, kinship, and intimate relations.

In their broad outlines, these circumstances characterize transnational migration in many parts of the world, raising the question of what if any-thing is peculiar to transnational African migration as it intersects with the conditions created by family-centered immigration regulations. The answer, we argue, lies in the way Africans have long adapted their kin-ship practices and even coming-of-age to facilitate mobility. Like the well-documented immigration flows from Mexico, the Philippines, and other parts of the world to the United States, African migration is partly a response to global economic restructuring. Like U.S.-bound migrants, Africans too seek to move across borders so that they can sustain their families who stay behind. And like these other migrants, they make ar-rangements to care for their children, forge romantic liasions, or adjust their relationships with kin or friends as they adapt to their new circum-stances. Unlike other migrants, however, many Africans hail from contexts in which mobility has long been central to the constitution of cosmology and social organization (see also Kopytoff 1987; Mains 2007; Newell 2005; Jónsson 2012; Manchuelle 1997; Whitehouse 2013). As a result, in contrast to much of the writing on kinship and migration, which emphasizes how transnational migration radically disrupts a range of social practices from marriage to gender relations and parent-child dynamics (Boehm 2012; Dreby 2010; Freeman 2011; Hirsch 2003; Parreñas 2005a), the essays in this volume collectively suggest that Africans draw on long-standing practices as they confront the new circumstances created by transnational migration. They also adapt and transform existing practices.

Our analysis of the exchanges through which Africans negotiate their intimate relationships makes two contributions to the study of immigration. With respect to African migration to Europe specifically, it offers an alternative to the narrative of crisis, suffering, and exclusion that dominates contemporary depictions. Despite the desperate lengths to which many people go to reach Europe, getting there is never an end in itself. Rather, African migration to Europe is a means to an end that often exceeds Europe as both a geographic space and a set of opportunities and ideals (whether or not migrants physically remain in Europe). Most people's journeys entail moral obligations toward kin and community back home or a desire to break free from these attachments (Lucht 2011; Plambech 2014). European states seek to limit migration to be sure (Streiff-Fénart and Segatti 2014). But migrants constantly adapt to or bypass these efforts in order to achieve their own goals (Kane and Leedy 2013). Many African migrants do manage to make lives for themselves in Europe despite enormous challenges. How they do so and the consequences for their kin ties and intimate relationships need to be considered alongside the suffering that so often captures both scholarly and public attention.

With respect to the study of migration more generally, the approach developed here provides a means of integrating the "sending" and "receiving" poles of transnational migration into a single frame. Scholars generally agree that transnational migration is not a one-way phenomenon and that those who leave often maintain connections to their homelands despite their absence, move back and forth between different countries, or eventually return home (Glick Schiller, Basch, and Blanc-Szanton 1992; Katz 2001). Nonetheless, only recently have the different poles of the migration equation begun to appear within the same analytic framework.[1] The attention to either the sending or the receiving context partly reflects the legacy of "methodological nationalism" (Wimmer and Glick Schiller 2002)—that is, the tendency to analyze migration from the perspective of the nation-state. It is also a result of the considerable diffi-culties associated with understanding multiple cultural, economic, and political contexts simultaneously. Yet both contemporary developments and the long history of Afro-European interconnections point to the im-portance of keeping an intercontinental focus and engaging across African and European field sites.

By attending to affective circuits—that is, the social networks that emerge from the exchange of goods, ideas, people, and emotions—the essays presented here encompass both sending and receiving contexts and draw attention to the interstices between countries, continents, and kin groups. All of the contributors to this volume have done multisited fieldwork in Africa and in Europe. Collectively, they show that the story of African migration does not begin in one nation and end definitively in another. Nor does it occur along clearly delineated paths such as work migration, marriage migration, or family migration, categories that are commonly used to frame analyses. It is an ongoing process that involves many different kinds of exchange, as migrants continually strive to re-generate and rework their intimate relations. Approaching these trans-national exchanges in terms of affective circuits opens up new ways of thinking about migration—in which the search for marriage or ties to kin can sometimes replace the search for work, sending photos and money can evoke powerful emotions or fulfill moral obligations, and joining a Pentecostal church or taking one's baby to the doctor can establish new ties of belonging.

Social Regeneration and Affective Circuits

In foregrounding migrant families and social networks, this volume joins a growing body of work that examines migration in relation to contempo-rary social reproduction, a term that generally refers to the different "ac-tivities and relationships involved in maintaining people both on a daily basis and intergenerationally" (Nakano Glenn 1992, 1). Much research that takes up the question of social reproduction builds on Marxist femi-nist insights into the tension between productive and reproductive labor. Studies in this vein argue that contemporary capitalism geographically separates production in the labor force from the social reproduction of families, effectively transferring wealth to places where migrants work (Katz 2001). Rhacel Parreñas (2001), for example, describes how Filipina women who go to Europe or the United States find employment as cooks, cleaners, and nannies for wealthier women who move into more highly paid jobs in the workforce. Migrant women in turn send their wages home to meet the needs of their own family members. In the contemporary translocal service economy, Arlie Hochschild (2003) argues, care is the new surplus value siphoned off from poorer countries to wealthier ones (see also Ginsburg and Rapp 1995; Kofman 2012; Nakano Glenn 1992; Parreñas 2001; Yeates 2012).

The importance of money transfers and global social and economic inequalities notwithstanding, it is also crucial to place the exchanges between migrants and their kin within the context of larger cultural frameworks and social dynamics (Åkesson 2011; Munn 1986; Parry and Bloch 1989; Weiner 1980). To that end, the chapters in this book examine the interaction between migrants' personal trajectories and broader political and economic structures, emphasizing the flexible nature of migrants' efforts to help their families. Collectively, they pay particular attention to the ways migrants honor, resist, or redefine inherited notions of social obligation as they reproduce, contest, and transform their social relations and cultural norms through different kinds of exchange, and they consider the ways other actors intervene in this process. Following Cole and Durham (2007, 17), we subsume these processes under the rubric of *social regeneration* to convey that they entail continuity as much as change.

We deliberately use "circuits" as a metaphor rather than "chains" (Hochschild 2000) or "flows" (Appadurai 1996) to capture the circular movements of people and resources both among migrants in Europe and between migrants in Europe and their kin or friends who remain in Africa. Many studies of transnational migration point to the central role of remittances—that is, the money and goods that migrants abroad send to their kin back home. Although the money and goods that migrants in Europe send to their kin in Africa are certainly important, so too are the medicines, photos, phone calls, and foodstuffs that kin at home send to their family members abroad (Abranches 2014). The circuit metaphor highlights this bidirectional movement.

Equally important, however, the circuit metaphor captures the potential for disconnection and conflict: it implies that the social networks through which objects, ideas, and people move are subject to regulation, slow downs, and blockage. State actors operating in concert with European immigration laws sometimes serve as circuit breakers, making it hard for people either to establish themselves in Europe or to move back and forth, with important consequences for migrants and their kin. Albeit powerful, state policies are not the only forces that regulate affective circuits. Kin, friends, peers, and lovers also seek to block, manage, or encourage exchanges for different reasons. The circuit metaphor, then, draws attention to multiple, overlapping dimensions of political and social control exercised by different agents operating at different levels.

We qualify these circuits as "affective" to capture the way the transactions that constitute them often combine material and emotive elements simultaneously such that love, obligation, and jealousy become entangled with the circulation of money, consumer goods, ideas, and information. Several recent studies have distinguished between the terms *affect* and *emotion* or *sentiment,* arguing that whereas *emotion* connotes particular moral meanings and individual intentions, *affect* refers to the sensations that precede formal cultural narration (Berlant 2011; Massumi 2002; Mazzarella 2010). Though informed by these discussions, we prefer to retain the ambiguity intrinsic to the colloquial use of the latter term, pointing to the way affective circuits make possible, and carry with them, specific culturally and historically elaborated emotions and potentialities, whether love, pride, shame, or jealousy, as well as the material manifestations of these feelings. The term *affective circuits* also usefully captures the inchoate ways that exchanges can themselves "affect" social ties, as the Deleuzian line of argumentation suggests, sometimes generating flows of energy and objects that exceed the boundaries of individual bodies and attach them to each other, at other times leaving bodies isolated and alone (cf. Deleuze and Guattari 1987).

Much as Marcel Mauss ([1950] 2000) argued that every gift carries with it traces of the giver, so too, the notion of affective circuits gestures toward the way material gifts (money, photos, herbs) carry with them traces of the relationship between sender and recipient, whether a spirit, a memory, or a social obligation owed. Likewise, immaterial gifts (such as a voice on the phone, a piece of advice, an amorous touch, a childhood memory of care) may in turn trigger the obligation to provide material gifts. Affective circuits involve sensory stimuli, such as the sight of a mother putting food on the table or the glimpse of a loved one's picture on a nightstand, that may evoke a migrant's debts to home. They also entail actions, such as a mother receiving cash from her daughter through Western Union or a woman shutting off her cell phone so she won't have to respond to her brother's demands. In affective circuits, the emotive elements of social relations combine with money and material goods, moving reciprocally or unequally between groups of kin, among friends, and between continents. In some cases, migrants may reinforce shared values and a shared sense of belonging through these exchanges. At other times, they may avoid, transform, or divert exchanges, perhaps transforming old relationships or creating new attachments in the process, as several chapters show.

Elaborating on these ideas, the contributors to this volume make three overlapping arguments with respect to how affective circuits operate in African migration to Europe. First, these circuits emerge from people's efforts to reposition themselves as nodal centers in wider networks of exchange, a process that is closely tied to migrants' efforts to achieve valued forms of personhood. Second, different conceptions of marriage and parent-child relations, both those enshrined in European laws and those migrants bring with them, underpin these circuits and influence actors' efforts to make or break them. Third, these circuits are gendered: men and women become emplaced within affective circuits in different ways. Before developing these arguments more fully, we examine the context in which contemporary African migration to Europe unfolds.

African Migration to Europe in the New Millennium

In their thoughtful essay on the emergence of migratory expectations in Africa, Knut Graw and Samuli Schielke (2012) ask why so many Africans want to leave Africa now. After all, while studies of African societies have long alluded to the importance of mobility, including long-distance trade, rural-urban labor migration, and movement stemming from fission within social groups and even from war, an intense desire to migrate to Europe, visible across social classes, is a relatively recent development. It was only around the turn of the millennium and shortly after that scholars and writers working *within* Africa began to consistently note both Africans' growing migratory aspirations and the expanding importance of having kin who lived in Europe or the United States. In *Expectations of Modernity*, James Ferguson (1999) used the term *abjection* to capture Zambians' sense of having been expelled from what they had assumed was a secure place within the modern world system. Only a few years later, similar kinds of characterizations, coupled with expressions of the desire to emigrate or to have kin who had done so, began to appear regularly in novels and popular writing about Africa. During a trip to visit her kin in Sierra Leone in the late 1990s, the British Sierra Leonean writer Aminatta Forna (2002, 298) was struck by the crucial importance of having kin abroad. "The more people I spoke to," she noted, "the more I realized that this had become the new measure of wealth in Sierra Leone: Not land, not goats or wives, and certainly not *leones* [the local currency]. No, a son or daughter who had successfully emigrated to the west was all that mattered." So too, numerous recent ethnographies depict Africans' search for paths abroad, whether by winning a visa lottery, finding a European spouse, or other, usually clandestine, routes (Cole 2014a, 2014b; Ferguson 2006; Groes-Green 2014; Johnson-Hanks 2007; Lucht 2011; Piot 2010; Venables 2008).

Given that Africans have long moved within the continent and that some Africans have also sojourned in Europe for military service, work, or higher education, why did African migration to Europe become such a visible social issue around the turn of the millennium? Part of the answer surely lies in the way European states have problematized immigration, constituting migrants and immigration more generally as social issues that they can then intervene in and control (Foucault 1997). But the heightened visibility is also likely tied to the ways that the structural adjustment policies of the 1980s and 1990s transformed everyday life and the ability to earn livelihoods across urban Africa.

Instituted by the World Bank and the International Monetary Fund in response to the debt crisis in Latin America, these economic policies sought to reduce African debt and minimize state control of the economy so as to encourage foreign investment. To do so, they compelled African countries to enact severe austerity measures to qualify for loans. As a result of these measures, states drastically reduced the value of local currencies and withdrew from public projects, including housing and schooling (Taylor, Watts, and Johnston 2002). In Senegal, Cameroon, and Madagascar, to take three examples relevant to this book, household revenues dropped by almost 50 percent between 1961 and 1991, while the gross national product declined by about 38 percent during roughly the same period (Antoine, Razafindrakoto, and Roubaud 2001). Although by the late 1980s there were many more people educated past secondary school than there had been at independence, the destructuring of national economies made state employment difficult for educated Africans to find (Hanlon and Smart 2010). Today in Ethiopia, unemployment rates for youth with a secondary education hover at around 50 percent (Mains 2012), and some estimates place youth unemployment in Mozambique at close to 60 percent (Brenthurst Foundation 2011, 14). The devaluation of state currencies has meant that those young people lucky enough to find jobs are increasingly poorly paid and unable to sustain the lifestyle to which they aspire.

These patterns of economic growth and employment, or lack thereof, vary across the continent. Nigeria and Kenya—to name two of the most evident economic success stories—have growing economies that appear to be fueling new patterns of consumption and a rising middle class (Kulish 2014). Some Portuguese citizens have begun to return to the former Portuguese colonies of Angola and Mozambique to escape economic austerity in Portugal (Smith 2012). Emerging forms of art and culture also testify to vibrant pockets of growth across the continent (Lee 2014). Nevertheless, for the vast majority of people, the growth celebrated in the *Wall Street Journal* or the *New York Times* has not smoothed the jagged edges of economic inequality, the suffering that occurs because of civil conflict, or the desire to find alternative paths to the kinds of futures that success stories and images of Western wealth inspire.

Movement and Becoming: Mobility and the Quest for Personhood

Although unequal economic growth and ongoing hardship are facts of life across the African continent and civil conflict has flared in the Congo and more recently in Mali and the Central African Republic, emigration is not simply a result of these circumstances. Economic theories that tie "push" and "pull" factors to labor markets or political crises are too general to illuminate the complexity and contextual meaning of people's journeys, as many of this book's chapters show. African migration to Europe is not merely a reaction to poverty and unemployment or a result of better job or educational opportunities in the global north.

Most analyses of migration that rely on push-pull models take for granted the individual, often conceived as a rational actor, as the primary unit of analysis. By contrast, conceptualizing migration in terms of affective circuits draws attention to the dynamic ways people are enmeshed in myriad social ties, influences, and obligations (see also Chu 2010). Thinking about migration from the perspective of more inclusive social groupings rather than the typical individual-state dyad is useful in many contexts, as efforts to develop analyses that focus on family networks show (Boyd 1989). But it is particularly pertinent to our concerns given that in many African settings, persons are conceived of as nodes in systems of relationships defined by mutual assistance and asymmetrical exchanges. In this conception, personhood emerges at the intersection between individual ambitions, on the one hand, and obligations to wider social networks, on the other. Pointing to personhood as something that is achieved gradually as one realizes oneself through relations with others, John Comaroff and Jean Comaroff (2001, 272) propose the concept of "being-as-becoming," while Charles Piot (1999, 18) tartly remarks that in many African contexts, people do not "have" social relations, they "are" their social relations. Ideally, an individual's achievement of personhood and the broader social regeneration of families intertwine.

It has typically been the case, however, that to successfully extend one's social influence and achieve valued forms of personhood, people engage in various kinds of asymmetrical exchange. In the precolonial past, when land was plentiful and labor was scarce, leaders sought to accrue "wealth in people"; labor provided the currency through which hierarchical relations of patronage were made (Guyer 1993; Miers and Kopytoff 1977). Over the course of the colonial period, administrators sought to free labor from the constraints of family and kinship, imposing taxes to compel people to participate in the cash economy (Cooper 1997). Despite their efforts, older ties of kinship and patronage continue to shape access to jobs and other resources (Bayart 1993; Ferguson 2013) as well as opportunities for migration (Groes-Green 2014). As economies have been transformed, the currency of community membership and social status has also changed, becoming increasingly tied to people's ability to display and consume commodities and associate themselves with other signs of modern status (Rowlands 1996). Fewer opportunities in formal labor markets, however, mean that people increasingly seek opportunities for social mobility in the informal economy. These circumstances leave many struggling to generate income, consume, and invest in their social relations (Makhulu, Buggenhagen, and Jackson 2010).

Men and women, young and old, experience this predicament differently. Unemployment and economic hardship undermine male authority, long premised on men's ability to provide for their dependents (Groes-Green 2012; Hunter 2010; Lindsey and Meischer 2003; L. Thomas 2003). Men's inability to fulfill their role as providers directly affects those who rely on them, often making women and children especially vulnerable. It has also become harder for young people to acquire the resources that enable them to marry and establish a new household, the traditional marker of adulthood in many places (Cole 2010; Comaroff and Comaroff 2005; De Boeck and Honwana 2005; Durham 2004; Mains 2013; Masquelier 2005; Weiss 2009). Many African youth feel stuck, frustrated by their inability to progress toward adulthood (Hansen 2005; Honwana 2012; Vigh 2006b). This feeling is particularly widespread among young men, as mass unemployment and the feminization of informal economies converge to make it harder for them to achieve a breadwinner role or fulfill long-standing ideals of masculinity (Francis 2002; Groes-Green 2009; Silberschmidt 2005).

In response, people seek alternative ways to prosper and attain normative life trajectories, transforming social norms in the process. In many countries, women increasingly participate in the transactional sexual economy of urban and peri-urban areas, sometimes forming relationships with Europeans who travel to Africa for work or pleasure (Cole 2004; Cornwall 2002; Fouquet 2007a; Groes-Green 2013; Hunter 2002; Leclerc-Madlala 2003; Newell 2009).[2] Young men may try to join patrimonial networks mobilized in war or turn to petty trade, theft, and hustling as a way to claim new kinds of masculinity that defy middle-class norms and conceptions (Agadjanian 2005; Groes-Green 2010; Hoffman 2011; Honwana 2012; Mains 2007, 2012; Newell 2012; Peters and Richards 1998; Rodriquez 2015; Vigh 2006a). Still other young people learn to represent themselves in particular ways in order to accommodate themselves to the demands of the NGO economy (Moore n.d.), perhaps becoming "youth for life" (Brummel 2015) so they can tap into new networks and opportunities brought by NGOs from abroad. And from among the options available to them in their search for success, some choose emigration.

Viewed from this perspective, transnational migration is one among many possible ways people across Africa seek to achieve full personhood (see also Fioratta 2015). As Henrik Vigh's chapter powerfully illustrates, the desire to "become somebody," that is, to be recognized by one's peers as capable of caring for others, prompts young men from Guinea-Bissau to undertake their dangerous journeys to Portugal as drug mules. Similarly, the young Malian men in Julie Kleinman's chapter set out for Paris on an "adventure," a heroic journey they hope will make them a "big somebody," that is, someone on whom others depend. And the Malagasy and Mozambican women featured in Jennifer Cole's and Christian Groes's chapters leave home with European lovers or husbands because they want to become "considered" or "a person," which means being able to enjoy what they perceive to be modern standards of living *and* help their families at the same time.

The way tensions between individual desires and collective demands animate affective circuits is partly captured by Jonathan Parry and Maurice Bloch's (1989) argument about the relationship between different moralities and cycles of exchange. According to their framework, individual acquisition, accumulation, and spending in a world of commerce and competition characterize short-term cycles of exchange. By contrast, long-term cycles of exchange reproduce the collective social and cosmic order in a particular community or social unit. The two transactional orders intertwine and feed off one another, since the long-term cycle depends on individuals' short-term acquisitions through jobs, hustling, and illicit practices of accumulation. These short-term, self-interested practices are only acceptable, Parry and Bloch contend, when they are subordinated to the reproduction of the broader social unit.

Applied to the context of migration, this type of analysis suggests that Africans who seek their fortune in Europe ideally do so within a short-term cycle that is constantly mediated and held in check by their transmission of gifts and money to kin in Africa, thereby fueling affective circuits and satisfying long-term ancestral obligations. Pamela Kea's chapter on how Gambian parents in London manage their relationships with children they have fostered with kin back in the Gambia provides a striking illustration of how these exchanges sustain long-standing ideals of parent-child relations. The migrant parents send money, clothes, bicycles, backpacks, and Gameboys to their children in part to perform responsible parenthood, while their children and their caretakers respond via Viber or Skype with photos showing them using those very items. This exchange of goods and photos, Kea argues, enables geographically separated parents and children to (re)perform their respective roles as providers and dependents as they seek to achieve the idealized model of intergenerational reciprocity that underpins Mandinka conceptions of kinship and personhood.

These positive effects notwithstanding, the expectations of reciprocity that sustain long-term cycles and ideally motivate these kinds of exchanges have a dark side as well, especially because those who fail to subordinate their individual desires to long-term cycles of exchange may be sanctioned, as Parry and Bloch (1989) observe. This dark side emerges, for example, in Carolyn Sargent and Stéphanie Larchanché's chapter on the flows of medicines and medical advice between Malians in Paris and their kin back home. Although they, like Kea, emphasize the solidarity-enhancing nature of the exchanges, it is notable that several of the patients mentioned in their case studies suffer from illnesses inflicted by jealous kin, revealing the social tensions integral to this dynamic. The threat of spiritual sanctions is also clearly part of what animates affective circuits among the Mozambican and Malagasy women depicted respectively in Groes's and Cole's chapters. The Mozambican women who accompany their lovers to Europe ultimately tend to subordinate their own needs to their obligation to support their mothers, while the Malagasy women feel compelled to return to Madagascar and participate in expensive ancestral ceremonies, in part because they fear they will suffer ancestral wrath if they do not.

Although these cultural dynamics motivate migrants' efforts to maintain affective circuits in some cases, whether and how people participate in exchanges varies. Sanctions such as ancestral wrath may encourage participation, but they do not guarantee compliance, as several of the chapters show. For example, the Malagasy women in Cole's chapter deliberately

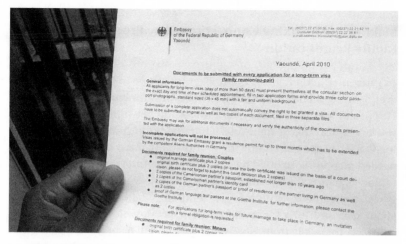

1.2 A young Cameroonian woman reading the official guidelines for family reunification, Berlin 2014. Family reunification provides one of the few remaining ways that migrants can gain legal entry and citizenship in European states. As a result, state authorities closely scrutinize demands for entry based on marriage or adoption. Photo by Elizabeth Beloe.

short-circuit exchanges and disrupt the flow of goods, care, and information by turning off their cell phones in France to avoid communicating with those at home and by planning the layout of their houses in Madagascar to better control their interactions with needy kin. Similarly, the Kenyan migrants depicted in Leslie Fesenmyer's chapter sometimes resist their kin's demands by adopting Pentecostal conceptions of personhood that emphasize possessive individualism. While one cannot assume that the length of time migrants have spent in Europe automatically leads to closer alignment with European models or to the attenuation of family ties, it is striking that both of these chapters deal with cases in which the migrants in question have lived in Europe for many years—the Malagasy women in Cole's chapter have been married to their French husbands for some time, while many of the Kenyan migrants in Fesenmyer's chapter came to Britain as students and grew into adulthood there. These examples remind us that the practices through which migrants constitute personhood and the conceptions of personhood that shape their efforts to build affective circuits are neither fixed nor incommensurable with European models (see Lambek and Strathern 1998). Rather, migrants use and negotiate new meanings of personhood "in *action* and *interaction*" with others (Jackson and Karp 1990, our emphasis) as they rework their intimate relations from abroad.

Making and Breaking Connections: The Promise and Perils of Family Reunification

To gain entry and establish themselves in Europe in the first place, however, aspiring migrants must engage with the immigration regulations of European states. Before the 1980s, migration between Africa and Europe was largely seasonal or rotational labor migration, and it was overwhelmingly male. In the years following World War II, many countries in Europe needed manpower to build national infrastructures and run factories. In response, national governments created guest-worker programs that allowed companies to hire men on temporary labor contracts. Between about 1945 and 1972, for example, French companies offered temporary contracts to people from North Africa and Mali to build roads, bridges, and buildings (Schain 2008). Great Britain recruited labor primarily from the West Indies and then from the Indian subcontinent, but many migrants also came from its African colonies (Bailkin 2012). In the 1960s and 1970s, Germany and Denmark ran guest-worker programs that facilitated the immigration of people from Turkey and North Africa to help build infrastructure and to work in industry (Lucassen 2005).[3] Following the oil crisis of 1972, this pattern began to change as contracting economies lessened European states' need for foreign labor. Great Britain and France, which had historically welcomed the largest numbers of foreign workers, halted the influx of temporary labor migrants, while Germany limited the number of guest workers it accepted. Generally, immigration policies across Europe moved from a regulatory logic based on labor to one focused on family reunification (Weil 2005).

Though premised on the right to family life, which is considered a universal human right, the laws and bureaucratic practices that underpin current European immigration regulations deploy conceptions of marriage and family that are far from neutral in their implications for transnational marriage and family reunification. To the contrary, they draw on culturally and historically specific ideas and practices and can thus be used selectively to influence the flow of migrants. Most European countries take companionate, monogamous marriage, which presumes the emotional and psychological unity of two individuals as opposed to the more heterogeneous material and social interests of families, as the norm (Hirsch and Wardlow 2006; Povinelli 2006). They also presume that blood and birth are primary for establishing filiation, just as a combination of blood and birth establish national belonging (and indeed just as the word *nation* comes from the Latin word *natio*, meaning "to give birth" [Herzfeld 1997]).

"Metaphorically," as Jessaca Leinaweaver (2013, 7) observes, "sharing the same nationality means being part of the same family." In conferring citizenship, most European states use the principle of jus sanguinis, which grants nationality through shared blood, as one of the main criteria, alongside jus soli, or being born in a particular territory (Brubaker 1992).[4] Aspiring migrants, like Europeans, also see kinship connections as central to belonging. But they sometimes draw on alternative ways of organizing kinship and configuring intimate relations, as many of the chapters show.

These potentially different conceptions of kinship notwithstanding, migrants were generally able to use family reunification policies to obtain entry and even citizenship in many European countries until the beginning of the millennium. Since then, however, most European states have sought to limit migration that occurs through family reunification. To borrow the terms used in recent French political debates, many states want immigration that is "chosen" (*choisi*) according to the needs of national economies rather than "suffered" (*subi*), the word French politicians use to depict migration determined by families (Cette France-là 2010). Consequently, state officials seek ways to limit the second type of immigration. In some countries, such as France, government directives encourage the slow processing of family reunification dossiers to reduce the number of people who gain entry (Ferran 2008), creating long delays that further divide—perhaps even break—families (see also Boehm 2012; Dreby 2010 for examples from the United States). They also deliberately deploy conceptions of marriage and kinship to limit immigration, making understandings of gender and family integral to the boundaries of the new Europe (Bledsoe and Sow 2011; E. Fassin 2010; Ticktin 2011). For example, to limit the number of marriage visas they distribute, European government officials deliberately demonize foreign spouses as unscrupulous gold diggers who profit from their European wives or husbands and the broader welfare system (*Le Monde* 2009; Les Amoureux au ban public 2008; Maskens 2013; Neveu Kringelbach 2013b; Wray 2011). They also use DNA tests to establish filiation when considering demands for family reunification, thereby restricting what counts as a parent-child relationship to a particular biologically based definition (Fassin 2009).

Although contemporary public discourse in many European countries, especially England, Denmark, and France, portrays binational marriage negatively, scholarly analyses offer more nuanced interpretations of how marriage articulates with state efforts to selectively control who enters and under what conditions. In contrast to popular perceptions and public discourse, many studies reveal the complex material and emotional entanglements that characterize these marriages, as they do marriage in any context (Constable 2003; Parreñas 2011). They also demonstrate how European efforts to regulate binational marriages potentially insinuate themselves into the lives of binational couples (Cole 2014c; Robledo 2011) and create new kinds of vulnerability as well as unexpected contradictions (Fernandez and Jensen 2014; Raissiguier 2010; Whithol Wenden and De-Ley 1986), a process that the three chapters on marriage and intimate male-female relationships confirm.

The contradictory effects of state efforts to regulate marriage migration and the way they shape migrants' efforts to build and maintain affective circuits is especially visible in Hélène Neveu Kringelbach's discussion of Senegalese men's migration to France. Once they marry, these men experience enormous pressure to materially support their families, and meeting this obligation often prompts them to emigrate. These men soon find, however, that the only way for them to legally move between France and Senegal, thereby maintaining their affective circuits and fulfilling their obligations to kin, is to marry a French woman. In response, they draw on Senegalese conceptions of and practices associated with marriage and family life, particularly polygamy, which has historically facilitated mobility within Senegal. Some of the men depicted in Neveu Kringelbach's chapter have long fantasized about marrying a white French woman as part of a grander migratory project. Others see themselves as belonging to a modern, Dakarian elite and want so-called modern love (Wardlow and Hirsch 2006). They take second wives with reluctance, doing so only because marriage to a French citizen offers the only way for them to fulfill their obligations to kin in Senegal. Ironically, French efforts to reduce paths to migration, which also block affective circuits, may encourage the very practices of polygamy that French policymakers decry.

In addition to indexing different social arrangements, conceptions of marriage and family bring with them different moralities of exchange—that is, ideas about who should give what kinds of gifts to whom and with what kinds of expectations for reciprocity. The way different moralities of exchange shape affective circuits emerges particularly sharply in the chapters by Cole and Groes, both of which analyze female migrants' intimate relationships with European men. Cole's chapter focuses on Malagasy women who have married Frenchmen and settled in France, while Groes's chapter examines Mozambican women who migrate with their Danish or Portuguese partners. The women in both cases expect their boyfriends or husbands to reciprocate their love and care with gifts and other kinds of financial support. Indeed, in both Madagascar and Mozambique, accumulating material and social resources through intimate relations with men is one way women can reposition themselves within local networks of exchange and gain status (Cole 2010, 2014a; Groes-Green 2013). While both Malagasy and Mozambican women see these relationships and their migration to France as a way to socially reposition themselves and fulfill long-standing material and moral obligations to their natal families, their Danish, French, and Portuguese partners are often less than enthusiastic about sharing household resources with their wives' extended kin, a point that emerges in Cole's analysis of how women mediate between their French and Malagasy kin networks. European men may also try to control their wives, perhaps demanding that they behave like traditional housewives, increasing women's financial and social dependence and preventing them from pursuing their own ideals of freedom and womanhood, as Groes's chapter shows.

Malagasy and Mozambican women handle this dilemma differently, revealing that migrants build and manage affective circuits in distinctive ways depending on their own circumstances and goals. In Cole's chapter, for example, we see how wives respond to their husbands' reluctance to invest money in Madagascar by expertly managing the flow of information to create particular impressions, a mode of regulating affective circuits they also seek to use with their kin. They rely especially on the control of social space and the performance of a modern identity, embodied most concretely in the layout of the houses they build in Madagascar. Mozambican women, who have not been in Europe as long as their Malagasy counterparts, tend to actively "resist marriage," preferring to risk their immigration status rather than forego their responsibilities to their kin back home. They appear much more willing than Malagasy women to adopt strategies such as maintaining relationships with multiple partners or combining the support received from partners with part-time work. Additionally, they tend to return to Mozambique once they have accumulated enough resources rather than move between the two places as the Malagasy women ideally seek to do. In both cases, however, conceptions of the proper behavior and moral commitments that define marriage or intimate relations and how these relationships affect one's commitments to kin help shape the circuits in which the women participate.

Much as conceptions of marriage simultaneously offer both a means to forge connections and a means to break them, conceptions of parent-child relations play an important role in the construction, maintenance, or blockage of affective circuits and the kinds of belonging they enable. Take, for example, Cati Coe's discussion of Italian soccer star Mario Balotelli. Born to Ghanaian immigrants in Italy, Balotelli was placed in foster care with a white Italian family. As a young man, Balotelli decided to disown his Ghanaian family and take Italian citizenship. His Ghanaian birth parents claimed they placed their son in foster care because of their difficult living conditions when they first arrived in Italy. Never intending to sever their relationship with him permanently, they continued to visit him while he was small. In his public statements, Balotelli tells a different story, claiming that his parents abandoned him in a hospital at the tender age of two and only sought to reclaim him after he had acquired both fame and fortune. Rather than maintain relationships with his Ghanaian and Italian parents, along with the different identities that these relationships provided, Balotelli chose to cut off his relationship with his birth parents, formalize his relationship to his foster parents, and define himself as entirely Italian.

Balotelli's biological parents likely drew on conceptions of parenting that are prevalent in Ghana and many parts of Africa according to which children belong to multiple mothers and fathers. Temporary placement of a child with another family—what is usually referred to as fosterage—has long been a stategy Ghanaian parents use to create new opportunities for their children without breaking the original biological relationship (Bledsoe 1990; Coe 2013; Goody 1982). It is part of how people thicken their social networks and multiply their social connections to expand their social prospects. By contrast, European conceptions generally figure the parent-child relationship as dyadic, occurring only between the biological parents and offspring rather than distributed among multiple caretakers. As a result, the legal mechanisms that enable people other than the biological parents to care for children rely on an "as-if-begotten" model, limiting the number of caretakers. Such conceptions of the child-parent relationship effectively curtail migrants' efforts to build affective circuits through their children, whether with other citizen families or their kin back home.

It is important to note, however, that just as the European ideals of marriage enshrined in immigration regulations sometimes enable migrants to gain entry and at other times are used against them, so too the conceptions of proper parent-child relationships embodied in European law and public institutions may enable migrant parents to establish new European-based connections through their children. For example, Pamela Feldman-Savelsberg's chapter on Cameroonian mothers in Germany shows how the birth of a child entitles the mother to certain benefits, setting off a cascade of interactions with officials. An expectant mother must contact her employer's office to schedule maternity leave, register the child's birth, and sign up for day-care vouchers and various other parental benefits. All of these interactions enable the exchange of goods, ideas, sentiments, and so forth. Moreover, if a migrant mother or her child's father has lived in Germany for more than eight years, the child is eligible for German citizenship, which may in turn confer citizenship on the mother. In this case, the understanding of parent-child relations embodied in European law promotes migrant Cameroonian women's integration into German society, albeit tentatively, while the difficulties of maintaining certain traditional birth practices far from kin weakens their ties to home.

Moreover, as Fesenmeyer's chapter on Kenyan migrants who convert to Pentecostalism illustrates, the adoption of new kinscripts may shape the way migrants manage affective circuits and reconfigure their connections with their kin. According to Pentecostal ideologies of family, Christians should privilege spousal relationships and parent-child ties over those with extended kin, much as the conception of family enshrined in European family reunification implies. Pentecostal discourse furthermore espouses a Christian conception of love that separates, rather than combines, love's material and immaterial dimensions (Cole 2009). Consequently, Pentecostal preachers promote a notion of relatedness that disentangles the moral and material dimensions of kinship. When family members in Kenya demand material aid, which they see as proof of their relatives' love for them, their migrant kin in London say they prefer to provide "assistance but not support." Rather than break off social relations entirely, they draw on the scripts offered by Pentecostal preachers to transform what relatedness means so that they can "love" their families without sending money home.

Gendered Emplacement and Parakinship

Although both men and women build and participate in affective circuits, how they do so, with whom, and to what ends appear powerfully gendered. Many of the chapters that focus on female migrants confirm the widespread observation that women play an increasingly important role in regenerating families across national borders (Kofman and Raghuram 2015), as reflected, for instance, in depictions of mother-child relations and dutiful daughters who remit home to their kin. Men who migrate, however, also sustain relationships through participation in affective circuits. The last three chapters in the volume focus on the struggles and adventures of men who emigrate, many of whom appear invested in building complex relations with parakin, that is, relations that are modeled on but extend beyond kin relations (see Newell, this volume). Sometimes migrants turn to parakin in their efforts to fulfill their obligations to family members back home. In other cases, however, the circuits migrants build with parakin appear to supplant those that move goods, ideas, and emotions among kin, generating new social networks.

Julie Kleinman's chapter examines the trajectory of Lassana Niaré, a young Malian man who spends his time with other West African migrant men at the Gare du Nord, the international train station in Paris. Although Lassana seeks to increase his social status and gain the respect of his kin, he finds that he cannot do so working as a contract laborer for French companies and living in a government-run hostel for foreign workers, as many Malians did in the past (Quiminal 1991). Instead, he and his peers seek job openings, social connections, and bits of useful information through their informal contacts at the Gare du Nord. To truly earn his family's respect, however, Lassana must convert the short-term relationships forged at the train station into more durable—and socially recognized—forms of wealth. He eventually does manage to help his siblings who remain in Mali, enabling him to move from being a dependent younger brother to being a "big somebody" within his kin network. But it is clear from Kleinman's analysis that he is unusual in this respect. For many, success and associated reintegration and positive emplacement within kin networks may take years or may never come. The precarious position occupied by male migrants whose only option is to operate within patrimonial networks of parakinship is especially vivid in the case of the young men depicted in Vigh's chapter, who work as mules transporting drugs between their home country of Guinea-Bissau and Portugal. These young men hope that by carrying cocaine to Europe they will acquire the resources to reposition themselves in the affective circuits that bind them to kin and thereby confer positive social recognition. They often find, however, that their journeys end with deportation back to Bissau, a volatility captured in the term *life's trampoline*. There, as deportees, they face considerable social stigma from their peers and kin.

Migrants who encounter difficulties in their efforts to reposition themselves in the affective circuits tying them to their families may build alternative circuits and generate new kinds of cultural practices and social ties, a point made especially clear in Sasha Newell's chapter on Congolese *sapeurs*. When the fashion-based subculture of *la sape* first emerged as a social phenomenon in the 1980s, the men involved in it moved back and forth between the Congo and France in order to expand their reputations and gain prestige by accumulating and displaying designer clothes (Friedman 1990; Gandoulou 1989). More recently, stricter immigration regulations in France and ongoing conflict in the Congo have blocked these circuits. Many *sapeurs* respond by remaining in France, where they create new kinds of father-son relationships and even a new *sapeur* style.

The forms of parakinship they establish provide an institutionalized support network to offset the relative absence of actual kin networks in Paris and help buffer these men from their kin's demands for material support. They also re-create long-standing aspects of Congolese culture premised on the importance of *ngolo*, or generative life force, and generate new ways of creating social distinctions that do not rely on the mobility between the Congo and Paris that was previously so central to *la sape*. Men may invest less in maintaining their connections with their kin, but over time the exchanges they engage in with parakin generate new, alternative social grids.

Although some of these men aspire to become family leaders, as both Kleinman's and Neveu Kringelbach's chapters show, when read against the many chapters that reveal the considerable lengths migrant women often go to to sustain their families, the men sometimes appear comparatively disconnected from their kin. Several explanations for this disparity come to mind. One is that women are constitutionally more likely to sustain their kin, an argument made by Carol Stack and Linda Burton (1994), who note that when it comes to *kinscription*—the ability to be conscripted for familial or reproductive labor—women generally appear to be more pliable than men. Another possible explanation draws on the work of postcolonial feminist scholars such as Ifi Amadiume (1987), Oyèrónké Oyewùmí (2011), Jìmí Adésínà (2010), and Signe Arnfred (2011), who argue for the profoundly matrifocal nature of much African kinship. They contend that instead of importing Western male-focused perspectives on gender and kinship, anthropologists should pay more attention to female-headed households, the status of female elders, and women's central role in social and cosmological reproduction. Read together, these perspectives suggest not only that women have a propensity to engage in kin work but also that the matrifocal nature of some African kinship systems may accentuate this tendency.

The problem with these kinds of ahistorical explanations for men's reduced participation in the transnational regeneration of families is that they are not supported by precedent, suggesting that more contingent political and economic factors may be in play. After all, many prior generations of African men migrated to Europe on formalized labor contracts, sent money home to sustain their kin, and usually returned to Africa upon retirement (Quiminal 1991). Nor do such arguments apply to migrant men within Africa today whose remittances pay for wells, electricity, and other infrastructural necessities in their natal villages (Whitehouse 2012). While we hesitate to privilege any single cause, it seems likely that transformations in the global economy, which make it increasingly difficult for young men to achieve the kind of social adulthood associated with providing for one's family, perhaps paired with the strong matrifocal ties that exist in some parts of the continent, converge with European migration regimes to make women more able than men to sustain regenerative connections.

In particular, with family reunification as one of the last loopholes left in European immigration policy, men may experience greater difficulty than women in establishing a foothold in Europe. For example, while both African men and women marry European partners, as the chapter by Neveu Kringelbach illustrates, the state officials who register these marriages and grant visas are especially suspicious of marriages between African men and white European women, making them more likely to reject immigration applications when the foreign spouse is the husband (Lavanchy 2014). Even though current laws mean that in Europe a foreign spouse must endure a temporary period of relative vulnerability as a legal dependent, doing so may still be preferable to pursuing some of the available alternatives. Perhaps when men cannot establish themselves securely through marriage, labor, or other recognized means, they invest in new kinds of social networks, sometimes at the expense of their families or extended kin. Particular conceptions of gender and race make it harder for men to articulate with categories and narratives imposed by contemporary migration regulations, further underscoring the gendered nature of affective circuits.

Affective Circuits: Beyond Afro-European Trajectories

Exchanges of money, goods, ideas, images, and people play a pivotal role in how African migrants regenerate their ties to one another and their kin at home as well as how they rework their relationships and produce new forms of belonging. It is precisely because most Africans travel to Europe to reposition themselves within the social networks that enable valued forms of personhood that we focus on the multifaceted exchanges through which they seek to achieve this goal. And it is precisely because these exchanges carry with them material resources, cultural meanings, and personal sentiments and because they are enabled and blocked to multiple ends that the metaphor of affective circuits is so appropriate for conceptualizing them.

Notions of marriage, kinship, and parent-child relations powerfully shape the development and growth of these circuits; these are also the idioms and practices through which Africans both make connections with one another and potentially articulate with the limited categories of belonging afforded by contemporary European migration regimes. In different ways, migrants, their kin, and European state agents all seek to regulate how these circuits grow and take shape. The circuits that exchanges give rise to are neither continuous nor all-inclusive. Although several of the chapters demonstrate the ways migrants regenerate their families and forge connections by building and managing affective circuits, it is also clear that not everyone succeeds in these endeavors. Ultimately, some migrants find it easier to become emplaced, which points to affective circuits as parts of wider patterns of inclusion and exclusion. To push the electrical circuit metaphor further, some fall off the grid.

Although the chapters in this volume elaborate these ideas with respect to African migration to Europe, the approach they take and some of the insights it offers are applicable to analysis of migration in other parts of the world as well. After all, African migration to Europe is only one part of a more general global reconfiguration of social regeneration. Now that labor migration has become increasingly difficult, marriage and intimate relations more generally have become important routes to mobility, blurring what used to be considered analytically distinct types of migration (Kofman 2012). Certainly mobility enabled by kinship and intimate relations is not restricted to Africans, as we have mentioned. Women from Cuba and the Dominican Republic dream of migrating to Europe and seek relationships with European men who visit the Caribbean as sex tourists (Brennan 2004; Cabezas 2009), while large numbers of Thai and Filipina women have married men in Germany, Denmark, and the United States (Constable 2003; Plambech 2010), enabling them to accumulate resources and help their natal families in Asia. Across East and Southeast Asia, work in strip clubs, brothels, or high-end nightclubs has become a common way for women to seek cross border mobility; women from the Philippines and Vietnam, especially, often make use of intimate relationships to migrate to wealthier countries such as Japan (Faier 2009; Parreñas 2011) or South Korea (Vu and Lee 2013). The global rise in female migration has also made the separation of mothers and their children, and alternative arrangements for care, an increasingly widespread and visible phenomenon (Coe 2013; Olwig 2012; Parreñas 2005a; Rae-Espinoza 2011). More generally, scholars agree that mobility has become increasingly central to establishing modern personhood while forced immobility appears to damage people's sense of self and their ability to fulfill roles in their families and communities (Bauman 1998; Fioratta 2015; Gaibazzi 2015; Lubkemann 2008; Rodriguez 2015). We also know that transnational exchanges among kin are a part of the way people sustain cultural cosmologies and contribute to the spatiotemporal extension of persons (Chu 2010).

How people from different parts of the world establish the networks of exchange that enable social regeneration to occur transnationally is likely to vary with conceptions of marriage, parenthood, and gender as well as with the moralities of exchange that accompany different types of relations. It may also differ according to historical relationships between regions as well as the specific migration regimes in place, which often present different paths to mobility. Nevertheless, with its attention to both the material and the affective dimensions of exchange as well as the social and political processes that shape exchange networks, the idea of affective circuits provides an analytic framework with which to illuminate transnational migration and social regeneration in Africa and beyond.

Notes

1. See Chu 2010; Coe 2013; Cole 2014a; Fink-Nielsen, Hansen, and Kleist 2004; Grillo and Riccio 2004; Groes-Green 2014; Krause 2008; Mazzucato 2008; Newell 2012; Saraiva 2008.

2. In some cases, men also seek to build relationships with European women. See Despres (2015), Ebron (1997), Meiu (2009), and Neveu Kringelbach (this volume).

3. Cold War alliances, meanwhile, fostered other kinds of mobility: thousands of Africans from socialist-aligned states such as Guinea-Bissau, the Democratic Republic of Congo, Madagascar, Mali, and Mozambique traveled to the Soviet Union and East Germany for education and professional training in the 1970s and 1980s (Covell 1989; Fikes and Lemon 2002).

4. Historically, Germany provided the paradigmatic example of jus sanguinis citizenship, while scholars often cite France as embodying the principle of jus soli (Brubaker 1992). In practice, however, most states use both principles to determine citizenship. For example, there have been times in the past when anyone who was born on French soil or to French parents in the overseas territories was automatically considered French, while today, for a child born on French soil to be considered French, he or she must have a parent who is of French nationality and must request nationality before the age of eighteen (Vie-Publique 2013). In Germany, meanwhile, reforms to citizenship laws that took place in 2000 mean that a child born in that country to noncitizen parents may acquire German citizenship if one parent has lived as a legal resident of the country for at least eight years (Bundesministerium für Justiz und Verbraucherschutz 2014).

ONE

Translations in Kinscripts: Child Circulation among Ghanaians Abroad

CATI COE

The well-known case of soccer star Mario Balotelli provides insights into how affective circuits can be broken and re-made as Ghanaians translate and adapt practices of child circulation taken from their home country to the cultural kinscripts underpinning social institutions and legal structures in Western countries. Born in 1990 to Ghanaian immigrants in Italy, Mario Balotelli was raised by a white Italian family from the age of three. Since his adolescence, he has claimed Italian citizenship, disowned his Ghanaian family, and refused to play for Ghana in international tournaments, causing much consternation among that nation's soccer fans (Williamson and Pisa 2010). His circulation into the Balotellis' household gave him a sense of belonging to the family and through them a public identification with Italy.

Balotelli's case is an unusual one because of his talent, visibility, and wealth, but it illustrates several points I make in this chapter about the experiences and dilemmas of more ordinary Ghanaian transnational migrants and their children. Ghanaians use practices of child circulation familiar to them from their own childhoods and adulthoods to support their migrations. These practices have been central to how generations of women who migrate within Ghana and elsewhere in West Africa balance work and reproduction and provide care across generations, a process Cole (this volume) terms *family regeneration*. Children's circulation into new households, where nonparental adults care for them, creates new affective circuits—that is, flows of love, words, moral support, advice, goods, money, and services produced in social networks (Cole and Groes introduction and Feldman-Savelsberg chapter, this volume). It also produces new ties of belonging and attachment, including attachment to national identities.

In Ghana, as elsewhere in West Africa (see, e.g., Alber 2003; Notermans 2004), children's circulation into new households is not meant to break their connections with their biological parents. Rather, the aim is to create a more complex and broader array of social connections along which material opportunities and emotional feelings will flow. Parents seek to add new (rather than replace old) identities and give children new, more desirable social class positions and urban/rural connections. In fact, child circulation not only connects children to new caregivers but also creates deeper connections between the biological parents and the fostering caregiver (Bledsoe 1990; Etienne 1979). Similar to the electrical currents created as electrons jump from atom to atom, new affective circuits between parents, caregivers, and children can be enabled and rerouted by placing children in the custody of new caregivers.

When Ghanaian migrants go abroad, they often seek to place their children in other households. Children tend to circulate to three kinds of households: those of nonkin citizen families in the country of migration; those of kin in Ghana; and those of migrant kin abroad. Parents and children alike work to maintain affective circuits despite physical distance, in part by maintaining flows of communication and material goods. However, as Balotelli's personal history dramatically illustrates, Ghanaian practices of child circulation translate imperfectly and unevenly into the scripts of family life that Ghanaians encounter in Europe and other Western countries. As Groes (this volume) recounts, a similar dynamic characterizes marriage, as Mozambican migrant women reject becoming "locked-up" housewives in Europe in favor of continuing "sponsorships" similar to those they initiated at home. Cultural narratives about kin relations, or kinscripts, shape the institutional and legal practices that "delineate and regulate kinship relations," including the family reunification routes by which Africans are allowed to immigrate into Europe (Boehm 2012, 60). Consequently, they also structure how social services provide help and how child circulation is legally regulated through fostering and adoption. I borrow the term *kinscript* from Carol Stack and Linda Burton (1994), but I use it more narrowly than they do to illuminate culturally patterned family narratives that shape conflict and care within families and policy related to family life.[1]

This chapter examines how cultural narratives about parenting, kinship, and care shape the maintenance and expansion—and contraction and breakage—of the affective circuits that Ghanaians create through transnational migration and child circulation. As the electrical circuit metaphor suggests, these flows can be blocked, slowed, dropped, and picked up again. Cultural kinscripts are key to interpreting the meaning of these flows as well as to deciding whether they should remain open or be shut down. The cultural frameworks that undergird the regulation of family life in Western countries resignify West African practices of child circulation, potentially generating new familial and national attachments. The fact that European law recognizes Western definitions of family and not African ones is a major factor in the short-circuiting of affective and material flows between African migrants and the children in their extended families. European laws' obliviousness to African kinscripts raises questions about legal pluralism, an issue I return to in the chapter's conclusion.

Ideologies Underpinning Ghanaian Child Circulation: Multiple Parenthood

In southern Ghana, children come to belong to multiple mothers and fathers (both biological and social) through practices of care.[2] Care takes the form of material support such as paying for food, clothing, medical attention, and school fees for the child. It also extends to emotional bonds, because love creates the desire to care for another in material ways (Coe 2011). Parenting can be distributed across many people without the child belonging to any one of them (Goody 1982). A Presbyterian minister from Ghana explained to me,

Many people help each individual to grow up. . . . So if someone wants us to help them, we look at our financial situation, and if we can help, then we help them to a certain place, and then someone else continues to help them. When that person grows up, he will also help someone. That's how we do things. Little by little, [we help one another]. . . . Like in this house, with the little children here, when he [his wife's nephew] finishes studying, he changes into a teacher, and they sit together and he teaches them. Or if he has a problem understanding his studies, he brings it to us and we teach him.

In part because the exchange of resources defines care (Thelen, Coe, and Alber 2013), multiple people can provide care during a person's life course, including older siblings and cousins. Furthermore, the child is expected to reciprocate this care, whether immediately—by cheerfully helping with household chores—or in the future, by contributing financially to the caregiver's well-being.

This cultural kinscript has been termed *fosterage* in the literature on Africa because of its distinction from the Western ideal—the coresidence of a biologically constituted nuclear family. However, fosterage is not always highlighted in contexts where the care of children is broadly distributed. In the town of Akropong, where I have done my fieldwork, there is no local term for raising a child one has not given birth to, speaking to its usualness, lack of exceptionality, and normality. After all, the child belongs primarily to the lineage and kinship group, not to the parents. Because care is distributed broadly, the ties to the biological parents are not severed, as they are in Western adoption. The parents' own parents or siblings are the most likely relatives to whom care will be distributed, and the child's relationship with the parents is likely to continue.

Through their practices of child circulation, Ghanaians deliberately seek to manage the affective circuits that connect parents and children. Children who are being fostered visit their parents on weekends or over school vacations, and their parents also visit them. Even children who are fostered from a very young age, as in grandmother fosterage, and who may not know that the person they call mother is in fact a grandmother or an aunt, eventually learn the truth: when they reach the age of ten or so, people in the neighborhood or other relatives will begin telling them that the person raising them is not their mother. Some people feel that this information will change how the child feels, that it will make the child worry about why he or she was given up; others feel that when care is satisfactory, the child will not be troubled to suddenly learn the identity of his or her biological mother. Parents and children use the cultural scripts available to them to manage their affective belonging when children circulate between households. Doing so is particularly important for those raised in a social parent's household from a young age, so that they can maintain relationships with multiple caregivers, including their biological parents.

Ghanaian Migrations: Past and Present

Transnational migration has been a valued route to advancement in Ghana since the colonial era, when Ghanaians traveled for work elsewhere in West Africa and for education in Britain, practices that continued after independence.[3] Migration from Ghana to Britain was once a sign of elite status, particularly when the purpose was a prestigious education. The dream of being educated abroad to become an important person in Ghana continues to animate many Ghanaians. Most international migrants have gone to other West African countries or elsewhere in Africa (Benneh 2004; International Organization for Migration 2009), but the United Kingdom and the United States each receive 5 to 7 percent of Ghana's emigrants, with migrants usually using initial travel to another African country to fund migration to a more developed country (International Organization for Migration 2009).

However, as international migration increased in the 1980s and 1990s, the opportunity to travel became democratized (Manuh 2006, 24). A broader swathe of the population, including students, teachers, lower-level civil servants, and skilled blue-collar workers such as mechanics and electricians, has become increasingly involved in transnational migration. Still, international migrants from Ghana tend to be from the more developed southern part of the country and to live in urban areas before their migration (Adeku 1995; Anarfi et al. 2003). What was once educational migration—even if only ostensibly (Goody and Groothues 1982)—is now clearly a labor migration.

As international migration has expanded beyond the educated elite, it has become increasingly characterized by struggle. The fruits of migration have shrunk for migrants both because the cost of living has increased in Ghana and because of the kinds of less-skilled jobs they do abroad. Moreover, because Ghanaians are relatively recent migrants to Europe, except to the United Kingdom, they usually do not have an extensive family network in place there to help with childcare and housing. In response, they have developed fictive kinship networks, particularly through churches (van Dijk 2002a) and hometown associations. Many work long hours in difficult and low-paying jobs, making their ability to contribute to and benefit from these organizations precarious. They often hope to return to Ghana once they have earned enough money to build a house or start a business there or pay for their children's education, but they find that their time away can stretch to decades, as some decide to remain abroad until retirement.

Historically, migration stimulated two different kinds of child circulation, both of which became more prevalent during the extensive urban migration in the 1960s and 1970s. One was known as grandmother fosterage, in which young women who traveled to urban areas for further education or work left their young children with their mothers.[4] Migrant women who used grandmother fostering in my survey were more likely to be young, unmarried, or remarried. For example, Belinda, fifty-three when interviewed, described how as a child in the 1960s she lived with her grandmother in Akropong because her mother was working in a nearby market town and had remarried. Her brother, meanwhile, went to live with their father. Grandmother fostering was also a common option for women who were transferred every few years because of their or their husbands' civil service employment and who wanted their children to have a more stable living situation. Elizabeth, a forty-seven-year-old nurse (born ca. 1961), described how her mother, then a young, unmarried woman, gave her to her grandmother shortly after her birth. She stayed with her grandmother because her mother, who worked for the social welfare department in Kumasi, was often sent to different stations across the country. Elizabeth never knew her father, and, in fact, her grandmother treated her as if she were her own youngest child. Such arrangements ideally provided care across the generations—to the mother, who could work and rest assured that her child was not being neglected; to the child, who was lovingly cared for; and to the grandmother, who was assured of her daughter's remittances and for whom the child performed household labor as she grew older. Relations between grandchild and grandmother strengthened the affective circuits between the migrant and her family at home because they ensured frequent visits and communication. Grandmother fosterage is one theme on which transnational migrants improvise, providing the model for Mario Balotelli's parents to foster their two-year-old out and for Ghanaian migrants to send their infants and young children to live with relatives back in Ghana.

Another kind of child circulation made more prevalent by the migration of adults was the movement of older children into urban areas, particularly into higher-status and more educated households, for the purposes of their education, exposure to urban life, and discipline, in exchange for which they contributed their labor to those households. As I witnessed during my fieldwork, the strategy of bringing relatives into a household was more common when the household included educated married women who were formally employed or when women were married to formally employed men, but it was also an important option for women traders, who appreciated having assistants to hawk goods around town (see also Schildkrout 1973). This kind of child circulation has been extended to justify adolescents' domestic servitude among nonkin or more extended kin, but it usually takes place between relatives, with more wealthy, educated, and stable siblings of the biological parent or of the child providing care to the child in exchange for the child's domestic labor, perhaps including care of younger children in the household. For example, Matilda, a forty-eight-year-old woman (born ca. 1960), went to live with her older sister, a nurse, for twelve years, finishing middle and secondary school while staying with her. Describing her sister's reliance on her in the household, she said that she helped prepare the meals for her sister's husband, something husbands usually insist that only their wives do. Young and teenage girls often helped their older and adult sisters or the sisters of their parents juggle their work and their household responsibilities and their older, more educated sisters helped them go to school.

In this scenario, the hierarchy of social class dovetails with a geographic hierarchy. In other words, parents see children as moving not only from a poorer household to a richer one but also from the village to the city, from a place that is less well regarded in terms of "civilization" (*anibuei*, to use the local parlance) to one that is better. "Civilization" is denoted by material conditions such as running water, electricity, cars and roads, better educational facilities, and habits related to cleanliness and disciplined behavior. Thus, children from village farming families are considered to have moved up in the world socially and economically simply by going to live in a town or city. It is this second kind of movement that transnational migrants are imagining when they attempt to bring their adolescent nephews and nieces or younger siblings to live with them abroad.

Parents often seek to extend established practices of child circulation, long pivotal to women's mobility in Ghana, to transnational migration, as the following example shows. A woman had begun taking care of her sister's child, Philip, when he was one and a half years old and his mother was working as an apprentice seamstress in Accra. When Philip was six years old, his mother traveled to the United Kingdom with her new husband, and Philip remained behind with his aunt. When Philip turned fifteen, his aunt wanted him to join his mother in the United Kingdom despite her own emotional connection to him, because "then she [the mother] can help him, because I have done my bit. And she also wants to help him with what is left [of his growing up], little by little." However, migrants soon find that building affective circuits and extending kinship links in Europe is far more difficult than they expect.

Ghanaian Families Encounter Western Family Law

Part of the difficulty results from the fact that the European states where Ghanaian migrants go to live and work take a very different approach to child circulation than Ghanaians do. Western cultural notions of the family undergird adoption and fostering laws as well as the state's provision of social services. Blood and birth are primary in establishing a child's rights and identity (Schachter 2009; Schneider 1968). Western understandings of parent-child relationships are encoded in legal mechanisms governing immigration, welfare, and social protection and discursively infuse everyday conversations and media representations. The legal and institutional mechanism that exists for the exceptional substitution of others for biological parents—aka adoption—is also premised on an "as-if-begotten" model (Schachter 2009).

One consequence of the as-if-begotten model is that the parent-child relationship is seen as dyadic rather than multidimensional (a child having multiple connections to many different kinds of caregivers who provide different kinds of care at different points in his or her life). For a child to acquire new parents, relations with the original ones have to be dissolved. Another consequence is that adoption is intended to be permanent. And finally, lacking the biological bond of blood and nature, an adoptive relationship between parent and child needs to be established by a formal contract between the adopting parent(s) and the biological parent(s) or the organization that brokers the arrangement (Schachter 2009). These measures illustrate adoption's deviation from the normal model of biological parenting even as they seek to render adoption invisible by making it conform as closely as possible to the biological model.

The Western view of kinship leads to plenary adoption that severs the biological parents' legal rights and emotional connections to the child, replacing them with a connection to social parents. Adoption in Western countries takes for granted that children will assume their adoptive parents' way of life socially, religiously, and nationally and privileges the bond between adopting parent and adopted child over that between biological parent and child (Briggs and Marre 2009). Because "adoption radically alters the adoptee's filiation, it involves the transmission of key markers of identity over time: name, kinship ties (such as siblings and grandparents), language, and nationality, as well as social, cultural, and ethnic affiliations" (Ouellette 2009, 76). In part, the restriction on multiple parenthood results from the historical use of adoption in Europe to provide people with heirs to their property (Goody 1969). That "the child becomes . . . a full member of the adoptive family, as if born into it" is predicated on the child becoming "a legal stranger to his or her birth parents and other birth relatives" (Ouellette 2009, 69). Adoption is thus premised on the severing of one affective circuit and its replacement with another rather than on viewing multiple affective circuits (between child and social parent, child and biological parent, social and biological parent) as enhancing and strengthening one another.

However, other practices of circulating children coexist with this model. In France and Belgium, courts occasionally authorize a simple adoption, in which the child acquires an additional family without losing his or her original kinship bonds (Ouellette 2009). Fostering, a less permanent arrangement, privileges the bond between birth parent and child over that of foster parent and child by maintaining the child's birth identity. However, fosterage often occurs coercively, under the supervision of social service agencies and child protection services, because of a mother's imprisonment, "neglect," or poverty, promoting the transfer of poor children to working-class and middle-class households or to foster-care institutions. Adoption can occur after a period of fostering, and many adoptions in the United Kingdom and the United States are not between strangers but between children coresident with a biological parent and an adopting stepparent (Bowie 2004). More recent movement toward open adoption would seem to undercut plenary adoption and recognize multiple parenthood. However, on the basis of her research in Quebec, Ouellette (2009) argues that the adopted child's medical need for genetic information drives the open adoption movement, not the belief that children can benefit from affective and filial bonds with multiple adults.

These Western understandings of family not only regulate family relations within national borders but are also encoded in international agreements, like the Hague Convention on Intercountry Adoption. To prevent the trafficking and exploitation of children, the Hague Convention conceives of adoption as a contractual agreement between entities who possess full knowledge of the agreement (Schachter 2009). Relations between birth parent and adoptive parent are expected to be nonexistent; these parties are anonymous to one another and are strangers (Schachter 2009). The Hague Convention considers international adoption "preferable only to orphanage care" (Yngvesson 2009, 109). However, international adoption, particularly of children who appear racially different from their new parents, has complicated some of the notions about blood and birth that normally make adoption invisible, as we see in the case of Mario Balotelli. In this context, complex processes of kinning adoptive children are necessary to incorporate them into both the family and the nation (Howell

2004; Leinaweaver 2013; Stryker 2011). Despite their greater recognition of the pasts children bring with them, adoptive parents in these cases still find their children's relationship with birth parents emotionally threatening, as if only one set of parents and affective circuits can exist (Yngvesson 2004).

When Ghanaians go to Europe, they encounter the legal and social frameworks of fostering, domestic adoption, and international adoption outlined above. They draw on these laws and scripts to try to further their own ends of raising their biological children and the children of their siblings. Below I discuss three strategies they use: fostering-out a child to non-Ghanaians in the country of migration (a translation to Western fostering), fostering-out a child to relatives in Ghana (an extension of child circulation in internal migration, which does not need translation and goes undetected by Western authorities), and fostering-in a child of siblings (a translation to Western international adoption). These strategies create different kinds of affective circuits—between biological parents, social parents, and children—and they also have implications for a child's social class position and sense of national belonging.

The Balotellis and the Barwuahs: Translating Multiple Parenthood into Fostering in Italy

The story of Mario Balotelli illustrates how the children of Ghanaians abroad sometimes circulate into the care of citizen families in "foster" arrangements when the migrant parents have trouble balancing work and family life in the absence of relatives who can help them. Initially perceived as temporary, these arrangements can become a source of tension as foster parents and child emotionally connect to one another. In some cases, they can threaten the relationship between birth parent and child, particularly when social services and the legal apparatus see the merits of the fostering arrangement for the child in terms of social class and/ or national identity. The story as I relate it here is taken from English-language media accounts in Europe and Ghana. In these accounts, the birth parents were much more vocal about their position than Mario Balotelli, who prefers not to speak about family issues. I have not personally interviewed any of the principals.

In newspaper reports, Thomas Barwuah explained how his son came to be fostered.[5] Mr. Barwuah was a metalworker with a job far from Palermo, where his family lived, and he "shuttled back and forth [between the two] every weekend on a twelve-hour overnight train." His wife, Rose, meanwhile, looked after their two children, Mario and a younger sister, largely by herself (Williamson and Pisa 2010). Mario was very sick and "in and out of the hospital as a baby" (Williamson and Pisa 2010). His condition fortunately improved, and the family moved from Palermo to Brescia, an industrial city where there were more employment opportunities for Mr. Barwuah.

In Brescia, as Rose Barwuah explained,

We lived with another African family in a one-bedroom apartment full of damp. I went to the social services and pointed out I had a sick child. There were no houses for us, so they told me it would be better to hand Mario [then age two] to a local family for a while. (*Daily Graphic* 2008)

Although they might have preferred to foster their son with a relative, no one within their kinship or social network was available to take him, so they turned to Italian social services. Rather than help the family stay together by giving them adequate housing, social services brokered the circulation of Mario to another family (see Feldman-Savelsberg, this volume, on the role of the state in making and breaking affective circuits). What happened to the Barwuahs, then, is consistent with dominant patterns of fostering in the West in which children are transferred from families either living in impoverished conditions deemed unfit for raising children or unable to balance their work with childcare to more stable and resource-rich households that can afford to live up to Italian ideals of childhood (Andersen and Fallesen 2010). The Balotellis were a wealthy couple with three children of their own who lived in an affluent town six miles north of Brescia (Williamson and Pisa 2010). Mr. Barwuah said the initial agreement was for a one-year foster placement, which was later extended by another twelve months (Williamson and Pisa 2010).

Mr. Barwuah described a kind of joint parenting arrangement between the two families, although his and his wife's affective connections to their son became increasingly tenuous over time.

At first we were not sure [about the arrangement] but we decided it was probably best for Mario. We saw him every week and we all got on really well. We thought that at some point, once things had sorted out, Mario would come back to us. But instead, every time we tried to get him back, the Balotellis kept extending the foster time. We couldn't afford lawyers to fight for us, so Mario grew more and more distant. He would come and visit and play with his brothers and sisters but he just didn't seem to have any time for us, his mother and father. We wanted him back for more than ten years but, every time we tried, the courts blocked it and as the years passed he became colder towards us. The Balotellis know people and are influential and we could do nothing. (Williamson and Pisa 2010)

Mr. Barwuah suggests that the fostering was intended to be temporary but turned into a more permanent arrangement because of the Balotellis' social status and influence. The more permanent arrangement led to Mario's increasing emotional closeness to his foster family, including his adoption of their surname. At the same time, the Barwuahs' reluctance to completely sever their relationship with their son meant that the Balotellis could not adopt Mario as they, and probably he, would have liked. The dyadic understanding of Western parenting worked against the Barwuahs' desire to maintain a strong relationship with Mario, but the contractual emphasis on obtaining their agreement to release their child enabled them to continue to impress their kinscript on the situation, because they would have had to agree to give up their identity as Mario's parents to enable the Balotellis to take their place. As a result, because of his fostering, Mario's national identity continued to be inherited from his birth parents, and he had to wait until he was eighteen before he could become an Italian citizen and play on the Italian national team (*Italy Magazine* 2008).

Mario Balotelli's public version of events differs from Mr. Barwuah's narrative of continued visits and contact: he tells a story of emotional and physical abandonment. His emotional response to his situation seems to have been framed by an "adoption" narrative. This narrative shapes his understanding that the Balotellis replaced the Barwuahs as his parents. Given this kinscript, he poses the painful question of why his parents gave him up (Yngvesson 2004). His answer to this question (as for many adoptive children) is that they did not care about him. In a television interview in 2008, when he joined the Inter Milan team, he said that his biological parents abandoned him at the hospital at the age of two and did not make efforts to contact him until he was sixteen and a rising young soccer star (*Italy Magazine* 2008). Because of their unloving act, in his view the Barwuahs are no longer legitimately his parents: they have no claim on him, and he has no obligations to them. "There is no bond between us and in my eyes they are just strangers," he has said (Modern Ghana Web 2008). Drawing on Pamela Kea's analysis (this volume), one could say he did not feel his birth parents had given a convincing parenting "performance."

Furthermore, he has accused his biological parents of wanting to be involved in his life because of his fame and fortune (Davies 2008; Williamson and Pisa 2010). It is the plight of celebrities to attract hangers-on, and Balotelli has slotted his biological parents into the category of false intimates. The Barwuahs' photos of Mario's childhood visits to their apart-

1.1   Mario Balotelli joyfully hugged his mother Silvia Balotelli after scoring a goal in the Italy
       versus Germany game in the 2012 European Championship in Poland. The hug became
       news in itself as a sign of Mario's Jewish and Italian heritage despite years of racist heckling
       from Italian fans. Screen shot of Polish television courtesy of the *Trinity Mirror*.

ment and his romping with his younger brother on their bed corroborate
their story of continued involvement (Williamson and Pisa 2010). Nevertheless, his narrative speaks to another kind of emotional truth—of abandonment and lack of love—with which some adopted children grapple.

Mr. Barwuah responded to Mario's accusations by envisioning a way in
which multiple parents could be involved in his life to different degrees of
intimacy and care. Among his son's social parents he includes his coach
José Morinho, with whom Mario was then embroiled in public confronta-
tions that were affecting his play on the Inter Milan team. Ghana's major
daily newspaper, the *Daily Graphic*, reported Mr. Barwuah as saying,

We do not care that he is now famous and we're not after money. Thankfully, we
have enough. All we want is that he remembers we are his parents, too. Tell the Inter
Coach, Jose Morinho, to look after Mario like a son. It's what he needs. We would like
to tell Mario that we have always loved him and are enormously grateful to the Balotelli family for raising him. But we'd also want an emotional connection with our son.
Above all, we wish to state that we didn't "give away" our child. Things happened in
a way that probably even Mario doesn't know about. (*Daily Graphic* 2008)

Such statements seem to reflect the Barwuahs' view that another family
had helped them in an hour of crisis—when their son was sick, they were
new immigrants, and they could not find or afford adequate housing. Ma-

Jo Boateng, Bracknell, 5 years ago

Most of people reading this article will probably not support the parent. However, if you've been an immigrant as the parents are you will most likely understand. One thing we shouldn't loose sight is that perhaps if he wasn't adopted he would never have reached this level. The parents couldn't have afforded a coach for him or perhaps he would have been pushed aside. Balotelli should understand that all things that happens in life happens for a reason and its all good...even IF the parents left him in hospital he should be grateful that they didn't leave him to die or even abort him due to their poverty. No one can go on without a history. He needs to understand is that whatever he chooses to be Italian or Ghanaian something will never change. You could have helped Ghana win the world cup rather than waiting to be in the Italian team...You may never be there...Get real!!! Be grateful to both your adopted parents and your biological parents. Period

Click to rate   24   2

1.2 Online comments on the *Daily Mail* story "Mario Balotelli's Double Life." There were twenty-eight comments on this story, representing a range of opinions, mainly from residents of the United Kingdom. Some, like this commentator, had Ghanaian names, but most of the commentators did not seem to identify as Ghanaian. Screen shot by Cati Coe.

rio's belonging could be multiple rather than transferred from biological parents to foster parents. The Barwuahs do not claim to be Mario's sole parents but rather want their son to remember that "we are his parents, too." They would be satisfied for him to continue to live with the Balotellis and visit them on weekends. The Barwuahs express appreciation to other adults who function as his social parents, both his foster parents and the coach of the Inter club. Their actions thus seem consistent with the premise that the care of a child can be distributed across many people without destroying the affective circuit between biological parents and their child.

On public comments sections of news websites, Ghanaians deployed scripts of multiple parenting and gratitude for care to encourage Mario to reunite with his biological parents. "Jo Boateng" in Bracknell, United Kingdom, for instance, told him, "Be grateful to both your adopted parents and your biological parents," because if his biological parents had not given him up, he might not be so famous or successful (in response to the story of Williamson and Pisa 2010). "Dogo" wrote,

The fact that he was raised by foster parents does not mean he should deny his biological parents when they are still [living]. . . . Yes the white couple did a great job in raising him and he cannot deny them either but he should not be ashame[d] of his biolog[i]cal parents. (In response to Ghana Soccernet 2013)

Tanko says:

August 21, 2013 at 2:59 pm

Folks: we all need to spare this dude! He didn't give birth to himself neither did he give himself to the foster home…. His parents might have taken that step to save and or rescue him from the illness that troubled him at early age. That's called destiny. After all, nationality is a FELING but not a passport. I was born and bred in Ghana but even before I left Ghana, I always thought I was American but in reality, I am NOT! Make sense??

Reply to this Comment

DOGO says:

August 21, 2013 at 4:35 pm

No!! You don't make sense. The fact that he was raised by foster parents does not mean he should deny his biological parents when they are still leaving. Do you think the parents would have given him up if they were in a position to take good care of him? I don't think so. Baloteli should know that he will remain black till the end of his life. He can never be white. Yes the white couple did a great job in raising him and he cannot deny them either but he should not be ashame of his biologcal parents.

Reply to this Comment

Tetteyfio says:

August 21, 2013 at 11:40 pm

Tanko, you are only American in your 'head.' You are Ghanaian whether you feel it or not, unless you have now become a US citizen. You may need to see a psychiatrist

Reply to this Comment

1.3 Online comments on the Ghana Soccernet story "Mario Balotelli Doesn't Like Talking about His Real Ghanaian Parents." The commentators responding to this story were likely Ghanaian. From the discussion that ensued, many revealed that they lived abroad. They used Mario's story to reflect on their own complicated identifications. Screen shot by Cati Coe.

Here, the commentators invoke frameworks that might enable the maintenance of affective circuits to biological parents despite ruptures caused by a sense of emotional abandonment or geographical distance.

While Balotelli's stardom makes for a particularly spectacular and public example, his case shares characteristics with others reported by Esther Goody and Christine Muir Groothues (1982) in their study of West African educational migrants in London in the early 1970s. Goody and Groothues present a court case from December 1972 in which the judge decided that the Ghanaian parents of a nine-year-old girl ("Ann") could not take her on their planned return to Ghana because she had been fostered since the age of three months by a white professional English couple. The two families engaged in negotiations over joint parenting similar to those involving the Barwuahs and Balotellis:

Two months later, when it became clear that the foster-parents assumed they would adopt her, Ann's parents took her home. After reassurances they allowed her to return to the foster-parents, but when she was four the foster-parents again pressed for adoption, and Ann was again removed by her parents. . . . Later an agreement was reached and the foster-parents understood that Ann was to stay with them until she was 18, and finish her education. When Ann's parents later decided to return to Ghana and wanted to take her with them, the foster-parents took action to retain custody over the child. (Goody and Groothues 1982, 217–18)

In part, the judge ruled in the foster parents' favor because he saw many West Africans fostering their children with English couples and because, through these arrangements, "a strong bond of attachment and love has been forged between the children and the foster parents" and "the children are brought up in and learn our British ways of life" (cited in Goody and Groothues 1982, 217). Although I have no specific information about the Italian authorities' reasoning in Balotelli's case, similar notions of what would be in the boy's best interest—based on his emotional connection to the Balotellis, the implied superiority of learning Italian ways of life, and growing up in a wealthier family—may have persuaded them to allow him to remain with his foster parents despite his biological parents' desire that the stay be temporary.

Fostering to nonkin citizen families in the country of immigration can thus lead to struggles over a child's belonging in which Western legal understanding of fosterage, adoption, and kinship can be brought to bear, shaping the child's narrative of his or her situation. Belonging, as Mario Balotelli's case shows, encompasses issues of national identity and citizenship status, naming, residence, and emotional connection as well as financial obligations and expectations between parents and children. It is also affected by social status, defined by social class and citizenship, as read by the law and social services. However, it is important to note that different kinscripts of parenthood and child circulation are not the only causes of struggle over a child's belonging; such struggle has long happened within contexts of shared kinscripts as well. Francis B. Nyamnjoh (2002), for example, describes an experience reminiscent of Mario Balotelli's. When Nyamnjoh was a youth in the Cameroonian Grassfields, his biological father and two social fathers each pressured him to change his name to theirs to reflect their individual connection to him. Similarly, the young Ghanaian man who served as my assistant during the survey research phase of this project, was simultaneously pleased and frustrated that his father began to show an interest in him once he had completed secondary school. The young man was conflicted because he primarily felt loyalty to his mother and her siblings, who had supported him his whole life. Such parental tussling may be most common when adolescent boys show great promise. Therefore, conflict between parents over the identity and belonging of a child in the context of distributed parenting is not a new phenomenon caused by international migration (see also Fonseca 2009), but Western normative scripts of parenting and their encoding in state laws in Europe and elsewhere have affected how such conflict is resolved and which affective circuits are strengthened.

Goody and Groothues wanted to find out how common fostering-out was among West African migrant parents. One study they cited found that 60 percent of the children in a sample of 143 private foster homes in Birmingham, England, were West African, far more than would be anticipated given the relatively small population of West Africans in the early 1970s. In their own interviews of 296 West African parents in London, they found that a third had left one or more children behind in the home country, 13 percent had sent one or more children home from England, and half had placed one or more children with English foster parents at some point, although at the time of the interviews only a quarter had a child being fostered by an English family. Thus, while fostering a child with a local family was one option for West African migrants in England, as it was for the Barwuahs in Italy, fostering one's child "in Africa" was even more common.

Fostering from Italy to Ghana: Felicia, Her Grandmother, and Her Parents

Another strategy Ghanaian external migrants use when faced with child-care difficulties is to foster their children with a mother or sister in Ghana, just as urban migrants in Ghana look to their children's grandmothers or aunts for foster care.[6] These transnational migrants describe a broader array of reasons for out-fostering than the kind of health-care crisis faced by the Barwuahs: among others, they want their children to learn their family's mother tongue, to know their relatives, and to receive proper training and discipline, which they feel are harder to obtain in the country of immigration. The practice of sending children back to the home country is quite common among West Africans and is not unique to Ghanaians living in Italy (Coe 2013; Kea, this volume; Whitehouse 2012). Out-fostering to relatives can create breaks in affective circuits between parents and children similar to that experienced by Mario Balotelli and the Barwuahs. However, because the foster parents to whom the child has become attached often want to maintain the child's relation to the biological parents (possibly also having experienced distributed parenting in their own lives), they may help the child expand his or her affective circuits to include unknown or unfamiliar parents, as exemplified in the following story.

I met Felicia in her secondary school in Ghana during a group discussion among the children of international migrants. A willowy sixteen-year-old, she described her experience as a child of migrants to Italy. Felicia had been born in Italy and been sent back to Ghana as a three-year-old child to live with her grandmother. Like Mr. Barwuah, Felicia's mother worked in a factory in Italy. Speaking in English, which secondary-school students preferred to use in the group conversations, Felicia described her mother's decision to send her to Ghana as driven by language concerns—so that Felicia could learn English and Twi.

She asked my Dad to take me to Ghana because she wanted me to learn the language, English rather than Italian. So she wanted to take me [i.e., she could have taken me] to any other country apart from Ghana to learn English, but she preferred to bring me to our homeland because she wanted me to learn our culture. She brought me to my grandmother, deliberately. To speak the mother tongue.

Her circulation to live with her grandmother shaped her attachment to Ghana ("our homeland") and her fluency in her "mother tongue" and English rather than Italian.

Probably to lessen her feeling of abandonment, her grandmother hid the fact that Felicia's parents were abroad, instead telling her that they were in the capital, Accra, and that they would be coming home soon. Yet when Felicia was ten or eleven, she began to wonder why she had not met her parents. Because her grandmother would not tell her, she asked one of her aunts about the situation, and her aunt told her the truth. Felicia had reached the age when children are seen as being able to absorb information about their true origins and can better establish relationships with multiple parents. The new information resulted in greater connection with her parents: she subsequently visited them in Italy over a summer vacation.

Her parents returned from Italy to stay in Ghana permanently when Felicia was twelve years old. Felicia described how she attempted to revise her emotions in view of her interpretation of appropriate family relationships.

It is like when they [her parents] came back, I had rather more love for my grandmum. Although I liked them, but then, I was too close to my grandmum. I was uncomfortable with them. I tried to stay with them, but it wasn't working. Later, I had to decide:

these are my parents, and I have to stay with them. Now [at the age of sixteen] things are okay, and I relate to them as a family.

She described how she consciously attempted to control her emotions to bring them in line with what she considered appropriate for "a family," for instance, telling herself that she loved her parents and ought to live with them rather than being "too close" to her grandmother. As we saw in Balotelli's case, Felicia's family script shaped her emotions; in her case, however, the result was a conscious effort on her part to create feeling for and familiarity with her parents (Hochschild [1983] 2003; Reddy 2001).

Unlike Balotelli, Felicia identifies with Ghana, not Italy. She described her vacation to Italy:

Going on a bus, going to board, and the bus comes, and you have to wait, you sit down, you're Black, and they want you to stand because you don't belong to the country. They can't tell you to stand, because you paid to get in [the bus], but they are looking at you in a way you don't feel comfortable. They try to move themselves so you know you are the only one [who is] Black. You feel like getting off.

In her story, the bus seems to function like a microcosm or symbol of Italy, prompting her to feel discomfort, a lack of belonging, and a desire to exit. Although she said she would like to visit Italy again, she was not enthusiastic about staying there permanently. Her attitude was influenced by her sense of how immigrants are treated in Italy, a perspective perhaps shaped not only by her own brief summer vacation but also by her parents' stories of their lives there.

In contrast to Mario Balotelli, Felicia is attached to her biological parents and to her social parents, including her grandmother and various aunts, who help her maintain a relationship with her parents. Her multiple attachments are enabled by her foster parent's kin relation to a biological parent. Relying on relatives at home to help care for their children seems to enable migrants to more successfully maintain multiple affective circuits than does foster care with nonkin citizens in the country of immigration, although disruptions do occur. Part of the reason for this relative success is that Western social services and legal mechanisms do not become involved in the out-fosterage of the children of Ghanaian migrants; it does not come to their attention, nor do they see it as under their purview. This under-the-radar fosterage contrasts sharply with what happens when transnational migrants try to foster-in their relatives: they run into legal obstacles quite directly.

45

Translating Fosterage into International Adoption in the United States and the United Kingdom: Akua and Her Nephews

Recent migrants—who are more unstable in their employment and housing—turn to out-fostering to enable their children's care and growth. However, migrants who are secure in their employment and have good housing abroad—and thus are generally more likely to have migrated a long time ago—try to step in to help their relatives in crisis in Ghana by bringing a niece, nephew, or younger sibling to live with them. In doing so, some try to translate fosterage into international adoption as the easiest way to bring a child who is not biologically theirs abroad.

As I note above, the Hague adoption convention establishes safeguards to protect the best interests of adopted children and prevent their abduction or sale across borders. In the case of non-Hague signatory countries such as Ghana, the United States sets a higher bar for intercountry adoption: adopted children must be orphans or the sole remaining parent must be "unable to care for the child and has, in writing, irrevocably released the child for emigration and adoption" (U.S. Department of State 2013).[7] If the child is not an orphan, then the prospective parent must have lived with him or her for two years before requesting a visa for the child. Furthermore, the child cannot be "abandoned, relinquished, or released to a specific prospective adoptive parent for adoption" (U.S. Department of State 2013). In other words, the biological parent cannot designate the adopting parent but must have an orphanage or adoption agency seek out and screen prospective adoptive parents. Finally, the child being adopted must be under the age of sixteen. Although the laws on domestic adoption in the United States allow relatives to adopt, the procedure on international adoption assumes that the prospective parent is working through a recognized adoption agency in the United States to adopt a stranger rather than a relative's child. This assumption makes international adoption a difficult pathway for immigrants who wish to foster a sibling's child.

Akua's case illustrates tensions inherent in translating practices of distributed parenting to a legal regime that does not recognize them (Coe 2013). In 2005, Akua, a forty-nine-year-old woman from Akropong, was working as a university administrator in the United States. In the wake of her mother's death in Ghana, she wanted to bring her two nephews, then aged thirteen and fifteen, who had been living with her mother since they were very young, to come live with her.[8] The nephews had been fostered by her mother because of their father's alcoholism and his divorce from their mother, who had migrated to the United Kingdom. I did not meet any other Ghanaian who had tried to adopt a niece or nephew abroad, but Chantal Collard (2009) reports that family adoptions from African countries have soared in Quebec since 2000.

Akua had wanted to adopt her nephews for a long time but realized that they were her mother's main companions. Then, as her mother's health began failing in February 2005, she initiated the process of getting approval to adopt from her state's social services, including having a home study done by a social worker and applying for visas for her nephews. In November 2005, immigration services denied her application to adopt, stating as the reason that her brother, her nephews' father, had written a letter formally giving up his relationship with his sons. This objection was curious, because U.S. laws require a living parent to write such a letter to enable his or her children to be adopted by someone else. According to Akua, the immigration authorities said that the letter was a sign that the father was still attached to the boys because he cared about putting them in the hands of a good person. Her brother's designation of Akua as the adoptive parent was another problem, according to her lawyer. Akua did not mention as a factor in the ruling that the boys had two living parents—one in the United Kingdom and one in Ghana—although it may have been one. She approached another lawyer, who told her that she could only adopt if the children were in an orphanage or if she had lived with her nephews for two years before initiating adoption proceedings. She appealed the decision, but the appeal was denied in September 2006, by which time the older nephew had turned seventeen. Akua was upset because she felt that U.S. immigration laws were inconsistent: although she was allowed to live in the United States, she could not bring her dependents into the country. "It doesn't make sense," she said.

Many aspects of U.S. law intended to protect birth families and children in intercountry adoption make international adoption policy incompatible with Ghanaian practices of child circulation within families; among the problematic provisions are requiring the biological parent to formally relinquish rights to the adoptive parent, prohibiting the biological parent from designating the adoptive parent, and restricting adoption to orphans or abandoned children. Another problem is that adoption is a highly legalistic and bureaucratic procedure, a contractual agreement dependent on signed documents, which is a culturally understood method of ensuring transparency, fairness, and ethical behavior in the United States. In contrast, Ghanaian practices and narratives of child circulation highlight flexibility, pragmatism, and informality to create a safety net at different stages of the life course. Flexibility and informality can come at the risk of exploitation of the child, as Ghanaians well recognize, but lack of permanence means that unhappy fosterage arrangements can be altered under social pressure. Finally, in international adoption, coresidence—rather than material practices of care, such as paying for health care, clothing, and school fees—establishes the bond between parent and child. Thus, because Akua had not been living with her nephews before her attempted adoption of them, she was not seen as their adoptive parent, regardless of the fact that she was responding to a changing family situation (i.e., her mother's death) and had been paying her nephews' school fees for many years, thus committing herself to being one of their social parents.

As Judith Schachter (2009, 61) notes, "Adoption in an international arena exposes the cultural imperialism that determines relationships within and across societies." Ghanaian practices of child circulation do not fit available straightforward legal categories, dropping into a legal "space of nonexistence" (Coutin 2003, 179). Fair and transparent application of a Western kinship script to regulate African families is a sign of Western power, which works to "universalize the structure and meaning of the human condition" from a Western understanding of self, other, and family (Clarke 2009, 232). Despite Akua's high level of education and familiarity with bureaucratic institutions, she responded to the straightforward and transparent application of these regulations with confusion and a sense of unfairness.

Feeling she had exhausted the legal possibilities of adoption in the United States, Akua ended up selling her house there and moving to England in December 2006. However, when she tried to adopt her nephews in the United Kingdom, the British embassy in Ghana asked why she was not living with the boys. She wrote in response that United States immigration laws had not allowed them to live together. As of December 2008, she was still trying to bring her nephews to Britain—as sponsored relatives rather than adoptees because by then her nephews were legally adults and no longer eligible for adoption.

Some Ghanaian parents seek to circumvent Western international adoption law by adopting nieces and nephews in Ghana, because the Ghanaian court system has been more open to local understandings of fosterage and its conversion to adoption. Although I did not encounter this particular strategy in my own research, Ulrike Wanitzek (2013) describes two cases brought before the high court in 2008 in which childless Ghanaian women resident in the United Kingdom adopted their sisters' children. In the first case, a deputy nursing manager who had lived in the

United Kingdom for twenty-two years adopted her six-year-old nephew and her eight-year-old niece after their father deserted them and their mother passed away in 2005. During the three years since the mother's death, the children had been residing with their maternal aunts, while the migrant abroad, like Akua in relation to her nephews, had been financially supporting their care. The Ghanaian courts allowed the nursing manager to adopt her niece and nephew even though a parent was still living and the children had not been living with her since the mother's death. Instead, her financial support was taken as a sign of her commitment to the children (as was not the case in Akua's American and British adoption proceedings). The court recognized that the migrant aunt was functioning as a social parent to these children through her remittances, not her coresidence.

In the second case, a nurse who had resided in the United Kingdom for twenty-four years adopted her sixteen-year-old nephew, whose mother was unemployed and whose father had disappeared after his birth. On the legal decision in this case, in which the child had been living with his mother, Wanitzek (2013, 236) comments that, "following the logic of international laws, the child was not deprived of his family environment and was not in need of 'alternative care.'" Whereas, in this case, the American and British courts would have followed international adoption law, the Ghanaian court did not. Instead, it drew on local norms of child circulation and distributed parenthood, in which the aunt's social parenthood had been established through financial support of the child. As Wanitzek (2013, 238) notes, "The challenge of reconciling these two different concepts of child adoption appears to have been solved by the court in a pragmatic way."

Ghanaians abroad seek to translate practices of fosterage into the kinscript of international adoption to enable their nieces and nephews to live with them. While American and British courts can thwart the circulation of children into the households of Ghanaians abroad by failing to recognize parenting generated through care practices and material support and insisting on legal and formalized procedures, Ghanaian courts more willingly convert informal fosterage arrangements into formalized international adoption for such migrants. These different legal practices have immense significance for the ability of migrants to be social parents and generate affective circuits with the children of their siblings and their own younger siblings.

Conclusion: Kinscripts and the Circulation of Children

Kinscripts for parenting and care shape the physical circulation and affective circuits of children. Ghanaians employ strategies of distributed parenting to support their migration to Europe, finding those strategies useful in the care of their own children and the children in their extended family. Distributed parenting provides a social safety net in cases of crisis and promotes certain goals migrants set for their children, particularly around language, discipline, and character. According to this script, differently positioned adults are best able to provide children with the kinds of care they need at different points in their life course. However, relying on Western practices of foster care and adoption to support these goals has proved risky or impossible even for Ghanaians who are successful cultural brokers in other areas of their lives. Migrants who turn to social relations and institutions in Ghana to supplement and support the care of their children have been more successful than those who do not in achieving desired ends, and those relations and institutions have allowed them to sustain affective circuits with the children they seek to care for to a much greater extent.

Such practices highlight the power of Western states to both inhibit and encourage certain affective circuits through immigration, social services, and international adoption. Western social service policies and laws do not seem to shift in relation to Ghanaians' needs; instead, it is Ghanaian courts and families that demonstrate flexibility and adaptation, for instance, in being willing to give the imprimatur of plenary "adoption" in cases of transnational child circulation.

Judges in Ghana have been sensitive to child circulation not only because they share cultural scripts about parenting and care with petitioners but also because the court system in Ghana is itself a hybrid product, shaped by colonial norms and traditional authorities. In the colonial Gold Coast, there was a two-tier judicial system in which chiefly tribunals became courts of the first instance for specific offenses and colonial courts functioned as appellate courts for chiefly tribunals. Roger Gocking (1997, 63) has described this situation as a "flexible and adaptive" one in which chiefly tribunals were influenced by the practices of the colonial courts and vice versa. In colonial Africa, Kristin Mann and Richard Roberts (1991, 3) note, the "law formed an area in which Africans and Europeans engaged one another—a battleground as it were on which they contested access to resources and labour, relationships of power and authority, and interpretations of morality and culture." Ghanaian courts, perhaps because of the history of colonialism, have been more willing to engage in cultural pluralism than European courts have been. Today, in the context of African migration to Europe, the law seems to be reemerging as a central battleground, as a place where the affective circuits of African transnational migrations are broken and renegotiated.

One of the consequences of Western institutions' failure to recognize West African practices of child circulation is that children are shifted out of the care of transnational migrants, whether or not they are the parents or other close kin, and into that of relatives (including biological parents) in Ghana or, more rarely, into the households of nonkin citizens in the country of immigration. This distribution has important implications for the children's sense of belonging, both as Ghanaians and as members of their family. Those who are raised in Ghana rather than in Italy or the United Kingdom by Ghanaian immigrants are denied the education and status associated with living "abroad," although they live transnationally, aware of a social or biological parent abroad (Fouron and Glick Schiller 2002). This means that even though they are the children of immigrants, many of the attributes and behaviors of second-generation immigrants do not apply to them. They are less likely than second-generation children to turn their backs on their country's language and culture, as Sargent and Larchanché discuss (this volume), and they are as moved by the smells, sounds, and language of their home country as their parents are. This habitus and sense of belonging as Ghanaian is intended by their parents. Should they eventually migrate abroad as their parents did, they may function more like a first generation, likely to maintain ties to the home country and to the caregivers who remain there. Through their multidimensional sense of identification, the children of migrants raised in Ghana are likely to remain Ghanaians in their hearts even if their citizenship status changes, rather than becoming, like Mario Balotelli, Italians in their hearts as well as in their legal status.

Acknowledgments

I am grateful to all those who participated in this project and to the rest of my research team: Kweku Aryeh, who assisted with the individual interviews; Joe Banson and Margaret Rose Tettey, who cofacilitated the children's focus-group discussions; and Rogers Krobea Asante, Joe Banson, Bright Nkrumah, and Emmanuel Amo Ofori, who completed the arduous task of transcription. This research was funded by the National Science Foundation and the Wenner-Gren Foundation for Anthropological Research. I am grateful to the editors and three reviewers who provided excellent suggestions for revision. All flaws and faults, of course, are my own.

Notes

1. Olwig (2007) and Súarez-Orozco, Todorova, and Louie (2002) similarly argue for the significance of cultural scripts in emotion work.
2. Because Ghanaians use stepwise migrations between African countries and Europe and often have relatives scattered across multiple nation-states, I do not distinguish strongly in this chapter between migration to Europe and migration to other countries in Africa, Asia, and North America. I conducted focus-group interviews in private and secondary schools in a midsize town and a large city in Ghana with seventy-nine children who had at least one parent abroad. Most of the parents had migrated to the United Kingdom (twenty-eight out of eighty-three) or the United States (twenty-six), but some had also gone to Germany (twelve), Italy (six), and the Netherlands (four). Children of migrants to Canada, France, Israel, Japan, South Africa, Spain, and Switzerland were also represented (one each). I followed up the focus-group conversations with individual interviews of children whose parents were in the United States, with their caregivers, and with the parents themselves. From that research, I obtained a sense of the emotional issues faced by transnational families (Coe 2008). I subsequently conducted a household survey of mainly Akan families in the Ghanaian district capital of Akropong to understand how child circulation in transnational families differed from that of families of internal migrants and to get a sense of change over time. Ultimately, this effort resulted in interviews with ninety-three caregivers and with eighty of the children they were looking after. The interviewed children were between the ages of eight and twenty-two years. Forty-five of these children came to focus-group discussions that were organized in their neighborhoods, at which they were also asked to draw images of life abroad. This research yielded data on the experiences of people of various social classes and ethnicities, reflecting the social and economic diversity of the town.
3. Though migration both within Ghana and to Europe is a long-standing practice, the payoff has shrunk in recent years. In the area of Ghana I know best (Akuapem, in the Eastern Region), people have traveled at least since the late nineteenth century to work on the railroads, in the cities on the coast and in the interior, in cocoa lands farther to the west, or in other parts of West Africa as skilled craftsmen and traders (Hill 1963). Many men and women migrate within Ghana today, moving between different places over their life spans as they cope with the contraction and expansion of economic opportunities and, particularly for women, with changing social relationships, whether marriage or divorce, a birth, or the sickness or death of a parent (Apt

1993; van der Geest 1998). Professionals such as teachers, nurses, accountants, and ministers are transferred to postings all over Ghana; farmers seek fertile land; and traders travel long distances to buy and sell commodities.

4. Brydon (1979) saw this as a new form of child circulation in Amedzofe in the Volta Region of Ghana in the late 1970s. Children were sent to live with the grandmother right after weaning, making them much younger than the usual fostered children (see also Etienne 1979).

5. One caveat to my interpretation of these events is that, unlike many of the Ghanaians with whom I have worked, the Barwuahs are not from Akropong but from Konongo, in the Ashanti Region.

6. Their practices of out-fostering are similar to those Whitehouse (2012) and Bledsoe and Sow (2011) describe for West African migrants in Congo and in Europe, respectively.

7. Ghana suspended intercountry adoptions "temporarily" in May 2013, until its policies could be reviewed by the Ghana Department of Social Welfare (http://travel.state.gov/content/adoptionsabroad/en/country-information /alerts-and-notices/ghana13-10-15.html). This suspension followed growing international concern about intercountry adoptions. The adoption proceedings I discuss in the text happened in 2005–2006, long before the suspension of intercountry adoptions by the Ghanaian government.

8. Akua could have applied for custody of her nephews through family reunification. However, the definition of family underlying U.S. policy is narrow, similar to that noted by Chantal Collard (2009, 122) for Quebec: "The definition of kinship enshrined in Canadian immigration law is too restrictive for many applicants, whose cultures recognize more extended kin relationships." In the United States, while dependent children and legally married spouses are given priority, more extended relatives such as the children of siblings can spend many years awaiting reunification (U.S. Department of State 2013).

TWO

Forging Belonging through Children in the Berlin-Cameroonian Diaspora

PAMELA FELDMAN-SAVELSBERG

Toward the beginning of our multiyear friendship and year of intense collaboration studying maternity, mobility, and belonging among African migrant women in Berlin,[1] my Cameroonian research assistant leaned her head toward mine, the coffee on the table we shared in the university library's café steaming up our glasses. A migrant mother herself, Magni confided, "We are always on the move, for ourselves and for our children."[2] We had just been discussing Cameroonian women who migrate to find better conditions in which to raise a family. They often find, however, that their migration simultaneously creates challenges to the social and emotional connections that constitute belonging—a complex mix of recognition by and attachment to a particular group and rootedness in a particular place. In the course of our work together, Magni and I heard many stories of migrant women's difficulties with respect to reproduction and belonging, summarized in their recurrent exclamation, "It's hard being a mother here!" Despite their complaints, our Cameroonian interviewees also clearly conveyed that their children enabled them to overcome the burdens of exclusion and forge new layers of belonging. Through their children, young women strengthened connections to kin in Cameroon and built new connections to Cameroonian diasporic communities and to German officials. Having and raising children in Berlin may have been hard and lonely for these recent immigrants, but it also helped them adjust to a new place. That morning over coffee, Magni told me how she too found her relations, her things, and her loyalties stretched between Cameroon and Germany. In fact, it was her carefully cultivated transnational connections that kept her and her children anchored.

This chapter explores how Cameroonian women in Germany seek to establish their belonging through birthing and caring for infants and what happens to their ties in places of origin and places of migration in the process.[3] This is partly a tale about integration—belonging in Germany—but it is also a story about belonging in new ways with Cameroonians back home and with fellow migrants in Berlin. Much of the literature on transnational families examines how women create and manage connections to others through the circulation of children via fostering, adoption, and other forms of distributed parenting (e.g., Alber, Martin, and Notermans 2013; Coe 2013, this volume; Leinaweaver 2008, 2013; Parreñas 2005b; Reynolds 2006). But what happens when mothers and children move together or when children born in the country of immigration stay with their immigrant mothers? In these cases, migrant women do not merely give birth to the second generation. Young children help their mothers maintain important connections with kin in Cameroon while simultaneously creating opportunities for them in their new lives in Germany by soliciting care from multiple directions.

In the tender phase of mother-infant care, mothers deploy their children to forge connections across a variety of social networks. Belonging "to" these social networks—kin groups and households, ethnic or migrant community associations, and states—encompasses a range of statuses and feelings (cf. Krause and Schramm 2011; Yuval-Davis 2006). Through their children, women may maintain or gain citizenship status, national or ethnic identity, emotional connection, and feelings of recognition, acceptance, and comfort. Women's and their children's belonging can be felt (an interior state), performed (by behaving according to certain codes), or imposed (e.g., when a bureaucrat categorizes a woman as deserving of aid). In interaction with family members stretching from Cameroon to Germany, with migrant associations, and with German officials, migrant mothers variably enact belonging through rights, duties, and expectations regarding financial transactions (remittances, fees, taxes); decision making (voting, advice); physical presence (residence and visits); bodily care (of themselves and infants); and use of symbols (including language choice and naming practices). Migration complicates belonging, stretching some connections to the breaking point while facilitating new ones.

Although Cameroonians often migrate to improve the conditions in which they regenerate families, transnational migration renders belonging as well as reproduction even more difficult. In migrating, African women make "choices for their future children and for their children's future" (Shandy 2008, 822). These choices entail sacrifice, as mothers leave behind the embrace of their families and familiar ways of being to face the material, social, and emotional challenges of starting anew in a strange place. Bureaucratic barriers as well as cost make it difficult to find partners, get married, and become pregnant in expected ways, forcing transnational Cameroonians to innovate. These same barriers make it difficult for extended female kin to provide physical and emotional care to new mothers and their infants. In addition, migration necessitates managing new sets of expectations, particularly those related to vernacular meanings of belonging through children that emanate from kin back home as well as from laws and bureaucratic procedures in Germany. The migratory context contributes to Cameroonian mothers' insecurity regarding physical, cultural, and social reproduction (Feldman-Savelsberg, Ndonko, and Yang 2005).

Women's efforts to overcome their reproductive insecurity and to seek support for themselves and their children generate new connections and forms of belonging. Finding partners, being pregnant, giving birth, and rearing children—practices of physical and social reproduction—tie mothers to families, to communities, and to states. For example, when parents care for their children, they fulfill family expectations while drawing on help from extended kin. Simultaneously, they receive entitlements from community associations and government social service agencies—benevolent branches of the same government that imposes immigration restrictions. Mothers purposefully build, maintain, and manage networks, sometimes across vast distances, through their reproductive practices (Astone et al. 1999). And mothers shape their reproductive decisions in part because they are striving for the sense of positive value and recognition that comes with belonging. Using reproduction to embed themselves in overlapping fields of social relationships, mothers actively construct their multilayered belongings.

The networks that women build up to establish belonging are maintained through ongoing interaction and exchange. We can picture the ties mothers forge as circuits through which money, goods, and medicines;

fostered children and visitors; and love, moral support, and demands all flow (see Cole and Groes, introduction to this volume). The metaphor of electrical current, subject to short circuits and regulated by circuit breakers, helps us appreciate the discontinuous nature of these flows: they can be slowed, dropped, blocked, and picked up again. They can, for example, be interrupted when pregnant women with shaky residence status avoid communicating the hardships of migrant life with their mothers in the home country. To push the metaphor further, these social flows not only vary in speed and strength but also occasionally shift from alternating to direct current. In other words, affective exchanges at times flow mostly in one direction despite—among kin—an ethos of long-term reciprocity. These flows constitute *affective* circuits (Cole and Groes, introduction), because the things that move along them are intertwined with—and indeed express—the emotive and loving elements of belonging to families and communities. Through birthing and caring for their infants and seeking care from others, Cameroonian women establish belonging by building up affective circuits with multiple social networks. However, the nature of these affective circuits and their operation differ depending on the sphere of interaction. As I show in this chapter, the flows that occur when mothers of infants interact with kin differ from flows through their circuits with hometown associations and with the state in terms of the things circulated, the emotional charge of the exchange, and its underlying logic.

Babies, Belonging, and Movement in Cameroon: Historical Roots of Migration to Germany

In Cameroon, local social practices around marriage and complex ethnic history have tightly intertwined women's reproduction with ideas of belonging. This is especially so for the francophone Bamiléké and their fellow Grassfielders from the anglophone Northwest Region who are the foci of my research.[4] Because of exogamous marriage rules, women from the Bamiléké and other Grassfields peoples have long migrated outside their villages and chiefdoms to bear children under socially acceptable conditions. They learned that to forge belonging in their new conjugal settings, they needed to bear children. Given the dual descent system, children simultaneously gave wives value in their husbands' kinship groups while further strengthening their ties to geographically distant natal families.

But birthing the children that forge connections is no easy matter. Hard labor, poor nutrition, and disease all make women's fertility fragile. In the late twentieth century, mothers in rural Cameroon commonly clapped and then opened their hands, palms up, to indicate "we have nothing"— not enough children, not enough food or material goods or conditions to grow healthy families. Rural women also feared witchcraft attacks due to competitive jealousies among cowives in polygynous households. Their physical distance from their families of origin often weakened the protection and support emanating from those sources, rendering reproduction yet more insecure. To top off the litany of hardships, from the colonial to the postcolonial era, Bamiléké have perceived the state as a threat to reproduction (Feldman-Savelsberg 1999; Feldman-Savelsberg, Ndonko, and Schmidt-Ehry 2000; Terretta 2007).

These patterns of reproductive insecurity have been exacerbated by political tensions colored by ethnic overtones since the mid-twentieth century. Once a German colony, Cameroon was divided during World War I between Britain and France by a League of Nations mandate; it gained independence in 1960 and became a bilingual federal republic in 1961. The francophone Bamiléké, currently 30 percent of the Cameroonian population of twenty million, became involved in armed resistance to the party in power in the years surrounding independence (1956–73). Many Bamiléké sought refuge from violence by migrating to join the urban Bamiléké diaspora. This Bamiléké history of political opposition combines with the group's reputation for entrepreneurial drive and high fertility to create ethnic stereotypes, summed up in continual references to the so-called Bamiléké Problem (Geschiere 2007, 2009; Geschiere and Nyamnjoh 2000; Kago Lele 1995). Anglophone Cameroonians, comprising 20 percent of Cameroon's population, share a similar reputation for entrepreneurial drive as well as a history of labor migration and domestic diaspora formation as "come-no-goes" (a Pidgin expression describing labor migrants who stay in work locales rather than return to their places of origin).

Cameroonian public discourse questioning both groups' loyalty to the state has sharpened with repeated economic crises. Those who are considered *allogènes* (strangers) by local communities face limited access to education, voting, and even urban market licenses (Geschiere 2009).[5] Anglophone and Bamiléké youth complain that corruption and lack of future perspectives—what Jua (2003) terms the loss of transitional pathways— impede founding and supporting families. Furthermore, since a constitutional change introducing multiparty politics in the 1990s, Cameroonian government services have become ethnicized, and expensive fees and bribes make accessing them, especially health care, difficult.

Higher education used to offer a way out of poverty. But young people in Yaoundé and Berlin told me that personal ties to powerful actors had become more important than merit in securing admission to coveted courses of study such as medicine. Migration is one way for Bamiléké to avoid Cameroon's discriminatory, anti-Bamiléké quotas for university admission and for Anglophones to overcome the paucity of options for higher education in English in a country dominated by the French-speaking majority. Indeed, the pursuit of higher education combines with histories of fractured belonging and struggle, pushing young Cameroonian mothers to seek well-being through transnational migration (see Stoller 2014). They become "bushfallers"—overseas migrants who seek adventure and fortune through their quest in the faraway "bush." They often end up in Europe (Alpes 2011; Fleischer 2012; Nyamnjoh 2011).

With its nearly free university education and the distant colonial connection that created an early if thin migratory path, Germany has become a particularly popular destination among Cameroon's emerging middle class (Fleischer 2012). Since the mid-1980s, targeted scholarships have led Cameroonian university students to both Germanys (the Federal Republic, or West Germany, and the German Democratic Republic, or East Germany; GTZ 2007, 7), establishing networks for later chain migration. Cameroonians also seek job opportunities in Europe's economic powerhouse. But because German immigration law makes legal labor migration nearly impossible, family reunification and educational migration are the most frequent forms of legal migration from Cameroon to Germany.[6] Many Cameroonian migrant mothers arrive as students or come to join a student spouse, gaining legal residency through laws governing family reunification (on highly educated migrants; see also Fesenmyer, this volume).

These migrant pathways shape the composition of the Cameroonian migrant population in Germany, which is young, of childbearing age,[7] relatively well educated, and disproportionately Bamiléké and/or Anglophone. Cameroonians continue to migrate to Germany in increasing numbers even as migration from other sub-Saharan African countries is declining. By 2012, over sixteen thousand Cameroonians were legally registered in Germany, well over two-fifths of whom were women (Schmid and Borchers 2010, 147; Statistisches Bundesamt 2013). Berlin itself hosts a sizable Cameroonian immigrant population, with 1,928 documented (and probably several times more undocumented) migrants geographically dispersed throughout the metropolis of 3.5 million (Amt für Statistik Berlin-Brandenburg 2013, 22).[8]

Encountering New Problems of Belonging in Germany

While Cameroonians migrate to create better conditions in which to build their families and raise children, they soon find that their problems are not easily solved by migration. Bih, a thirty-three-year-old graduate student at a prominent university in Berlin and mother of a preschooler, told me, "Oh, I have big dreams, but the problem is how to accomplish it. Everyone dreams, right?" With her dry comment, Bih hints at a key reality of migrant motherhood—moving to Berlin in search of greater security paradoxically creates new problems.

The new difficulties Cameroonian migrants face in Berlin are related to a range of issues from immigration rights and regulations pertaining to foreign students to existential questions of food, shelter, and health-care access, finding and maintaining relationships with fellow Cameroonian migrants, and satisfying family members' expectations. An overwhelming series of laws and bureaucratic procedures greets migrant mothers arriving in Germany. Students, for example, must meet German visa requirements, including depositing a year's living costs (ca. €8,000) in a blocked German bank account (DAAD 2016). Despite the challenges of studying in a foreign language and an unfamiliar system, they must maintain good academic standing to qualify for scholarships and must stay in school to keep their visas. Somehow, new migrants must learn German rules related to rent deposits, residence registration, and health insurance. Mothers must make the rounds of numerous offices to register their children's birth, attend mandatory well-baby checkups, and later manage a complex school placement system. Accessing health care can make pregnant women living in Germany without a proper visa visible to immigration authorities. Discovery usually occurs when irregular migrants cannot pay for their obstetric care, drawing the attention of hospital billing departments; the Residence Act (Aufenthaltsgesetz) "mandates that persons residing illegally in Germany be reported to the authorities if they seek services at public facilities" (Castañeda 2008, 344).

Everyday interactions with the social actors who enforce these German rules remind Cameroonian mothers of their foreignness. Even the most well-intentioned bureaucrat must categorize migrants as noncitizens and thus as people subject to special regulatory constraints. But some practice everyday forms of racism (Kilomba 2008; Sow 2008) that underscore mothers' nonbelonging in emotionally painful ways. Hannah, an engineering student, proudly brought her newborn daughter with her to the International Student Office to pick up some papers. The secretary made a face at the baby, remarking, "What a *kleine Affe* [little monkey]," leaving Hannah shaking in anger. Relating this story to me several years later, Hannah said, "It is hard every day to have to fight."

Cameroonian mothers circulate such cautionary tales to help one another cope with the difficulties they face as migrants. Building new, informal affective circuits among their fellow migrants, newcomers learn from earlier arrivals about practical affairs such as finding one's way to the Foreigner's Office. Already established migrants encourage newcomers to attend hometown association meetings. They share good comebacks to "kleine Affe" remarks. But life among fellow Cameroonian migrants does not always flow smoothly. As in any relatively small group, there are likes and dislikes, inclusions and exclusions. Information about jobs may be shared with some and jealously guarded from others. Migrants may monitor each other's child-rearing practices to see whether they are in line with Cameroonian norms. Formal rules regarding descent, membership fees, and attendance determine who may or may not belong to hometown associations. Within these associations, celebrations honoring newborns foster conviviality, but mistrust—generated by gossip and possible reporting of immigration irregularities—weakens diasporic networks (Cole 2014b).

Newly arrived Cameroonian women discover that keeping in touch with kin is also problematic. Yearning for empathy, they find that their parents and siblings have little sense of the challenges they face in Berlin. Instead, kin dream of a Europe overflowing with easy opportunities. When parents have made huge sacrifices to finance a child's migration, they expect that child to seize these opportunities and eventually to send remittances home. Migrant students feel this pressure; educational success therefore carries an emotional burden. Managing obligations to repay while remaining in school is particularly challenging for young women who are simultaneously juggling schoolwork with occasional jobs, romantic relationships, pregnancy, and childcare. Difficult pregnancies may cause women students to dematriculate and lose their legal immigration status. Divorce may also lead to loss of a precious visa for women who have migrated to join their student husbands. Some Cameroonian mothers keep calls home short and sweet to avoid sharing their hardships with parents.

So'nju, for example, was reluctant to let her mother know how difficult her life was in the distant European "bush," avoiding communication when she became pregnant.

But even if I am pregnant I don't always say until I deliver . . . because when you tell they will ask every time you make a call. . . . Until I deliver after two days I call and tell. Yes, my mother is always angry about that, . . . she is always angry when I am pregnant when I don't tell. "I am your mother, I am not your aunt or your stepmother, I am your mother, you could have told me."

So'nju's struggle with truth and distance (Baldassar 2007) short-circuited her transnational exchanges with her mother, impeding the expected flow of maternal care for her as a pregnant daughter and subsequent care for her newborn. So'nju's mother's lament, "I am not your aunt or your stepmother, I am your mother," referred to a common taboo against discussing a woman's current pregnancy with anyone other than close kin. So'nju's mother was desperately reminding her daughter that fulfilling expectations for communication, that is, participating in affective circuits, is an essential part of belonging to a family.

Migrating to Germany thus engenders difficulties of belonging in several spheres of Cameroonian women's lives. Young mothers find it challenging to meet their kin's expectations and to maintain practices— such as giving birth in the presence of female kin—that reinforce the obligations and sentiments of belonging to families. When mothers seek out their fellow Cameroonians, they find a population geographically dispersed across a vast metropolitan area instead of a tightly woven community. The hometown associations in which they seek solidarity meet only once monthly. Associations' ability to alleviate migrants' sense of alienation in Germany is thus limited. Instead, regulatory regimes and such everyday questions as "where do you come from?" underscore migrant mothers' foreignness.

Making Families and Forging Belonging

In response to these difficulties, Cameroonian migrant mothers modulate their reproductive practices and forge new ties of belonging. By birthing and caring for children, mothers form multiple ties to kin who remain in Cameroon as well as to fellow migrants and to representatives of the German state. Each of these ties creates a different type of circuit along which emotions, support, goods, and money flow—often asymmetrically— among mothers, their babies, and related sets of actors.

All Alone: Imperfect Maintenance of Kin-Based Circuits

Although Cameroonian mothers of newborns in Berlin miss the social and practical support of female relatives who can easily travel to and care for a new mother and her infant, they go to great lengths to maintain ties with their kin—phoning, visiting, and sending and receiving packages. Distance, though, thins out connections with family "back home," changing the intensity and content of flows along affective circuits. Childbearing has an ambiguous effect on the affective circuits that Cameroonian migrant mothers maintain with kin.

On the one hand, having a child and caring for an infant strengthens ties to kin who remain in Cameroon. Migrant mothers deploy a newborn (*mɛn fi*, or "fresh person") to strengthen the exchange of loving words with kin back home. They build on repertoires and expectations that female kin help out after childbirth—visiting, taking over housework, passing the new baby from lap to lap, and making eye contact with the infant to integrate it into a world of social relationships.[9] Lily is a case in point. She grew up in Cameroon and France before joining her husband in Berlin. Active in her Pentecostal church, Lily is busy completing a diploma in business administration, and she is supervising her oldest child's homework. Struggling to juggle the demands of her hectic life with the birth of her third child, Lily phoned her mother nearly every day. "As for advice, in Cameroon, *les mamans* are there, they have their experiences, and that helps a lot. But even us here in Europe, we need the experience of our *mamans*, who can tell us if we need to do this, do that."[10]

On the other hand, bearing a child while overseas also makes obvious to a woman and her relatives just how much distance and bureaucratic barriers weaken kin ties: "your mother, your sister, your girl-cousin . . . they are far, far. The telephone, even Skype, it's not the same." In both practical and emotional terms, transnational communication via mobile phones and Skype does not substitute for physical presence (see Kea, this volume).[11] Several women told me that the flow of visits, food, handcrafted baby clothes, and bodily care that, in Cameroon, promoted newborns' belonging to kin groups was reduced in Germany to "mere words." The resources that flow through migrant mothers' affective circuits with kin are more limited than they are for mothers in Cameroon; distance, cost, and bureaucracy act as circuit breakers blocking the flow of the physical care, transmission of knowledge, and shared enjoyment of the baby's developmental milestones that depend on copresence. Mothers express the situation in their laments that the immediate postpartum period is a particularly lonely time. As Christine, a Bamiléké political refugee, explained, "In Cameroon, every evening we drank, we ate, there were visitors. . . . [They] held the baby. . . . For a month there were always lots of people. . . . But here . . . alone."

Some mothers, however, make heroic efforts to reproduce the physical presence of close female kin. They coordinate work, schooling, and relations with spouses to forge connections of care and belonging across great distance. When female kin cannot come to them, these mothers travel to their female kin, as Bih did. Bih became pregnant while both she and her Cameroonian husband, James, were enrolled in graduate programs in Berlin. Bih strongly wished she could follow the tradition of returning home to spend the perinatal period with her mother, but both her parents had died young. If Bih were in Cameroon, her female siblings would substitute for their mother's presence—but these sisters were spread across five nations on three continents. How could she coordinate her wish to spend her first birth under the tutelage of a female elder with her drive to complete her education and her need to maintain her residency permit in Germany? Coordination of multiple life-course imperatives at the vital conjunctures of pregnancy and birth is a common feature of the transition to social motherhood in Cameroon (Johnson-Hanks 2006). Bih's heroic juggling act reflects her efforts to maintain several types of belonging simultaneously—to her distant kin and their notions of the proper way to be part of a family and to the institutions and actors surrounding university life in Germany.

With her due date falling during the break between semesters, Bih studied ahead and arranged to take her final exams early. Seven months pregnant, she traveled to the United States to stay with James's mother and sister. Moving temporarily from Germany to North America meant disrupting her medical care. Bih's treatment at an American public hospital was harsh, characterized by delays in making appointments for necessary tests. At this delicate time of first birth, Bih also endured a three-month separation from her husband, with whom she had a close, companionate marriage; on his end, to fund Bih's travels and save for their new family, James worked three jobs while maintaining his laboratory research for his dissertation.

Although in an unfamiliar environment, and lacking the "traditional" visits of multiple female kin and friends, Bih placed herself in the company of two female affines who guided her through pregnancy, birth, and early infant care. She returned with her one-month-old baby to her husband and studies in Berlin just in time for the start of the next semester. With the help of a small maternity stipend Bih reeived from a student organization, she and James managed to get by financially. Ties to other Cameroonian women through a Grassfields hometown association and through a student housing project kept Bih from feeling "all alone" after her return to Berlin. These "Cameroonian sisters" substituted for kin, sharing information and childcare, permitting each other to survive motherhood in a strange land.

Even if Lily, Christine, and Bih are nervous about losing a sense of closeness with their kin back home, each unequivocally feels that she "belongs" to her family. Christine and Lily exchange words of advice, solace, and even scolding with their parents and siblings who have remained in Cameroon. This flow of words and occasional small gifts maintains belonging in the absence of other exchanges. The signal passed along their affective circuits is weakened by distance; it becomes more single stranded—words and a few things rather than people who can travel. Nonetheless, the flurry of communications surrounding the birth and care of a new baby helps rejuvenates migrant mothers' sense of belonging to their extended families. Bih's travel to her globally scattered kin represents an extreme attempt to maintain family ties and a sense of doing what is culturally right in relation to a birth. Because so many kin have also migrated to Europe and North America, mothers like Bih maintain their belonging to their families and cultural origins by building and maintaining ties with other Cameroonians abroad.

"Shake Your Shoulders with Us": Conviviality and Caution in *Community-Based Circuits*

Through their newborn babies, mothers receive affirmation and access formal entitlements in Cameroonian diasporic associations during community events characterized by a precarious mix of conviviality and caution. The birth of a baby is a joyous occasion to share with the population of nonkin hailing from the same part of Cameroon and now living in Berlin. Scattered across the city, this "community" meets monthly in place-based cultural and development associations,[12] most of which are registered simultaneously at the German administrative court and at the Cameroonian embassy. The pleasurable sociability and formal obligations of association meetings are immediately concerned with the construction of belonging, the management of birth and illness, and the challenges of cultural reproduction among a mobile, diasporic population. My interlocutors describe the associations as "islands of home," although the boundaries of "home" are drawn more generously in Berlin than they would be in Cameroon. Members rarely knew each other before migrating to Berlin, and they may or may not see each other outside formal monthly meetings.

Mothers forge extrafamilial connections when they maintain formal association memberships, participate in monthly meetings, make claims on association resources in times of need, and in turn—as association representatives—deliver gifts and aid to others. They fulfill obligations of

2.1 "Shake your shoulders with us." Family and hometown association members dance together at a Born House celebration held in honor of a newborn infant, Berlin 2010. Hometown association members wear matching *pagne*, or cloth wrappers. The association's gift to the baby's parents shines in the glaring lights of the rented hall. Photo by Pamela Feldman-Savelsberg.

belonging through children when they give birth and throw an elaborate Born House party (*Jeunes Mères* in Cameroonian French) honoring a new baby as a member of their hometown's diaspora. Associations reciprocate through the obligations their members feel toward mothers and children. As Lola, a nurse and mother of five, explained,

The child is the responsibility of the whole village or a whole society, so we as an association, we feel the responsibility when a child is there. And there are some social benefits; we try to support them, the parents. Born House is like the presentation of the child to the society or the association.

At one Born House celebration, I met Shelly, the wife of an association officer. Struggling to converse above the din of Cameroonian music played by Petit Pays et les Sans-Visas, we compared Born House celebrations in Berlin with festivities we both knew from Cameroon. Back home, the new mother invites relatives, friends, and other well-wishers to see and hold her new child. The event is held in the mother's house, about two months postpartum. Attendees eat a dish made of plantains harvested from the tree under which the baby's umbilical cord was buried. Prepared with copious amounts of bright red palm oil, the dish symbolically links the child to the land of its ancestors and to the mother's experience of birth. A tiny taste of the sauce reassures the baby that it is "among kin and kith who care about his well-being" (Nyamnjoh and Rowlands 2013, 143).

In Berlin, migrants' apartments are too small and their neighbors are too concerned with noise, Shelly explained, to allow for an exuberant celebration in an intimate, family setting. Instead, Born House ceremonies are elaborate civic events drawing together diverse community members in a semipublic space. Because it takes time (and resources) to prepare, most parents meld Born House with the child's first birthday celebration. Parents rent a hall, hire a band, buy and cook food, and serve drinks. In turn, association officers present a gift, such as a car seat or cash, predetermined in the association's bylaws. Association officers, friends, and guests pronounce blessings and offer speeches wishing the baby love, peace, and prosperity. They encourage mother and father to teach their child perseverance and respect for elders and extol the virtues of community belonging. Born House creates an exchange between parents, who invest resources to host a party centered on their new child, and association members, who contribute material and emotional resources to the parents and child.

Part of the fun at Born House parties in Berlin is the showcasing of neo-traditional performances and an exchange of gifts that underscore a sense of cultural belonging among all participants. During the event I mention above, at a cue from the master of ceremonies, the hired band fell silent as association members donned matching wrappers. Past and current association presidents sang and danced in a circle around two drummers, joined by the hosting mother, father, and baby daughter. The MC invited guests to "shake your shoulders with us." Association officers and other guests presented gifts in an atmosphere of joyously raucous sound, tastes of home adapted to host-country ingredients, and lighthearted conversation in familiar accents. Cash, food, layettes, and conviviality flowed along circuits created and reaffirmed through the day's festivities. In contrast to kin-based affective circuits, at Born House parties the items flowing through the circuits and the timing of the exchange are formally defined. Parties are held within a year of birth, gifts are predetermined entitlements, and advice comes in the form of solemn oratory.

The emotions flowing along community-based circuits are not always so convivial. Monthly home association meetings—when the treasurer compares demands for Born House, aid for ill members, and wake-keeping contributions against the association's balance sheet—can also become occasions for contention. As one Bamiléké father told me, "People go to their meetings to have an island of home, to be comfortable and laugh with others. But trust is a different matter. We rarely talk about our private lives at meetings."

While friends and kin may attend the same home association meetings, most of those present are only occasional acquaintances. Because new mothers are not very familiar with people they meet at community events, they worry that other attendees may be judgmental of their attempts to manage the challenges of reproduction in a strange land. Even at relatively informal events, such as an association's year-end party, friends interrupt personal exchanges when a mere acquaintance approaches. I observed this happen at one year-end party when I was sitting with with Marthe and her best friend, holding Marthe's baby on my lap. Radiant as we admired her child, Marthe had sought advice from her friend, sotto voce, about her daughter's sudden refusal of solid food. The moment another woman joined us, Marthe and her friend changed the subject from a backstage concern to chattier frontstage matters (Goffman 1959).

Adapting their presentation of self to a new audience, Marthe and her friend revealed that diasporic associational life is marked simultaneously by conviviality and caution. Marthe could never know how news of her troubles might travel along circuits within the diasporic community or even to her family and friends in Cameroon, possibly casting her maternal skills—and more—in a bad light. Because association members are not as close as kin and friends but are nonetheless close enough to gossip within socially relevant circles, Bamiléké and anglophone Grassfielders' place-based organizations in Berlin are sites of cautious communion. As Lola later told me, "No, confiding [about reproductive or family problems], no. We can exchange matters about school, daily activities, just sit and think about some things in Africa." Mistrust within Cameroonian community settings emerges, on the one hand, from migrants' legal and emotional vulnerabilities and, on the other hand, from migrants' wish to control the flow of information (including gossip) along transnational networks (Feldman-Savelsberg 2011; cf. Cole 2014b). Mistrust acts as a circuit breaker, temporarily interrupting affective flows among Cameroonians in Berlin as well as between Berlin and Cameroon. Women's ambivalent relationships to fellow migrants in their hometown association subtly reshape the nature of ethnic belonging from a self-evident even if complicated part of everyday life in Cameroon to an achieved status in which one can choose to embed oneself to varying degrees in Germany.

Circuits with and around German Others: State Regulation and Tentative Belonging

Pregnancy and childbearing create opportunities for women to forge ties with German public and private institutions and individuals. Pregnant migrants, new mothers, and babies interact with multiple authorities, change their immigration status, visit doctors, and submit health-insurance claims. Thus, having children is one way Cameroonian mothers connect to German institutions, obtaining rights and protection. The person with whom a woman bears a child has consequences for that woman's visa status. How a mother bears and rears her children determines whether she receives benefits or punishment. Bearing a child affords a woman several official maternal protections. In exchange, she must follow child protection rules (e.g., regarding mandatory pediatric checkups) to avoid sanctions.

The birth of a child precipitates a cascade of visits with and applications to German authorities. In a photocopied handout, the Berlin office of the family planning organization ProFamilia lists six steps to take before and ten steps to take after a birth to access the entitlements of the welfare state. Stops along the *Behördengang* (the long pathway of administrative errands) include the Registry Office to obtain the child's birth certificate, the employer's personnel office to arrange maternity leave, Youth Services to apply for a day-care voucher and parental benefits, the Employment Office for the child benefit (*Kindergeld*), the Housing Authority for housing benefits, and the medical insurance company for coverage of the midwife's home visits and help with household chores. Although insurance companies and physicians are not state actors, mothers experience them as such; indeed, documentation of preventive medical care in the yellow pediatric checkup booklet (*Untersuchungsheft*) is required by law for children from birth through age six (§26 SGB V).

As Lily tells us above, Cameroonian mothers of newborns in Germany must manage this bureaucratic maze on their own. Family reunification regulations make it difficult for certain categories of kin—such as adult sisters—to care for new mothers through extended visits. Submitting to the rules of the state, then, interferes with kin-based circuits, allowing things but not people to cross borders. In the absence of kin, recently arrived mothers learn how to navigate the German social services labyrinth from migrants who are more settled and experienced (Kohlhagen 2006). Occasionally, instructive stories exchanged at migrant community gatherings are also stories of betrayal, relating how some migrants found themselves anonymously reported, and even deported, for immigration violations. Ariane, a single mother and hometown association officer, told me,

Here there have already frequently been cases that no one knew how to explain. Sometimes a Cameroonian who . . . is perhaps at a party or visiting a friend or even just at home, and suddenly the police come, there is a simple control, and then they arrest and take the person and repatriate them.

Ariane explains that these stories of betrayal add to Cameroonian mothers' reluctance to reveal their needs for reproductive health care and social services to women in their hometown associations. The shadow of the state looms over women's relationships with their fellow migrants, contributing to the circuit breaker of mistrust within community-based flows. So off mothers go to the Registry Office, "all alone."

When her newborn is eligible for German citizenship, registering its birth and paternity ties the mother to state authorities in a special way. Rose was one of several mothers who told me that she had birthed a "German child." Her young son's citizenship gave Rose a sense of safety by regularizing her own residency status. The German Nationality Act (Staatsangehörigkeitsgesetz) of 2000 reformed the former jus sanguinis descent-based citizenship law. Today, a child born in Germany to noncitizen parents may acquire German citizenship if one parent has lived as a legal German resident for at least eight years. This rule allowed Rose to stay in Germany after a long and traumatic pathway cut off kin ties that would have allowed her a dignified return to Cameroon. Rose arrived in Germany as the spouse of a Cameroonian with a student visa, having given up a pink-collar job in Yaoundé. Rose's "papers" and livelihood thus depended on the longevity of her marriage. Although Rose's husband was infertile, her mother-in-law blamed her and encouraged the husband to chase Rose from the childless marriage. With divorce, Rose lost her claim to legal residence. During the difficult period that followed, Rose became pregnant by another African migrant who had lived in Germany for over eight years. The son she subsequently bore thus has a German passport, allowing Rose in turn to obtain a residence permit as the custodial parent (Ausübung der Personensorge). Baby Serge, then, shaped his mother's relationship with German immigration authorities, rescuing her from deportability if not from a lasting, nervous "illegality habitus" (Huschke 2013, 120).

Baby Serge also shaped Rose's relationship with German voluntary organizations. Like many Cameroonian migrants, Rose worked as a hotel chambermaid, a relatively insecure service-sector job. When she was eight months pregnant, she lost both her job and her health insurance. She was then recognized by a clergy member as a "woman in distress"; Rose's categorization as "deserving" secured her the assistance of a Catholic charity (Huschke 2014). This nonstate actor arranged emergency housing, legal aid, and perinatal care with a medical charity serving the uninsured. Indeed, the German social welfare system, based on the principle of subsidiarity, delegates the provision of benefits across a complex network of public, quasi-public, and private and voluntary agencies (Solsten 1995). As a result, Cameroonian mothers must place themselves into the categories that will get them access to needed services from particularistic service providers (see Bledsoe and Sow 2011).[13] Consciously or not, they perform deservingness in exchange for help through the affective circuits they build with German social service workers.

Attitudes toward the state regulation of childbirth and infant care held by German volunteers working in charities such as the one Rose visited and by other service providers contrasted sharply with those held by Cameroonian migrant mothers. Dr. Fritz, the director of the charity clinic Rose attended, issued her a *Mutterpass* (mother's passport), carefully noting a scheduled series of prenatal tests and checkups. Dr. Fritz worried that her African patients, having witnessed many "natural" births "in the village," would find the medicalization of childbirth alienating. She did not know that Cameroonian migrant mothers like Rose come from urban settings and, even if that were not the case, as women who had not yet borne children, they would not have been allowed to view a birth *au village*. Rose insisted that childbearing is *medically* easier in Germany than in Cameroon. She and other migrant mothers relished the highly regulated perinatal care offered, indeed *required*, through the German health and child welfare system. While worried about being reported to Youth Protection Services if they missed an appointment, mothers praised the "thorough" series of pediatric checkups tracked through their child's *Untersuchungsheft*.

While bearing and caring for infants can provide Cameroonian women a form of medical citizenship in Germany (Castañeda 2013), the emotional tenor of interactions keeps them from feeling accepted by broader German society. Relationships between Cameroonian mothers and their German bureaucratic and medical interlocutors create conditional belonging (Boehm 2012). Mothers are allowed to stay legally in Germany as long as they maintain their student or employment status and/or as long as they retain custody of their German citizen children. They must provide and care for their children in ways congruent with current, historically specific German notions of childhood as a protected and playful life stage free from authoritarian disciplining (Durand 2004). No matter how well

2.2   A mother's passport (*Mutterpass*), Berlin 2011. This passport was issued to a Cameroonian mother during her pregnancy to record her attendance at prenatal visits as well as birth outcome and the results of perinatal checkups. Dr. Fritz issued a similar *Mutterpass* to Rose in 2009. Photo by Elizabeth Beloe.

they achieve this balance, how accent free their German may become, and how thoroughly they fulfill the conditions for German citizenship "for the children's sake," Cameroonian migrant mothers' German belonging remains tentative.

Making Belonging through Babies

Movement is a normal part of marriage, childbearing, and child-rearing in Cameroon, but transnational migration makes it difficult to maintain the statuses (e.g., citizenship) and feelings (e.g., comfortable acceptance) that constitute belonging; Cameroonian migrant mothers respond to these challenges by purposefully building varied types of affective circuits. The period of birth and infant care is a delicate time in which mothers forge connections with kin, with fellow migrants, and with Germans. Such connections help them deal with the difficulties surrounding reproduction. Simultaneously, these interwoven relationships undergird mothers' belonging, solving the problems that make it so "hard being a mother here." Women carefully manage these connections to adapt to their changing circumstances as young mothers within the Cameroonian diaspora. They try to control the kinds of information, goods, money, and emotions that flow between them and three sets of actors: kin who either remain in Cameroon or are scattered in other migration destinations, fellow migrants organized into hometown associations, and German state and humanitarian actors. Although these spheres of interaction may influence one another, each has a characteristic structure of feeling, operates on its own logics of reciprocity, and circulates a distinct set of resources.

Affective circuits with kin operate on the logic of nonspecific delayed reciprocity. When migrant mothers are young and have just given birth, they send the happy news, upbeat words, and photos back home to kin. In exchange, they receive informational, emotional, and material support—as well as some pressure to conform to socially established expectations. Older female kin in particular send parenting and medical advice and kind words of encouragement. Cost and immigration regulations prevent them from providing bodily care. Some grandparents in Cameroon compensate by sending cash or gifts to their new grandchildren. Eveline, a Bamiléké refugee, lived in an asylum camp for a time, during which her contact with her family was temporarily cut off. After receiving asylum and moving to Berlin, Eveline was able to pick up this circuit once again. Eveline's mother, unable to provide physical care to her tiny grandson, sends small packages, material gifts that express love and connection to him. "Especially when she sees someone who is coming [to Germany], she'll put together a little package. And me, I send . . . I don't send her much, because I'm not working yet, it's a little hard." At this stage, the mother-infant pair receives more than it sends. In an emic understanding of intergenerational wealth flows (Caldwell 2005) that emphasizes morality over economic calculation, kin in Cameroon expect that over time the directional flow in these affective circuits will reverse, with migrants sending remittances, goods, and care in their direction.

Affective circuits within migrant community associations are based on formality. Belonging to the community is defined through membership in the association and regulated by bylaws regarding descent, fees, and regular attendance at monthly meetings. The material items that flow through community-based circuits are also formally defined. Benefits, gifts, and even formal visits to the mothers of newborns are regulated by the association's constitution. The timing of exchanges is more sharply defined than in kin-based circuits; membership fees are due on certain dates, meetings occur on a specific schedule, and Born House celebrations are staged within a limited time range. The emotional charge of these exchanges ranges from the warm conviviality of sharing a dish of Born House plantains to the seriousness of passing along stories that instruct recent arrivals how to get along in a new place to the extreme caution people exercise regarding potential gossip. This caution is heightened by fears of betrayal to German authorities for immigration violations.

Affective circuits with German state and humanitarian actors also operate on a largely formalistic logic. German bureaucrats enforce norms that place Cameroonian mothers into categories of citizen/noncitizen, legal/illegal, and self-sufficient/needy. The humanitarian impulse of nongovernmental medical charity and social service providers is also rooted in categorization and control (cf. Fassin 2011; Ticktin 2011). Sometimes women learn to fit themselves into categories of deservingness—by paying taxes, bearing children with the "right" kind of citizen or a permanent resident father, living up to German codes of good parenting, or performing a needy or vulnerable role. Playing these roles well means that one can receive secure residency, social services, and quality medical care. But performance is a tricky task that comes with the threat of disaster—losing custody of children, being deported—if it fails to convince the state and nonstate actors who decide on deservingness. Because the stakes are so high, Cameroonian mothers' interactions with German officials are usually businesslike but tense. Taut faces bespeak the self-control that migrants muster in such encounters, only too aware of the power difference between those who do and do not belong to the German state.

A striking feature of the German context is the dense network of social services that allows most Cameroonian mothers to keep their children with them rather than "posting" infants to be raised by relatives in Africa (Coe 2014). Because children stay with their mothers—in almost all cases throughout their school years—they become essential players in their mothers' social integration in a new place. Infants begin this process by eliciting the care and interest of several types of actors, stimulating exchanges that flow along various affective circuits. The needs of infants and the status they give their mothers sometimes overcome the circuit breakers of distance, mistrust, and law that threaten to interrupt these flows. Cameroonian mothers in Germany use their children to manage these complex, emotionally charged circuits of exchange and thus their struggle through the dual difficulties of reproduction and belonging in the diaspora.

Examining different domains of practice related to infant care, we discover that belonging emerges through not one but several types of affective circuits. Operating on different logics, these circuits create a tenuous, ambivalent, and multilayered belonging for migrant mothers and their children. Managing such complex sets of relationships is part of what is hard about being a Cameroonian mother in Berlin. It is also part of the genius of migrant mothers, who make great sacrifices to seek social mobility "for the children," as they say, by coordinating their reproductive lives and relationships with the effort of being "always on the move."

Acknowledgments

The U.S. Department of Education, the National Science Foundation, the Wenner Gren Foundation, and numerous grants from Carleton College generously supported research in Cameroon, while the Wenner Gren Foundation, a Hewlett Mellon Fellowship, and a Small Faculty Developmental Grant from Carleton College supported my research in Berlin. Thanks to Jennifer Cole, Christian Groes, Cati Coe, Heide Casteñeda, Alma Gottlieb, and three anonymous reviewers for their insightful comments on previous drafts of this chapter and to Elizabeth Beloe for her research assistance in Berlin.

Notes

1. Research for this contribution took place in Berlin, Germany, over fourteen months during 2010 and 2011 with additional visits in 2009, 2012, 2013, and 2015. Participant-observation occurred in people's homes, at life-cycle events, and in home associations and community organizations. I also conducted fifty interviews with thirty migrant mothers and one couple. I undertook research in Cameroon in the fondom of Bangangté during 1983 and 1986 and among members of six Bamiléké women's home associations in Yaoundé between 1997 and 2002.
2. All names are pseudonyms. In most cases my interlocutors chose their own pseudonyms as part of the informed-consent process. To further protect privacy, I have occasionally altered inconsequential but potentially identifying details.
3. Other researchers on Cameroonian migration to Berlin have focused on

men who marry German women and women who bear the children of German partners to overcome restrictive immigration rules (Casteñeda 2008; Fleischer 2012). In contrast, none of the women among my interlocutors had borne a child with a German partner, and only four women had ever been married to Germans; two Cameroonian fathers had previously been married to Germans. Most Cameroonian women arrive and stay in Germany through other pathways.

4. The Grassfields area, *Grassland* in German, comprises a mountainous plateau stretching over two provinces: the Northwest Region and the West Region. The Bamiléké and the Bamoun live in the francophone eastern Grassfields (administratively, the West Region), while numerous groups—such as the Nso, Kom, Bafut, and Bali—live in the anglophone western Grassfields (the Northwest Region). In popular usage, *Grafi* (Pidgin for *Grassfields*) sometimes refers exclusively to Anglophones from the Northwest Region. Considerable intermarriage as well as a long history of internal migration complicate these ethnic, regional, and linguistic identities.

5. *Allogène* in contemporary Cameroonian French, or *come-no-go* in Pidgin, is a relational term categorizing people of other ethnicities who originate in other parts of the country and who are strangers vis-à-vis local *autochthones* (original, indigenous dwellers or—considering long histories of migration in this part of Africa—first comers).

6. Of 2,010 Cameroonians who migrated to Germany in 2012 (1,044 with temporary residence permits following the new residency law), 636 came as students, 250 via family reunification, 219 as asylum seekers, and only 53 with work permits. The total number of Cameroonian students registered in Germany in 2012 was 6,016, representing 27.2 percent of all students from sub-Saharan Africa (Josha Dick, personal communication, January 12–14, 2014; Stefan Rühl, personal communication, information from the Federal Office for Migration and Refugees [Bundesamt für Migration und Flüchtlinge], October 2013).

7. Between 2005 and 2012, 8,961 Cameroonian births were registered in Germany (Stefan Rühl, personal communication, information from the Federal Office for Migration and Refugees [Bundesamt für Migration und Flüchtlinge], October 2013).

8. Some concentrations of Cameroonians are starting to emerge in the districts of Mitte (especially Wedding), Reinickendorf, and Lichtenberg.

9. For discussions of the effect of West African and German infant care practices on attachment and social embeddedness, see Gottlieb (2004); Keller, Voelker, and Yovsi (2005); and Durand (2004).

10. The term *maman* refers not only to one's own mother but also quite possibly one's mother's cowives, older female kin, and nonkin blessed with the wisdom of experience.

11. See Baldassar (2007, 403) for a comparative analysis of copresence in trans-

national caregiving. She and Wilding (2006) find that the kin work of regular contact through small media builds greater expectations for family visits.

12. While this collectivity is not a community in the sociological sense, both Cameroonian migrants and German researchers, activists, and officials speak of "die kamerunische Community" and even "die afrikanische Community," using the English word to denote a particular migrant population defined by ethnic, national, or even continental origin.

13. Writing about European family reunification policies, Bledsoe and Sow (2011, 182) refer to such presentations of self as acts of selection, as individuals prospectively emphasize "attributes that qualify them for membership in groups offering the most desired pathways of opportunity."

THREE

Photography and Technologies of Care: Migrants in Britain and Their Children in the Gambia

PAMELA KEA

When I visited Gambian friends and acquaintances on my first stay in Brikama in 1993, my hosts would offer me *attire*, a very strong sweet green tea, or send a child to fetch a can of soda before insisting that I have some lunch, prepared earlier that day. I would sit for several hours on a settee in the front parlor or in a large armchair outside in the open courtyard, watching children play, listening to the BBC World Service, and talking to my hosts. Partly prompted by my interest in photos displayed on the parlor cabinet, my hosts would invariably pull out old family albums that bore the traces of heavy use. They would then relate details of ceremonies and festive occasions and explain how they were related or otherwise connected to the people in the photographs. In so doing they conveyed a sense of the importance of showing and circulating photographs to affirming bonds between the photographic subjects and their viewers and also of the significance of photographic narratives in defining and connecting family and friends.

At that time few homes had telephones and televisions, as they were the preserve of wealthier compounds. Needless to say, mobile phones were not yet a part of the technological landscape. Every week I would walk to the local branch of Gamtel, the national telephone company, to make an overseas call in a hot, dark booth. There were three computers at the Gambia teacher training college in Brikama where I worked. However, these prized machines were rarely used, and students were banned from the room where they were kept.

On my last visit in September 2012, I found the technological landscape completely changed.[1] There was an Internet café in Brikama, largely frequented by local youth, and many more dotted throughout the coastal towns and holiday resorts. It was not uncommon to see groups of people in compounds gathered around a computer Skyping with distant relatives. The old Gamtel site, although still in use, had become a testament to outmoded means of communication. Mobile phones were virtually ubiquitous, and I often saw inhabitants of Brikama stroll through narrow lanes, hop in and out of bush taxis, pause at market stalls, and precariously steer their cars while talking or sending text messages and pictures on their mobile phones.

Given increasing levels of national and international mobility in the Gambia, these new technologies have become important not only in the organization of everyday life but also in supporting communication in long-distance relationships. Many Gambians migrate to the United Kingdom to meet expectations of intergenerational care that cannot be met at home given existing economic conditions. Through hard work, they hope to maximize the money they can send home so as to better fulfill their obligations to others. Because many migrant parents cannot afford to pay for childcare or to sacrifice wages to look after their children themselves, they frequently take children back to the Gambia at the age of six months to three years—either for a few years or indefinitely—to be cared for by grandparents and/or other extended family members, thereby having to parent from a distance. In turn, they seek to build affective circuits (Cole and Groes, introduction to this volume)—that is, flows of goods, money, information, love, and advice—through which they maintain connections to their children and their carers.

In this chapter I examine the role of technology (mobile phones, computers, and photographs) in the maintenance and transformation of affective circuits. Much of the existing literature on the use of technology in maintaining connections between family members highlights how rapid expansion of communication technologies since the early 1990s has helped migrants and their families to communicate with greater ease, speed, intensity, and regularity (Carling, Menjívar, and Schmalzbauer 2012, 203), allowing migrants to better replicate the everyday connectivity and intimacy of home. At the same time, technology may be used to discipline, assert authority, control behavior, and reinforce obligatory ties. It may serve as an oppressive force, particularly when migrants seek to distance themselves from their families (Bacigalupe and Cámara 2012, 1433). Studies generally show that technological devices are not simply objects but are appropriated, domesticated, and integrated into the practice of daily life (see, e.g., Miller and Slater 2000; Silverstone and Hirsch 1992). Such findings highlight the context within which technology becomes embedded and the cultural values and practices that are central to its use. Additional literature has focused on how technology mediates social interaction (see, e.g., Chouliaraki 2006; Couldry 2008; Madianou and Miller 2012). In a dialectical process of mediation, people appropriate and domesticate technology, and the latter, in turn, mediates social relationships.

As Madianou and Miller (2012, 141) argue in their study of migrants' use of technology to sustain family bonds, all kinship relationships are mediated and have three dimensions: normative notions of the ideal, that is, a socially directed script defining the behavior appropriate to a specific kin position (Lubkemann 2005, 265); the behavior of the actual person who inhabits that kin position; and the disparity between the two. Moreover, parenting can be partly understood as performance. Photographs, and technology more generally, are key props in this performance and in the enactment of familial relations, central to which is the expectation of intergenerational reciprocity. Consequently, to better understand the role of technology in the production and maintenance of intimacy in long-distance parenting relations as well as the affective circuits that technology both supports and gives rise to, we need to be attentive to these three dimensions.

As children are usually babies or toddlers when they are taken to the Gambia, separation from parents occurs before their development as persons who occupy specific kinship roles. Often children and parents may develop familial relationships and bonds with each other only through the use of technology that enables them to recognize one another's images and/or voices. I argue that parents and their children resort much more to normative notions of the ideal father, mother, son, or daughter in their technologically mediated relationships than they would were they together. Parents' and children's use of technology and photographs may generate tension and conflict at times, highlighting the complexities of long-distance relationships. However, in attempts to build affective circuits, both adults and children work hard to fulfill the ideal through their strategic use of technology. Indeed, photographs are used to enact identity, unify the family, and engage idealized conceptions of the family (Barthes 1981; Bourdieu and Bourdieu 2004; Hirsch 1997; Smart and Neale 1999).

Following Fedyuk (2012, 283), I argue that through exchange, photographs become a part of the relationship in itself (see also Drazin and Frohlich 2007, 55) because their circulation constitutes part of a larger exchange relationship that is central to intergenerational relations and ideals of parenting, care, and the household moral economy. In this sense, photographs are "put to work in social relations" (Edwards 2012, 226). Yet, to understand how they do this work, we need to move beyond a focus on photographic images and explore how they are experienced and embodied as sensory objects, the meanings of which are constituted through social practices and context (Edwards 2012, 228). Following Gell's theory of the agency of art objects and objects more generally, I conceptualize photographs, mobile phones, and computers as agentive objects. Material objects coalesce with persons through their social relations with those persons as well as through their mediation of relations between different people (Gell 1998, 12). In their capacity as social agents, material objects generate knowledge, make meaning, evoke emotions, and carry affective traits. At the same time, there is an expectation that people interact with objects in deliberate and intentional ways that are informed by existing social practices and contexts (Edwards, Gosden, and Phillips 2006, 13).

In what follows, I analyze the emotions, knowledge, and particular forms of somatic engagement that the transnational exchange of photographs engenders and the photographic narratives that are central to this process in the context of the affective circuits that parents and children generate and maintain. Although I examine the way in which one form of technology—whether mobile phones, computers, or photographs— feeds into and supports another, recognizing that the use of varied forms of technology can facilitate a deeper and more intense connection, I focus my analysis on photographs, both analog and digital. Just as the distinct nature of handwriting in letters can convey the sense of a person and place, evoking intimacy and (dis)connection, so too, photographs as material objects and visual relics (Edwards and Hart 2004; Tall 2004, 37) that can be held, lingered over, displayed, and treasured possess a permanence that escapes more transient forms of communication technologies. Before turning to the role of the Internet, mobile phones, and photographs in sustaining affective circuits between parents and their children, I explore key Mandinka concepts that are central to the household moral economy, intergenerational relations, and the project of migration.

The Mandinka Household Moral Economy

Historically, Mandinka communities have been made up of wards or patrilineal kin groups. These, in turn, are made up of compounds where members of an extended, three-generation family reside, with men having up to four wives (Kea 2010, 59).

Two moral dimensions underpin the everyday dynamics of Mandinka households, parent-child relations, and kinship relations more generally (Watts 1993, 185; Wootten 2009). *Badingya* (mother childness) conveys group harmony, cooperation, obligation, stability, and kinship. Those who share the same mother often feel a stronger sense of kinship for each other than those who share the same father and are socialized and brought up by different mothers. *Fadingya* (father childness) conveys conflict, individuality, and personal ambition (Jansen 1996, 661). The qualities associated with *badingya* highlight the sense of allegiance and closeness that is expected from those who share the same mother, unlike the sense of individuality, fragmentation, and selfishness (*fadingya*) that characterizes those who share the same father. An individual's reputation and sense of self come primarily from the father and the patrilineage. To exercise and develop *fadingya*, an individual must surpass the reputation and achievements of his or her father and ancestors. This capacity for action is embodied in the Mande hero—one of the best known of whom is Sunjatta Keita, founder of the Mali Empire—and emerges in epics about the Manding imperial past (Kea 2010, 67). Group cohesion, stability, and cooperation (*badingya*) are central to the reproduction of the group and its gendered and generational hierarchies. Hence, it is important for women to rotate cooking duties, with junior wives undertaking the bulk of the least desirable domestic work.

The relationship between *badingya* and *fadingya* conveys a tension between the individual and the group that is central to domestic life (Bird and Kendall 1980, 14–15) and the moral economy of the household. Further, these two moral axes underpin Mandinka social structure and serve as a unifying ideology of the Mande, to whom the Mandinka trace their ancestry (Bird and Kendall 1980, 14).[2] Although group cohesion, cooperation, obligation, and stability (*badingya*) are privileged in domestic life, *fadingya* is seen as facilitating change and "the driving forces necessary for the advancement of the group as a whole" (von Braun and Webb 1989,

516). These opposing forces are complementary and equally valued in Gambian domestic life.

In keeping with these values, parents cultivate *fadingya* in their children by encouraging them to work hard at school and to be exemplary Muslims, as Islam is a central feature of Mandinka identity (Kea 2013, 104). Although everyone recognizes that some people exhibit more *fadingya* behavior and others *badingya*, children are taught to value these complementary forces as well as other resources and attributes that inform the moral economy. Being a good Muslim and bearing many children—to extend the patriline and secure the prestige and future support that children ideally provide—have historically been core features of Mandinka female identities and key features of the Mandinka way (Kea 2013, 109).

The Gambia, an agrarian neomercantilist state in crisis, is one of the least-developed countries in the world. Worsening economic conditions have made it increasingly difficult for Gambians to fulfill intergenerational obligations and Mandinka ideals. Since the 1970s, the devastating effects of desertification on the Sahelian region have had a profound effect on Gambian agrarian and pastoral livelihoods, encouraging many to migrate to the urban coastal regions, to neighboring countries, and abroad in search of work (D. R. Garcia 2006, 409). In 1985 the Gambian government began a process of structural adjustment in order to receive additional loans from the World Bank and various other private commercial banks to service existing debt. Related policies have included privatization of corporations and industries, cuts in public spending, the introduction of user fees for education and health, and the removal of subsidies on particular food items and agricultural inputs (Little and Dolan 2000, 62). With a rise in the cost of living, unemployment, and the cost of domestic foodstuffs, Gambians have become increasingly impoverished, thereby further compromising their ability to fulfill intergenerational obligations (Chant and Evans 2010; Kea 2010).

The majority of Gambians combine farming, the sale of horticultural produce in local markets, and livestock care with nonagrarian livelihood strategies. Yet, faced with increasingly low financial returns from farming—a mainstay of the Gambian economy—and few opportunities in the burgeoning tourist sector or in government, people find it increasingly difficult to fulfill the intergenerational contract at home (Kea 2013; cf. Gaibazzi 2015). Consequently, migration has become an increasingly desirable and sought-after alternative (Kea 2013), to the extent that many Gambians may spend years planning trips, building up funds for travel to Europe or the United States, and cultivating networks with family and friends overseas in order to acquire a visa.[3] There is a collective recognition of the power of the remittance economy in helping to fulfill intergenerational obligations. Indeed, remittances to the Gambia, as a percentage of GDP, have been among the highest in sub-Saharan Africa (Kebbeh 2013). Bourdieu (1990, 167) refers to "an economy of material and symbolic exchanges between the generations," as children both adhere to parental socialization and, as adults, help to meet the material needs of their parents. The Mandinka concept of *dali* ("to become accustomed" and "the complexity of an enduring relationship"; Robertson 1987, 252) underscores the complex and ongoing nature of an exchange whereby children are effectively owned by their lineages (Bledsoe and Sow 2011, 9) and are indebted to them. The expectation of care in relation to parent-child and carer-child relations informs the intergenerational contract. Further, the act of fostering—in which children are entrusted to relatives or friends to affirm relations, as an additional source of labor, and to attend school and acquire additional skills—is a common practice throughout West Africa. Within this context, raising children is seen as a collective responsibility (Bledsoe and Sow 2011, 748; Goody 1982). The notion of wealth in people, a key feature of the Mandinka moral economy, informs the practice of entrustment through the importance attached to investing in people: an investment in people and the claims on people to which such investments give rise serve as a form of wealth and a way to accrue status (Berry 2002, 112; Guyer 1993). This notion of entrustment has no doubt served to facilitate and normalize migrants' practice of sending children back to be cared for by grandparents or other members of the extended family (Gaibazzi 2013, 269). Further, fosterage is about establishing relations of patronage between adults within a wider kin network, thereby affirming particular sets of kinship relations (Bledsoe 1990). Indeed, entrustment signals a sense of continuity, cooperation, and group cohesion (*badingya*), an ethical imperative that should drive the migrant's behavior. At the same time, migrants need to work hard and exercise *fadingya* in their migratory journeys. Part of the social imaginary, migration is seen to lead to economic and social mobility, prosperity, and recognition of the fulfillment of, or attempts to fulfill, *fadingya*.

On the Move: Fulfilling the Intergenerational Contract

Gambian migrants traveling to Britain have encountered increasingly strict immigration laws, visa regulations, and border controls. Many are refused entry on arrival or given visas for work, study, family reunification, and tourism (Bledsoe and Sow 2011) only to have their movements subjected to strict regulation and control. Increasing numbers of migrants have gained entry illegally, overstayed, and/or resorted to asylum (Gibney 2004, 122). A significant proportion of skilled workers, particularly doctors and nurses, leave the Gambia. In 2010 estimates put their numbers at approximately sixty-five thousand (4 percent of the population; see Kebbeh 2013). Although some Gambian migrants will continue to work in their professions once in the United Kingdom, many qualified and educated Gambians are forced into low-paid and unskilled work such as care work, domestic work, cleaning, hairdressing, shop work, and manual labor. Despite the unskilled jobs and frequently unsociable hours that many are forced to work, migration offers the opportunity to exercise *fadingya*, with potentially greater opportunities to provide for children and extended family (*badingya*). It can provide mothers in particular with a wider range of earning opportunities and increased income, thereby enabling them to act as instigators of change as well as to fulfill the role of provider in novel and empowering ways (Carling, Menjivar, and Schmalzbauer 2012, 193; Coe 2008, 223; Hondagneu-Sotelo and Avila 1997, 557). Yet the difficulties of combining full-time work and/or study with parenting as well as covering the high costs of childcare while attempting to fulfill *fadingya* and maximize income for remittances served as one of the main rationales for sending children back to the Gambia. Many parents were keen to immerse their children in the linguistic, cultural, and religious life worlds of their homeland. Framing their responses to questions about their decisions in positive and agentive terms, they highlighted the significance of Mandinka culture and personhood, belonging, home, and kin (Lubkeman 2005, 264).

Sending Children Back: Culture, Nostalgia, Sociality, and Discipline

Although parents usually approach prospective carers, grandparents occasionally offer to look after their grandchildren. Further, many grandparents and extended family members benefit from migrants' remittances, they appreciate that such remittances are partly dependent on the support they can provide to migrant family members, and, thereby, they willingly assume responsibility for raising migrants' children. In many carers' compounds, I observed the inhabitants building new houses, tiling pathways and terraces, upgrading roofs, and making full use of the additional financial resources that came from remittances. As the ability to financially provide for one's children is paramount, remittances invariably increase when children are sent back, as parents allocate money specifically for their education, clothing, food, and other related expenses.

Jabou, a Gambian woman in her early thirties, was fostered to her father's brother and grew up with him and his wife in the Gambia. She initially came to the United Kingdom in 2001 to give birth to her son, and later she pursued an education. Her husband, an accountant, got a job at UNESCO in 2004, and they then moved to Paris before she had finished her studies. Jabou gave birth to her daughters Awa in 2007 and Adama in 2009. She felt unhappy and unfulfilled living in France. She talked at length about her desire to go back to the United Kingdom to get an academic qualification. She initially planned to go there with her kids and a helper, but the helper was unable to get a visa. She then decided to leave the kids in Paris with the helper, but this proved to be an unsatisfactory arrangement, and she took them to the Gambia shortly after. Jabou sat very close to me during our interview in a busy café near London Bridge station. Her facial expressions conveyed a range of emotions—from excitement and enthusiasm to apprehension, loss, and pain—when remembering the moment she left her daughters in the Gambia.

Jabou: I thought, let me take them to my mum [in the Gambia]. My Aunt is the one I call mum because she is just like my mum. So, I said to my husband, I'll be more comfortable if they are with her than leaving them in France. My helper would take care of them, but she would not be able to bring them up. You understand. . . . Taking care of them, dressing them, taking them to school, giving them something to eat, is different from raising them. All I want is to keep that bond. I left them in February and stayed with them for one month so they could adapt. That was the time you had that family setting again. I saw myself as very selfish. This breakage is just because of me. It was very hard.

Pamela: When you were going to send them back, did you ask your mother, or did they offer?

Jabou: I asked them, and I was so reluctant asking them because culturally you have to stay with your husband, and my dad is like so much into my husband and into the culture. For them women shouldn't have that education. I was so scared my dad would say no. I know that the environment is very good for the kids. I know my aunt is very good at raising the kids and taking care. I've lived with her since I was four in that compound. So, that was the only place I wanted them to be. I really appreciate the way she brought me up and the values she put in me. Teaching my kids to have that same thing. If I can't do it I think she is in a better position to do it.

When Jabou states that her "helper would take care of them [her children], but she would not be able to bring them up," she conveys a heartfelt distinction between someone who can dress and feed her children and someone who can socialize or raise them. Constrained by gendered patterns of authority, she experienced feelings of selfishness, guilt, apprehension, and uncertainty as well a sense of liberation and autonomy at the prospect of "improving herself," effectively pursuing *fadingya*. Such contradictory emotions must be situated in a patriarchal context in which Jabou's request—one she is reluctant to make—has to be sanctioned and approved by her husband before her father (uncle) agrees to it.

Many informants emphasized the importance of sociality in Gambian relationships as well as nostalgia for home in recounting their decisions to send their children back. The people, festive occasions, and key social referents such as the gardens (small plots of land used for farming), the compound, the market, the bush, and the materiality of daily life encapsulate the topography of Gambian Mandinka life worlds. Despite de-agrarianization and increased mobility, many of the informants affirmed these referents and a visceral connection to the soil established through the hard labor of farming or clearing the land to build a family compound. The Mandinka have worked as farmers in the Senegambian region since the fourteenth century (Carney and Watts 1991, 654). Consequently, farming and land have historically been attributed a mythical quality that lies at the heart of what it means to be Mandinka (Kea 2004, 367). Agrarian social practices and images are central to nostalgic representations of Gambian Mandinka family and domestic life. When I asked Jabou how she felt her children would benefit from being sent back, she said,

Culturally, that is going to stay with them for the rest of their lives. Even my son left Gambia just before he was three, but still now he's got some values. We have a belief that he still knows how to deal with people, how to talk to people. You know, relate to people and all that. And the girls as well, by going back home they've seen both worlds at this young age. And whether it's implicit or they've learned something, they've met their cousins. Because here you have that individualism, you have that nuclear family, just you. They've seen so many people. It's so extended both on my side and their dad's side. They've got this routine that I never set for them before. They've seen other underprivileged kids as well. I know I missed them, and maybe when they come I will know if it has affected the bond, but I don't think it has affected my bond with them.

For Jabou's children, knowing their culture entailed learning Mandinka, exposure to Islam, and developing relations with relatives and friends, thereby ensuring that they would feel comfortable in the Gambia when they visited and/or returned at a later date. Knowledge of Islam and the

Koran, discipline through prayer gained from attending Koranic school for a few hours a week, as well as the ability to pray in Arabic are seen to instill particular ethics rooted in Islamic moral precepts. Further, Jabou juxtaposes Gambian sociality, as represented in familial relations, friendship networks, parenting, and domestic ideals, against the individualism of British society. This tension speaks, on the one hand, to the complex ideologies that inform local cultural attributes and values, partly captured in the Mandinka concepts of *badingya* and *fadingya*, and, on the other hand, to increased mobility, globalization, and commodity culture, both of which are central to Gambian life worlds. The increasing commodification of goods and services in part creates pressure to migrate. Mobility allows migrants to better meet their families' material needs as well as to (re)imagine family and their life worlds through a transnational perspective. Similarly, representations of the hardworking Mandinka farmer resonate with those of the migrant whose labor helps to provide for family and close friends.

We see a similar concern with the importance of exposing children to Mandinka culture, sociality, and discipline in Awa's reflections on how her son benefited from being sent back to the Gambia to live with her parents. I interviewed her in a second-floor, two-bedroom council flat situated on a leafy and quiet estate in Woolwich, Southeast London. Awa came to the United Kingdom in 1997 just after marrying her cousin, Mustapha, who lectures in accountancy. She works evening shifts at a nursing home in Woolwich two or three nights a week. The couple had three children— Muhammed, aged thirteen, Abdoullah, aged eight, and Mariamma, aged four, and were expecting a fourth when we spoke.

Awa: The nursery provision is really expensive. For Muhammed that's the reason why I took him [back to the Gambia]. So that I could study, because we lived in a shared accommodation as well. We were not in a position to look after him properly. Mustapha was studying and I wanted to study as well.
Pamela: How do you think he benefited from being there?
Awa: Discipline wise. He listens to me more than this one. [*She points to Abdullah.*] He knows the language as well. He's aware of the love surrounding him because he was brought up by the grandparents, and everybody loves him. The attention. I think he enjoyed that. Also, he's more sociable than the others. You can see the difference. When we went for holiday, he was excited, like me. He was happy. It's benefited him by giving him a good foundation in terms of behavior.

Significantly, many parents send their children back because of their strong feelings about the interfering role of the British state in child-rearing practices and domestic relations (see also Coe 2008; Whitehouse 2009). In light of these feelings, many emphasized the importance of discipline and good manners—more easily instilled at home in the Gambia—as both were seen to reflect on the parents' and carers' parenting skills, which affected the reputation of the family more generally (cf. Coe 2013). However, Awa recognized that Muhammed would be spoiled by his grandparents because of the joking (*anaweyaa* or *dangkutoo*) and informal relationship that is said to exist between grandparents and grandchildren. (This joking relationship is said to diffuse conflict and to generate social bonds and cooperation.) In this sense, grandparents, although ready to discipline and enforce good behavior, provide a particular form of care, support, and socialization that is recognized and valued by parents. Further, Awa and Muhammed's shared nostalgia for Gambian sociality and a sense of belonging serve to unite mother and son in a way that is simply not possible for Awa to share with her other children who were not sent back to live in the Gambia. When I asked Muhammed what he liked about living in the Gambia, he stated, "You could go out when you liked. You could talk to anyone. Here, you have to stay inside all the time. But I have friends here. And there are more opportunities here, and the technology." When parents entrust their children to their parents and/or extended family members, they take advantage of existing and familiar disciplinary cultures (Bledsoe and Sow 2011, 748–55), relying on the sense of mutual exchange and support that entrustment and *badingya* convey (see Coe on grandmother fostering, this volume). Nostalgia for their own experiences of care and socialization invariably informs their motivations for sending children back, thereby affirming group cohesion, obligation, and collective welfare (*badingya*; Kea 2013, 109). Yet the migrant is driven by ambition, hard work, and a need to work on and develop a successful and aspirational self (Horst 2012, 63), embodying the qualities associated with *fadingya*. To embrace *fadingya* with no regard for *badingya* can result in "a domestic or community anomie" (Watts 1993, 184). Indeed, it is this tension that migrants grapple with in their migratory projects and in managing and maintaining affective circuits with their children and other family members. Hence, the importance of the exchange of photographs and the use of technologies with children and family back home in demonstrating migrants' achievements as well as their ongoing commitment to the household moral economy.

Communication and Visual Technologies: The Affective Dimension of Transnational Connections

Sending children back may act as a panacea that soothes the often drastic dislocations migrants experience in lifestyle, environment, and everyday life. It may also help to fill an emotional void that is created when migrants leave home because it enables them to (re)connect with the sense of a place. As Feldman-Savelsberg (this volume) illustrates, Cameroonian migrant mothers in Berlin create belonging and affirm local and transnational ties through their children. Similarly, Gambian parents in the United Kingdom establish connection and continuity with kin through their children, thereby creating the possibility or setting the stage for their own return. The child comes to embody home. Significantly, technology allows migrants to relive their experiences of daily life in the Gambia, evoking the sense of a place and people, another feature of affective circuits. Awa talked at great length about her feelings of loneliness when she first moved to London in 1997 after marrying Mustapha. It was too expensive to speak on the phone at the time, so photographs of her family and friends were of great comfort to her. In recounting these details, Awa and others affirmed collectively valued and frequently idealized aspects of Gambian culture and life worlds and their own connections to those worlds. Technology allows parents to partake in Gambian sociality, to participate—as observers—in their children's social worlds and in so doing to (re)imagine Gambian familial relations. Further, technology as a prop in the performance of parenting helps to overcome physical distance and supports migrants' efforts to secure recognition of parent-child bonds as real and legitimate.

When I visited Abi, a middle-aged Mandinka woman, and Isatou, her eight-year-old niece, in Abi's large compound in Brikama on a hot and humid afternoon in September, Isatou was keen to show me their recently acquired laptop computer, brought from the United Kingdom by a friend of her parents. "So that we can Skype," she explained. Isatou saw the computer as proof of her parents' ability to provide materially and of their commitment to parent from a distance through daily communication.

Abi: Almost everyday they call and they talk.
Pamela: What do you talk about?
Isatou: I am here. Send these things for me.
Abi: She tells them I want this. I want that. I have this laptop here but normally on
 telephone. But we all Skype together with them. Sometimes we sit there for an

hour. Normally we do it at the weekend. Sometimes when I go on Skype I find her mother and we just talk, or she phones me and tells me to go on Skype.

Isatou, who would convey news about school, friends, and extended family, occasionally let her parents know that she missed them by expressing feelings of loneliness and sadness, yet she tempered such expressions with talk about the prospect of reunion. By interacting with her parents in such a manner, Isatou conveyed what was expected of her, thereby fulfilling normative notions of the ideal child. Here, technology elicits particular types of behavior. Significantly, children would frequently ask their parents to send them clothes, bags, and other goods, telling them precisely what they wanted. In doing so, they not only recognized their parents' role as providers but also affirmed the material dimensions of affective circuits and the link between parental obligations, intimacy, and financial support (see also Sargent and Larchanché, this volume, and Coe 2008). In most cases parents would meet these demands because they were financially able to do so and were keen to occupy the role of remitter, thereby providing a clear rationale for their initial migration and fulfilling normative notions of the ideal parent. Further, the ability to provide for their children appeases feelings of guilt, loss, and remorse during separation from them. From the child's perspective, technology helps to provide an ongoing sense of parental presence, material provision, and well-being as well as a way to help make sense of family at a distance. Further, requests for material goods may mirror the interactions, familial tensions (Miller and Slater 2000, 58), anger, and frustration that take place within a household where children and parents have not been separated, thereby affirming the normality of familial relations. Such occasions may involve negotiation and conflict as those involved attempt to marry differing expectations and to reconcile the differences between normative notions of the ideal parent and/or child and the person who inhabits the actual kin position (Madianou and Miller 2012, 141).

As well as facilitating processes of negotiation and conflict, technology can be used to support the performance of a particular kind of self. In an examination of the aesthetics of Ghanaian migrants living in London, Fumanti (2013, 211) highlights the importance of photographs and video recordings in capturing and recording festive occasions. Displays of "self-fashioning" captured in these images are crucial in garnering recognition of migrants' achievements and success to family and friends back home. Filipina female migrant domestic workers in Hong Kong, for instance, are depicted in full sartorial splendor in the photos they send home, these images showing no sign of the toil and tedium of their work (Margold

2004, 59). In the Gambian context, parents, children, and carers may conceal information, bad news, ill health (as in the case of a child who was suffering from malaria while in the care of her grandparents in the Gambia), the tedium of work or lack of it, poverty, and general proof of the inability to live up to notions of the ideal. Similarly, when bad news is conveyed to a migrant, as in the death of a friend or extended family member, there is an expectation that that person will respond immediately, conveying grief, extending emotional and moral support, and providing financial assistance where necessary.

When a family has ready access to the Internet—many of my informants did not and had to borrow laptop computers from relatives, thereby highlighting the structural inequalities inherent in the use of technology (see also Parreñas 2005b)—there is continuous movement between mobile phones, computers, and photographs (both hard copies and those sent via mobile phone and e-mail). The ubiquity of mobile phones means that communication is more immediate; there is less preparation involved. Emotional intimacy is distinctive because of the sense of immediacy and copresence that it affords (Miller and Slater 2000, 57). Significantly, free web-based, real-time video telephone systems, such as Viber and Skype, enable users to engage in lengthy, everyday exchanges. However, power outages in the Gambia mean that there is frequently "no light" (electricity), thereby encouraging many informants to use mobile phones, moving between them and Skype, with one form of technology supporting and reinforcing the other. A parent may phone the carer and tell the person to go on to Skype if there is "light" or an available laptop.

The ring of the mobile phone, the blinding luminosity of a computer screen that has been switched on in a dark parlor room, and the renewed low hum of a fridge—indicating that electricity has been restored—provoke a range of embodied responses and emotions (excitement, expectation, anxiety, relief, apprehension, etc.) that characterize the fabric of daily life. The everyday use of technology provides a means of regular engagement and the space to work on and (re)produce a sense of badingya. It confirms that children are being well cared for and properly schooled in those aspects of Gambian culture and Islam that served as one of the motivating forces for sending them back in the first place (see also Carling, Menjivar, and Schmalzbauer 2012). The mobile phone and computer, as agentive objects, facilitate relations between different persons (Gell 1998, 12), thereby helping to allay concerns, fears, and anxieties as well as vindicating parental decisions to send their children to the Gambia to be looked after by carers. This ongoing process is crucial to the establishment and maintenance of transnational affective circuits. Further, the generation

and expression of certain feelings and emotions is central to the fulfillment of normative notions of the ideal. For instance, when talking to her
father on the phone, a young girl, conveying emotions of loss, attachment, intimacy, and expectation, says, "I miss you. When will I see you?"
In so doing she conveys emotions that children who are separated from
their parents should ideally feel. Similarly, when children are sent back as
babies, their parents invariably experience feelings of loss, as Awa's case
shows, as well as a sense of achievement and pleasure because, in most
cases, their children appear to be happy and thriving gowing up in the
households of kin.

When Awa and Mustapha sent their son Muhammed back to the Gambia, they did not have access to a computer and so, to connect with him,
relied on the exchange of photographs and on news from friends who
were residing in the United Kingdom and had recently visited the Gambia.

Awa: In the end it was very difficult. I used to call a lot. Because he couldn't talk I
was worrying all the time—what was happening to him and what was he eating.
I would be watching on the street looking at other people's children. You know
it was really hard.
Pamela: Did they send photographs of him?
Awa: They would send me pictures of him when he was walking, sitting [*laughs*].
Pamela: And did you send photos there, or was he too little?
Awa: Yes, we sent pictures as well. We visited him twice for two weeks and then three
weeks. Not much.

Photographs, in the contiguity between the image and the referent, create
a sense of the present (Benjamin 1979, 243). Photographs of Muhammed
on his own, with other family members, and attending social functions
helped to allay Awa's feelings of loss, anxiety, and sadness by generating
a powerful connection to him. Here, photographic images, in their materiality and permanence, provide ongoing sustenance to affective circuits
(Fedyuk 2012, 290).

It was precisely their feelings of loss, generated in part by the exchange
of photographs, that were central to the fulfillment of Awa and Mustapha's notions of ideal parents. (Similarly, Awa's parents were very upset
when she informed them that she and Mustapha wanted Muhammed to
return to the United Kingdom. The profound sense of loss they experienced highlights another feature of familial separation as well as some of
the tensions and dilemmas that can arise in the collective socialization of
children.) Awa pointed to a small side table with two framed photographs
of Muhammed as a toddler in the Gambia. Her mother sent photographs

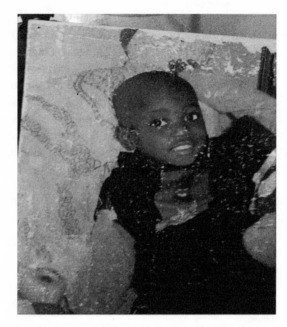

3.1 Photograph of a young boy who was sent to live with his grandparents in the Gambia. Brikama, The Gambia, 2012. Caretakers in the Gambia frequently send photographs of the children entrusted to them to their parents in Britain, who proudly display them on side tables, parlor cabinets, and desks. These photographs typically portray the children as loved and well cared for, thereby affirming parents' decisions to send their children to live in the Gambia. Photo by Pamela Kea.

documenting the various stages of his development, generating knowledge that enabled Awa and Mustapha to parent from a distance. Photographs were particularly important to the couple because Muhammed was too young to speak to them. Here, photographs, as agentive objects, are placed next to each other on the side table. As bearers of affective traits, their materiality and positioning allows Awa and Mustapha to experience and bear witness to the various stages of their son's growth, nurturing the feelings of love and intimacy that are central to affective circuits. Awa, in turn, sent photographs of herself and of Muhammed's younger brother and father to the Gambia.

Carried in purses and displayed on tables and on cabinets (Bello 2007, 9), photographs confirm Awa's and Mustapha's status as parents. They are shown to and held by relatives and friends for acknowledgment and recognition. In its tactility, a photograph is "a material vestige of its subject" (Sontag 1999, 81). Consequently, there are morally correct practices for the treatment of photographs. As material objects with biographies,

3.2 Arrangement of photos and other valued objects in a Gambian compound, 2012. Gambians often display photos and other valued objects in their parlors. The positioning of the photographs frequently reflects the social relations of those depicted in the images. Photo by Pamela Kea.

photographs generate an affective and sensory response beyond the actual images they capture (Edwards 2012). Their biographies document the relationships in which they are enmeshed, giving rise to different forms of sociality. They evoke strong feelings (of love, attachment, tenderness, happiness, frustration, loss, etc.) through exchange and visual and tactile engagement because they constitute and are constituted through social relations. Unlike telephone conversations, their materiality ensures distribution and use (Fedyuk 2012, 283–88) as well as a lingering presence and a degree of permanence. Technology helps to provide public recognition, and the range of emotions such recognition generates (e.g., pride, contentment, generosity, etc.), of the exemplary fulfillment of kinship relations (*badingya*). (More prosaically, it confirms the existence of a kin relationship in the first place; Carling, Menjívar, and Schmalzbauer 2012, 203.) It is public in the sense that, in its various forms, it does not simply enable communication but also generates information and knowledge about the nature of relationships. This information is rendered public when photographs are displayed in sitting rooms in the Gambia and England, with parents, children, and carers providing narrative detail about the contents to friends and relatives. As parents, carers, and children proudly pass around mobile phones displaying photographic images and share the contents of telephone conversations they have had with each other, they further publicize and seek recognition of their relationships. Further, in their power to document and represent family life, photographs serve as social proof of the continued bond between parent and child and the fulfillment of intimacy and affective circuits.

Pa, a ten-year-old boy who is cared for by Adjie Bintou, his mother's mother, in a large open compound on the outskirts of Brikama, was taken to the Gambia when he was one. He is an only child whose parents have lived in the United Kingdom for the past eleven years and have been unable to return to the Gambia to visit him. When I asked about the photographs grandmother and grandson exchanged with Pa's parents, Adjie Bintou proudly pointed to the large collection displayed on the parlor cabinet. Pa was keen to show me a recent photograph of his mother, which had pride of place on the cabinet. In his eagerness to show it to me, he sought both to affirm a maternal bond with his mother and to have the bond and its implication of a successful relationship recognized. As displayed domestic items showing formal individual and group portraits, photographs can convey a sense of familial "togetherness" and a sense of absence, when some are not pictured or are pictured but are not physically present (Rose 2010, 12). Yet the presence of those who have migrated is reinscribed through remittance practices and the maintenance of affective circuits and wider exchange networks. Familial "togetherness" is performed, and domestic space is established as Adjie Bintou, Pa, and other members of the compound place photographs next to each other on the cabinet and side tables, look at the photographs together, and exchange them with one another. Each of these acts and practices of exchange—which make up an ongoing performance—produces a sense of closeness and connection evoking the affection, tenderness, and sense of cooperation that are central to *badingya*. If a child's siblings have gone abroad to live with their parents, the siblings may send back photographs of their school awards and achievements, not simply exchanging images of people but mementos of daily life. As a result, they further contribute to the everydayness, normality, and intimacy of familial relations.

Photographs may also provide the opportunity for a critique of caring practices. They are increasingly sent via mobile phones, resulting in a virtually instantaneous connection between the referent, the photographer, and the viewer. Further, the ubiquity of mobile phones ensures that photographs are always to hand and easily shared with others, as the interview with Jabou illustrates:

Jabou: They send me photographs on Viber, most of the time. There was this Eid, you know, Tobaski.[4] But I wouldn't want them to stay that long in the Gambia because it's always different the way you want to bring up your kids. Like this photo that I'm telling you with their makeup. I wouldn't do that. I wouldn't want them to do something like that. I wouldn't want them to put relaxer on their hair. And then those are things that I don't want to be telling her this is what I want to do. I just want them to come back to me and I do whatever I want with them. You understand. Like this. [*She shows me a photo of her daughters with makeup.*] It's cute, but . . .

Pamela: Who put the makeup on?

Jabou: It's my cousin back home. They just sent me these photos. They were going to a birthday party.

Pamela: You don't like the makeup?

Jabou: Maybe it's just kids and it's fun, but I don't know.

Pamela: I suppose they're quite young.

Jabou: Yeah, that's what I don't want. And these kids, they're very aware, so I wouldn't want them to . . . I just want them to be kids. Look at the eye shadow. You know, stuff like that. I'll show you the other photos they sent me. For their birthdays I always send them to celebrate. This one is of Adama's birthday. This is her going to school.

Pamela: That's so lovely. That's a really sweet picture.

Jabou: Happy Birthday. That was her cake. That's them at home.

As Jabou shows me photographs of family occasions and events, Islamic holidays and birthday parties, in which family togetherness is represented, she performs parenting, proudly pointing out Adama's birthday cake and beautiful dresses and expressing disapproval of her cousin's decision to let her daughters wear makeup and have their hair straightened. Jabou maintains that "a child should be a child." As she challenges small acts, she parents from a distance. Although the makeup image is significant, the act of looking at and commenting on it is just as important (Bal 2003, 9) because it confirms Jabou's status as a discerning and protective mother who knows what is best for her daughters. Here, Jabou focuses on the complete somatic singularity of her daughters, a privilege that she, as mother, readily assumes (Rose 2010, 54). Her statement clearly conveys that she does not want her daughters to grow up too quickly, as this would only contribute to her feelings of loss while they are separated from her.

A well-placed critique of her cousin's behavior allows Jabou to convey her seemingly ideal and exemplary parenting standards.

Conclusion: Photographs and Affective Circuits

Technology helps to support parents' and children's attempts to produce and maintain affective circuits. It is used to work through and negotiate tensions as well as to satisfy the ideals of parent-child relations informed by the Mandinka household moral economy and personhood. Similarly, as parents and carers assume collective responsibility for raising children, they affirm intergenerational ties and networks of exchange that are central to the household moral economy. It is clear that mobile phones, computers, and photographs, as agentive objects, have a performative dimension in terms of the way they allow parents and children to enact their roles and maintain social relations. In this sense, technology creates the space for the generation of emotions, which are both embodied and part of the social fabric. "In . . . affective economies, emotions *do things*, and they align individuals with communities—or bodily space with social space—through the very intensity of their attachments" (Ahmed 2004, 119). The emotions generated through the use of technology "align" and intensify migrants' "attachments" to their children, extended kin, home, community, and friends. Here the use of technology facilitates the realization of desires fashioned on existing ways of life or a sense of self (Horst and Miller 2006, 6). From the migrant's perspective, developing the project of the self partly entails maintaining intimate relations with one's children and fulfilling ideal notions of parenting. Technology serves to affirm existing notions of the Mandinka moral economy and person-hood, to be sure. Yet it is also used to represent desired and novel identities in which an individual seeks to achieve a reputation surpassing that of his or her ancestors, a central element of *fadingya*.

As Drazin and Frohlich (2007, 51) note in their analysis of photographs in English homes, these images "materialize intention." The variety of ways of showing photographs—in albums, framed on cabinet shelves, taped to the wall, and virtually on mobile phones and computers—constitutes a "network of intentionalities" that can be displayed indefi-nitely. Photographs, computers, and mobile phones can be used to convey the intention to fulfill normative notions of the ideal and a commitment to home, revealing successes and concealing failures. Significantly, the ex-change of photographs encapsulates a larger exchange relationship that is central to kinship relations and personhood. In short, the exchange of photographs in maintaining affective circuits is about the making of persons and relations between them. Through their exchange, photographs make a unique contribution to the maintenance of affective circuits. Further, as exchanged and displayed objects, photographs reflect a "network of intentionalities": the intention to fulfill normative notions of ideal parent-child relationships based on the household moral economy as well as the intention to produce novel identities and change (*fadingya*). Yet the two aims are not wholly distinct, because the new possibilities that migration and mobility offer influence normative notions of the culturally constituted ideal. Part of what Margold (2004, 50) terms "diasporic memory-making," photographs allow migrants to refashion themselves to host and home communities as well as to confirm their improved financial standing, which will ultimately benefit their children and future generations. Imagined identities may be rooted in dreams of material wealth, a transnational social imaginary, and a new and empowered sense of self—all of which form the basis for aspirational lifestyles. Yet photographs and communication technologies generate a sense of continuity with the Mandinka way of life by materializing intentions rooted in ideal parent-child relations and an ongoing commitment to the Mandinka household moral economy.

Acknowledgments

Ethnographic research for this chapter, funded by the Rockefeller Foundation, was carried out from February 2012 to December 2013.

Notes

1. During my 2012 research, I interviewed seven Gambian migrants (six parents and one child) in the United Kingdom and twelve adult carers and five children in the Gambia, all of whom belong to the Mandinka ethnic group, the country's majority ethnic group. In one case, having interviewed a mother in the United Kingdom, I was able to interview her children and their carer in the Gambia. A coresearcher carried out interviews with Nigerian migrants in London and Lagos. This chapter focuses exclusively on Gambian migrants.
2. See Kea (2010) for a more detailed discussion of the ethnic groups that make up the Mande.

3. Bryceson (2002, 725) highlights the process of de-agrarianization, or "rural income diversification away from agricultural pursuits," that has occurred in sub-Saharan Africa in the last fifteen years as a result of market liberalization.

4. Tobaski, feast of sacrifice, takes place approximately 70 days after the end of Ramadan. A sheep is slaughtered in ritual sacrifice.

FOUR

Transnational Health-Care Circuits: Managing Therapy among Immigrants in France and Kinship Networks in West Africa

CAROLYN SARGENT AND STÉPHANIE LARCHANCHÉ

Transcontinental migration carries no guarantee against acts of sorcery across time and space. What happened to Oumou, a young bride who followed her husband to France, is a case in point. Oumou has long suspected that malicious spiritual forces caused her to miscarry three babies and to lose a fourth at birth. She arrived in Paris from the Malian capital of Bamako at the age of twenty-three to join her much older husband, Mamadou, a labor migrant who had lived in France for over twenty years. He was proud of his legal immigration status, which enabled him to bring his new wife to France. Both were divorced: after Mamadou found his previous wife in bed with another man, he phoned his brother in Bamako to ask his help in finding him a "serious girl" to marry. Oumou, divorced from an abusive husband and with custody of her four-year-old daughter, seemed an ideal candidate. Oumou had suffered two miscarriages before the birth of her daughter, and when she married Mamadou, she was already pregnant again. Oumou left her daughter in Bamako when she traveled to Paris, where—six months pregnant—she suffered her third miscarriage. She was seriously depressed and wondered which of her relatives might be implicated in this tragic event. After all, she had heard from an elder relative that her husband's older sister had consulted a marabout.[1]

A marabout is a ritual specialist who draws on Islamic doctrine to divine, diagnose (in the case of illness), and resolve dilemmas (Monteil 1931; Tall 1985). Some West African marabouts in France prescribe herbal remedies as well as ritual interventions. They offer advice on a wide range of personal and social problems, including those involving health, love, academic or professional success, and rivalries of all sorts (Kuczynski 2002; Pordié and Simon 2013). Oumou's sister-in-law, it seems, was engaged in *maraboutage*—that is, ritual acts designed to harm Oumou. Her elderly relative had even told Oumou to obtain cowry shells blessed by a specialist in Bamako as a protective measure. She phoned her grandmother to ask for protective ritual and herbal preparations to safeguard her home and her body. In an effort to assuage her grief over her recent miscarriage, her husband agreed to send for Oumou's four-year-old daughter to join them in Paris.

Within months, Oumou was pregnant again and happy, though anxious. The baby, a boy, was born preterm, weighing a scant 1.3 pounds. After a year's hospitalization, against all odds, he was released in reasonably good health, and the family prepared to move from a twenty-two-square-meter studio apartment to a new two-bedroom apartment in a housing development nearby. While Oumou was pregnant, her grandmother in Bamako had asked a diviner to throw cowries, and she was told that as soon as the baby was born, he should have blood spilled on the ground for him—that is, his mother should hold a sacrifice to ensure his well-being. Oumou and Mamadou found the means to arrange a sacrifice in a suburban worker hostel near Paris, obtained some ritual substances from Mali by phoning a marabout in Bamako, and did the sacrifice in four places: in the hostel, in their old apartment immediately before they moved, along the road as they drove in a taxi to their new home, and in the new apartment. The ritual was made possible through both regular phone calls to relatives in Mali and the help of a friend who was traveling from Bamako to Paris and who brought the requested medicines with him.

In recounting these events, Oumou noted that she made sure to bless the pediatrician who cared for the baby and who had intervened to arrange for the new apartment. In an aside, she whispered that she also had sent to the marabout for medicines to ensure her husband's love and guarantee the family's health, for leaves to use in protective washing of the children and for fumigation, and for a special *gundo* (secret) for herself.[2]

4.1   Malian-owned general store in Paris that imports medicinal products from Mali, 2015. This store, selling medicinal plants and herbs, is one of many located in the Chateau Rouge area of Paris (18th arrondissement), which is considered to be the city's African neighborhood. The area hosts a large market and numerous stores offering a variety of products, including foods, textiles, cosmetics, books, music videos, and religious items. There are also numerous bars and restaurants, tailors, hairdressers, nail salons, and "taxi phones." Photo by Stéphanie Larchanché.

These treatments—which include love potions, medicinal plants to protect the health of children and adults, and plants to burn for the therapeutic value of the smoke—are all commonly used in Mali and continue to be valued among Malians in France.

In both places, they are intended to ensure stable marriages, fidelity, health, and well-being among family members. Hence, they are perceived as intrinsic to social reproduction and affective ties among kin and intimate friends.

Oumou's case serves as an introduction to our discussion of the role of transnational therapeutic circuits in the process of social reproduction that occurs between migrants from the Senegal River Valley region and France.[3] Between 1945 and 1974, labor migrants from former French colonies such as Mali, Mauritania, and Senegal flooded into Paris and neighboring cities. Entrenched poverty in this region propelled young men to France in search of employment, usually in construction, street sweeping, and other forms of unskilled labor.[4] The fundamental migratory goal was to send money to kin in Mali and eventually to build at least one house in one's community of origin.

After 1974, when the French government officially ended its guest-worker program (Hamilton, Simon, and Veniard 2004), family reunification legislation allowed wives and children of labor migrants to legally reside in France. The men in the first generation of migrants now reflect on how much they suffered, living in degraded worker hostels and stretching their slim budgets to provide financial assistance to family in West Africa. Even today, when labor migration is officially restricted to certain highly skilled immigrants, undocumented workers continue to enter France, where they join relatives in hostels or apartments and work in difficult conditions on the black market.[5] At the same time, many families who reunited under the post-1974 legislation have attained French nationality or long-term residence permits; they describe their everyday lives as comfortable. These patterns of transnational migration, however, have stretched kin networks and created new kinds of problems as people try to adapt to changing legal, economic, political, and social pressures. In recounting their histories, most immigrants encountered in our research focused on the ultimate goal of reducing the suffering of kin in Mali and on the pride they experience by achieving this objective.

It is clear that immigrants provide financial, medical, and other forms of assistance to kin, but what kinds of reciprocity exist?[6] Some studies of migration and transnational relations have emphasized the moral obligations of kin to provide care and support for one another as well as the constraints immigrants face as they try to maintain reciprocity (Abranches 2014; Grillo 2008, 13–14; Grillo and Mazzucato 2008; Groes-Green 2014; see also Fesenmyer, this volume). These studies notwithstanding, much of the scholarly literature on immigration and health focuses on the structural violence and health-care inequities immigrants encounter or on how immigrants' explanatory models of health clash with those of more dominant local biomedical institutions (Sargent and Larchanché 2007, 2011; in the context of France, see also Chauvin and Parizot 2005; Fassin 2000; Kotobi et al. 2012; Musso 2005; Sayad 1999). Few scholars explore how advice and resources related to health might circulate between immigrants and their kin in societies of origin (exceptions include Abranches 2014; Baldassar 2008; Krause 2008). Nor do scholars explore the implications of therapy management (Janzen 1978) for sustaining a sense of cultural intimacy (a term we elaborate momentarily) and solidarity. Yet, as is well known, in many African societies healing attends not only to the physical body but to the social body as well (Feierman and Janzen 1992; Sargent 1982; Turner 1968).

Consequently, most Malian immigrants, like their kin in Mali, conceptualize illness as more than an individual affliction (Janzen 1978). Rather, kin, close friends, and the specialists on whom they rely for advice work collectively to diagnose and manage treatment for the sick. We call these groups "therapy management groups." They may draw on local understandings of spiritual causes of misfortune and appropriate interventions as well as on biomedicine. As a result, therapy management groups, whether in Mali or across transnational borders, allocate material resources. They also facilitate knowledge sharing about sickness etiology and treatment, caregiving, and the interpretation of misfortune. Transnational therapy management networks reinforce affective circuits between migrants, kin, and friends and the viability of both biomedicine and ritual and herbal specialists (Cole and Groes, introduction to this volume). This reinforcing of intimacy and proximity may carry with it some degree of ambiguity in that the impetus for activating transnational therapy management groups may be the need to face dangers such as jealousies or rivalries that result in acts of sorcery or other potentially harmful actions. Yet these affect-related ambiguities do not detract from the significance of connecting with kin for protection. Hence, we propose that the management of illness sustains transnational connections—material, spiritual, and affective. Malian immigrants often interpret illness as a sign of the need to draw on and rework various spiritual and social forces. Even those immigrants who systematically rely on biomedicine in France turn to therapy networks, creating them transnationally, to collectively strategize about illness causation and treatment, including ritual and herbal interventions (Krause 2008).

We propose that these networks create spaces for a "shared repertoire of cultural intimacy" (Herzfeld 1997; Reed-Danahay 2008, 82) that emerges in the pursuit of successful therapeutic interventions and, more broadly, management and prevention of crises and misfortunes when migrants go to Europe. By cultural intimacy, following Herzfeld and Reed-Danahay, we refer to ways immigrants and their domestic networks of kin and friends in West Africa sustain emotional ties on the basis of shared group knowledge—in this case, understandings of illness—and collective decision making.[7] Transnational therapy management—through kin support, strategies of healing, and spiritual protection—assures the maintenance of a common sociality, the reinforcement of affective ties, and the creation of a sense of belonging (Reed-Danahay 2008, 82) linking immigrants and their home communities.

As we show in this chapter, for those living in France and in Mali, collective engagement in managing illness episodes has the potential to reconfigure and disrupt but also to cement kinship obligations and intimate relations (see Feldman-Savelsberg, this volume, on how "migration complicates belonging," and Fesenmyer, this volume, on how Kenyan migrants in London "navigate the changing nature of relatedness"). We suggest that transnational therapy management strategies contribute greatly to maintaining cultural intimacy among immigrants and their kin in West Africa despite the obstacles posed by distance and generational tensions. Therapy management may involve sending medications by mail or by courier between the two contexts. Pharmaceuticals, herbal preparations, amulets, and other protective or curative products travel in both directions, as does advice from ritual specialists, herbalists, and biomedical clinicians (Abranches 2014; Saraiva 2008).[8] As much research has shown, in the presence of more than one medical tradition, those seeking health care commonly use diverse modalities, whether simultaneously or consecutively. Thus, as our case studies indicate, immigrants residing in France often rely on nonbiomedical intervention as well as the French national health system, and their kin in Mali value biomedicine in addition to local healers. Finally, we note that state regulation of immigration both constrains and creates possibilities for immigrant health-care strategies, shaping the particularities of therapy management in specific instances.

Therapy Management in Mali

In his groundbreaking work on therapy management networks in Zaire, Janzen (1978) notes that the individual sufferer is deeply embedded in the dynamics of kinship networks and the representation of sickness as a symptom of tensions within a social network. His and subsequent work on this subject, especially as it relates to healing rituals, builds on the seminal work of Turner (1968, 1969) on the ritual process and its social functions. For example, in her work on Dogon narratives of healing in Mali, Slobin (1998) observes that treating illness is a way of repairing social ruptures, restoring health, and ensuring social reproduction as well. She relates the story of a young woman suffering severe menstrual problems who turned to her fiancé, her mother, her grandmother, her brother, other elderly women in her family, and several friends for advice. After consulting healers recommended by those in her therapy management network, she concluded that the roots of her ill health lay in the hostilities between her, her fiancé, and his first wife. Slobin interprets this case as illustrating how, by means of therapy management, individual suffering is reinterpreted in the context of family tensions and the need for resolution (see also Janzen 1978; Turner 1968).

Correspondingly, Castle (1994) examines the relationship of mothers' kin and community power relations to the process of diagnosing children with fatal illnesses in rural Mali, primarily in Fulbe households (for a monograph on this subject, see Holten 2013). She notes that senior women in Fulbe patrilineages collectively act as therapy management networks (Castle 1994, 315). Most women, especially young mothers, have daily contact with their mothers-in-law. In this patrilineal, endogamous society, most women have frequent interactions with their natal families as well as their husband's kin (Castle 1994, 317). The analysis of child deaths demonstrates how accountability for sickness is transferred from the individual to the community when illnesses are seen as social rather than solely biological or natural processes. Therapy management network engagement thus sustains power relations and pathways of information transmission within the community (Castle 1994, 331). Such engagement may produce ambivalence as it carries potential constraints and limitations on individual decision making while it positively reinforces group cohesion.

Kane (2010) describes the transfer of medications and medical advice between migrant associations in France and migrants' villages of origin in the Senegal River Valley. Referencing in particular the Halpulaar and Soninke, Kane suggests that new technologies of communication such as cell phones and the Internet are opening a virtual realm of diagnosis and healing. Not only do immigrant village associations send pharmaceuticals "to kin and others in their social network, [but] immigrants [also] routinely receive 'traditional medicines and marabouts' talismans" (Kane 2010, 2) as part of the flow of healing objects. Members of these village associations are not only from the same communities in the Senegal River Valley but are often kin as well. Such networks persist in the context of transnational migration and generate possibilities for immigrants and families in West Africa to inhabit different social worlds while retaining a sense of mutual connection and cohesion (Vertovec 2011, 89) even though the logistics involved may also entail exposing immigrants to additional distress in the process of diagnosis, proposed treatments, and debates regarding sickness causation.

The West African Community in France: Context and Tensions

When male workers from the Senegal River Valley region (Mali, Maurita-nia, Senegal) first arrived in France in the 1960s, they were usually housed together in hostels (*foyers*) and were mainly employed as low-skill labor in industry, public services (i.e., as street sweepers and garbage collectors), and construction (Quiminal 1991). With family reunification legislation enacted in 1976, male immigrants residing in France could legally bring spouses, children, and other relatives to France. At the same time, family reunification policies limited the possibility of circulatory migration between France and Africa (La Documentation française 2006).

The influx of immigrant families since the early 1980s has prompted a rise in xenophobia, public concerns about a threat to French national identity, negative stereotyping, and discrimination. In a context of eco-nomic instability and high unemployment rates, immigrant families have been accused of living "off the largesse of welfare payments" (Wieviorka 2002, 132). The government has pursued the restriction of immigration flows, moving toward a policy of "zero immigration" (Viet 1998).[9] A series of laws and amendments addressing gender, marital status, and family composition have thus successively threatened African migrants (Sargent 2006). Such restrictive policies have increased economic precarity in the migrant population (Fassin, Morice, and Quiminal 1997; Ticktin 2011; see also Neveu Kringelbach, this volume).[10]

A substantial body of research has documented the complex socio-economic difficulties confronted by West African immigrants, such as the scarcity of affordable housing (Péchu 1999), educational segregation (Durpaire 2006), and unemployment rates twice those of the rest of the population (Meurs, Pailhé, and Simon 2005). In both the industrial and the service sectors, West African migrants were (and are) discriminated against in such areas as job training, promotion, and bonuses. One study reported that more than 30 percent of migrants from the Senegal River Valley are unemployed or participating in the black market. In terms of housing, they, like many other migrants, find themselves segregated in low-income housing projects in the banlieue, neighborhoods located on the periphery of Paris (Quiminal and Timera 2002, 23).

Therapy Management in France

Most Malians living in France expect that the experience of migration will reconfigure their relationships to their kin back home. As Cole (2014b, 286–87) observes with respect to Malagasy migrants in France, they also hope to sustain relationships and to creatively manage two distant social worlds by using transnational telecommunications (see also Kea, this volume). Cell phones render possible the circulation of medical counsel, medications, and collective therapeutic decision making (Sargent 2006; Sargent, Larchanché, and Yatera 2005).[11]

The opportunities offered by new communication technologies for transnational therapy management also produce ambivalence. Although many Malian immigrants describe the sentimental pleasure of hearing the voices of loved ones, they also experienced distress at the prospect of sharing news of misfortunes. Thus, some withheld information about their life situation in Paris to spare family members the distress of knowing they were unemployed, undocumented, or ill. Eventually, however, as we see in our case studies, serious illness becomes a matter for collective consideration. Requests for therapeutic advice and intervention at both ends of the transnational circuit reinforce understandings of everyday realities and engage kin in strategies to resolve health-care dilemmas. The use of phones, ritual advice, medicinal plants, and remittances all become part of transnational affective circuits where things, technologies, and knowledge circulate and intersect with mixed senses of obligation, pressure, haranguing, pleasure, love, and healing processes, in Mali as well as among migrants in France.

When we compare the possibility for communication between France and the Senegal River Valley region in 1965 and in the 2000s, we see a remarkable transformation in the intensity and frequency of contacts. Elderly migrants in Paris today still reflect on how difficult it was to communicate with family when they first arrived in France. In the 1970s and 1980s, news of an illness or death arrived by mail or courier and often took months. By contrast, cell phones have made possible—for better or for worse—the immediate and direct transmission of important information among kin and members of a broader domestic network. Phone contact implicates kin—both immigrants and extended family in Mali, Mauritania, and Senegal, whether literate or not—in multiple facets of everyday life: conflicts among cowives, disputes among brothers, financial crises, marriage arrangements, illness, and death.

The highly regulated nature of immigration to France, however, constrains transnational connections—specifically, therapy management networks—in different ways. Of particular importance with regard to health-care access are restrictive policies that limit visas for those seeking entry to France specifically to obtain health care and that require undocumented immigrants to wait three months to obtain health insurance.[12]

Illness Episodes as Opportunities for Family Reconnection and Transformation

Kinship obligations remain fundamental to migrants in Europe. Yet they may also be transformed, as sons and daughters who were formerly peripheral to family decision making become central in terms of sustaining and reproducing families by providing lifesaving interventions for kin in West Africa. Even undocumented migrants with intermittent employment find themselves central to sustaining a sense of family belonging and material stability.

Badri, thirty-four years old, is one such migrant. He has been in France for thirteen years. He arrived at a time when immigration policies had become highly restrictive and significantly reduced chances for those residing illegally to obtain legal residency. Despite being a *sans papiers* (undocumented immigrant), he has managed to find work—albeit in difficult conditions. Although he has been separated from his family for over a decade, he has maintained close ties to his parents and brothers in Bamako. They converse by phone at least once a week. Badri has always been forthcoming with his family in Mali about his situation in France, his difficulties making ends meet or finding decent housing. Sensitive to his economic situation, his parents have never requested remittances. One day in 2006, however, one of his brothers called to let him know his father had been transported to a clinic in emergency after he had suddenly become paralyzed. Badri learned by phone that his father had been diagnosed with advanced type 2 diabetes. Badri recalls that his first concern was whether his father should be flown to France for care or to another, more competent clinic in West Africa. A direct conversation with the doctor in charge of the case sufficed to reassure him that his father could receive the care he needed in Bamako provided he could follow the prescribed treatment. Badri decided to contribute to medical expenses, sending a blood glucose measuring device and organizing money transfers for doctors' visits and acupuncture. When asked about his position as the financial caretaker, Badri described his filial obligation:

Financially speaking, considering my father was ill and my mother no longer worked—she had retired—and none of my brothers worked . . . [. . .] the fact that I was in France, that I worked at the time, all of that was a positive thing, for future medical prescriptions and hospital fees.

One of Badri's brothers sends him scanned copies of medical referrals, prescriptions, or checkup results on a regular basis. Thus, although he is not the eldest son, Badri has taken on a particularly important role in managing his father's health, which has much improved. He argues that managing treatment decisions and financially providing for care is not particularly tied to his status as an immigrant and the economic advantages this status may offer in the eyes of kin back home. Rather, he contends, it reflects his responsible behavior and his position in the family before he left Mali.

As far as I'm concerned, I can't say that it [migration] changed my status. Because even when I was in Mali, I was always stubborn in terms of decision making. And considering our culture, if it had something to do with the family and I was somehow concerned, then people asked for my opinion . . . I always was someone . . . I always gave my opinion on things and . . . well, I can't say that coming to Europe changed my position in my family . . . no, no . . . Things would have gone the same way. I would have gone to see the doctor, ask for explanations.

However, we see a reworking of Badri's narrative as he continues to analyze his responsibilities and decisions. He eventually states that the financial resources tied to his work opportunities in France were key in positioning him as the problem solver and hence decision maker in his father's medical care, despite his status as younger brother:

I knew that if expenses had to be made, I could take care of them. And immigration helped me in that sense. [. . .] My brother told me that if I didn't send money then, that no one else had the possibility to pay. Not even my father's younger brother who works at the clinic.

In the end, what emerges from Badri's narrative is a reconfiguration of kinship obligations based on the distribution of material resources, which in turn reflected counsel Badri obtained in the French biomedical system on his father's behalf. Badri sustained emotional ties with his family during his ten-year absence by sending money, medications, and advice. At the same time, his influence in the family subtly shifted as he assumed primary responsibility for his father's health over the years despite his position as younger brother (cf. Fesenmyer, this volume). Badri's story exemplifies how affective circuits incorporate emotive and material elements simultaneously as well as how they sustain reciprocity through space and time. Affective circuits work to regenerate family members' sense of belonging while they also allow and give coherence to the reconfiguration of preimmigration family organization and norms.

Expressing Belonging beyond Shared Explanatory Models of Illness and Healing

The identification of an illness often determines the constitution of transnational therapy management networks. Many migrants argue that some illnesses respond well to biomedicine, while other sicknesses, including those associated with sorcery accusations and curses or otherwise "sent" by spiritual agents or human antagonists, do not. Chronic illnesses and psychopathologies may also be considered ambiguous in terms of appropriate treatment. Therapy management for such illnesses in the immigrant population in France may vary over the course of the sickness, its relapses and remissions. However, explanatory models of illness and healing may shift or differ between immigrants in France and their kin at home. In such circumstances, cultural intimacy may be sustained despite diverging interpretations of illness causation and treatment, as Djibril's case demonstrates.

Djibril had suffered lower abdominal pain in Mali. He came to France in 2006 to join his wife and children. When he decided to make the trip, he had already received medical treatment for the pain. In the context of an infectious disease screening in France, his doctor diagnosed stomach cancer. For an entire year he underwent chemotherapy and radiotherapy treatment.

Djibril, who has studied at the university level, believes that diseases like cancer are not, as he said, mastered back home and cannot be handled effectively by traditional healing techniques, although others in his therapy network in Mali disagree. He noted that people in remote or rural areas may still find external causes for the disease. For instance, Djibril said,

When I was diagnosed with cancer [in France], friends would call from home and tell me things like "Someone who wishes to be in your situation in France sought to cause you wrong and cast a spell on you," but that's their own interpretation. I did not really understand their position.

An unexpected conversation we had with a close friend and coworker of Djibril cast a significantly different perspective on his situation. The friend lamented the return of Djibril's symptoms and confided his suspicions that the illness was indeed the result of sorcery "sent" by a disgruntled former employee in Mali. Contrary to Djibril's contention that he has no fear of sorcery, his friend noted that Djibril had often talked about the need for ritual protection in addition to biomedical intervention.[13]

In his youth in West Africa, Djibril was initiated as a hunter. He is thus very familiar with what he referred to as "traditional" medicinal treatment that one can seek when one falls ill in the bush (la brousse). "There are many plants that can heal a fever, a bad cough, a general state of fatigue. Shea butter, for example, is very efficient to get rid of a cough or to relieve fatigue." In France he never gave his children biomedical treatments for fever, diarrhea, or teething. In neighborhoods of Paris such as the 18ième arrondissement, numerous shops import and sell remedies for such everyday complaints. And friends and family return from trips to Mali or Senegal with shea butter and other medicinal products. Cancer is not responsive to such traditional treatments. Yet it is clear that, should Djibril relapse, those in Mali who constitute his therapy management network are likely to urge him to consult local healers in addition to pursuing his own preferred biomedical interventions. And although Djibril expressed his lack of confidence in medicinal plant therapy for cancer, he also spoke affectionately of his mother's caretaking at a distance. She sent him monthly packages containing herbal preparations. He said he never ingests them or washes in them, but he values them nonetheless. He would never tell his mother that he does not believe in the therapies she sends with such concern.

Djibril's case nuances the extent of the power of kin in the therapy management network. By presenting himself as an educated person, Djibril emphasized both his biomedical knowledge and his ability to make individual choices. Although he deeply values the biomedical treatment he has received in France and disdains medicinal plant therapies, he does rely on ritual interventions to protect himself from the risk of a sorcery-induced relapse (for which he needs the assistance of his kin and close friends in Mali). As Cole and Groes emphasize in the introduction to this volume, the affective circuits metaphor does not imply that transnational networks and social relations remain smooth and coherent. Rather, it implies that these relations are subject to regulations and stoppages at different levels. In Djibril's case, at the individual and emotional level, affective circuits involve constant negotiation of different explanatory models of health and healing, which activates mixed feelings of shame, misunderstanding, and loyalty. Indeed, kin back home proposed alternative interpretations of his illness and therapeutic strategies that both they and family and friends in France debated. Regardless of disagreements regarding efficacious treatments, such discussions sustain emotional connections and a sense of belonging. The case also shows that the knowledge or perception that relatives may be jealous and intend harm, in some cases perhaps using spiritual forces, does not negate the significance of connecting with kin to manage illness and seek protection from other spiritual forces and potential harm. Accordingly, transnational therapy management reinforces sociality and cultural intimacy even when it has a negligible effect on therapeutic strategies.

Therapy Management for a Chronic Illness

When a much-loved family member has an intractable illness, kin may be mobilized for extended periods in fruitless attempts to find a successful therapeutic intervention. Immigration status, financial resources, and cross generational ties sustained over decades have shaped the transnational therapy management strategies deployed for Moussa's chronic illness. One individual, Aminata, mobilized kin transnationally in a continuing effort to achieve a lasting cure for Moussa. Aminata has lived and worked in France for almost forty years. She is now a dual citizen of France and Mali, and so are her nine children. She has a son living in Mali who takes care of the house she constructed there. She travels to Mali regularly and maintains sustained family bonds in France, Senegal, and Mali. Approximately four years ago, on a cold winter night, her grandson Moussa had a psychotic episode. Moussa lived with his mother (Aminata's oldest daughter) and other siblings in the northern suburb of Paris where Aminata herself resided. His mother had often indicated that Moussa sometimes behaved strangely and had trouble sleeping at night. That night, dressed in a T-shirt, Moussa suddenly left the house and headed to the center of town. He stopped by a church and climbed to its rooftop. His mother and uncle, who had gone to look for him in the neighborhood, found him there and called emergency services. After the police and firemen managed to get Moussa down, he was taken to the hospital, where he was admitted to the psychiatry ward. As Aminata reported,

But for us, when they put him in a hospital, the family he came from, his grandfather's family—not his family directly, but his mother's—they are the kind of family who live with spirits back in Africa . . . well, here they don't, because people who are born here, grow up here, they don't know. But in Africa, it's the B. family, the family that lives with spirits. When someone is ill, we take it to them so they can assess what is going on. So right away, we called the family to let them know what happened, that he [Moussa] is at the hospital, we told them everything. "Of course not!" the elders told us, "of course not! You shouldn't have taken him to the hospital! This is an illness from home, we could have healed him. We would have healed him with the help of spirits, we would have healed him with plants, we would have called such uncle or such person." They would have sent us leaves and told us how to proceed. [. . .] But here we don't have a choice. Especially under those conditions. [. . .] Ten days later, I was supposed to go to Africa. I couldn't cancel my vacation, but I went and asked the doctors whether I could take him with me to get him a treatment over there. [. . .] They wouldn't let me, arguing that he could be in danger. He could hurt someone, or hurt himself. So they kept him. And after a few months of hospitalization, they released him.

Following his biomedical treatment in France, Moussa seemed to improve. But Aminata, together with kin in Mali, thought it likely that an inherited spirit possession illness had caused his malaise. Aminata, her eldest son in Mali, and assorted relatives in several countries debated his diagnosis and prognosis. Given his trajectory of relapses and remissions, the family doubted the efficacy of his health care in France, including the diagnosis. Aminata recalled,

Here, doctors did not tell us the name of the disease. They gave treatments. Sometimes they were very heavy, and they had to be modified. Sometimes the treatment was too weak . . . [Moussa] had to adapt to the treatment. [. . .] We also consulted people here. People from the family who can heal [although they lack the medicinal plants they would use in Africa].

Accordingly, Aminata arranged for Moussa to travel to Mali for treatment by a well-known ritual specialist whom the family often consulted. Relatives in Bamako took responsibility for his treatment there. After Moussa spent a few months at his uncle's house undergoing treatment, his health stabilized, though he kept having hallucinations: "We cared for him, we tried everything, but it did not go away," Aminata said.

Moussa later returned to Paris to resume treatment there and to engage once again with work and family in France. Meanwhile, his mother heard about a renowned healer in the Gambia who could cure Moussa. She and Moussa went to the Gambia and stayed for two weeks. She had such high expectations of this healer that she stopped the hospital treatment without informing the doctor. A few weeks after they returned to France,

Moussa had to be hospitalized again. This time he was very aggressive with his doctor, who suspected that Moussa had not followed his treatment regimen. His mother would not admit that the family had stopped the treatment and instead told the doctor that as far as she knew, Moussa had continued to follow it. On the day we interviewed Aminata, Moussa had been hospitalized for over a month. When we asked her whether this downturn had changed the family's perspective on Moussa's illness, she responded,

In Africa they say it's the spirits. [. . .] As far as we are concerned, we think that . . . to tell the truth, there were important men, our elders, our grandfathers, our uncles . . . these men, they had a gift. They could heal with no difficulty with the help of plants, and it went away. But today, you can no longer find these persons. [. . .] Even those he saw back home, even if it was good, it's not the same as it used to be. You pay money, they give you plants, you cleanse, you do everything, but it doesn't go away. So now I think that, after this experience . . . [. . .] I think that a good decision to be made is to continue with the medication and see the doctor from time to time, see if it gets better.

The shared management of Moussa's illness between France and Africa lasted almost ten years. During this time various family members took responsibility for his care—they provided plane fare, lodging, paid herbalists and diviners, and accompanied him to consultations. Aminata was the first to accompany Moussa to Mali, but her son in Bamako also cared for him for two years.

It was a big responsibility. When he [the uncle] heard about a person who could heal him, he would take Moussa there. When someone heard "this person was ill and he went to that village where he was cured," then his uncle would take him there . . . but in the end nothing happened. Frankly, we wasted a lot of money. Plane tickets, money for healers, ritual sacrifices, and in the end, no outcome.

Nevertheless, Aminata explains, "little packages" are still periodically sent to Paris from home. She says the situation was handled just the way it would have been had the family been in Africa:

Everyone mobilized. People in the family called other persons so that they would pray for him and make sacrifices. Even friends of people we know who can do things came to see us. I think if a thorn had to be taken out of the foot, it would have been gone long ago.

In this case, we see that kin in Paris, in Bamako, and in Senegal have worked to maintain customary notions of appropriate kinship responsibilities and sentiments. Because Aminata and the Paris-based family are all French citizens with pensions or full-time employment, they can easily finance frequent trips between France and West Africa. The social context, in terms of administrative and economic stability, was determinant in easing affective circuits for Aminata and her kin. The case also gives us insight into the ways family members simultaneously and consecutively use diverse (herbal/ritual/biomedical) treatments, thus creating a repertoire of therapeutic possibilities. The family made decisions pragmatically, using biomedicine in France and ritual interventions in Mali as complementary modalities. The relapsing and remitting features of the illness and the possibility of a hereditary component related to possession were instrumental in guiding discussions and decisions among those managing Moussa's therapeutic trajectory. It may well be that the history of possession in Aminata's husband's family over generations, indicating an explicit connection between the illness and kinship relations, contributed to the engagement of a widespread network of kin with Moussa's illness trajectory.

Sustaining Cultural Intimacy across Generations

Increasingly sophisticated transnational communication technologies have enabled consecutive generations of labor migrants and their families who joined them in France to remain in close contact with family and friends in West Africa. This regular contact has in fact been shown to consolidate kinship networks on a transnational scale and across generations (Cole 2014b; Teixeira 2008; see also Kea, this volume). Currently, French-born and raised children of immigrants may access the same affective circuits their elder relatives do when facing illness episodes. However, considering the tensions inherent in intergenerational relations, in this section we explore the extent to which cultural intimacy can be sustained cross generationally.

Coumba, age nineteen, for example, defines herself as "purely French." She was born in Mali but raised in Paris, the child of an undocumented Malian father and one of his three undocumented wives, also from Mali. She has thirteen brothers and sisters. Her father arranged her marriage to a thirty-year-old man who lived in Mali but traveled to Paris frequently for business. The fiancé had presented bride wealth to Coumba and the family, which they accepted. One day, Coumba asked whether we had noticed that she was pregnant (we had not). The father of the child was not the official fiancé but rather her boyfriend, the son of a Malian émigré to France. The two had asked their fathers for permission to marry. Both parents had reacted similarly: the boyfriend was of noble ancestry and Coumba was of the blacksmith clan; under these circumstances, marriage was impossible.

Coumba was furious. She cited the French Constitution, the Bible, and the Qur'an as evidence that there was no legitimate reason to prevent the marriage. Ultimately, her boyfriend left her, and her father fell ill. Partially paralyzed and diagnosed with a stroke, he consulted by phone with family in Bamako about possible therapeutic interventions. Kin in Bamako and Paris blamed Coumba for having caused the stroke through her irresponsible behavior, although her father also suspected sorcery "sent" by someone in Mali who was envious of him. Coumba's father recovered enough to travel to Mali to seek help from a ritual specialist. Meanwhile, in Paris Coumba found a social worker who helped her find an apartment. She left her parental home, hoping to reconcile with her boyfriend. Toward that end, she has consulted a marabout in Paris to obtain a product to induce undying love. She says she would never travel to Mali for medical care, does not know her relatives there, and were she to fall sick, would see a doctor in Paris. However, for romantic purposes (like those motivating Oumou above) and for routine childhood illnesses, she would consult a marabout in Paris or simply purchase products imported to Paris from Africa, such as shea butter.

In a sense, Coumba's story reflects the sort of conflicts that often arise when immigrant children born and raised in France try to impose ideas and practices that older members of the family have difficulty accepting or negotiating. We regularly hear young, French-born adults express scorn for the significance their parents attribute to maintaining affective circuits. They claim not to comprehend their relatives who contact kin in Mali for advice in the context of illness episodes. Like Coumba, they assert that they would never live in West Africa or seek advice from relatives there. They often accuse their parents of being "maladjusted" to life in France or of clinging to "primitive" customs that are embarrassing. However, as Coumba's case also shows, such critiques do not necessarily hinder adherence to their parents' explanatory models of misfortune when they find it relevant to do so. Indeed, consultations with ritual specialists in Paris for romantic, financial, or academic problems are commonplace among younger generations born or raised in France.

How these generational conflicts play out or affect therapeutic circuits is far from linear. Affective circuits encourage cultural intimacy and solidarity, yet the potential for conflict remains depending on class, generation, education, and immigration status (see also Fesenmyer, this volume). Children who are born to and raised by immigrant parents in France do not necessarily reject the medicinal therapies or rituals favored by their parents, although they are likely to also rely on biomedicine. The conditions under which some remain connected to social support networks in West Africa and retain confidence in the therapeutic interventions that so effectively sustained older immigrant generations are not entirely clear. However, it seems that those whose parents have remained in close contact with kin and friends in Mali and those who have themselves visited or lived in Mali continue to value transnational affective ties and material exchanges.

Awa's experience illustrates how accepting therapeutic counsel from extended family can produce a sense of belonging and sustain cultural intimacy. As in Djibril's case, in Awa's we see that immigrants and family residing in Mali may not agree on treatment priorities. Yet the process of negotiating treatment in itself enhances social solidarity. On one of our trips to Mali, we accompanied Awa, the twenty-two-year-old, French-born, French-raised, and university-educated daughter of our host in Bamako. She had not returned to Mali since she was two years old. She described herself as a "stranger" becoming acquainted with her own relatives. She became close to a cousin of the same age, who took her on a tour of town on his motorbike. During their excursion, they had a minor accident. Awa badly scraped the side of her foot on the road. What initially appeared to be a bad scratch, however, turned into a possibly dangerous infection, as Awa's foot became increasingly swollen. Her mother, a hospital interpreter who has lived in France for thirty years, decided to take action and called on a well-known healer who happened to be in Bamako at the time. The man came to the family's house with his healing objects and medicines, and after carefully observing Awa's foot, proceeded to heat up mutton grease and rub it energetically onto the wound.

Awa sat, silently biting her lips, in obvious pain. The session with the healer ended when she cried, "Stop!" The treatment relieved neither Awa's pain nor her increasing fever. Finally, Awa expressed her own opinion for the first time in days, saying, "I want to see a 'real' doctor." Her older brothers initially questioned what she meant by a "real" doctor but eventually acquiesced and took her to a biomedical clinic. There she received daily injections of antibiotics for a week.

Throughout this episode, Awa had sought both to respect her mother and uncle's advice and to signal her belonging to her family residing in

4.2 The healer applies hot mutton grease to Awa's wound, Bamako 2005. Members of the hunters' clan in Mali are renowned healers. Initiates develop skills that allow them to communicate with animals, who are considered wise and knowledgeable. These animals are said to bestow their knowledge of healing on initiates. Photo by Stéphanie Larchanché.

Mali. After almost twenty years of absence, she sought to reconnect with her kin and establish a closer relationship to her eldest brother and his family. Therapy management became the context within which she could symbolically express her desire for that reconnection. There were obviously limits to her willingness to adhere to her therapy network's decision when her condition became serious. By that time, however, her demand became acceptable, as the network itself seemed to have exhausted its own therapeutic options. While the pain Awa experienced and the emergency nature of the situation tested the boundaries of affective circuits, they did not threaten them.

Another of our informants, Djenebou, transformed her Paris apartment into a medical office for a visiting Malian herbalist in a similar effort to signal her investment in the healing repertoire of her Malian family. Djenebou came to France at age ten and subsequently received biomedical training and became a supervisor in charge of cleaning and sanitizing labs and operating rooms in a large section of a public hospital. Her employment in a hospital and her comprehension of biomedical principles did not prevent her from supporting her husband's request that they welcome the herbalist for an extended professional visit to Paris.

This specialist is a relative of Djenebou's husband, and the two have maintained contact by telephone for years. The healer resided at the couple's house for ten months, seeing clients on a daily basis. On his business card, he introduced himself as a phytotherapist who collaborated with the department of traditional medicine in Mali (Institut national de recherche en santé publique [INRSP]) and as someone who specialized in general medicine and obstetrics. He is Bambara but speaks French, English, Soninke, and Pulaar as well. His clients include Bambara, Halpulaar, and Soninke immigrants; some clients are also Algerian and French. Most of his clients seek treatment for illness, particularly mental illness, but he also treats problems related to love, immigration papers, school, work, and finances.

By inviting a specialist in West African medicinal plants to see patients in her living room, Djenebou, who had acquired the reputation of working in the biomedical sector, found a way to express the enduring relevance of "traditional" healing and to display her adherence to "a repertoire of meanings" (Reed-Danahay 2008, 83) shared with her immediate family in France and with kin in Mali. A resident of a suburban housing project, she symbolically conveyed her familiarity with medicinal plants and the value she placed on herbalism, thus reinforcing cultural intimacy and the affective circuits on which it relies.

Therapy Management, Transnational Belonging, and Cultural Intimacy

Our analysis of transnational therapy management networks takes us back to Janzen's (1987) assertion that health is closely intertwined with sociality as well as to other works that have discussed its continued relevance in the context of transnational migrations (Krause 2008). In addition, it delineates another layer of meaning that, beyond the description of readily apparent social dynamics, relates to deeper emotional stakes. As it does for Malians, transnational therapy management involves negotiating social hierarchies as well as sustaining emotional connections. In the course of communicating about an individual's illness, kin, friends, and ritual specialists who engage in therapy management experience a sense of belonging. This healing process sustains mutual interests and affective ties across distance and time despite the inevitable doubts, suspicion, and uncertainty that may accompany therapeutic interventions.

Therapy management generates exchanges of material resources such as money and medications but also of medical information. Immigrants in France may share advice they receive from doctors at French hospitals or from kin and friends in France with intimate others in Mali who participate in therapy management, and they may in turn receive advice, ritual interventions, and medications such as medicinal plants from those participants. This common process is nuanced individually by such factors as age, immigration status, or economic precarity. But throughout, the management of illness is a key vehicle for sustaining shared repertoires of cultural intimacy based on flexible notions of illness causation, diagnosis, and treatment. These shared repertoires shape and are shaped by affective circuits that include exchanges of knowledge, counsel, and caregiving. Transnational reciprocity involves gifts of valued medicines, whether pharmaceuticals, herbal remedies, or ritual objects, as well as financial resources. This continuous flow both reflects and shapes the emotions and sentiments that make possible the social reproduction of the family.

Notes

1. Across North and West Africa, the term *marabout* (French, from Arabic *murābiṭ*) refers to Islamic ritual specialists. The precise meaning varies according to local context. For example, a marabout may be a revered religious figure, the head of a Muslim brotherhood such as the Mourides, or a teacher in a Qur'anic school for children. Immigrant discourse about marabouts in Paris often includes reference to the possibility that they are charlatans rather than devout and learned Muslims. Those who claim to have spiritual powers to confront or engage in sorcery are particularly suspect.

2. *Gundo* is a generic term for *secret*. It can refer to mundane, secular secrets or to powerful knowledge, incantations, or a secret substance prepared by a ritual specialist, whose purpose is known only to the specialist and the client. In this case, the informant referred to having obtained a *gundo* from a marabout.

3. Our research focused particularly on immigrants from Mali living in France. They include Soninke, Bambara, and Fulbe populations. The majority of West African immigrants to France are drawn from the Senegal River Valley, from portions of Mali, Mauritania, and Senegal in which these ethnic communities reside. This region has served as a source of migrant labor for France since the World War I era. Malians still constitute the largest population of

West African immigrants in France, followed by Senegalese and immigrants from Côte d'Ivoire, Cameroon, Guinea, and Mauritania. Currently, an estimated 120,000 Malians (including undocumented immigrants) live in France, the majority in the Île-de-France, greater Paris, agglomeration (Vincent 2013). Most in the first generation of immigrants were men. The state family reunification policy established in 1975 allowed wives to join their husbands and children their fathers, as we see in the case of Oumou.

4. West African migrants have been present in France since the mid-nineteenth century, and a Malian community has existed in Paris since World War I (Cordell, Gregory, and Piché 1996). Emigration from Mali, a landlocked West African country, to France has been the product of rural poverty, desertification, and population growth over a period of decades. See Abdallah (2000), Diouf (2001), Manchuelle (1997), and Timera (1996) for historical origins of migration from the Senegal River Valley to France.

5. The term *black market* here refers to employment of immigrants without work permits, in violation of state labor regulations.

6. The significant contributions of Malians in France to families in Mali are evident in the remittances sent home, which in 2009 amounted to approximately €300 million; remittances quadrupled between 2000 and 2009 (Gonin and Kotlok 2012). Yet it is important to remember that immigration is at its roots often a family project and a collective investment that begins with the financing of travel to Europe (Manchuelle 1997; Riccio 2008, 221; Timera 1996).

7. Herzfeld's original conceptualization of "cultural intimacy" was adapted by Reed-Danahay for the analysis of immigrant "belonging." Here we focus on cultural intimacy as it produces an "assurance of common sociality" (Herzfeld 1997, 3) rather than as a source of embarrassment, although it may elicit that response (see the case of Djibril discussed subsequently in the text).

8. As Saraiva (2008, 254) eloquently remarks, "The study of migration cannot be limited to the circulation of goods and people, but has to take into account the circulation of symbolic universes, including religion and the ritual practices that heal [the] states of affliction."

9. The term *zero immigration* was coined in 1993 by the French conservative government's interior minister, Charles Pasqua. The expression was later qualified to mean zero illegal immigration.

10. Several authors have argued that restrictive immigration policies have led to an increase in undocumented migrants (A. Garcia 2006; Sanket and Ratha 2011; Ware 2015). Presumably, the reasons for this increase are similar to those generating legal migration from West Africa: rural poverty, urban underemployment and unemployment, and historical migration trajectories such as those of the Soninke. However, as Cornuau and Dunezat (2008) observe, statistics on illegal immigrants are estimates at best. In 2006, Sarkozy estimated that between two hundred thousand and four hundred thousand "clandestine" migrants were living in France and between eighty thousand

and one hundred thousand were expected to enter France each year (A. Garcia 2006). Cornuau and Dunezat (2008, 17) offer a scathing assessment of the limitations of French census data on entries into and departures from France. They assert that the legal uncertainties confronting immigrants should not lead to the conclusion that immigration is declining but rather that there is an increase in undocumented migrants.

11. In a study of nine men's worker hostels in Paris (Sargent, Larchanché, and Yatera 2005), we found that residents from the Kayes region of West Africa had invested an estimated €10,000 to install a satellite dish in one remote community to facilitate communication. On an individual level, even those who were underemployed or working on the black market invested from €50 to €240 monthly to "call home." Callers on both ends of the circuit were thus constantly engaged in the same dilemmas and pleasures of everyday life, from the mundane to the dramatic. One young man interviewed at a worker hostel, for example, lamented his inability to send money to his father, who had just lost two cows to theft, while another was encouraged by his younger brother's school successes.

12. Documented immigrants have the right to the same basic national health insurance (Couverture maladie universelle [CMU]) as French citizens. Undocumented immigrants who can provide evidence that they have resided in France for three months have the right to Aide médicale d'état (AME). All immigrants, regardless of immigration status, have access to care for emergencies, a category that includes injuries, acute infectious disease episodes, pregnancy, and childbirth.

13. Djibril likely emphasized his status as a university-educated, scientifically knowledgeable person to distinguish himself from less Europeanized, more "superstitious" immigrants.

FIVE

"Assistance but Not Support": Pentecostalism and the Reconfiguring of Relatedness between Kenya and the United Kingdom

LESLIE FESENMYER

Sustaining relations transnationally is not only a moral issue but also a material and deeply affective one. It raises difficult questions about what it means to be related, the answers to which are subject to debate within families, across generations, and in wider society. During my research with Kenyan migrants in London, I found that many struggled with defining and managing their ties to kin who remained in Kenya. "We put it on ourselves," Beatrice, a divorced forty-year-old woman originally from Kiambu District, said to me, referring to the pressure to support family members in Kenya.[1] Later that evening, Beatrice's paternal cousin Charles dropped by her apartment in Forest Gate, East London, where I was staying for the weekend. Interested in his views on the subject, I mentioned my earlier conversation with Beatrice. A married man in his early forties, Charles told me he "tries to help where he can." If he helps one day, he said, he does not expect to have to help the next day, adding that "you can't help everyone, but where do you stop?" His question highlights a moral dilemma facing many Kenyan migrants in London:

they feel obliged to "help everyone," yet they sometimes find they lack the capacity and/or desire to do so. Like Charles and Beatrice, many of their Kenyan peers sought answers to such questions in Pentecostalism.

This chapter examines the role of Pentecostalism in migrant Kenyans' efforts to navigate the changing nature of relatedness. As a form of evangelical Christianity, Pentecostalism requires new congregants to be "born anew," reject their old lives, develop a new self-image, and adopt a new code of moral conduct. Accordingly, it demands that they "make a complete break with the past" (Meyer 1998, 316). Yet, if Pentecostal discourse asserts a complete break, scholarship on the topic shows a far more complex picture. As Meyer (1998, 340) has argued, "Rather than exchanging the 'past' identity with its emphasis on family ties with a new, individualist identity, [Pentecostalism] offers members an elaborate discourse and ritual practice to oscillate between both and to address the gap which exists between aspirations and actual circumstances."

To analyze how Kenyan migrants in London draw on Pentecostalism to reconfigure their relationships with their kin in Kenya, I bring together a processual approach to kinship with recent work on Pentecostalism. According to a processual perspective, kin relations are dynamic and "always under construction," and understanding them entails attention to the sociality of everyday life and the agency of individual kin (Carsten 1995, 1997, 2000). Indeed, much research on Pentecostalism, both in Africa and in the African diaspora, focuses on the ways it allows for various kinds of transformations of meaning with regard to persons and relations (Bochow and van Dijk 2012; Cole 2010, 2012; Daswani 2010; Engelke 2004, 2010; Englund 2004, 2007; Gifford 2004; Lindhardt 2010; Marshall 1991, 2009; Maxwell 1998; Meyer 1998, 1999, 2004; van Dijk 1998, 2002a, 2002b). In this chapter I show how migrants draw on Pentecostal discourse and practice to maintain their familial relationships while at the same time trying to rework them (Bochow and van Dijk 2012; Cole 2012; Lindhardt 2010; Meyer 1998; van Dijk 2002a).

The notion of affective circuits (see Cole and Groes, introduction to this volume) enables us to see how migrants in London and their nonmigrant kin in Kenya make, remake, and unmake kin relations across space. According to this idea, money, goods, information, and other resources move within circuits together with aspirations and expectations. So too, love, affection, and concern flow through them, as do frustration, guilt, and resentment. Yet, much as kin relations are dynamic and constantly reconfigured, the affective circuits through which persons constitute their relations also change and are negotiated over time. Though Kenyans have historically understood the moral and the material to be intertwined in affective circuits, I contend that Pentecostal ideas and discourse help migrants disentangle the moral from the material aspects of kin relations. More specifically, I argue that Kenyan Pentecostal migrants attempt to limit the material resources, such as remittances, that flow from London to Kenya without jeopardizing their own moral standing or cutting off their kinship ties. By (re)defining whose material well-being they are responsible for to include only their spouses and children, they prioritize the Pentecostal ideal of the nuclear, conjugal family over the extended, multigenerational family. Nonetheless, although Pentecostalism provides a compelling moral rationale, it cannot insulate migrants from the emotional complexity of such familial negotiations. Defining what it means to be related is inevitably a dynamic and contested process.

Migrants' reworking of familial relations occurs not only transnationally but also vis-à-vis other Kenyan migrants in London and wider British society. As they distance themselves from their kin, they cultivate a new set of reciprocal moral relations with other Pentecostals in London, among whom staying engaged transnationally has a particular social and moral currency. Viewed within the wider context of migrants' lives in London, I suggest that maintaining, rather than breaking, affective circuits can be seen as a mark of success. Those (few) who can fulfill newly defined (i.e., narrowed) familial expectations *and* build their lives in London are doubly successful in a situation where the chance of doubly failing is much higher. Doing so thus serves as a commentary on the success of their migration projects relative to those of other Kenyan migrants, giving rise to a social hierarchy within their nascent moral community. At the same time, it enables migrants to position themselves as morally superior vis-à-vis British society, which they perceive not to value "family," and to rebut the accusations of their nonmigrant kin that they have "become British."

To explore how migrants rework their relations with kin they leave behind,[2] I begin by considering the context of changing familial relations in Kenya. I then turn to migrants' lives in London, the challenges they face, and the Pentecostal churches where they spend much of their time. Focusing on the guidance offered by Pentecostal pastors and doctrine, I consider how migrant Kenyans translate Pentecostal ideas into practice vis-à-vis their kin in Kenya and the ambivalence such negotiations can engender. Finally, I examine how migrants' emplacement in a new moral community in London contributes to the reconfiguring of affective circuits. Though I pay greater attention to migrants, my intention is not to privilege their experiences. Rather, it is to highlight that they are morally and socially obliged to explain their actions in ways that nonmigrants are not because those who move bear the greater burden when it comes to staying in touch (Hage 2002).

The Changing Nature of Relatedness among Families in Kenya

To understand why many migrants turn to Pentecostalism, it is important to understand family dynamics and patterns of intergenerational reciprocity and how they have changed and shifted over time. Fulfilling obligations to one's family and wider community has long been central to ideas of moral personhood in Kenya (Lonsdale 2003). Among Kikuyu-speaking people who predominated in my research, a man traditionally became "an upright member of society" by starting a family and managing his own household (Kershaw 1973, 47). The sternest test of one's "self-mastering moral agency" (*wiathi*) was mastery of one's "own home" (Lonsdale 1996, 19). Similarly, Luo speakers from western Kenya valued "hard work, self-discipline and respect for others" as well as having many children and well-stocked food stores to support not only their own families but also those of others in times of crisis (Oruka 1992, 122; see also Oruka 1990).

Yet colonialism long ago transformed households throughout Kenya as the bases of production, distribution, and consumption, challenging the centrality of kinship to people's lives and livelihoods. Increasing land shortages during the colonial era, especially in Kikuyu-speaking Central Province in the heart of the White Highlands, home to many of my migrant interlocutors, contributed to internal migration, weakening the links between "town" and "country" (see also Frederiksen 2001; Lonsdale 1992, 356–58). Decades of rural-urban migration, along with the rise of an urban middle class in Nairobi, with its Christian ideal of a conjugal nuclear family, further challenged the salience of wider kinship ties as sources of support (Gordon 1995). The sputtering and later declining Kenyan economy of the 1980s and 1990s exacerbated the situation as people struggled to sustain livelihoods.

Nonetheless, the boundaries of many so-called nuclear families remain permeable. Extended kin continue to stay for varying lengths of time in the homes of (distant) relatives as they finish their educations or search for work (Stichter 1988, 185–86). Kenyans also still "exercise rights and . . . [are] subject to obligations which are normally thought of as economic beyond the household in which they live" (Guyer 1981, 98). Consequently, a normative expectation of generalized reciprocity among families is prevalent in Kenya, if often unrealized in practice, and carries significant moral weight.

In the name of kinship, relatives make moral demands on each other, on their autonomy and resources, marking the entanglement and circulation of affection and (moral and material) obligation (Cole and Thomas 2009; Peletz 2001, 418–19; see also Fortes 1969, 232–42). The migration of Kenyans during the 1990s and early 2000s stretched these moral economies of relatedness across space.[3] I would suggest that for their nonmigrant kin in Kenya,[4] it brought renewed hope in kinship ties being a possible means—and not simply an ideal—of securing their own well-being and realizing their aspirations. As David Parkin (1975, 149) pointed out with regard to his work among Luo-speaking rural-urban migrants in the 1970s, "They [migrants] are even greater sources of patronage for rural kin than they might otherwise be had they remained at home." The opportunities thus imagined to be available in a wealthy country such as the United Kingdom have only fueled familial expectations of support.

The generation of Kenyans who migrated in the late 1980s and 1990s on the cusp of social adulthood had yet to engage in reciprocal relations with kin. Prompted by the uncertainty and instability in Kenya during this time, they sought to move to places where they could realize their own aspirations, a yearning shared by many of their contemporaries elsewhere in Africa (Christiansen, Utas, and Vigh 2006; Cole 2004, 2010; Vigh 2006b). They largely moved from middle- and working-class estates and informal settlements in Nairobi, such as Kasarani, Langata, Riruta, and Kawangware, or from towns and villages in Kiambu District, adjacent to the capital. In London they joined a growing and diversifying African diaspora (Koser 2003).

"We Came to Work and Study": Migration and Life in London

Many migrants I encountered during fieldwork in London found that the burden of familial obligations, experiences of discrimination and marginality, and increasingly restrictive (im)migration regulations undermined their ability to pursue a normative path to adulthood. The migration project of a woman named Lucy helps illuminate this point. I first met Lucy, a petite forty-year-old woman with long, thinly braided hair and a diffident but friendly gaze, at a Pentecostal church service in Greenwich one overcast Sunday morning in December 2009. Not long after, we met for coffee in central London near the university where she was enrolled in a master's level management course, and she shared with me how she came to live in London.

Raised by her widowed mother, who worked as a police officer, and her grandmother, Lucy moved between their households in Nairobi and a Kiambu village. Lucy insisted on studying abroad—a good student, she imagined it would be "better to go out" to continue her studies. With the help of her mother and her cousin Rosemary, who lived in Athens, she moved to Greece in 1988 as a nineteen-year-old. But, with no proficiency in the Greek language, she could not enroll in a university, and she fell into a series of low-wage jobs working as a nanny and later a waitress. Lucy's relationship with Rosemary became strained almost immediately because Rosemary "took her paycheck" and expected her to cook, clean, and care for her children on her days off. Meanwhile, Lucy's brothers eagerly awaited her help with their own migrations, and her mother anticipated remittances with which to start a business. On the verge of being deported for violating the terms of her student visa, in 1993 she managed to scrape together enough money to buy a plane ticket and move to London, where a childhood friend lived, rather than return to Nairobi and face social humiliation.

In addition to familial expectations and obligations, Lucy and her peers in London struggled to balance the demands of education and work. Some trained to become nurses and teachers; Lucy continued her studies in business management in addition to working as a security guard and later a hotel receptionist. The availability of jobs in London that paid higher wages than one could hope to earn in Kenya made schooling appear unnecessary to some for achieving their aspirations. Charles, for instance, stopped his studies and became a plumber. Others I met worked as carers, cleaners, store clerks, cooks and servers, and administrative assistants. Such jobs allowed them to earn additional income by working overtime and night shifts. However, what initially seemed like good jobs to them have emerged as largely low-status ones that leave little leisure time, much less the means for them to "better themselves" or to help their families. In fact, these jobs reveal the segmentation of the labor market in London, in which people with a diversity of migration experiences predominate in a range of largely low-wage occupations (Wills et al. 2010). They also reflect stereotypes based on nationality, ethnicity, and/or gender regarding those who are (or are not) "ideal workers," which can serve as additional occupational barriers to social mobility (McDowell, Batnitzky, and Dyer 2007).

Visa regulations further complicated many migrants' lives. Most Kenyans I met initially migrated on some kind of temporary visa, for instance, student, worker, or visitor. From the 1990s through the mid-2000s, the British government introduced numerous parliamentary measures aimed at tightening requirements to obtain permanent residence. While most Kenyans had not given much thought to how long they would stay in London, instead seeing the act of migration as *the* achievement, the prospect of having to leave when they had not (yet) realized their aspirations was unwelcome and prompted many to try and find ways to stay. Some eventually secured the right to remain by applying through one of two routes: after ten years of continuous lawful residence in the country or after fourteen years of "continuous residence of any legality," which can include periods of being undocumented.[5] For instance, Lucy applied to regularize her status in 2009, more than two decades after she first left Kenya. Though eligible to apply two years earlier, she had to delay her application until she could cover both the legal costs and increased application fees. Thus, the interval between the 1990s, when many migrated, and the start of my fieldwork in 2009 coincided with a period when many obtained permanent residency or were in the process of doing so. Unsurprisingly, however, some migrant Kenyans remain undocumented, their numbers impossible to determine. An important consequence of the time entailed in obtaining residency is that many of my interlocutors did not visit their families in Kenya for a decade or more after they first migrated.

Taken together, overwhelming familial expectations, labor market segmentation, and tightening immigration regulations have frustrated the ambitions of many migrants and left them stuck in time and space, a predicament not unlike that of their peers in Kenya (Carling 2002; Frederiksen 2000, 2002; see also Vigh, this volume). Understanding more about their postmigration lives necessitates shifting attention to the churches where they spend much of their time in London and to fellow congregants with whom they have developed reciprocal moral relations.

An Emerging Kenyan Pentecostal Community in London

Though born into the mainline Christian denominations of their parents, thirty- and fortysomething Kenyans in London largely attend Pentecostal churches.[6] While some were Pentecostals at the time of migration, others became Pentecostal after migrating in the 1990s, and still others rededicated themselves to God after a period of "backsliding" (see also Meyer 1999). For example, Lucy became born-again as a teenager in Nairobi and then rededicated herself not long after she became a single mother in London in the late 1990s. Migrants' adherence to Pentecostalism coincides with its surging popularity among Kenyans, including some of their kin (Gifford 2009).

While Kenyan migrants have settled all over London and beyond, many of the churches they attend are located in East London in the boroughs of

Newham, Redbridge, Greenwich, and Barking and Dagenham. A Kenyan pastor typically leads the churches, and other Kenyans predominate among congregants.[7] The churches hold two- to three-hour services, primarily conducted in English, every Sunday. During the week, women's, men's, and youth fellowships hold meetings and organize activities. Congregants also host weekly prayer meetings and Bible study in their homes. Periodically, there are multiday conferences that bring together Pentecostals from various parts of the United Kingdom. The time that participation in church activities entails is not insignificant for church members, most of whom work long hours and often live far from their church and other congregants. Consequently, they spend much of their free time with other Pentecostals, cultivating a community from which they can draw support and guidance.

Pastors in particular figure importantly in this regard. In their sermons, they address congregants' aspirations and dreams, difficulties and challenges, worries and suffering. In doing so, they engage discursively with wider British society and generate an alternative basis of authority rooted in Pentecostal beliefs that offer migrants new ways of defining and valuing themselves (cf. Cole 2012). During one service I attended in Ilford in northeast London in early 2010, the pastor spoke of each of us as an asylum seeker,[8] which he defined as one "seeking cover" whether for safety or economic reasons. He encouraged us to focus on who we are and who God made us to be rather than on what others say about us. He said doing so was especially necessary because "when we say we are British in response to the question 'what are you?' people doubt us because of our accents." This doubt can be very hard to deal with, he went on, because "it makes you feel bad, like you do not belong." The pastor concluded by saying that it was important to believe in yourself and what you can do because no one else will; you must follow your own path guided by God. His emphasis on personal agency reflects an understanding that one must accept individual responsibility for choosing one's life path rather than see oneself as a victim of circumstances beyond one's control (see also Daswani 2010; Pype 2011, 281, 298). This thinking challenges an image of congregants as powerless in the face of British racism and discrimination.

An often-mentioned topic of conversation is how Pentecostals engage with their nonmigrant kin and handle their familial obligations. The advice of a Pentecostal Kenyan pastor I met many times, who is a prolific speaker and writer on family-related issues, conveys a religiously informed logic:

The in-laws think of it as their right to benefit from their son's or daughter's riches and especially if they are doing well. That could be a good assumption and naturally it's expected that those who have material possession share with those without.

Nevertheless, a husband should discuss with his wife how to help their in-laws. Some in-laws are quite demanding and if there is no good plan then there will be pressure in the marriage. Understand that you cannot carry all the problems of your clan or tribe. . . .

On investment, it is important to remember that all what you have belongs to you and your wife/husband and not with others. This means if you waste your resources with your people then your wife/husband will be deeply wounded. If you are to give anything to your family then involve your spouse also. If you are to invest at home then take care not to over trust your relatives. Some have done it and got wounded. Think of having an overall manager who is not related to you and your relatives could work under him if at all they are to be involved. This will ensure that respect remains and you will not be wounded. . . . Let not cultural stand or practices ruin your marital relationship while you could have used it to strengthen your relationship.[9]

Several aspects of the pastor's guidance are notable. He places the husband-wife dyad at the center of the social universe. In doing so, he draws attention to the potential for one's kin to come between spouses, a worry that suggests an understanding of one's spouse and kin as potentially at odds with one another. The pastor warns against wasting one's resources on one's people and overtrusting them, indicating a wariness, if not outright suspicion, toward kin. To manage familial relations, the pastor proposes maintaining distance from kin. Such distance not only preempts being taken advantage of but also, importantly, ensures that respectful relations among kin are sustained (see also Cole, this volume). Lastly, the pastor suggests that a "cultural stand" and "practices" are not inherently harmful and can instead "strengthen" marital relationships. For example, at the time of their weddings, most Pentecostal couples I met consented to their families negotiating bride wealth as part of the marriage process. While they expressed some ambivalence as to whether the practice constituted the "buying" of a person, they nonetheless wanted to stave off what one pastor referred to as "generational curses" and, thus, to secure the blessing and support of their families. Engaging in selective customary practices on newly defined terms, I would suggest, is at the core of how migrants negotiate familial obligations.

"Assistance but Not Support": Putting Pentecostal Logic into Practice

In following the guidance of their pastors, migrants aim to "assist but not support" their nonmigrant kin. More specifically, they are willing to provide "assistance," which means sending occasional remittances of varying amounts, rather than remitting the same sum of money on a regular basis as if it were a steady income. In doing so, migrants seek to uncouple the moral from the material, that is, to remain moral persons without being completely responsible for the material well-being of their nonmigrant kin. In what follows, I consider the ways migrants draw on particular Pentecostal ideas to determine how and whom to assist.

Honoring One's Parents

One Sunday after church, John, a man in his early forties from Kiambu, and his Nairobi-born wife invited me to join them for lunch with their two children at their home in Dagenham in East London. They both moved to London in the mid-1990s, he with the intention of becoming a lawyer and she with training as a nurse. She now works in a National Health Service (NHS) hospital, but John lacked the money to complete his law degree and instead took an administrative job in the local council. As we talked about keeping in touch with those in Kenya, John remarked,

Once you go abroad, it's a blessing and a curse. When you live out, people expect you to support them. They may do nothing to help themselves. They act like you owe them. Coming to [the] UK causes problems for many families.

He went on to share his logic for handling the pressure to remit:

I send money to my parents . . . but I do not support them. It would go against God if I were forced to choose between supporting my parents over my own children since God wants me to care for and nurture my family. Supporting my parents would disrupt things because I would become a parent to them. To support them would take a kind of power away from them and disrespect them. It is easy to abuse that power.

In raising the subject of intergenerational reciprocity, John recasts the relationship between children and parents: while adult children traditionally assumed responsibility for the needs of aging parents, John instead seeks to reposition himself vis-à-vis his parents (see also Lindhardt 2010). In this alternate view, his refusal to support his parents does not reflect callous disregard but rather is a measured decision intended to show respect for his parents' authority. Moreover, the reference to becoming a "parent" to his parents has an important cultural corollary, namely, that Kenyans see themselves as "bringing forth their parents" (Kershaw 1973, 47). Kikuyus traditionally considered four children, preferably two sons and two daughters, to be the ideal number to ensure the rebirth of both maternal and paternal grandparents (Herzog 1971).[10] Here, however, John invokes God to limit what "bringing forth one's parents" means in practice. More specifically, restricting giving ensures that a child does not usurp his or her parents' power, and, thus, the child's restraint can be considered an expression of respect toward them. Such thinking further suggests a different conception of money in the context of familial life: rather than being a means of fulfilling reciprocal obligations, money is morally dubious and has the potential to corrupt relationships.

Respecting Gender Roles

One afternoon while at John's house for a social gathering, he and I picked up a thread in our ongoing conversation about transnational kin relations. He mentioned that some Kenyan women he knows in London only send money to their mothers to "empower" them. However, in his view this is dangerous because if mothers have money, they do "not need to rely on the father anymore. This can tear up the fabric of a family." In raising this concern about the gendered balance of power within marital relationships, John invoked what he said was the traditional role of fathers as the head of the household among Kenya's historically patrilineal, virilocal peoples. If he were to give to his mother, according to his logic, he would displace his father by becoming her provider.

At the same time, his concern aligns with Pentecostal ideas about the complementary gender roles of men and women (Maier 2012; Marshall 1991; Mate 2002). Men are the heads of families and women are their designated "helpmates." Congregants describe married couples as a body wherein the man is the head and the woman is the neck or the rest of the body. In the view of the pastor quoted above,

A relationship that will emulate God's initial plan will be characterized by mutual respect between a husband and wife. In this relationship each spouse will look at the other as a valued member of the family unit and each one will be fully involved for the welfare of said unit.[11]

Accordingly, there is no need to give only to one's mother because one's father, if fully embracing his role as provider, will not abuse his "natural" power by not caring for her.

Beatrice could be one of the women to whom John referred. She worries about her mother, who she feels is not well cared for by her father, not least because he has had several mistresses over the years. Beatrice said that it can be a struggle to meet one's needs without the help of one's spouse. She herself migrated to London in 2002 not long after her divorce, taking up a better-paying nursing position in the NHS after she completed additional training in the United Kingdom.[12] Sympathetic to her mother's predicament, Beatrice asked her pastor for guidance, much as van Dijk (2002a) found among Ghanaian Pentecostals in the Netherlands, whose pastors provided "moral supervision" of their reciprocal relations. Mirroring John's logic, her pastor encouraged her not to interfere and "disrupt" her parents' relationship. Nonetheless, Beatrice decided that she would send what money she could to her mother.

Here, we see how the deployment of Pentecostal ideas can be adapted to the specificities of a particular situation, thus accommodating personal interpretations of how to proceed. Though Beatrice felt guilty for not following her pastor's advice, she believed God would understand her dilemma. She invoked traditional gender ideals of men as providers, asserting that her father's failure necessitated her intervention. In this way she sought to morally insulate herself from criticism that she was not a "good" Christian. At the same time, her decision to assist her mother reflects the lived experiences of many families in Kenya, where women are primarily responsible for distributing income and running the household (Amadiume 1987; Stichter 1987, 1988).

Providing for One's Family

Pentecostal discourse encourages married couples—the foundational social and spiritual unit of the church and community—to work together as a team, especially regarding financial decisions. At a wedding reception in East London, I listened as the father of the bride instructed the couple, Stella and Isaiah, "not to treat things as 'mine' and 'yours' or say half of everything of yours is mine and vice versa. No, everything of yours is mine and everything of mine is yours." I talked with the newlyweds not long after their wedding and learned how they were trying to honor her father's words. Stella, a petite woman in her thirties, moved to London from Nairobi to study hotel management in the mid-1990s but did not complete her course because she lacked the money for her fees. A thirty-five-year-old man with a slight build, Isaiah migrated several years later with the intention of studying, but he too had to put aside his studies to start working. However, unlike Stella, whose father (a civil servant) and mother (a teacher) "do not need, so they do not ask," Isaiah faced requests for help from family members in Nairobi and in his natal village in Kikuyu-speaking Nyeri District.

Reflecting on their own situation and that of others they know in London, Stella commented that the pressure to help stops people from studying and "bettering themselves." Isaiah added that many "have no lives [because they work nonstop and remit most of their earnings]. This means they can't invest in their futures, which stops their productivity and holds them back." From the start, they explained, they made each other their priorities because they did not want his family's needs "to come between them" or to let anything "pull their new family behind" (Marshall 1991; Mate 2002). They decided together that "it was their responsibility to help" but to do so on their own terms. As Isaiah remarked, "It is better this way, not to be their provider." Their actions reflect their agency, expressed through Pentecostal logic, to shape how they handle their familial obligations.

Similarly, when Charles married a Kenyan woman he met in London in the early 2000s, he decided to stop sending much of his income to his parents and siblings. Before that point, his remittances could be considered "support" in that he tried to send a consistent sum of money (roughly £200) on a regular basis (monthly) to his parents for daily household expenses and school fees for his younger siblings. However, Pentecostalism's privileging of the new family forged through marriage offers couples a means to renegotiate their position and status vis-à-vis their nonmigrant kin. Upon marriage, Charles said, nothing should be allowed to come between oneself and one's spouse, a sentiment that reflects a Pentecostal hierarchy of relations: "the next person to you is your wife, followed by your children, and then your parents come third."[13]

Unlike the Mozambican women among whom Groes (this volume) works, migrant Kenyans cultivate a Pentecostal-inspired conjugalism in an ongoing effort to disembed themselves from wider circles of intimate relations. John, for example, insists on preserving his parents' authority by not assuming the role of their provider. Doing so, in turn, ensures that he, like Isaiah, Stella, and Charles, can prioritize supporting his spouse and children. Framed in this way, the logic intertwines with traditional ideas about authority and the importance of the family and household to notions of personhood. It resonates with the pastor's guidance that (selective) "cultural practices" can "strengthen" rather than "ruin" marital relationships. At the same time, it narrows the definition of who is considered kin in the sense of whose material well-being one bears responsibility for. Similarly, these gendered ideas of authority and personhood reflect a traditional emphasis on male authority while denying the gendered complementarity that has been prevalent at the level of practice (see also Nelson 1992, 112–13; Robertson and Berger 1986, 11). Kenyan migrants continue to convey respect for "family" discursively while redefining who is considered kin and what being related entails, signaling discontinuity in practice.

Ambivalence in Affective Circuits

In intertwining Pentecostalism with existing cultural ideas, migrants develop a culturally intelligible moral discourse, but intelligibility does not ensure its acceptability. Rather, acceptability is contingent on negotiations between migrant and nonmigrant kin. The reconfiguring of affective circuits necessitates their mutual willingness to remain implicated in moral economies of relatedness. Yet these negotiations are emotionally fraught and can generate feelings of ambivalence on both sides, which can fray affective circuits. For example, Faith, a married woman in her midthirties living in East Ham, told me that while she and her husband had to prioritize their children's needs, she nonetheless worried about her widowed mother and still unmarried brother Thomas, who did not have the resources to pay bride wealth or finish building a house in his family's homestead. At the same time, though, she expressed a frustrated wish for Thomas to be more enterprising like their youngest brother.

Her Anglican mother, whom I met in their Kiambu village, voiced a Christian-inspired acceptance of the situation: "I know she [Faith] helps as much as she can. We pray to God that they [Faith and her husband] will be able to boost us more." In contrast, Thomas expressed resentment toward his sister, an irony given that he too is Pentecostal. Referring to Faith's migration in 1998, he said, "It was my idea to go. I tried first. I finished school and applied to go [to the United States] but was rejected." He mentioned a friend who moved to the United Kingdom with the assistance of his brother; the implication seemed to be, why wouldn't Faith help him? Yet, alongside his feelings of envy, Thomas also expressed contrition, commenting that he knew the visa process could be unfair.

These two siblings are differently positioned in a transnational moral economy, and their social locations shape their interpretation of Pentecostal ideas. More specifically, Thomas did not see asking Faith for money to be incompatible with the Pentecostal emphasis on the nuclear family. His view reflects Harri Englund's (2004, 307–8) point that persons whose livelihoods are inextricably intertwined with those of others cannot afford to cut off their ties. Arguably, Faith's concern and frustration stemmed from her own financial constraints and ambivalence over how to resolve this moral dilemma, but, unlike her brother, she was not dependent on kin to realize a particular aspiration, at least in that moment.[14] By trying not to let their difference of opinion or hurt feelings rupture their relationship, they both sought to practice the Christian values of forgiveness and understanding, intimating that for them, Pentecostalism is expansive enough to accommodate both of their viewpoints.

In contrast, Lucy's experience illustrates what happens when efforts to reconfigure affective circuits are unsuccessful. Talking with Lucy about my plans to travel to Kenya in 2010 prompted her to recount her last experience there. When she returned for her mother's funeral in 2001, the "whole village" welcomed her back. She said, "All my aunties and uncles were looking at me like I was a savior, their savior." Relatives whom she "didn't know and had never seen before" requested money for everything from school fees, business capital, and medical expenses to sodas, sweets, and "new" clothing from the local secondhand market. Their claims, made in the name of kinship, arose from her being an unmarried migrant woman: her marital status meant she was still considered part of her natal family, and her migrant status signaled her great(er) financial resources.

Though Pentecostalism emphasizes the nuclear, conjugal family, it nonetheless offers single women, especially mothers, a way of making sense of and managing their kinship obligations without forgoing their moral standing and capitulating to requests. Lucy said she tried to explain to those who asked for help that she could not prioritize "parenting" her elders and extended kin over caring for her own child. Her logic emphasized her primary responsibilities as a mother in her nuclear family (albeit one consisting of herself and her son), not her role as a sister, aunt, or cousin in the wider extended family. Unable to stave off their requests, she chose to sever her ties with those in Kenya.

Disconnecting is itself a social act. As James Ferguson (1999, 238) asserts, "The state of . . . [being] disconnected requires to be understood as the product of *specific structures and processes of disconnection*" (italics in original). Lucy felt implicated in a moral economy of relatedness yet frustrated and powerless to reconfigure it. She justified cutting her ties in terms that echo Pentecostal ideas about extended family impeding one's ability to flourish and create a future for one's nuclear family (Maxwell 1998; Meyer 1998; van Dijk 2002a): "Extended family is what holds Kenyans [in London] back. Rather than save £100–200 per month, they send it home. This means they can't save and invest. And, the cycle will never stop." Notably, she did not mention her own tenuous legal status at the time or her low-paying job, both of which arguably constrained her capacity to help her relatives. Through Pentecostal ideas, Lucy redefined what being related entails while refashioning her sense of self (see also Cole 2012). Nonetheless, her tearful recounting of this story underscores how emotionally complex such experiences are. Her ambivalence points to the value of conceptualizing affective circuits in these instances as dormant and kin relations as lapsed rather than irrevocably broken, for it is through such emotions that circuits may eventually be recharged and relations rekindled.

Negotiating Moral Standing vis-à-vis Kenyan Pentecostals and British Society

Pentecostalism not only helps migrants reconfigure the affective circuits linking them to Kenya but also serves as the basis of a moral community of belonging in London (Englund 2004; van Dijk 2002b). The conjugal nuclear family formed through marriage and privileged in Pentecostalism is important to migrants' efforts to redefine those for whom they are materially responsible, just as it is central to the social hierarchy in this nascent community. Maintaining reconfigured affective circuits can be seen as a commentary on the success of migration projects such that how one balances obligations to one's conjugal and natal families is subject to moral scrutiny.

Moreover, migrants' prioritization of "family" allows them to distinguish themselves from wider British society and refute their nonmigrant kin's accusations of "having changed." Nonmigrants are morally insulated by the symbolic power of Kenya as "home," whereas migrants to the United Kingdom—Kenya's former colonial ruler—live in a place viewed with envy and curiosity but also ambivalence and moral criticism. In disentangling the moral and material, migrants do not want to be accused of "forgetting where they come from" or "becoming British."

Consistent with the high regard with which they hold "family," migrant Kenyans view marriage as the highest social and moral ideal. As I have argued elsewhere (Fesenmyer 2014), in wider conversations about the morality of different kinds of intimate relationships, migrants and nonmigrants alike discursively juxtapose marriage with what they refer to as "come-we-stay," or cohabiting, relationships. A key point of distinction between marriage and cohabitation is evident in how cohabiters (are understood to) handle obligations to extended kin in Kenya. In contrast to Pentecostal marriages, "come-we-stay" relationships are relationships of convenience that arise in London as a means of managing some of the challenges related to migration, such as the strain of trying to earn money to build a life for oneself that includes marrying *and* fulfilling transnational familial obligations (see also Pasura 2008). Each person in a cohabiting couple assumes responsibility for supporting his or her own family, unlike couples in Pentecostal marriages who (are encouraged to) make decisions jointly. They thus build "separate" lives rather than create a life together as a couple. In this way, cohabiting relationships illustrate how "cultural practices," that is, supporting one's nonmigrant kin, can impede the formation of a conjugal, nuclear family. Nonetheless, because being Pentecostal entails an ongoing commitment to God, it can accommodate periods of backsliding followed by rededication. Accordingly, cohabiters who are Pentecostal will assert their intention to marry in the future as a way to blunt such criticism.

Of course, handling one's kin obligations separately is not confined to cohabiting partners. Each spouse in a marriage might support his or her own family, but doing so would cast a negative light on the state of their marital relationship. The broader point is that how migrants manage their obligations can be read as an indicator of whether they are "good" Christians. This moral evaluation in turn contributes to a social hierarchy among Kenyan Pentecostals in London in which married persons who are able to disentangle the moral from the material in affective circuits are positioned at the apex.

At the same time, staying engaged transnationally allows Kenyan Pentecostals, including cohabiters, to distinguish themselves from wider British society. As born-again Christians, (Kenyan) Pentecostals do not withdraw completely from the society in which they live. Rather, they continue to live in the wider world with non-Christians, cultivating a critical distance discursively and in practice. By staying engaged, they embark on a "reverse mission" to bring the United Kingdom back into the Kingdom of God (Adogame 2010; Fumanti 2010; Krause 2011). In identifying as Christians and aligning themselves with the United Kingdom's Christian history, they resist the structural position available to them in British society as racialized ethnic minorities, migrants from a geopolitically weak country, and largely low-wage workers.

As part of their newborn personhood, they seek to distance themselves from "immoral" and disrespectful British ways. In addition to maintaining that "excessive" drinking, unfaithfulness, and divorce threaten the sanctity of families, they often cite British treatment of older relatives as evidence of disrespect for families. They point to everyday examples of disrespect, such as children not offering their seats on the bus to an older person or arguing with their parents (see also Kea, this volume for similar concerns among Gambian migrants in Britain). My interlocutors who are care workers shared stories of elderly patients whom their families "forgot," by which they meant their patients did not receive (enough) visitors often enough. Ironically, such sentiments find parallel expression in nonmigrant kin's complaints that migrants "send nothing," which generally means they send less than nonmigrants think they should rather than sending nothing at all (Åkesson 2004; Carling 2008, 1460). Migrants' identification with what we might call a nonmigrant position underscores the relational and situated aspects of such moral arguments.

One carer, Phillip, a thirty-nine-year-old married man born in Nairobi to civil servant parents from Luo-speaking western Kenya, remarked to me over coffee, "The BNP [the far-right British National Party] might want to get rid of us, but then who'll care for their grannies?" His comment takes aim at what he saw as a contradiction embedded in public and policy discourses about migration in the United Kingdom: migrants may be unwelcome, yet they perform vital, often low-status jobs that British people are unwilling to do for kin or for elders more generally, and they (try to) do so without forsaking their families in Kenya. That Phillip is male *and* a carer is also significant because Kenyan men do not typically perform this role (see also McGregor 2007); his doing so recasts this so-called women's work as having moral value and thus as befitting a man. His criticism alludes to a larger perceived moral discrepancy: British people say they value families, but in practice they do not take care of their own elderly relatives or allow migrants to care for their own by bringing them to the United Kingdom. Through such commentary, migrants underscore that care still remains central to their understanding of relatedness even if, ideally, it does not include full responsibility for their kin's material well-being.

Social belonging is in part created through acts of boundary drawing that separate "us" from "them" while also (re)constructing a moral universe. Migrants themselves do not want to "forget" their families, but many have neither the ability nor the desire to meet all of their family's expectations. By invoking Pentecostal ideas about the centrality of "family," they assert that they have not "changed" while negotiating social distance from their kin in Kenya. In maintaining affective circuits, they differentiate themselves from other migrants who are unable to sustain kin relations transnationally and from wider British society, which they perceive as disrespectful toward families.

Conclusion: Pentecostalism and the Reconfiguring of Relatedness

I have shown that, rather than break off their transnational ties, migrant Kenyans seek to redefine, through Pentecostal logic, what being related entails. They attempt to disentangle the material and the moral in affective circuits without dismantling the wider moral economy of relatedness. At the same time, Pentecostalism plays a crucial role in developing new reciprocal moral relations in London. As migrants distance themselves from their nonmigrant kin, they cultivate ties of fictive kinship with other Pentecostals through new affective circuits in which the moral and the material flow together. Nonetheless, staying engaged transnationally is indexical of their moral standing among their coreligionists in London. It is thus possible to see how migrant Kenyans draw on Pentecostalism both to create and limit affective circuits and, in doing so, manage their engagement in multiple contexts.

Families are of course not stable and coherent social units but instead are shaped by wider historical forces *and* by kin themselves, who debate what it means to be a good kinsman or kinswoman. Doing research among transnational families inevitably means working with families whose members have maintained relations. While Pentecostalism may facilitate the renegotiation of social distance among transnational kin, it does not shield migrants from the emotional, affective, and psychological complexity of kin relations. The perspectives of migrant and nonmigrant kin that I gathered tended to convey sentiments that shift between understanding and frustration, empathy and disappointment, acceptance and resignation. People's emotional oscillation, I argue, reflects their ambivalence as well as their ongoing implication in these moral economies of relatedness.

The patterns of reconfiguring affective circuits revealed in this analysis may change over the life courses of these transnational families and their individual members. In managing familial relations across space, kin engage with each other from particular social positions, drawing on different sources of power to assert their claims and defend their interests. Their social positioning, however, will inevitably shift over time as will the contexts in which they live. Coupled with the contingency of circumstances, this point underscores the importance of not taking the Pentecostalism of migrant Kenyans to be static, much less monolithic. Rather, it is better understood as an ideological resource and moral framework that helps them make sense of their lives in a specific social and historical moment.

In the future, migrants and their young families in London may engage more deeply with those who remain in Kenya. As their parents age, they may need care, which will create new expectations and demands for help. As migrants themselves get older and contemplate retirement, some may decide to build houses in Kenya. It is unclear, though, whether they will return there. After all, many see their London-born children as "British" and, therefore, as likely to remain in the United Kingdom, so they too may decide to stay there. If some do decide to move back, they will certainly need people to whom they can return.[15] Reconnecting with those in Kenya may entail reinterpreting Pentecostal ideas such that the moral and the material become intertwined once again in ideas of relatedness. It is thus necessary to adopt a diachronic approach to the study of affective circuits to track how they are recharged or left to fizzle out and how, through them, ties of relatedness are deepened, broken, or rekindled across space.

Acknowledgments

I thank the Godfrey Lienhardt Memorial Fund, St. Antony's College, Oxford and the Economic and Social Research Council for financial support during the researching and writing of this chapter.

Notes

1. Names of persons and neighborhoods have been changed to ensure my interlocutors' anonymity. With regard to place names in Kenya, my use of Kiambu District is consistent with how the area was referred to during my fieldwork there in the first half of 2010. However, since the August 2010 passage of the new constitution, Kiambu District is now referred to as Kiambu County.
2. The argument presented here is based on fourteen months of fieldwork in 2009–2010 among transnational families whose members live in London, Nairobi, and/or Kikuyu-speaking Central Province, Kenya. My London-based interlocutors identified as Pentecostal Christians, whereas their kin in Kenya are Christian but not necessarily Pentecostal. Kikuyus predominated in my research, though my interlocutors also included Luos and Luhyas. In London and Kenya I spent time with family members at their homes and at social gatherings, church services and activities, and weddings.
3. See Fesenmyer (2013) for a lengthier discussion of why Kenyans' migration projects can be productively understood as cases of family migration even though typically only one family member migrates rather than the entire family, which is how family migration is more commonly conceptualized.
4. I use the term *nonmigrants* to refer to those who remain in Kenya, even though they may include persons who have migrated within that country. In using the term, I acknowledge the inadequacy of defining persons in the negative—that is, by what they are not—as it implies that being a migrant is the normative state among Kenyans, which is not the case.
5. As of July 2012, the fourteen-year route was replaced by a twenty-year residency path (Home Office 2012, 64). This change is only one example of how immigration regulations have continually become more restrictive.

6. Some interlocutors attend several churches, including mainline ones, because of multiple religious affiliations, a particular church's proximity to home or work, the timing and appeal of particular services and activities, and/or more idiosyncratic reasons, such as the pastor's style of preaching and interpersonal relations with other congregants more generally (see also Adogame 2009).

7. While it is difficult to determine the overall number of such churches, the London-based Misterseed.com website listed thirty-one "Kenyan churches in United Kingdom" in 2009 (http://www.misterseed.com/link%20pages /kenyanchurches.html, accessed June 25, 2009; no longer posted; see also Parsitau and Mwaura 2010). Additionally, though many congregants spend time with other conationals and even coethnics, as Kikuyus predominated in the churches I visited, it would be a mistake to presume that these churches see themselves as "Kenyan," much less as Kikuyu, churches. Doing so would suggest that they are not international or cosmopolitan in ambition as well as obscure the socioeconomic differences among congregants that make either a national or an ethnic identification reductionist (see also Krause 2011, 421).

8. I use the term *us* because the pastor explicitly included me as one of the asylum seekers, my American accent marking me as not British.

9. "Culture and marriage." http://misterseed.com/familyrebuild /familyrebuild2008.html (accessed October 3, 2013; no longer posted).

10. According to Neil Price (1996, 423), young Kikuyu couples in Kiambu consider it "irresponsible" to have so many children, a sentiment seemingly shared by my London-based informants from Kiambu, who tend to have only two or three children per family.

11. "Understanding our roles in marriage: Part 1." http://misterseed.com /familyrebuild/familyrebuild2008.html (accessed October 3, 2013; no longer posted).

12. The recruitment of highly skilled workers, in this case nurses, was part of the Labour government's efforts to link business interests and migration to advance Britain's position globally (Flynn 2005). Data from the United Kingdom Nursing and Midwifery Council (2004, 10) show that Kenya was the eleventh largest sending country in 2001–2002, the peak year for overseas recruitment.

13. http://www.misterseed.com/familyrebuild/familyrebuild2008.html (accessed October 3, 2013; no longer posted).

14. Concern about curses and other forms of witchcraft did not arise among my migrant interlocutors with regard to their nonmigrant kin nor was it prominent in church services, which focused more on cultivating congregants' personal relationships with God.

15. See Fesenmyer (2016) for a comparative discussion of how older Kenyan women migrants in London handle the question of return and the moral and material obligations it entails.

SIX

The Paradox of Parallel Lives: Immigration Policy and Transnational Polygyny between Senegal and France

HÉLÈNE NEVEU KRINGELBACH

In Dakar, everyday conversations are filled with entertaining stories about the adventures of returning migrants. One common theme involves the visit of a Senegalese man who has returned from Europe with a foreign spouse. The most entertaining part of the story comes when the man's family and friends go to great pains to conceal the existence of another wife and children in Senegal. In one version, the Senegalese wife is introduced to the European one as the husband's "sister" or "cousin," thereby deceiving the European wife into believing that the children in the household are her husband's nieces and nephews whereas in fact they are his own children (see also Salomon 2009). The most appreciated elements of the story are usually the tricks deployed by various family members to maintain the illusion of a biological relationship between the husband and his "sister." The truth is finally revealed when, for example, a child, a family member, or a jealous rival reveals who *really* is who.

Whether fictionalized or not, this type of narrative points to the fact that many Senegalese migrants establish households in destination countries even though they have left a spouse and, sometimes, children back home. In France, these parallel family arrangements, which may be called *transnational polygyny*, are usually presented in public discourse as the remains of age-old African practices or as instrumental ways of bypassing immigration laws. Although there is a degree of truth to these assertions, this chapter presents an alternative interpretation of these marriages. Some of the spouses involved in them are former Senegalese migrants who have acquired French citizenship; however, the majority of the French spouses I interviewed were born as French citizens.[1] Consequently, this contribution focuses on transnational polygyny involving what are usually referred to as binational or "mixed" families.[2]

The role of European immigration policies in shaping transnational family life is crucial. Following the end of labor migration schemes in the 1970s in old immigration countries such as France, Germany, and the United Kingdom, marriage to a citizen or resident and family reunification more generally were among the few remaining routes for non-EU citizens to acquire long-term legal status (Beck-Gernsheim 2011; Charsley and Liversage 2012; Schmidt 2011b; Wray 2011). In France in 2011, family reunification accounted for 80,500 visas for stays of at least a year, or 40 percent of all visas granted; meanwhile, student visas accounted for 33.7 percent and work visas 9 percent (Comité interministériel de contrôle de l'immigration 2012). Undocumented migrants or migration candidates may feel that they must marry at all cost to regularize their status. Similar observations have been made in other EU countries. Fernandez (2013), for example, shows how Danish family reunification policies work against their own imperative of avoiding so-called forced marriage by making marriage the only option for binational couples to live together in Denmark.

That marriage to a citizen is one of the few legal ways to enter and establish citizenship in France may be the main reason migrant family practices have been increasingly targeted by French state regulation in the past two decades. In fact, it is increasingly through the definition of acceptable family practices that the boundaries of citizenship are redefined (Anderson 2013; Ferran 2008). In the French case, as Cole (2014c, 529) points out, public discourse on marriage and migration has generated "two kinds of opposition, one between love and money, the other between 'French' and 'immigrant' kinship." Among the many types of immigrant kinship, polygamy—or more specifically polygyny, because it usually involves situations in which a man has several wives—has become a particular target of opprobrium in the French public sphere.

Anxieties around polygamy in Europe are not new and have long been driven by concerns with managing immigration costs, women's rights, and the perceived link between successful integration—which usually means adapting to European ways of life—and European family ideals (Charsley and Liversage 2012).[3] But these anxieties have also intensified with rising anti-Muslim sentiment. In France, recent public discourse invariably presents polygamous men as individuals with low moral standards whose insufficient adherence to republican values makes them undeserving of either residency or citizenship. Several right-wing politicians blamed the 2005 French riots on the anger and moral decline produced by immigrant childhoods spent in poor, polygamous households. French Academy member Hélène Carrère d'Encausse joined the bandwagon when she explained to a TV reporter that polygamy was to blame for France's social unrest (Millot 2005):

Those people, they come directly from their African villages. But Paris and other European cities are not African villages. For example, everybody asks, why are African children in the street and not at school? Why can't their parents buy a flat? It's obvious why: many of these Africans, I'm telling you, they are polygamous. There are 3 or 4 wives and 25 children in a flat. They are so overcrowded that they are no longer flats, they are . . . God knows what! Then we know why these children roam the streets. (translation mine, from French)

In 2010, the right-wing magazine *Le Point* ran a feature on a Parisian banlieue that portrayed polygamous men as immoral oppressors. It was later revealed that the interviews with a polygamous man and with a wife in another polygamous household were carried out over the phone after the magazine failed to find individuals willing to be interviewed at home; the whole feature turned out to have been a hoax. The magazine issued an apology a few days later, but it is significant that the editors expected this negative portrayal of polygamy and immigration to appeal to its readers.

This kind of discourse lumps together all individuals of African descent regardless of their region of origin, religious affiliation, and actual citizenship (many of the individuals concerned are French citizens). It also powerfully stigmatizes Muslims of African descent by presenting their family practices as the main cause of France's increasingly palpable social unrest. Most importantly for my purposes here, however, it portrays polygamy as an atavistic practice resistant to change.

As I argue in this chapter, however, polygamy is neither atavistic nor resistant to change. Rather, family arrangements and immigration rules are mutually constituted. The increasing restrictiveness of European immigration policies means that African migrants now spend longer periods of time abroad undocumented (De Haas 2008). Without legal papers, they find making a living exceedingly difficult, a situation that has been

6.1 *Le Point*'s feature on polygamy in a Parisian *banlieue*, September 2010. Entitled "One husband, three wives," the article offers a lurid depiction of polygamy meant to titillate French readers. The article starts, "Cité des Bosquets in Monterfermeil (Seine-Saint-Denis), Building 5. In the 3-bedroom flat, on the 3rd floor, a dozen children, and two women who share the same husband, a Malian man of about sixty, live crammed together" (translation mine).

further exacerbated in France by a new law that makes employing an undocumented migrant a criminal offense. With marriage to a citizen or resident of Europe one of the few remaining paths to regularization, some Senegalese men find that only by establishing a new family abroad to achieve legal residence can they continue caring for their families back home. Ironically, though French public discourse condemns polygamy, state regulations encourage the practice. Polygamy encompasses a wide range of practices, as Charsley and Liversage (2012, 60) note, "some of which are new constructions arising from the specific conditions of transnational migration." For many Africans in Europe, family life is not simply organized according to culturally determined practices. It is also heavily shaped by immigration regulations.

To build my argument regarding the mutual constitution of immigration policies and transnational family practices, I draw on ethnographic material collected in France as well as in Senegal. Although both Senegalese men and women marry French citizens and migrate to France, I focus particularly on the dilemmas of Senegalese men because they are more likely than women to accumulate spouses and thus better illustrate the mutually constitutive relationship between immigration regulations and family practices.

Family Reunification Laws and Kinship Forms

My analysis builds on a substantial body of anthropological work that demonstrates how South Asian family practices and migration regulations have long shaped each other (e.g., Ballard 1990; Charsley 2005, 2006, 2013; Gardner 1995; Rytter 2013; Shaw 1988, 2000, 2001). Taken collectively, these studies establish migration patterns to Britain from specific areas in the Indian subcontinent as rooted in the employment of sailors on British ships, postwar labor policies, the mass displacement of populations due to the partition of India in 1947, the war between Pakistan and Bangladesh in 1971, and development projects across the region. In the early 1960s, for example, one hundred thousand residents of the Mirpur area of Pakistan were displaced following the construction of the Mangla dam. In 1961, Pakistan removed its restriction on emigration so that five thousand dispossessed villagers might move to the United Kingdom before passage of the Commonwealth Immigrants Act in 1962 (Charsley 2013). Thereafter, access became restricted to the family members of those already settled in Britain, which reinforced migration from certain parts of Pakistan to specific areas in the United Kingdom (Shaw 1988).

Because there were few other legal options for migration and because of a preference in Pakistan for endogamous cousin marriage or marriage within status groups, transnational marriage became the norm among British Pakistani families (Shaw 2001; see also Ballard 1990; Gardner 1993 for analyses involving migrants from other parts of the Indian subcontinent). Even laws that required migrant spouses to demonstrate that they did not marry for the sole purpose of emigrating to the United Kingdom did not deter Pakistani transnational marriage (Wray 2011). During the 1960s–1990s, then, restrictive immigration policies and family reunification rules actually encouraged transnational marriages arranged by relatives, which often involved siblings marrying off their children to each other.

Now that transnational marriage has become more restricted across the European Union and it is much more difficult to sponsor a spouse from Pakistan, these types of marriages have gone from being the norm in Britain and other European countries in the late 1990s to being much less popular (Charsley 2013). In part, their decline is due to a rising public focus on forced marriage, which has led to a shift in how some younger Pakistani women evaluate the nature of parental influence on marital choices (Charsley 2013, 11). Some women who did not describe their marriage as "forced" a few years ago do so now, and divorce is openly talked about as a possible exit from arranged marriages with relatives "back home." Mikkel Rytter (2013) also observed a decline in transnational marriage between Danish Pakistanis and spouses from Pakistan in the wake of Denmark's implementation of strict marriage migration rules in the early 2000s. Both Charsley and Rytter document a shift toward marriages between young diasporic Pakistanis, sometimes across European national borders.

These studies point to the malleability of kinship practices as they interact with social, economic, and legal changes. But they also show that kinship practices can be more resilient than expected because people feel strongly about transmitting their notions of relatedness to the next generation. Indeed, people may even use legal or economic changes to protect valued practices, as has been the case among some South Asian groups in Europe. Less well documented are the ways state policies affect marriages that cross linguistic, ethnic, and national boundaries between people who represent "the first links between families and social entities sharing little common culture or heritage" (Williams 2012, 32). Yet such mixed marriages are increasingly common globally, giving rise to new "world families" involving multiple forms of boundary crossing and intimacy at a distance (Beck and Beck-Gernsheim 2014). In addition, binational and cross-cultural marriages are likely to throw what Carol Stack and Linda Burton (1994, 157) call "kin-work"—that is, the "labor and the tasks which families need to survive from generation to generation"—into particular relief, because it is often when boundaries are crossed that people work the hardest at ensuring social reproduction.

Between Family and the State: Senegalese Men and Transnational Polygamy

When discussing parallel families with Senegalese men and women in France, I remembered conversations I had taken part in while doing fieldwork with performing artists in Dakar. On one occasion, in the mid-

2000s, I sat in my flat with a small group of male performers I knew well. As often happened when they met, the conversation soon turned to their dreams of mobility. These men found that their applications for visas that would allow them to travel abroad for dance festivals were all too often rejected, and they bitterly resented the immobility that was forced on them. One of them announced that he intended to find a European woman to marry—as a second wife, given that he was already married and had children in Senegal. He hoped to meet a woman holidaying in Senegal so that she might do the work of applying for a spousal visa for him, a common pattern among the young men who forge relationships with older European women in the region's coastal resorts (Ebron 1997; Salomon 2009). But he was also prepared to court someone while on tour abroad. He explained to me that marrying a European woman would make it possible for him to travel freely and succeed in his artistic career, ambitions he shared with the other men in the group. Besides, he said, he was tired of working hard for little gain and felt he needed to experience something new.

A lively debate on the pros and cons of polygyny ensued as some of the men expressed similar desires to marry Europeans while others warned against the risks inherent in the practice. The oldest in the group, a married Catholic man in his late thirties, agreed that migrating legally was far more desirable than going off into the world undocumented. Many performers who had done so had been forced to give up their artistic dreams. However, he added, polygyny was never a good arrangement because it took "at least ten years off" the lives of most men: cowives were known to engage in occult practices to harm their rivals or their children. Polygynous arrangements, he explained, were ultimately harmful because "something [had] to be sacrificed," usually at the expense of the husband's well-being. The others agreed, their laughter echoing against the walls of the small flat. One of them pointed out that the speaker's view was that of a Catholic who had to make the best out of being bound to a single woman, an unfortunate fate indeed. Others added that they could never afford the marriage payments and bridewealth required to wed several brides let alone the daily expenses needed to support multiple households. One man added, amid general laughter, that it might be less costly to marry a divorcée or a mature and wealthy woman.

By then, the conversation had become heated, with the men's voices growing ever louder. The performer who had first spoken of marrying a European was beaming with pleasure, pointing out that the others' arguments just proved that his was an excellent idea: having a wife in Europe in addition to his Senegalese spouse would allow him to travel freely as well as grant him prestige, all without requiring a bride price (the men all concurred that European women did not like to be "purchased"). Moreover, a European woman, they agreed, would be unlikely to engage in occult practices. How could marrying one not be an attractive proposition? At the time, I thought the initial speaker was joking. A few years later, however, he traveled to France with another dance group, overstayed his visa, and eventually married a French woman, much to the dismay of his Senegalese wife. The marriage to the French woman soon failed, but by then the man had been granted settlement in France, and he initiated a relationship with another French lady. While his Senegalese wife had tolerated the first relationship, I was told that she requested a divorce when he found a second French partner instead of returning home, as she had hoped he would. The problem with the situation in which she found herself was not simply that her husband was away but that, according to the Wolof preference for patrilocality, she and her children lived with her in-laws. Far from enjoying the autonomy one might expect a migrant's wife to have, she had been forced to trade her husband's companionship for the surveillance of his relatives (see also Hannaford 2015).

Although the man in this case emphasized his personal dilemmas, Senegalese men's migration is always a family matter (Barou 2001; Beauchemin, Caarls, and Mazzucato 2013; Riccio 2001). Senegalese migrants have always been expected to care for their families back home, and, if anything, translocal and transnational marriages have increased rather than diminished these expectations (Cole and Groes, introduction to this volume). Families expect that migrant kin will send monetary remittances, take responsibility for the education of younger siblings, pay for the treatment of sick and aging relatives, or finance the pilgrimage of a parent to Mecca (Buggenhagen 2012; Gasparetti 2011; Riccio 2001). In addition, family members expect their migrant sons and husbands to keep in touch with them by phone and through Skype (see also Fesenmyer 2012; Parreñas 2005a). Communication may be considered just as important as money transfers, particularly if those left behind include spouses, children, and aging parents (see also Kea, this volume). Several migrants' relatives whom I visited in Senegal remarked on those who continued to communicate regularly after years abroad. Family members often suspect those who fail to do so of either not caring about them or trying to conceal their engagement in criminal activities. At any rate, lack of communication compromises migrants' reputations. Such expectations weigh most heavily on men, although increased female migration means that women too are expected to care for their families and to communicate on a regular basis.

The expectations placed on migrants cannot be entirely explained by relatives' assumption that they earn a good living abroad, although this is obviously an important factor. In addition, parents and kin who contribute to a person's education and opportunities for travel expect to enjoy reciprocal forms of care when that person achieves success (Coe 2013; Cole 2010; Groes-Green 2014). Migration, or, more accurately, achieving a mobile lifestyle, is a costly endeavor because migrants must often pay intermediaries substantial sums of money to acquire even a short-term visa. Migrants, therefore, not only must live up to social obligations of exchange within their families but also are indebted to all those who have lent them money toward the migration project. These multiple levels of debt and social obligation often place unbearable pressure on migrants, many of whom struggle abroad for years to make ends meet, particularly if they end up with undocumented status. In recent years the economic decline in much of Europe has exacerbated these difficulties, particularly for those Senegalese living in countries such as Italy and Spain and more recently Portugal and Greece (Beauchemin, Caarls, and Mazzucato 2013; Heil 2013; Riccio 2001). Although Senegalese at home have become more aware of the hardships migrants experience, not least through the testimonies of those who have returned or been deported, there is nevertheless an enduring association between spatial and social mobility: success in life involves the capacity to move freely. But aspirations of mobility are often thwarted by the severe restrictions placed on migration by European states. Migrants must overcome these restrictions if they are to meet their family's expectations and succeed.

Senegalese Kinship and Marriage Repertoires

My friend's conviction that finding a French woman to marry as a second wife might solve his mobility problems draws from some long-standing practices in the region. Although the statistics should be treated with caution,[4] the most recent Demographic and Health Survey notes that 35 percent of married women in Senegal live in polygynous unions,[5] three-quarters of which involve two wives (ANSD 2012). The use of a single term to designate a wide range of marriage arrangements, however, conceals the dynamic character of the practice cross-culturally (cf. Charsley and Liversage 2012; Clignet 1987; Zeitzen 2008). David Parkin's (1978) pioneering study of social change among Luo speakers in Kenya in the 1960s and 1970s, for example, showed how, by rotating wives between rural and urban households, Luo adapted polygyny to facilitate rural-urban migration while protecting land ownership. In the Senegambian region, low population density, caused in part by the transatlantic slave trade, led to a relative shortage of labor (Searing 1993). These circumstances likely made polygyny attractive as a way for big landowning lineages to accumulate women and children (Ames 1955; Diop 1985). From this perspective, polygyny became the ultimate expression of the "wealth-in-people" ethos well documented across Atlantic Africa (e.g., Guyer 1993).

Although it is likely that polygyny has always encompassed a wide range of practices, in the past few decades its role in facilitating spatial mobility has grown in importance. Having households in several locations can enable men to migrate while also retaining claims to land and belonging in their regions of origin. With mass migration to Senegalese cities occurring from the 1950s onward, polygyny became valued as a way of facilitating translocal family life (Antoine and Nanitelamio 1995; Buggenhagen 2012).[6] But it was also transformed because the cost of living in cities did not always allow migrant men to establish new households there; in several cases I have come across, men who had married and established their own household in their region of origin had moved into an urban wife's compound, which had either been inherited from her parents, received from a previous marriage, or built for her by a migrant son. In these cases, mature men who had migrated to the city as young men but had not yet accumulated sufficient resources to establish second households benefited from the prestige of polygyny without paying the costs.[7]

Just as polygamy has a long and varied history in the region, so too does marriage with Europeans. During the slave trade and the early colonial period, many French traders and military officers developed relationships with African women (Jones 2013; White 1999), who came to enjoy a privileged status as intermediaries in coastal cities (see Bois 1997 for a similar pattern in Madagascar). The creole families that emerged from these unions subsequently enjoyed a special status as a midlevel bourgeoisie during the colonial period. With the establishment of formal colonial rule, the French administration discouraged these unions, but they were soon replaced by interracial marriages with a different gender dynamic as Senegalese men began marrying French women during prolonged stays in France. My interviews with several generations of informants, as well as the biographies of prominent Senegalese figures throughout the twentieth century, indicate that such unions initially involved Senegalese who had traveled to France to study (Neveu Kringelbach 2015). Following World War I, sailors and former soldiers from all over francophone West Africa who traveled to France met women and established families there. For a long time, then, marriage with a French woman was perceived as the prerogative of elite Senegalese men.

Did polygyny exist in Euro-Senegalese marriages in earlier generations?

6.2 Senegalese-French couple in Marseille, 1956. This studio photograph was taken against a
backdrop representing the SS *Normandie* ocean liner. The husband was a real sailor. His
French wife had a West African grandfather. Photograph courtesy of Martine Tall.

According to my interviewees, it certainly did but it has not been documented in scholarly studies. It is however, depicted in novels, most famously Mariama Bâ's *Un chant écarlate* (1984). In this tale of ill-fated love,
the Senegalese novelist powerfully captures the intrusion of polygyny into
a Franco-Senegalese marriage. Ousmane and Mireille, the novel's young
couple, live in Dakar, where they met as students. Unhappy with their
daughter's choice of partner, Mireille's French expatriate parents reject
her. But it is ultimately the arrival of a second wife, encouraged by Ousmane's mother, that destroys the union. My interviewees noted that the
need to obtain legal immigration status seldom encouraged polygamy in
earlier generations. Rather, it seems to have occurred when Senegalese
men who had married in Europe during their youth returned to Senegal
later in life and sought to reinsert themselves into local networks and fulfill familial expectations.[8]

In more recent years, marriage to Europeans has extended beyond the educated elite to include performers (Neveu Kringelbach 2013a), people employed in the NGO sector, football players, former soldiers, school leavers with secondary-level education, and many others.[9] At the same time, urban Senegalese are increasingly aspiring to companionate marriage, a trend captured in songs and other forms of popular culture. Among Wolof-speaking populations there used to be a marked preference for cross-cousin marriage (Buggenhagen 2012; Diop 1985), reflected in the use of the old-fashioned Wolof term *wurusu jabar*, or "wife of gold," to designate a cross-cousin. I have come across many such cross-cousin marriages in Dakar, particularly among individuals now in their fifties and older. Today, however, there is a clear movement away from cross-cousin marriage and from marriages arranged by relatives more generally, across all ethnic groups and social classes (see Dial 2008, 74–79), a pattern consistent with rising aspirations to companionate marriage in other parts of Africa (Cole and Thomas 2009) and globally (Hirsch and Wardlow 2006). As "a marital ideal in which emotional closeness is understood to be both one of the primary measures of success in marriage and a central practice through which the relationship is constituted and reinforced" (Wardlow and Hirsch 2006, 4), companionate marriage is usually understood as incompatible with polygamy. Yet, in urban and rural Senegal alike, rising aspirations to companionate marriage coexist with polygyny, a coexistence that men, in particular, may valorize (Antoine and Nanitelamio 1995). In fact, men's marriage ideals have diversified: whereas some men prefer monogamy, others still hold polygyny as an ideal but with wives of their choosing and with several years separating each union. In many parts of the country, men still see having two wives as a sign of success, although they rarely have the resources to accumulate wives before they reach their late forties (Mondain, Legrand, and Delaunay 2004).[10] Given the long history in the region of marriage to Europeans, it is easy to see how some Senegalese men may want to practice transnational polygyny as a way to benefit from family reunification rules and therefore migrate (or remain abroad if already there) legally.

Transnational Polygyny as a Migration Strategy: Djamal and Amadou

Djamal's and Amadou's stories exemplify how the demands of family life in Senegal converge with current European laws to make finding a European wife a possible migration strategy. I had known Djamal in Senegal for several years before he started traveling to France on a regular basis, using his existing connections there to obtain short-term business visas. At first, Djamal told me he traveled specifically for business, and he did make useful connections abroad. However, he actually spent more time visiting friends and trying to make new acquaintances than conducting formal business. He eventually admitted that his main objective in traveling was to meet a European (though not necessarily French) woman whom he could marry. He also explained that his wife back home, whom I knew well, approved of his plans: "She's a good friend to me, she understands me. She has followed me into everything since we got married. I trust her," he said.

It turned out that Djamal told me about his quest because he hoped I might introduce him to a suitable person: he wanted to meet a generous and selfless woman who would accept his devotion to a minority movement within the Tijaaniyya, one of Senegal's main Sufi *turuq*, or "paths." He also expressed his fear of being stuck in a bad relationship with a woman with mental health problems, as he said had happened to a number of his friends.

Many of the women who are interested in us [African men] over here [in Europe], they're a bit lost. Some of them are crazy, like my friend's wife whom I told you about. I met her parents at the wedding. They're good people, but she's . . . she's not well in the head, you know. And it's tough for him [the Senegalese husband]. I'm very afraid of that. Because the women we met over here, you know, often they're the ones who have problems.

Migrant men like Djamal often place their wives back home under intense remote surveillance, as Hannaford (2015) has also observed. Ironically, they also complain about the surveillance that European wives and girlfriends subject them to, which they think compromises their masculinity.[11]

Djamal's request that I help him find a good woman, then, was an attempt to minimize the risk of making a poor choice in a cultural context in which he found it difficult to assess women's qualities during his short visits. Another somewhat younger Senegalese man, in his midthirties, expressed similar concerns to me but focused more explicitly on the perceived risks of such a relationship.

Most of the women here, once you're married, they want to be the boss. They want to decide everything, and they want to know everything you're doing all the time. Like [name of his girlfriend at the time]. If I'm going into town, after fifteen minutes she calls me to know what I'm doing. If I don't answer the phone, then later she yells at me. It's really hard with white women. Back home it's not like that, you're not accountable to your wife all the time like that.

When I visited Djamal's wife on a subsequent trip to Dakar, I discreetly brought up the topic of transnational polygyny. She looked at me inquisitively and asked whether I knew that her husband was indeed hoping to find a wife in Europe. She then explained that she had nothing against his plans since she had always expected to have a cowife at some point. For her, a European cowife was preferable to a Senegalese one close to home.

It's OK if he's going to take another wife, I don't have a problem with that. But when you love someone, and you see him with another woman, no matter how much you're prepared, it hurts . . . So it's better if she's far away.

While Djamal sought a European wife during his trips to Europe, Amadou, a tremendously gifted drummer I knew from my previous research, was able to find a European spouse to enable his migration without ever traveling abroad, thanks in large part to his artistic talent. When I met him, he was openly courting women from various parts of the world who traveled to Senegal for drumming lessons. He had relationships with several of them, and during my visits to his home, I sometimes heard him engage in long-distance phone conversations with them. His wife of many years, with whom he had several children, did not seem to mind the frenzy of female activity around her husband, and Amadou confirmed to me that she agreed with his plan to marry a foreign woman. Like Djamal's wife, she believed that a foreign wife living far away was less likely than one nearby to cause domestic trouble. But she also supported him, Amadou said, because she believed a mobile life for him would ultimately be beneficial to the entire family.

Sustaining relationships over the phone proved more difficult than Amadou had expected, and most ended within months of the women returning to their home countries. His quest was eventually successful, however, when a woman who was already a trained drummer came to take lessons with him. She came not from France but from a country where a musician Amadou knew had settled, married, and taught West African drumming. Amadou had been recommended to her as an excellent teacher, and she came with high expectations. In fact, she told me so herself when I met her, a few weeks after she had arrived. By then, she and Amadou had already married through a ceremony performed at his local mosque. Amadou described her as a generous woman with high moral standards who was keen to help his first wife and children improve their living conditions. The new wife spoke little French and no Wolof at all, and she marveled at the thought that she and Amadou had fallen in love at first sight even though they did not share a common language. She also praised Amadou's first wife, now her cowife, whom she found to be a "wonderful, very welcoming" person. A drumming teacher herself, she was also thrilled at the prospect of going back to her drumming school with a musician of Amadou's caliber.

I was surprised at the speed with which their relationship had developed. People in the performing scene in Dakar seemed less so, but the news that both Amadou and his new wife seemed to have found what they were looking for was the talk of the town for a short while. After waiting many months for his visa, Amadou moved abroad with his second wife, leaving his first wife and children behind in a compound they shared with several of their relatives. Since then, Amadou and his new wife have had a child, he has pursued a fairly successful transnational career as a musician, and having been granted settlement in his new country of residence, he is able to travel back home every year. When I last heard about him, he was planning to bring his eldest child to live in Europe with him.

As I suggest above, French public discourse often portrays African Muslim men as immoral, oppressive husbands, unable to move on from obsolete family practices such as polygyny. In contrast to this perspective, Senegalese men such as Djamal and Amadou often frame their search for a European wife in moral terms. In fact, their discourse offers the mirror image of French public discourse. They often describe themselves as being morally upstanding individuals who risk falling prey to abusive relationships in a social context in which the new wife will enjoy a considerable advantage: she will be the one on which their legal status depends, and she will be "at home" in her own culture and will likely have the support of her family and friends should the relationship fail. Some men also feared that the wife's family would be racist and suspicious of their real intentions. Much like the Malagasy and Mozambican women depicted respectively by Cole and Groes (this volume), they often emphasized their moral qualities by speaking about their concern for their families back home. They also emphasized the particular human qualities they looked for in their future European spouse. These qualities included generosity—so that the new wife would not object to their sending remittances back home—and openness to the Muslim faith (but not necessarily the will to convert to Islam, because having a Christian wife is not usually regarded as a problem). Most thought it important that marriage not interfere with their own religious practice and hoped that any potential children would be raised as Muslims.

Parallel Families as the Outcome of "Forced Immobility"

While Djamal and Abdou sought polygamous marriages to facilitate their mobility, the story of Djibril, a young Senegalese man who grew up in Dakar and came to France in the late 2000s, illuminates how polygamy may in fact be a response to prolonged immobility. When Djibril arrived in France, he expected to work for a year or two and save money to bring home to his young wife and child in Senegal. He had lost his job a few months earlier, and with few formal qualifications, he had felt stuck. He and his wife had been able to rent a small flat of their own in Dakar, but without a regular income they had been forced to move out, and his wife had returned to her parents' home. Djibril also felt a duty to care for his aging and ill mother, who he said had "suffered a lot in her life." Like many of his peers, Djibril believed that he had no choice but to look for work abroad.

After several attempts, Djibril eventually obtained a short-term visa to enter France, and then overstayed it. He soon found small jobs, but after two years, he had been unable to save anything. His wife sent him photographs of their growing child, and they spoke by Skype and mobile phone, but this contact hardly soothed the pain of separation. As a child, Djibril explained, he had been sent away to be raised by a relative and had suffered because of the separation from his parents. He had not, therefore, wanted to impose the same experience on his own child. At the same time, his family discouraged him from returning home empty-handed, for then the sacrifice of his departure would have been in vain. Moreover, his family feared that leaving before he acquired legal status would prevent him from ever being able to return to Europe. Djibril complained often that they did not understand his predicament. Indeed, his family members in Senegal remarked to me that if life was hard in Europe, surely it was worse in Senegal. They argued that Djibril ought to pray and be patient, that a few years of hardship abroad must eventually be rewarded with legal status and a better income.

As the years passed, Djibril confessed to me that the thought of marrying in France as a way of obtaining legal status had crossed his mind. His first marriage was a Muslim one that he had not registered with the town hall. As there was no civil record of it, it would not stand in the way of a second marriage when the French state demanded proof of his "capacity to marry" as part of the civil procedures required for marriage by French law. Even when a first marriage in Senegal has been (legally) registered, people sometimes manage to bribe officials to issue a certificate attesting to their unmarried status. Djibril eventually met a young French woman who soon became pregnant by him. A lawyer assured him that fathering a French child would likely entitle him to live in France, at least temporarily. The couple did not marry officially, but Djibril arranged for a Muslim wedding to be held for them in Senegal, a common practice in which the couple are wed in absentia by an imam at a mosque in the presence of chosen witnesses. Shortly thereafter, Djibril was granted legal status on grounds of paternity. But he was now caught in a situation he had not wanted: he had two wives, neither of whom knew about the other. He was torn because he did not want to abandon either woman or child, and he still felt the pain of not being in Senegal to see his child there grow up. With Skype as their only connection, he said, there was little left of the bond that a shared everyday life provided, and his child sometimes refused to speak to him.

Having been granted a temporary visa, Djibril traveled back to Senegal to visit his family. In many ways the trip was everything he had wanted it to be. He had been very moved to see his mother again, even though it was also painful to see how much her health had deteriorated. During his years abroad, whenever they had spoken over the phone she had expressed her fear that she might never see him again, and his decision to go back as soon as he could legally do so had much to do with her declining health. The reunion with his first wife had been emotional and difficult (as had his reunion with his child) because he had decided to tell her about the existence of the French wife. She had not taken the news well, but after a tense period, her parents intervened on Djibril's behalf: they convinced her to forgive him because he was ultimately trying to live up to his familial duty. He had no choice but to marry so as to regularize his situation in France, they argued, and as a good wife she ought to stand by him. Upon his return to France, Djibril hoped that life would be a little easier now that one of the wives knew about the other. As he explained, "If the African wife knows about the other one, that's OK. She will stay because she has no choice. But if the European wife knows about the African one, she'll just dump you. Women here can't accept that." As Amadou's story suggests, not all European women reject polygamy, but Djibril had correctly identified the power that his French wife held to determine his residency status. Much like the Malagasy women Cole depicts (this volume), he felt the strain of constantly having to manage the flow of information about his past life in Senegal to secure his future in France.

Djibril's case exemplifies the way polygamy may result from men's efforts to negotiate a protracted period of precarity with little hope of acquiring regular status and, therefore, a dignified life as someone able to care for his family back home. Djibril had not planned to have another family in France, and had he been able to move back and forth fairly freely, he would most likely have gone back to Senegal earlier. He had always aspired to a companionate marriage with a young wife he loved, and, his own desires aside, in Dakar he would have been too young to have several wives. Ultimately, Djibril's choices were motivated by his emotional attachment to both wives and children as well as to his aging mother. That his relationship with a French woman enabled him to gain legal status, allowing him to return home to honor his commitments to his kin in Senegal, illustrates the mutual constitution of immigration rules and marriage practices.

Djibril's Senegalese wife chose to stand by him despite their joint aspiration for a nuclear family because he continued to care for her from abroad and they remained emotionally connected. In other cases I have encountered, however, the wife "left behind" did not feel sufficiently cared for to endure years of separation. For example, Aby, a young woman in her late twenties whose husband traveled to France the year after they got married, lived for several years at his parents' home in Dakar while he was away. By then, they had a young child together. Like Djibril and many other men, her husband had only planned to be away for a couple of years at most, but he was unable to save enough to return quickly and ended up staying on in France. As an undocumented worker, he found it difficult to get decent-paying jobs and only occasionally sent money to his wife and his mother. He eventually married a French woman and moved in with her, but because he did not want her to know about Aby, he rarely called home. He instructed Aby not to try to contact him. Uncared for by her husband and under the constant surveillance of her in-laws, she went back to her parents' home, leaving her child with her in-laws. Although I did not speak to the husband, his family told me that the situation was not what he had wanted. But for Aby and her husband, living parallel lives simply put too much strain on the relationship.

The Paradoxes of Transnational Polygyny

Although anthropological literature on kinship has long underscored the way states and religious institutions seek to shape families, one of the most distinctive features of the contemporary period is that families are increasingly transnational and therefore that "kin-work" (Stack and Burton 1994, 157) is increasingly contingent on cross border mobility. Senegalese migrant men find themselves caught between three forces in tension with each other: the moral economy of kinship back home, ideas about love and nuclear family in their new households, and French and other European states' desire to limit migration by setting rigid standards for what constitutes appropriate forms of love, intimacy, and family. New family arrangements and immigration rules are mutually constituted but not in a balanced way because destination states have the legal power to decide which family practices will be regarded as acceptable (Wray 2011). Increasingly, sovereignty involves the capacity to simultaneously control human mobility within a given territory and impose specific family values and arrangements.

Alongside the resilience of polygyny in Senegal, forms of marriage in the region have also grown more diverse, and polygyny itself has been transformed by regional mobility. Younger generations, particularly women, have increasingly expressed aspirations to monogamy and companionate marriage. These aspirations are often frustrated by familial pressure on young men, and increasingly on young women, to travel abroad for a few years and send remittances back home. Because family often instigate migratory projects, many individuals end up feeling compelled to sacrifice their marital life to broader imperatives of care for the extended family. This means that men sometimes give up dreams of companionate marriage to a wife in Senegal so that they can stay in Europe. In fact, in some of the cases I have encountered, families in Senegal pressured men already married in Europe to take a second wife back home in part to ensure that the migrants' resources were not completely absorbed by their new household abroad.

In some cases, transnational polygyny in which Senegalese men have a European and a Senegalese wife emerges as migrants extend older practices of translocal polygyny to facilitate transnational migration. In other cases, however, transnational polygyny is less a premeditated strategy than an accommodation to an increasingly restrictive context. While these patterns seem to support French government discourse about African men trying to cheat the system (and their French wives) to obtain visas, I suggest that criminalizing these strategies or seeing the men who employ them as immoral is far too simplistic. Not only are these strategies produced by the absence of alternatives for regular migration, as I have argued, but marriage aspirations and ideas of love in Africa, as elsewhere, are almost always linked to a complex blend of material and sentimental concerns, including hopes for social and geographic mobility (Cole 2010; Cole and Thomas 2009; Fouquet 2007b; Groes-Green 2014; Salomon 2009). It does not make sense, therefore, to see genuine emotions and material benefits as incompatible or to assume that the men involved do not care for their European families simply because marriage is also tied to a migration project. They often feel a strong emotional attachment to their new family abroad, especially when children are born. Men end up being caught up between two families with whom they must share their resources, which inevitably leads to tensions. This is especially the case when they remain dependent on their European spouse to renew their initial residence permit.[12] Men's very real concern for the welfare of multiple households places tremendous strain on them that European social climates, which are increasingly hostile to Muslim men, further intensify. In the Senegalese context, however, where polygyny has come to be associated with translocal migration, having a spouse and children in two places makes sense in moral terms. The entertainment value people find in stories of migrants' multiple spouses comes from the fact that the European spouse does not understand the local codes, not from the existence of parallel families.

Multiple paradoxes and contradictions follow. French public discourse condemns polygamy as immoral and incompatible with human rights, but French immigration laws actually reinforce the practice by pushing individuals into polygamous marriage if they want to stay in France so that they can support families in Senegal. The inadvertent promotion of transnational polygyny by European states also reinforces gender inequalities in Senegalese families: whereas for women, marriage to a European man excludes a marriage in Senegal, men may marry both Senegalese and European women and thus live away from home while still fulfilling familial expectations. Senegalese women who "marry out" are often forced to make more decisive choices, which may be one reason why such marriages are regarded with more ambivalence than the ones described in this chapter. This gendered inequality may also explain why, as Dan Rodríguez García (2006) has shown for Senegalese-Spanish couples in Spain, Senegalese men who marry European women tend to be better incorporated into Senegalese communities abroad than are Senegalese women who marry European men. And immigration laws also work against the ideal of companionate marriage that the French state seeks to promote and that many Senegalese women, and some Senegalese men, also want but cannot achieve given current legislation and family pressures. Just as the Danish government did not intend its laws to "force" binational couples into marriage and the British government did not intend for its immigration policies to encourage Pakistani cousin marriage, so too, the French government certainly did not intend for its policies to promote de facto polygamy. Ultimately, one may ask what the consequences will be for social morale in European nations when significant numbers of migrants, themselves often future citizens, are pushed into certain practices only to be stigmatized for doing so.

Acknowledgments

The Leverhulme Trust generously provided funding for the first leg of this project (2011–2013) as part of the Oxford Diaspora Programme. I thank Robin Cohen and my colleagues in the Oxford Diaspora Programme and at the African Studies Centre, University of Oxford, for their encouragement and support. Thanks are also due to Jennifer Cole and Christian Groes for their tireless editing. Fieldwork in Dakar over the years would never have been possible without the hospitality of my friends Aminatou Sar and Jerôme Gérard.

Notes

1. This chapter draws on nine months of fieldwork in France, ongoing fieldwork in the United Kingdom, and two months in Senegal between 2011 and 2013. Research was conducted through semistructured interviews, informal conversations, and volunteer work with les Amoureux au ban public, a French civic association providing legal advice to binational couples. Study participants included approximately fifty couples, thirteen of whom were divorced or separated, and equal numbers of francophone African men and women and their French spouses. Individuals ranged in age from their twenties to their eighties. My own identity as the child of a French mother and Senegalese father facilitated access but may also have skewed testimonies toward the more positive aspects of binational marriage. All informant names are pseudonyms, and some biographical details have been changed to preserve anonymity.

2. The term *mixed* here refers to binational couples who perceive themselves as such, that is, in which one spouse was raised in Europe and the other in Senegal, as opposed to cases in which the European spouse is a Senegalese migrant who has acquired European citizenship through a previous marriage or several years of residence.

3. French law prohibits polygamous marriage, and living in a polygamous arrangement was banned altogether in 1993. Figures are unreliable, but the last official survey, conducted in 1992, estimated that there were about eight thousand polygamous families, involving ninety thousand individuals, living in France (Tribalat, Simon, and Riandey 1996).

4. The figures must be approached with caution because they obscure the

tendency for people to move in and out of polygamy over the course of their lives (cf. Clignet 1987; Houseman 2009). Surveys only give a snapshot at a particular time and are therefore not entirely accurate ways of measuring polygyny because they do not reflect marital trajectories as a whole (Mondain, Legrand, and Delaunay 2004). In fact, most marriages in Muslim Senegal are monogamous for an average of twelve to fifteen years, after which men may take second wives (Antoine and Nanitelamio 1995; Mondain, Legrand, and Delaunay 2004). A second marriage may lead one of the wives to choose divorce and to herself marry again later, often into a new polygynous arrangement (Dial 2008). Another factor causing bias is that men may tell census surveyors that they have several wives because of the prestige attached to the practice even though they only have one wife at any given time for much of their married lives. In such situations, women are likely to give a similar response so as not to contradict their husband in front of a stranger.

5. This number reflects a decrease from 1993, when 60 percent of Senegalese women over thirty-five were in a polygynous marriage (Ndiaye, Diouf, and Ayad 1994).

6. For a much earlier study of transnational polygamy in France, see Fainzang and Journet (1988).

7. This observation resonates with Fatou Dial's (2008, 86–87) observation that urban family arrangements have become more complex than in the past because of the unaffordability of housing. Household heads are still assumed to be men, who are understood to have moral authority (*kilifteef*) over household members and dependents (*surga*). In Dakar, however, the lack of formal employment, a high rate of divorce, and male migration mean that household heads are increasingly women. Yet these same women often choose to maintain the illusion of compliance with male authority to protect their reputations and the social networks they facilitate (cf. Bocquier and Nanitelamio 1991; Bop 1996; Buggenhagen 2012; Lecarme 1992).

8. For example, one woman now in her midthirties, born of a Senegalese father and a French mother, explained how her mother had found herself in a polygynous situation a couple of years after the whole family had moved to Senegal. Her parents had met in France, where her father had been a student and had worked during the 1960s and 1970s. At the time, he had adopted a French lifestyle, regarded himself as a nonpracticing Muslim, and been committed to monogamy. Not long after the couple moved to Senegal with their three children, however, the husband met a younger Senegalese woman and began sharing his time between his first household and her home. They eventually married in a Muslim ceremony. My interviewee says that her mother knew about the relationship from the beginning and felt as if she had a cowife even before the Muslim marriage took place. She had asked her husband to end the relationship, but he had refused, and she felt that his family's pressure on him to take a second wife worked against her. After sharing her husband for a couple of years, she decided to return to France with

the three children. The couple only divorced much later, and, according to my interviewee, her mother never made peace with the way she had felt "pushed out" of the marriage. I was told of other cases in which the arrival of a second Senegalese wife or the discovery that there had been a first wife all along created serious tension within a marriage but did not bring an end to it. In all of these cases, the European women had had children with their Senegalese spouses, and they chose to come to terms with the polygynous situation rather than let the family dissolve altogether. The survival of these marriages in the face of polygyny involved many individual factors, but it seems to have been linked to the place of residence of the different parties: when the two households lived in different countries, the polygynous arrangement was more likely to endure even when both wives knew about each other. When polygynous arrangements involved a European and a Senegalese wife both living in Senegal, however, breakdown of one of the relationships was more likely. This pattern may not be very different from that associated with Senegalese polygynous families, as studies such as Dial's (2008) have shown that polygyny in contemporary urban Senegal is associated with a high rate of divorce.

9.   Whereas men who meet their European spouses abroad are usually middle class (because migration requires resources), those who meet their European wives in Senegal may be from less-privileged backgrounds. Moreover, in recent years the gender balance has shifted, as rising numbers of Senegalese women now marry European men. Much as anthropologists have noted in other parts of Africa, Senegalese men's declining ability to establish their own households in a context of economic liberalization has made marriage to European men increasingly attractive to women (Cole 2010; Groes-Green 2013).

10. Predictably, women's perspectives often differ: they too increasingly aspire to companionate marriage, but because being married is key to establishing status, many feel that they have little choice but to get married at any cost, even if doing so means becoming a second or third wife. Some of the women on whom a second wife is imposed, as is often the case, choose divorce to get out of unhappy polygamous marriages (Dial 2008).

11. Salomon (2009) noted a similar inversion of gender roles in her study of intimate relations between Senegalese men and European women on the coast south of Dakar.

12. Different countries have different rules, but there is a general tendency across the European Union to extend the probationary period, with renewal of one-year visas subject to people's ability to demonstrate that they still live together as a couple and have sufficient resources to support themselves. In France, the probationary period was extended from two to four years in 2006.

SEVEN

Men Come and Go, Mothers Stay: Personhood and Resisting Marriage among Mozambican Women Migrating to Europe

CHRISTIAN GROES

During one of our many conversations, Leila, a twenty-four-year-old Mozambican migrant who had settled in a suburb of Lisbon, told me about the difficulty she was having finding a man to take care of her.[1]

I have been looking for a man who can take care of me after Pedro and I broke up because this cleaning job [I have] is badly paid. But I don't want to get married and be locked up [*ficar preso*] in a big house with a husband and with nowhere to go, understand? I still want my freedom [*liberdade*]. I have these things I want to do in life, but I also need to use this opportunity, being here in Lisbon, do some good, help the family. Surely if I cannot find a good job I will need a man to take care of me, but one thing my mum has taught me is that men come and go, your family stays. You can't rely on a man forever. You need alternatives. But my mother stays my mother. She is the reason I exist. I must make sure she and the little ones are OK.

Leila's story nicely captures some of the dilemmas young Mozambican women face when they migrate to Europe with predominantly older white men they have met in Maputo, Mozambique's capital. Traveling to Portugal with Pedro, a forty-eight-year-old engineer, Leila had no fixed idea of what she wanted from her relationship with him, what would happen when she moved into his house in Lisbon, or what kind of life awaited her there. All she knew was that accepting his offer to take her with him to Portugal was a once in a lifetime opportunity for adventure; she hoped she might even achieve the career in modeling she had always dreamed of. She had heard of other women who had gone to Europe and come home rich or found love there. In fact, she told me, one of her cousins had married a Frenchman who had provided for the cousin's whole family. Later, her cousin returned to Maputo and bought a beauty salon using the money she had saved up in France. But Leila was not able to follow her cousin's example. After arriving in Portugal, she quickly sensed that it would be a mistake to marry Pedro. She was not in love with him and found him too controlling.

Leila entered Portugal on a three-month visa; she knew that after it expired she could only remain in the country legally by one of two means: marrying a Portuguese citizen, thereby fulfilling family reunification requirements, or getting a job contract, which would allow her to apply for a three-month visa extension. For Leila to get a visa extension, Portuguese immigration laws required that she be able to prove that she was financially self-sustaining—that she had sufficient funds to cover expenses of up to fifty euros per day and that she had found and had the ability to pay for permanent housing. To get a one-year prorogation of her visa after the three-month extension, she would need to prove that she continued to meet these criteria. After five years of successfully fulfilling the temporary residence requirements, she could apply for a permanent residence permit. Periodically having to prove that they live up to the visa extension requirements makes migrants' lives very precarious. Fortunately, Leila found a job as a cleaner, but the salary was very low, and she could not pay her rent, making it impossible for her to satisfy the requirements. To make matters worse, she had no money to send home. After struggling for a few months, she met Marco, who became her casual lover. Marco agreed to pay her rent and support her until she found a better job. This assistance enabled her to meet official requirements to stay in Portugal.

Unlike Pedro, Marco let Leila lead her own life and did not insist on marriage. With a visa and the support of a less controlling partner, Leila was free to pursue her dream of becoming a model and living indepen-

7.1   A *curtidora* and her *patrocinador*, Maputo, 2013. *Curtidoras* usually meet their
patrocinadores in the bars, nightclubs, and restaurants in Maputo's city center. Photo by
Jesper Milner Henriksen.

dently; she could also frequently send money to her mother via Western
Union. Her cleaning job and her casual relationship with Marco provided
her with an alternative to marrying Pedro and living in a relationship that
she felt limited her *liberdade*.

In many ways, Leila's relationship with Marco was similar to those
she had had with European men in Maputo who are locally referred to as
sponsors (*patrocinadores*). In Maputo, sponsorship implies casual sex and
love affairs in exchange for money and gifts; the men involved are mostly
older, sometimes married, and ususally uninterested in a serious relationship. Having a male sponsor is quite common among younger women,
and these men are often also referred to as their lovers (*pito* or *amante*).
Women who have sponsors are often referred to and sometimes refer to
themselves as *curtidoras* (from the expression *curtir a vida*, "celebrate life").

As the name implies, being a *curtidora* is associated with going out at night to bars and restaurants frequented by European men and spending money obtained from the men on drinks, appearance, fashion, friends, and adventure seeking.

More recently, being a *curtidora* has also become associated with the possibility of meeting a white man who will provide access to a life abroad. Most women I discuss in this chapter have been part of the sexual economy in Mozambique, having left the poor suburbs for the city center, where they seek sponsors as a way to achieve social mobility and support their kin. As *curtidoras*, often coming from poorer backgrounds, their orientation to sexual-monetary exchanges, a life of *liberdade*, and ability to support kin is distinct from that of other groups of Mozambican women who migrate abroad with a partner. For example, I also meet Mozambican women from more educated middle-class backgrounds who marry Europeans, and their relationships are less dependent on the men's ability to support the wife and her family. This difference in orientation may explain why curtidoras think about marriage as one of several options and seek alternative avenues to support themselves and kin.

Beyond Couples: From Marriage Migration to Affective Exchange Triads

Leila's struggle to stay in Portugal by means other than marriage is echoed in many of the stories I gathered during my fieldwork among ten Mozambican migrants living in Portugal and Denmark and sixteen migrants I met in Maputo who had returned there from different European countries to visit families or to resettle. Danish immigration regulations are stricter than Portuguese; to stay in Denmark longer than the three months allowed by a tourist visa, migrants must meet the requirements for family reunification. Thus, marrying and staying married to a Danish partner is the only solution. Only when they have been married for five years, giving them access to a permanent residence permit, can migrants divorce without being deported (Udlændingestyrelsen 2014). Despite strict immigration policies all over Europe, half of the twenty-six women in my study sidestepped marriage or filed for divorce from a partner with whom they had migrated, fully aware that doing so put them at risk of deportation.

But why do so many of these women end up avoiding marriage or getting divorced before obtaining a permanent residence permit to stay in Europe? One of the answers, I argue, lies in how these women's migratory projects relate to their broader goal of achieving full personhood. To reach this goal, they need to simultaneously support kin, thus becomimg a respected family member, and achieve what they call *liberdade*, a sense of freedom understood as pursuit of personal ambitions and the recognition that comes with the ability to spend freely, to purchase consumer goods and be seen by others as an independent person. However, when they find that their original migration strategy does not allow them to help kin and achieve *liberdade* simultaneously, women tend to look for other means to reach these goals. Some avoid marriage altogether or get divorced. They also look for other ways of sustaining themselves and their families through unskilled work as bartenders, cleaners, maids, and in some cases as sex workers. Others do end up finding men who live up to their expectations. If none of these options are possible or desirable, women may return home to start over, either on their own initiative or because they are deported. By creatively finding alternative solutions for reaching their goals, women often resist the prerequisite of marriage as a means to migration.

To understand their behavior when they move with men to Europe, I suggest situating these women within a wider network of affective circuits (see Cole and Groes, introduction to this volume). Drawing on my earlier work (Groes-Green 2013; 2014), I use the concept of *affective exchange triads* to encompass exchanges vis-à-vis European partners, on the one hand, and kin, on the other. By *affective exchanges*, I refer to transactions that are at once emotional, social, corporeal, and material and in which such qualities as love, desire, and obligations are entangled with monetary, consumer, and material interests (see also Cole and Thomas 2009; Zelizer 2011). Financial support is experienced as an expression of care and necessity and produces affective attachment in both the giver and the recipient. And social support, care, and intimacy bolster affective ties and reproduce social obligations toward a collectivity of others. These exchanges are also affective in the sense that they have the power to affect people's bodies, minds, ambitions, and trajectories. Exchange triads are often asymmetrical because of the monetary power (often older) European men have over young Mozambican women and because of the economic role that migrants play as providers in relation to demanding families. Hence, affective triads imply entangled material and emotional exchanges that are shaped by complex moral obligations linking the women to kin, on the one hand, and to male partners, on the other. When women migrate, they become mediators of affective-material distribution and redistribution between male partners, who are both sources of material support and receivers of care, and their kin, who are recipients of support through moral and affective obligations.

Addressing affective exchange triads is part of an effort to move beyond what I call *methodological conjugalism*. Methodological conjugalism is the tendency to see marriage as the norm, the ideal, and the natural end point for women from the global south who migrate with Europeans and settle in Europe. This hegemonic stance is powerfully reflected in European nation-states' ideologies and policies, whereby family reunification laws make immigration dependent on marriage, a stance that we, as scholars, inadvertently risk reproducing if we uncritically take marriage as a point of departure in migration research. Thus, I suggest, methodological conjugalism is a logical extension of methodological nationalism, which takes the nation-state and its policies and ideologies as the point of departure in analyses of cross border migration (Wimmer and Glick Schiller 2002).

By contrast, looking at migrants' exchanges with family and with intimate partners within the same framework, without privileging either one of these affective relationships, allows for moving beyond a narrow focus on migrating couples or individuals and contributes to revealing the broader moral economy shaping the choices of women migrants. The women in this study prompt us to look at a broader field of intimate migrations—understood as migration through sexual, emotional, and material ties to shifting partners—and to take into account how intimate ties to kin and children, for example, influence migration. As the women's resistance to marriage illustrates, so-called marriage migration cannot be seen as unilinear. This nonlinearity can best be understood if movements toward Europe are seen against the background of affective exchange triads in which different forms of intimacy with men and kin are negotiated differently according to levels of obligation and notions of personhood. In this light, marrying a man merely becomes one migratory option out of many, as there are always alternatives to marriage and obligations beyond the conjugal.

The argument I present here draws from fieldwork conducted primarily in Maputo, where, since 2007, I have done participant-observation and interviews among women in the sexual economy, their families, and male sponsors.[2] It also draws from shorter fieldwork among Mozambican migrants in Portugal and Denmark in 2012 and again in 2015.[3] Because I conducted most of my fieldwork in Mozambique, where I gathered stories from women who had returned to Maputo to visit families or resettle or who had been deported, my account tends to privilege the returnees' perspectives, although I attempt to include as many accounts as possible of migrant women still living in Europe.

Personhood and the Sexual Economy in Maputo

In contemporary Mozambique, entering the sexual economy and building a relationship with a foreign man is one of the few routes to valued personhood available to poor young women. Formal work is hard for young people to find even if they have completed secondary school. Many young women are not satisfied with the prospect of informal work such as selling vegetables or nuts on the street or secondhand clothes in the market, which are common sources of income among their female kin. Looking for adventure outside Maputo's poor suburbs and eager to help their struggling families, many head to the more affluent city center. There, they use their social connections to try and meet white European men who are willing to support them. Yet women see such liaisons as more than a way of contributing to the household. They also believe that having a relationship with a white man (*mulungu*) is the easiest way to secure their own fortune and achieve a better life than their relatives and neighbors have. Cole (2010) records similar attitudes among young Malagasy women who seek social mobility through a connection with a white man (see also Cole, this volume).

Having a sponsor, whether a local man or a foreigner who gives them access to status and social mobility, affects women's ambitions. It often gives them an appetite for more status, freedom, and recognition that migration only stimulates further. Many express a wish to become or to be seen as "a person" (*uma pessoa*), meaning being respected and gaining status in society and among family members, neighbors, and friends. Growing up in the *bairro* (neighborhood), many felt neglected and depreciated. Their new life makes them visible and important. Being a person, some argue, also implies having their own money (*seu próprio dinheiro*), which they can spend freely on themselves or distribute to kin as they choose. Some *curtidoras* only receive gifts or cash from sponsors when they ask for it or when the sponsors feel they deserve it. But in more stable liaisons women commonly receive a monthly allowance (*mesada*), which is deposited in their bank account. In many cases *curtidoras* transfer a portion of their money from sponsors to a mother or an aunt who also has a bank account and who then redistributes some of the funds to other kin or uses the money on household expenses, food, clothes, or school fees for the children. Some kin also invest these funds in property, land, or small businesses.

Sponsorships in which men supported younger women were common in Maputo before the arrival of large numbers of Westerners. Today, however, foreign men in general have more economic power than local men. The influx of relatively affluent foreigners since the end of the civil war in 1992 is partly due to neoliberal reforms and structural adjustment policies that opened Mozambique to foreign investment and the development industry. At the same time, these policies have worsened unemployment rates and economic hardship in poor areas. The combination of restricted access to income for poor women and men and a growing number of wealthy men willing to support younger women has altered domestic economies. Neoliberal reforms affect gender roles in households as jobless fathers become ever more marginal as breadwinners for their children and wives. As fathers' financial power crumbles and households struggle to make ends meet, young women take over the role of provider through sponsorships in the expanding sexual economy (Groes-Green 2013).

Looking for sponsorship by a white man is more than a means of achieving wealth and social mobility. The sponsor's whiteness also brings a promise of spatial mobility, freedom, and the excitement of a life abroad. His capacity to take a partner with him to famous and dreamed-of places in Europe makes such a man deeply attractive. Finding a white sponsor among development workers, diplomats, and businessmen by hanging out in bars and restaurants is not only seen as a young woman's easiest way out of poverty but it has also become a path to faraway places she might never visit otherwise. To many *curtidoras*, being intimate with a white man means getting closer to achieving the promise of a better life (*uma vida melhor*) in a wealthier country.

Women find sponsorships rather than marriage or sex work appealing because these flexible arrangements allow them to both support their kin and enjoy considerable freedom. As twenty-three-year-old Maria said,

If Roberto leaves me, I can talk to John, or ask François for assistance. If you marry you are stuck, even if you love the guy, you have to rely on him only. But I also don't want to be a prostitute; then you have to take whoever comes by. I want a few sponsors I can choose between and who let me have my own life.

However, the boundaries between having a sponsor, being a sex worker, and being married to a white man can blur. In Maputo, where intimate encounters between local women and foreign men are common, women tend to generate an income through a broad range of intimate relationships over the life course. To ambitious young women, marrying a local man from the poor suburbs is not an option. *Curtidoras* give two main reasons for wanting a sponsor instead of a local man. First, it is increasingly difficult to find a man with a steady income in their neighborhoods.

Even finding a man who can pay the *lobolo* (bride wealth) expected by a family can be challenging (Granjo 2005). Encountering a well-off Mozambican man willing to marry them is seen as impossible; such men look for women from their own social class. Second, once they have experienced the relative independence they believe sponsorship gives them, many cannot imagine going "back to scratch," as some termed the prospect of marrying locally and becoming a poor wife with few options in life.

Milking Sponsors and Sponsoring Mothers: The Dynamics of Affective Exchange Triads

Affective exchanges between *curtidoras* and foreigners are highly gendered, and the moral notions that underlie them are deeply rooted in men's and women's ideas of obligations and rights. First, as in much of Africa, local opinion holds that intimacy entails material remuneration, especially of a woman by a man, and particularly if the man is older and richer (Cole 2010; Groes-Green 2011, 2013; Hunter 2009; Tamale 2006). Women in Maputo's suburbs generally agree that men they sleep with are obliged to give them what they need in material and financial terms and that it is their right to receive gifts from men. This right, they say, applies just as much to a man with whom they have a one-night stand as it does a sponsor, a lover, a boyfriend, or a husband, although to different degrees depending on the level of intimacy. A man who can afford to assist a woman or cover a woman's expenses but who refuses to do so is seen as ungrateful and as having no respect for women. Such refusal indicates that the man does not appreciate a woman's company and does not care about her well-being. As Leila said,

The men are indebted to us for what we give them. If we stay with them, they must make sure we can eat well and look nice, and if they don't they are simply rude, especially if they have money to give.

Others described feeling abused when a man refused to help them. This highly gendered notion of financial obligation, of course, applies to many settings around the world, particularly where the exchange of money and sex is less restricted, where poor women's access to jobs and incomes is limited, and where social inequality is deep. In Mozambique it also often gains legitimacy by reference to tradition and ancestral laws. Thus, some women in the suburbs regarded *lobolo* as emblematic of women's higher material value relative to men's. *Curtidoras* and their kin frequently explained that the *lobolo* was remuneration for the loss of a woman to a family just as money was remuneration to a woman for sex. Such forms of compensation, they said, did not apply to men.

Payments by sponsors are not only a result of men trying to abide by local norms of remuneration or trying to attract and keep the most popular *curtidoras*. It is also a result of *curtidoras'* active efforts to extract money and material goods from them. Indeed, *curtidoras* often told me that men are weak and vulnerable to women's sensual moves and tricks. Many women talked about the erotic and spiritual practice popularly called "putting a man in the bottle" (*por um homem na garrafa*) or, in the Ronga language, as "tying a man" (*khotsolar*). This expression implies making a man dependent on a woman, emotionally and sexually, to the extent that he becomes weak and docile and more easily gives in to her demands for money, support, and independence (Groes-Green 2013). In everyday vernacular, using erotic tricks to extract money from men is also referred to as "milking" men (*senguer*) or as "scaling the fish" (*escamar*; see also Hawkins, Price, and Mussa 2009).

The morality of exchange between *curtidoras* and their kin follows a different logic than that involved in sponsor relations, one tied to notions of kinship, gender, and generation. As a daughter grows up, she is expected to provide for her mother and female kin whenever they need support materially, socially, or in terms of assistance in the household. Because of fathers' and sons' lack of access to work, mothers and, especially, daughters have increasingly taken over responsibilities for ensuring a family's income. Thus, when daughters find men to support them, they are obliged to distribute part of their income to their mothers, and in some cases to their aunts and siblings as well. The mother often sees it as her responsibility to then redistribute some of this income to other needy relatives.

The morality of this distribution derives from a fundamental obligation toward kin and ancestors. Not assisting one's family if one has the opportunity to do so is believed to lead to bad luck (*azar*), implying a possible sanction or retribution from ancestral spirits or kin, occasionally through witchcraft. Any instance of misfortune, such as falling ill or having an argument with a husband, can be interpreted as *azar* caused by lack of support for kin and neglect of ancestral bonds (see also Cole, this volume; MacGaffey and Bazenguissa-Ganga 2000; Sargent and Larchanché, this volume). The obligation toward kin is thus much more fundamental than that toward lovers and spouses. It is unconditional and infinite, the essence of being a person (Groes-Green 2014). When *curtidoras* were young, they helped families do household tasks, took care of siblings, and sold

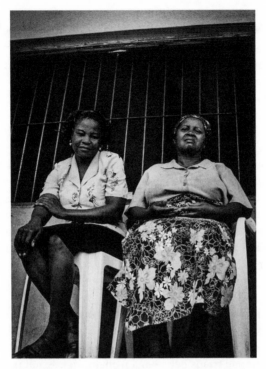

7.2 A mother and a grandmother sitting on the front porch, Maputo 2013. Female kin play a central role in maintaining close relationships with Mozambican migrant women in Europe. Photo by Jesper Milner Henriksen.

vegetables on the street; now they support families with cash and valuable gifts. But affective exchanges naturally go both ways. Kin provide daughters with advice, comfort, and a safe base they can return to when they have trouble with lovers or boyfriends or when they no longer have a man to support them. Female kin also assist them with advice about extracting money from men, teaching them about herbs, erotic techniques, and spiritual ceremonies that can be used to put men in the bottle. Bibi, a twenty-three-year-old woman, provides an example of how these exchanges and moralities play out in affective triads:

We went to Coconuts, where I met this Spanish guy, Sergio. I asked him for a drink, and we danced all night. I charmed him by dancing in front of him, and I made him jealous flirting with others. When he went over and said I should be with him, not the others, I knew he was hooked. I said, "You must show you want me, then I might be with you." Next day he promised to help me out and invited my friend and me to move into an apartment he owned. He was married, and we met secretly twice a week. He agreed to send me an allowance (*mesada*) once a month. This meant that I could now support my family and my aunt who is sick. I go back to the *bairro* every Sunday to go to church, and then I give them what I have. But I also have my own life now. I have my own apartment and money to invite friends over for drinks without having to ask my mother for permission. Sergio even wants me to go visit him when he goes home. Yes, life is OK. I am respected and loved by everyone.

Bibi's story succinctly conveys the dynamics of affective exchange triads between *curtidoras*, their partners, and their kin: material assistance, gifts, and luxuries flow from white men to *curtidoras* and are seen as signs of care and affection. In return, *curtidoras* provide love, attractiveness, and company. *Curtidoras* then share some of the gifts they receive from men with their female kin, who show gratitude and, over time, treat them with respect as their status grows.

Moving to Fortress Europe: Transnationalizing Affective Exchanges

Affective exchange triads between a woman, her sexual partner(s), and her kin are refigured when the woman migrates to Europe. In recent years, nation-states have tightened immigration policies, making it more difficult for non-EU citizens to legally enter and stay in Europe. In particular, family reunification laws requiring that a migrant marry an EU citizen before being allowed to stay and work sometimes force couples to marry who would not otherwise do so. To enter Denmark on a tourist visa, Mozambicans must be accompanied or invited by a Danish citizen, and they often also have to convince the Danish embassy in Maputo that they have an intimate relationship with this person. Getting a visa to enter any country in the European Union almost always requires an interview at the country's embassy; this is the case for the many migrants going to Portugal. This policy aims to prevent migrants from staying illegally or without money and to prevent marriages of convenience. The consequence of such policies is that migrants become equally dependent on the state's and their husbands' willingness to have them in the country. In some circumstances, husbands and nation-states in a sense become allies, forming a conjugal regime that places migrants and European citizens on different levels in a hierarchy of gender, race, class, and access to support, citizenship, and rights. The state's insistence on marriage also effectively creates the conditions governing migrants' ability to meet kin's demands for support and as a consequence the extent to which they feel stuck between meeting those demands and the demands of the state. This is not to deny that some husbands do help wives get jobs or an education or that the state does assist migrant women once they marry. Nevertheless, such assistance is predicated on the women's willingness to remain dependent on their European husbands. In this light, resisting marriage requires great strength, persistence, and creativity from migrants and constant maneuvering between possible paths to personhood even in situations in which dreams of *liberdade* cannot be fully realized.

As a consequence of tight immigration policies, migrants have to navigate between demands from the state, demands from kin, and personal dreams when they settle with a husband in Europe. One of the most frequent fears they expressed was that, by marrying, they would lose their independence and not be able to live up to their own ambitions and their families' demands.

The Fear of Being Locked Up

Regardless of the country to which they had migrated, most women told me stories of male partners who controlled their whereabouts or decided how they should spend their time. They conveyed this experience through the notion of being locked up (*ficar preso*). Leila, whose story opens this chapter, explains that she did not feel right about staying with Pedro in Lisbon:

He took me to his big house with a nice swimming pool. We sat and had a drink by the pool. He said he wanted to give me all this if I married him and stayed by his side all the time. But I did not want to get installed in that house. I did not go to Lisbon to get tied up with someone [*me apertar com alguém*]. If I become tied to someone, I want to decide who that is.

Leila frequently rejected offers from men who wanted to marry her, and, then, one day she found Marco, who worked as a real estate agent in the city. He treated her well and supported her but did not ask her to marry him because, as she said, "he understands my situation." Like Leila, Malika ended up rejecting a man she was going to marry. She insisted that choosing her own way and having a more casual relationship was more important than getting rich or playing the role of servant for a man.

I won't marry to end up being locked up. Even if I have to go back to Mozambique to live in a hut [*cabana*] and plant whatever in the fields. I don't want any man to take control of me. If I was to go back, well, I have friends to assist me. I don't want to clean dishes all my life, as wife or as maid.

As Leila's and Malika's stories illustrate, being locked up should be understood both in the *physical sense* of partner control—being prevented from leaving home to go out and meet friends, to find jobs, and to seek adventure—and in an *existential sense* of being stalled and not getting ahead in life, measured in terms of achieving personhood by simultaneously supporting kin, gaining status, and being relatively independent in their life choices. Just because many migrants do not know where they will end up once they leave Mozambique and are often disappointed to find they have less freedom than they expected, however, does not mean that they are naive or that they do not make their own decisions. In their resistance to control and domestication and their insistence on pursuing the double aim of personal independence and fulfilling obligations toward kin, they demonstrate a high degree of assertiveness as individuals and as members of a social collective.

Isolation from kin and the difficulty of making friends with other Mozambicans further contributes to migrants' sense of being locked up. The women's experiences in this regard differed for migrants in Portugal, Denmark, and other countries as well as between those living in the countryside as opposed to cities. In Lisbon, for example, employment, even if only bartending or cleaning jobs, offered women some independence. Also, the Mozambican diaspora is much bigger in Portugal, Mozambique's former colonial ruler, than elsewhere, so migrants more easily established a network of friends there.

In Denmark women's ability to make friends and have a life of their own was often more limited, partly because of the marriage requirement. The fact that they had to rely on a man's willingness to marry them, and stay married until they could get a permanent residence permit, made them vulnerable. Some were hesitant to see friends outside the home and build their own social network for fear of provoking their husband's jealousy. In some cases when couples divorced, the Mozambican partner risked deportation. Some migrants also felt constrained by their Danish husbands' narrow expectations of their role as housewives. The sense of isolation and entrapment was exacerbated by the fact that African diaspora populations in Denmark are generally smaller and more fragmented than in Portugal. Some migrants said lack of community made the experience of loneliness and everyday racism harder to cope with and the distance to kin more unbearable. The fact that these women, who have experienced social mobility in Maputo by associating with wealthy and influential men at five star hotels, casinos, and restaurants, now live a life of exclusion from higher levels of society or isolation from the majority population aggravates the extent to which they feel they are no longer recognized and seen as respectable persons. The admiration and status they won through participation in Maputo's sexual economy has all but disappeared, only to be replaced with a sense of being back to scratch, even when they have easy access to luxury. Some said they literally felt like they were back in the *bairros* where their journey began, with few options for moving up in society. Having money and living in a beautiful apartment was not experienced as success in itself. Rather, the fulfillment of personhood depended on one's ability to be seen as having success—by others in Danish society as well as by people at home—by dressing nicely and showing off one's status in public and being recognized for doing so. Even migrants who were deeply in love with their partners or husbands sometimes ended up realizing that emotional intimacy was not enough to conquer the feeling of being trapped. This feeling sometimes intensified when a woman realized that her husband could no longer provide the same kinds of gifts and allowances he had given her when they lived in Maputo. As Tania said,

I woke up one day and saw that Peter was not the Peter I knew in Maputo. His flat in Berlin was small, he no longer got that good salary from his organization. It was like he could not help me anymore. Of course I loved him, but we were in a bad situation. The excitement and magic of our life back then was gone. We could not even go shopping or see a concert anymore.

Disappointment over the lack of status and spending power ensued with the awareness that they could no longer afford the grooming and fashion that enabled them to be seen and respected by others, as they had been in Maputo.

The case of Mariana clearly reveals how women seek to negotiate between having to stay in a marriage and cope with the economic and social limitations their husbands place on them and supporting a family as well as pursuing personal career or educational dreams.

Caught between Kin, Men, and the State

When Mariana arrived in Denmark with Thomas, her life was far from what she expected. At first the two went shopping and traveled, and they had a romantic wedding. But soon the excitement wore off. Thomas did not like the idea of her working and preferred that she stay at home. He also asked her not to go out at night to have a drink and advised her not to become friends with people in the village where they lived. She was sad and lonely and missed her family, especially her daughter, whom she had left with her mother. Thomas worked all the time. Matters got worse when he suddenly refused to assist her with financial help for her daughter and family. He also asked her to talk less with her mother because of the high phone bill. Because she was not allowed to work, she could not find a way to continue supporting her family. This was her main reason for considering divorce.

It was because of his lack of acceptance that I wanted to help my daughter. He controlled my money transfers, minimized my *mesada* (allowance), and asked me not to call home too often or too long. I felt suffocated here and useless in the eyes of my loved ones.

Mariana ended up staying with Thomas because she hoped to convince him to be more kind and generous and because she needed to remain married for five years to qualify for a permanent residence permit. She knew that she risked being deported by Danish authorities if she did not stay married to him. However, she decided she could no longer remain in the marriage when, one day, Thomas became violent toward her. Although she was afraid of how he would react and anxious about the prospects of having to leave the country, she found the courage to call the police, who sent her to a women's shelter. Divorce followed. Afterward, Thomas asked the municipality (*kommunen*) not to allow Mariana to attend Danish language courses and encouraged authorities to send her back to Mozambique. But Mariana had a friendly lawyer who told her that processing her application for residence might take months or even a year, meaning that she could at least stay in the country for that period. She also helped her continue taking courses in Danish and start an education as a care worker. Although she knew she might one day have to leave Denmark, Mariana described this time as the best of her life. She moved to a bigger city, went out with Danish friends, and had a good time. One day she received a letter from the immigration office saying that she had to leave the country immediately. The message shocked her, and she struggled to find ways of avoiding going home. She considered staying in the country illegally and working as a cleaner, and one day she desperately asked a man she was dating whether he would help her stay by marrying her. Nothing worked out, however, and she saw this a sign that the time had come for her to go back to Maputo and start all over.

Soon after Mariana returned to Mozambique, her daughter died from tuberculosis. Some time after her death, while Mariana was living with her mother, an engineer she knew who was visiting from Denmark asked her out for a cup of coffee. They soon fell in love, and Mariana became pregnant. She did not see this intimate encounter, her pregnancy, and her daughter's death as coincidences. Rather, all of these incidents showed her that she might have one more chance to achieve the life she wanted. She agreed to move with the engineer to Denmark, where they married. She enjoyed much more freedom in her second marriage than she had in her first. Her husband did not interfere with how she spent the money he gave her or the people she went out with on weekends, and he allowed her to take up work in a kindergarten and, later, a nursing home. With her own income and the contined support from her husband, she was able to support her mother and at the same time save up money for herself.

As Mariana's story illustrates, affective exchange triads become dysfunctional when the flow of affection and support is withheld or limited at one point in the circuit. Thomas, Mariana's first husband, decreased his social and financial support of her (not giving her allowances, controlling her whereabouts) and limited her affective transactions with her kin (stopping remittances and phone calls). He also stood in the way of her working and attending language school. Divorcing Thomas enabled her to reestablish the flow of affect through a new triad when she found a man who acted more generously and less controlling and who accepted her wish to work and get an education. Her family accepted her decision to get divorced because her husband blocked her support of them and because of her sense of isolation. As in other cases involving intimate and marital affairs, her mother and aunt were involved in the decision. They subsequently supported her marriage with the engineer because Mariana continued to send them money and because contact with her was more regular by phone and by Skype as well as through her visits to Maputo. The birth of Mariana's child with the engineer convinced the family that the marriage would last and that her future was more or less secured. Even if her new husband should leave her or she him, she would at least receive child support, enabling her to live well in Mozambique, and she was saving up enough money to allow her to begin a new life.

Mariana's case also reveals how state authorities complicate migrants' pursuit of *liberdade*, by privileging their Danish spouses in the event of domestic problems. When the Danish police arrived at the house after Mariana reported her husband's abuse, she asked them to take her with them to protect her. Instead, they turned to her husband and asked him to explain what had happened. He denied the abuse, and they believed him. Only when Mariana showed them the bruises on her head and her back did they take her request seriously.

With Mariana controlled by her husband and unable to help her kin, the affective exchange triad, ideally built on continuous flows of affection and support between the migrant, her family, and her husband, was effectively blocked and damaged beyond repair. This case illustrates the tacit alliance between Danish citizens and the state versus migrant women, which is one of the major obstacles migrants face when trying to achieve their goals. Mariana's difficulties should be seen against the backdrop of Danish immigration policies, which are among the most restrictive in Europe. As in many other European countries, Danish authorities frequently view foreigners from the global south who marry Danish citizens with suspicion, in particular because they are concerned with preventing so-called marriages of convenience (Rytter 2011).

Sania's story is similar to Mariana's. She was twenty-three years old when she entered Denmark on a tourist visa. She married her thirty-four-year-old Danish fiancé so that she could stay in the country. But she missed her kin and her independence and realized she would not find a job. Instead of becoming a lonely housewife, she decided to leave her husband and go back to Maputo. There she found an Italian man whom she married and with whom she stayed in Mozambique.

Two of the three migrants in my study went to Denmark with a partner from whom they were later divorced. This in itself suggests a high divorce rate among Mozambican women who come to Denmark as spouses. According to official statistics, forty-five Mozambican women immigrated to Denmark from 2000 to 2014. Twenty-seven of these married Danish men, and during the same period twenty-five Mozambican migrant women divorced Danish husbands (Danmarks Statistik 2014).[4] Although some of the latter had married before 2000, the nearly equal numbers of marriages and divorces during the same period signal a high divorce rate among Mozambican migrants in general. The regulatory regime of the Danish nation-state makes it harder for migrants to fulfill their goals of supporting kin and achieving a sense of personal freedom.

Going to Portugal: Liberal Policies and Alternative Options

In Portugal, as I have noted, immigration laws are less restrictive than in many other European countries, although growing nationalist sentiments might soon lead to tighter regulations. To stay beyond the three months allowed by a temporary visa, a migrant must marry a Portuguese citizen or prove access to enough money to be self-sustaining. However, migrants are not allowed to work during their first three months and therefore must have savings or be provided for by a partner or husband to demonstrate self-support. These policies create possibilities not available to migrants in Denmark. In particular, they give migrants alternatives to marrying and living with a partner, which, as I illustrate below, women use to their advantage. Even so, many are forced to find a man to support them at least during the first three months. High unemployment and the low-paid work available also make marriage more desirable for some women.

Halfway to Personhood: From Housewife to Bartender and Sex Worker

Although marrying a European allows women to stay, it often only gets them halfway to their goals of achieving personhood. It usually allows them to support their families, gain status vis-à-vis kin, and pay their debt of care to their mothers. But even if they succeed in these goals, many still find themselves constrained by their husbands, who often prevent them from working or pursuing an education. Women also complain that they miss the everyday recognition that comes from spending and showing off one's luxuries, an essential part of the *curtidora* lifestyle in Maputo. The following case shows how migrants find alternatives to marriage.

Twenty-seven-year-old Sadia had explicit hesitations about marrying the partner with whom she moved to Portugal. As she said, when her boyfriend revealed that he wanted her to be a housewife, she knew she had to find a way out:

The second week after we arrived, Caldo said to me, "I'm glad you agreed to bring your daughter here because then you will be able to relax, not go out so much as before. You will be *dona de casa* [housewife]. I asked you to bring your daughter so you no longer have to wander about at night and get lost with men." I didn't like that, how he wanted to set me up as *dona de casa*. So I moved out with my daughter and struggled to find another place and money to survive.

Wanting to avoid a life as a housewife, Sadia broke up with Caldo, moved in with friends of friends from Mozambique, and tried to find other ways of surviving. She met a woman from Cape Verde who worked in a discotheque. One day when she was on Facebook, Sadia learned that the woman's boss was hiring, so she applied for a job and passed as a bartender. The discotheque was part of a tourist hotel, so many of the customers were from other countries. Being accustomed to the *curtidora*'s transnational setting of dancing, drinking, and flirtation, Sadia felt more at home. Sometimes she did sexual favors for money. Occasionally, for short periods, she worked full-time as a stripper and sex worker because she needed the cash. Despite the illegality of and risks associated with the work as well as the shame it might put on her daughter, she wanted to stay open to any alternative to becoming a housewife. Her decision not to marry was very much related to her own wish for a more independent life.

In this case it was the migrant herself who, by backing out of a relationship, played a central part in blocking the flow of affective exchanges. What triggered her decision was her realization that her dream life in Europe would not be fulfilled by living with Caldo. A consequence of leaving him was that she could no longer send remittances home. Some relatives complained she was forgetting them. Only because of her periodic sex work was she able to satisfy kin, save up money for herself, and go shopping or eat out with friends and colleagues.

Establishing Transnational Sponsorships and Expanding Ties of Dependence

Finding unskilled and illicit work is one way for a woman to avoid feeling locked up. Finding a local sponsor in Europe is another. Having a sponsor allows the woman migrant to secure financial support without necessarily having to live up to all the obligations imposed by a marriage, such as doing what the husband wants and being faithful. While having a male sponsor is common in Maputo, in European countries such arrangements are condemned as prostitution or as exploitative sugar-daddy relationships. In Denmark, sponsorship is not even an option for resolving immigration problems because only marriage enables the migrant to legally stay in the country. In Portugal, however, where migrants must prove they have enough money to support themselves and be able to pay rent as they wait for a permanent residence permit, it is a viable alternative. Bibi's story shows how keeping a lover-sponsor can be an alternative to marriage.

When Bibi met with her lover Claudio in a downtown bar in Maputo, she told him about her longtime dream of going abroad. He suggested she go to Portugal and told her he would talk to a friend who could help her find work there. Claudio bought her plane ticket and gave her pocket money for the trip. However, when she arrived in Lisbon, Claudio's friend refused to help her because she was not willing to have sex with him in return. Having little money herself, Bibi looked for work and a cheap place to stay. One day she realized that she only had enough money to stay another week, and there was no work in sight. So she called James, an older Englishman in Maputo, who had helped her financially during their love affair some years earlier. He immediately wired her €1,000 and promised to send her some money once a month. Half a year later another ex-lover then living in France visited her, and he also pitched in. Bibi explained,

I don't forget these guys, because one day you might need them again. I have my list of men I know. Yes, we do have feelings, and sex when we meet, but most of our feelings are based on memories and fantasies.

Thus, to stay in Europe without compromising their desire for personal freedom, some migrants draw on the safety net of former or current lovers and sponsors in Mozambique or Europe. Paradoxically, then, the search for independence in Europe can be ensured by expanding the ties of dependence on men across continents and national boundaries.

Candela's story illustrates another version of this strategy. In 2008 Candela met Mauricio, a forty-five-year-old man working for an international corporation.

He thought I was beautiful and charming. We quickly fell in love. When his contract ended we agreed I should go with him. In Portugal he took me to wine castles, museums, romantic dinners. We talked about marriage. But one day he left me to go back to his ex-wife.

Although Candela was very sad and disappointed, she still felt deeply indebted to Mauricio because he helped her get an extension of her visa and still sent her money. Also, he had agreed to prove to the immigration office that he could provide for her during her stay. But once her extended visa expired, she could no longer stay legally without either marrying or getting a work contract. Mauricio told her he could not live without her and proposed to her. But Candela, who had lost faith in him as a future husband, refused. Out of desperation to make her stay, Mauricio proposed that she go to work in his company. So he drew up a work contract she could show the authorities to satisfy immigration requirements. As Candela explained, "He employed me as driver, but of course it is just on paper, because I cannot drive, and also he does not need a driver. He pays me a salary instead of giving me an allowance." She was happy about the agreement because it meant she could stay in the country without marrying Mauricio, and the deal kept her afloat while she looked for other options.

Some women went to Portugal with a sponsor who did not intend to marry them because he already had a wife there, but they found ways to maintain his support. Other migrants tried to find new sponsors in Portugal but realized that this was no easy task. When these Mozambican women migrate to Europe, they find the model of having lovers who allow them their freedom as well as pay them a monthly allowance hard to reproduce. The lifestyle of the *curtidora* in Maputo—having a network of lovers and not committing completely to a single man—cannot be easily transplanted to places such as Portugal or Denmark. Although they are aware that Europeans think about sex, love, and money differently than Mozambicans do, some migrants are puzzled by how men they meet react to ideas of sponsorship. Having a sponsor, they learn, is almost unheard of and largely unaccepted, and they cannot expect a man to remunerate them in a relationship. When they go out, they notice that other women do not ask men for drinks as readily as women do in Maputo, and that a man more rarely pays for a woman's dinner or gives her money or clothes as gifts, even if he becomes her lover or boyfriend. These behaviors reflect complex differences in conceptions of exchanges of intimacy and money. As Bloch and Parry (1989) have argued, intimate and monetary exchanges may be regarded as mutually reinforcing in some settings, particularly in African countries, while in other settings, such as Europe, money is believed to destroy love and sexual intimacy. By contrast, women in my study, much as the Malagasy women depicted in Cole's chapter, saw economic support by men as a sign of care, love, and dedication. Some migrants understand men's unwillingness to pay and be their sponsors as part of European culture, and instead of complaining, they try to explain to men that, "in Africa, men pay women." Nevertheless, different notions of what affective exchanges can entail undermine the *curtidora* lifestyle. Because being a *curtidora* is next to impossible in Europe and because finding a well-paid job there is difficult, migrants often find that their only options are to marry or scrape by as a hotel cleaner, a bartender, or a sex worker.

Returning Home: Affective Investors or Failed Daughters?

Given the obstacles to staying in Europe, going home is a common out-come. Some women are deported, and some leave because they are dissat-isfied with their marriage or cannot find alternatives to marriage to enable them to stay. In some cases, the sense of personhood migrants look for can more easily be fulfilled back in Mozambique and the exchanges that define affective triads are more easily reproduced there. Some migrants are able to save money in Europe, which they then invest or use to buy property or a shop after they return to Maputo. Others go home regularly to visit family and friends. Doing so, however, depends on their partner's willingness and ability to pay the airfare, because flying to Mozambique is expensive. For migrants who are fortunate enough to have sufficient funds, going home to Maputo on holiday trips or moving home more permanently is at once an opportunity to confirm their status and an op-portunity to revitalize affective ties. As Leila explains,

When I go home, I buy T-shirts saying "Portugal," small pieces of jewelry, nice shoes. I plan a party for family and friends. I show them how well I am. . . . Coming home in my new clothes and nice stories from Lisbon, people see me, respect me. They treat me with admiration and envy.

The kind of respect, status, and admiration Leila finds when she goes home to Maputo is not easy to achieve in Europe. As mentioned, a range of factors such as partner control, isolation, racism, and lack of access to jobs and education stand in the way of migrants experiencing such rec-ognition. In Mozambique, women can more readily achieve the status they desire by displaying their wealth and symbols of freedom: they dress nicely and fashionably, spread wealth among kin, give gifts to relatives, and generally make sure everybody tastes a bite of their success. Some returnees also try to maintain their high status by opening small busi-nesses or making investments. Leila was one who did so: "When I saved up enough money," she told me, "I went back and opened a massage par-lor." For migrants who are unskilled and have little education, buying and opening a shop in Europe is complicated, just as finding a well-paid and respectable job is. In Maputo, migrants find increased entrepreneurial opportunities because of the strength of European currencies and cheap local labor and because migrants have much broader social networks there. Going back, migrants revitalize affective ties to kin by spreading their wealth and involving families in their investments. Mariana, for example, went home on a holiday and bought a house, which she allows her aunt to live in. She also opened a chicken farm, which her brother manages for her. The fulfillment of personhood upon returning to one's home country as a conspicuously successful migrant has been discussed by Newell (2012) and Cole (this volume), who show how returnees from France to Côte d'Ivoire and Madagascar strengthen social bonds at home and become emblems of the European dream.

For those return migrants who saved enough money and who left their husbands or partners in Europe, affective triads were transformed into affective dyads. Upon their return home, the main channel of material-affective exchanges ran between them and their kin, while their partners had a more peripheral role. No longer dependent on a husband or on a number of sponsors for support, such women seemed to choose relationships ever more freely, having casual affairs and appearing less concerned with finding a man of status and financial capacity.

Other return migrants were not so lucky, especially those who were deported or were otherwise unsuccessful. Once back in Maputo, they often found that opportunities were more limited than they had been prior to migration. Breaking up with a man and not saving money meant that they had to interrupt the flow of support within affective exchange triads. As a result, they were often seen as having neglected their duties as daughters and as wives, and they risked being scorned for not exploiting their opportunities abroad. They could be accused of possession by hostile spirits, be forced to work hard in the kin household to make up for their failure, or be effectively excluded socially and asked to live alone outside the family compound.

Intimate Migrations from Africa to Europe: Affective Circuits and Assertive Women

While researchers have examined marriage migration and intimate migration in Europe (e.g., Charsley 2012; Rytter 2011; Schmidt 2011a), Asia (e.g., Constable 2005; Palriwala and Uberoi 2008; Plambech 2010), and Latin America (e.g., Brennan 2004; Fernandez 2013; Oso Casas 2010), intimate migration from Africa to Europe is still understudied. The dearth of investigations of binational couples who migrate from African countries to the global north is especially conspicuous. There has been a bourgeoning scholarship on transactional sex and sexual economies in urban and peri-urban Africa (e.g., Cole 2010; Cole and Thomas 2009; Cornwall 2002;

Hunter 2010; Groes-Green 2013; Leclerc-Madlala 2003; Masvawure 2010; Newell 2009). Yet we know less about how intimacy between wealthy foreigners and local women in the emerging sexual economies in African cities leads to migration northward as well as how intimate relationships are transformed when couples move abroad. Specific research has targeted relationships between local African men and white female sex tourists (Meiu 2009), young Senegalese women who use dating sites to look for a man in Europe (Venables 2008), Malagasy women who form liaisons with white men and go to France (Cole 2010), Mozambican women who marry or who use male sponsors to travel to Portugal or Denmark, and Senegalese men who move to Europe with foreign spouses (Neveu Kringelbach, this volume). Yet little research attends to the way intimate migrations shape and are shaped by affective exchanges with partners and with kin when Africans manage to move to Europe.

Inspired by Wimmer and Glick Schiller's (2002) plea to move beyond methodological nationalism, I suggest we move beyond *methodological conjugalism*: the tendency to focus on marriage, couples, and dyads within the largely Eurocentric framework of the nation-state. By addressing affective exchange triads and shifting emotional ties in their multiplicity, we can avoid naturalizing couplehood, assumed to be the outcome of intimate migration sanctioned by the state. From this perspective, intimate migrants can no longer be seen a priori as engaged in continuous, monogamous, and stable relationships (see also Roseneil and Budgeon 2004). Moving beyond methodological conjugalism also means avoiding a view of migration as necessarily linear, planned, and agreed on by two compatible partners and instead being attentive to unpredictable journeys sustained by ties to shifting partners, lovers, and sponsors and to kin or others to whom migrants are affectively related. As I have shown, migration is not always intentional or supported by a single intimate partner. It often arises from multiple and sometimes transitory intimate encounters.

As Beck and Beck-Gernsheim (2010) argue, some studies tend to portray women migrants who move with Westerners as largely powerless and coerced. These assumptions do not acknowledge the possibility of migrants rejecting men whom they find oppressive. If we ignore the selectivity involved in women's migration, we obscure the agency, courage, and creativity they exercise in the face of adverse conditions (Beck and Beck-Gernsheim 2010). Beck and Beck-Gernsheim (2010) point to another questionable scholarly tendency to focus on intimate migrations as based either on love or on self-interest, the latter being suspicious and instrumental. The former reflects a Western conception of marriage as the ideal form of male-female intimate relationship and of love as its ideal content and condition (Beck and Beck-Gernsheim 2010). This line of thought upholds the Western nation-state's privileging of egalitarian love-based marriage over and in opposition to partnerships defined by kin, rank, and social inequality or to asymmetrical gendered exchanges between men and women (see also Fernandez 2013). As Fernandez argues in her study of Cuban-Danish marriages,

These ideals of a love-based companionate marriage rooted in autonomy and indi-vidualism are evident in Danish family reunification policy and political discourses against forced migration and marriage of convenience. [Unions not solely based on romance] are seen as immoral and threatening to the state. (Fernandez 2013, 274)

Thus, by approaching marriage migration as ideally love based, we risk reproducing the core principles by which states define, control, and ideal-ize some forms of migration, family building, and intimacy over others. Consequently, we must be attentive to mechanisms in state regulations through which methodological conjugalism is reinforced.

Attention to broader affective circuits, as Cole and I suggest in the intro-duction to this book, allows us to acknowledge how migrant women seek ways to maintain and generate material-emotional flows that ensure their sense of personhood and to track how men, kin, and the state may block these circuits. In contrast to seeing these women as passively submitting to men's wishes or to immigration laws or as silently accepting unwanted marriage as a way to gain legal immigration papers, we recognize them as actively trying to shape their trajectories. Maneuvering between demands of men, states, and families in precarious situations, they show different degrees of assertiveness.

Even as some resist the framework of marriage and male control, they must still live up to certain expectations at home in order to achieve per-sonhood. Their sense of obligation toward kin is often more deep-seated than their pursuit of personal goals, and the choice of a male partner de-pends on his ability to help them support their kin, codified in the saying "Men come and go, but mothers stay." This focus on kin can be under-stood through Parry and Bloch's (1989) theory of short- and long-term exchange cycles. While short-term cycles relate to temporary transactions, consumption, and personal satisfaction, long-term cycles are defined by the obligation to pay back one's ancestors for continued reproduction of the family to whom one is indebted for life. The short-term cycle is always subordinate to the long-term. Thus, if the short-term transactions of an individual are not seen to serve the long-term purpose of the social unit—that is, they are nonreciprocating—the individual will be deemed insufficient, and the guardians of the social order will respond with strong censure (Parry and Bloch 1989, 25). Migrants who could no longer provide for kin because their partner withheld their allowances or because they had left a partner often had an especially ambivalent relationship to their kin in Mozambique (see also Groes-Green 2014). This tension was reinforced if families suspected that the migrant kept money for herself or wasted it on parties, her personal appearance, and her own individual desires. Affective exchange triads, then, may be unsettled by a male partner's whims or unwillingness to provide or by his restrictions on the woman's freedom. But the balanced flow of support might equally be tempered by the migrant's poverty and unemployment or by her prioritization of her own quest for freedom and spending power over her familial obligations.

Although Mozambican women have migrated with men to Europe for a long time, everyone in Maputo agrees that the phenomenon has increased over the past fifteen years. The informants I followed had only been in Europe for periods of up to three years. Further research is needed to understand what happens to migrants who stay longer in Europe.

Addressing intimate migrations from Africa to Europe, and migration more broadly, via a careful analysis of affective exchange triads and larger affective circuits is a useful avenue for future investigations of transnational movements. Such analysis enables us to acknowledge the political, social, and economic forces driving or blocking migrants' search for respected personhood in a world where more and more people imagine a life in the global north as an alternative to a lack of opportunities at home.

Notes

1. To ensure anonymity and protect informants from authorities, families, and partners, all names are pseudonyms, geographical details have been changed or omitted, and personal details have been blurred.

2. Fieldwork in Maputo lasted a total of twenty-two months, from 2007 to the end of 2012. Migrants in this study went to Portugal (seven), Germany (four), Denmark (three), Italy (three), France (three), England (two), Spain (one), Holland (one), Ireland (one), and Sweden (one), countries that are representative of *curtidoras'* main destinations when they move to Europe with a partner.

3. This article draws mainly on experiences of migrants going to Portugal and Denmark because they illustrate broader trends among Mozambican women

migrants going to Europe. In addition, the two countries have different immigration laws and policies, which allows for instructive comparisons and contrasts to be drawn. Fieldwork in Denmark and Portugal lasted two months each.

4. Of 167 Mozambicans living in Denmark, 111 are women (Danmarks Statistik 2014).

EIGHT

Giving Life: Regulating Affective Circuits among Malagasy Marriage Migrants in France

JENNIFER COLE

By the time I met her in 2011, I'd heard about Philomène from so many other women in the wider network of Franco-Malagasy couples scattered across southwestern France that I felt like I knew her already. Philomène's husband worked as a salaried employee taking care of cattle on a dairy farm; she worked as a maid at a hotel. Together they had bought a small house in a village in south central France. Built into the side of a hill, their house overflowed with used clothes, muddy boots, and boxes of supplies. What the house lacked in orderliness, however, it quickly made up in warmth: it was always filled with Malagasy women, usually somehow related to Philomène (if only fictively), and with various French people coming and going.

Philomène's fame (what Malagasy call *laza*, from the verb "to declare") in the wider community of Franco-Malagasy families stemmed largely from the depth of her social networks, her warmth, and her modest material success. As she told it, her parents had coerced her into marrying her first husband, a Malagasy man many years her senior. Dissatisfied with the marriage and hoping to find happiness elsewhere, she begged her paternal grandmother, who had married a French sailor and settled near Marseille, to bring her to France from Madagascar. It was the mid-1990s, and the laws regulating immigration were not as strict as they were to become under French president Nicolas Sarkozy (2007–12). Nevertheless, even back then it was still the case that to acquire residency, Philomène had to marry a French citizen.[1] Her grandmother helped her come to France on a three-month tourist visa. At the time, the use of Internet matchmaking sites had not yet become widespread, and most people still relied on personal ads placed in magazines such as *Le Chasseur Français* (The French Hunter), which circulated widely among provincial men, to establish liaisons. The grandmother placed an ad in her local paper on her granddaughter's behalf. Shortly before her tourist visa ran out, Philomène found a husband, married, and regularized her legal status. The couple had two daughters. The man turned out to be an alcoholic, however, and the marriage ended after several years. By then, Philomène had acquired French residency and citizenship. She had also returned to Madagascar and brought her two Malagasy daughters from her first marriage to join her in France. Two years later, when she felt ready to marry again, Philomène searched the personal ads in the local newspapers and found Jean-Luc. A divorcée, Jean-Luc was only able to see his own daughters on weekends and during vacations; his ad specifically mentioned that he wanted to have a household with "lots of children." The two met, fell in love, and married. Though they never had children of their own, together they raised her four daughters and his two. They also bought and paid off their house. Meanwhile, Philomène worked tirelessly to help her family back in Madagascar. Over the years, and despite the imposition of ever more restrictive French immigration policies, she managed to find husbands for many of her female relatives, enabling them to migrate to France. She also arranged with several of her sisters who had settled near her to rebuild her father's house in their hometown in Madagascar. And she sent money to help her brothers and their many children and regularly traveled home to participate in ancestral ceremonies or attend to family business.

Philomène is among the thousands of coastal Malagasy women who have married Frenchmen and migrated to France since the 1990s.[2] These women go, as they so often put it, to "search" (*mitady*) and to "find their lot" (*mitady anjara*) in life—Malagasy expressions that refer, respectively, to seeking one's fortune and to finding one's marriage partner or mate, their combined use suggesting how, for women, the two are intrinsically linked. Like Philomène, many of these women have previously been married to Malagasy men and have borne children. Some have borne children out of wedlock, which, while common, makes it harder for them to enter a desirable second marriage locally. Given ongoing economic hardship in Madagascar and their relative lack of education, which further limits their opportunities, marrying a Frenchman and migrating to France is one of the best ways these women can reposition themselves within and transform their social networks. In Madagascar, women who marry Frenchmen, whether or not they migrate, are referred to as *vadimbazaha*, a Malagasy word that literally means "the spouse of a European" (see also Bois 1997). Malagasy sometimes say that by supporting their French and Malagasy families, *vadimbazaha* "make them live" (*mahamelona*).

In this chapter, I analyze how these women, whom many might dub marriage migrants, "make live" or "regenerate" their families in both France and Madagascar. I also show how this regeneration is central to these women's projects of self-fashioning. It is a part of how they become "considered" (*consideré* [Fr.]) or "achieve the first word" (*toa teny*), an expression that refers to someone who has earned the right to speak first in social gatherings and who can mobilize his or her extended family. Through an analysis of the way *vadimbazaha* mediate between nationally and culturally distinct kin networks, I offer a framework for thinking about how transnational social regeneration in binational and bicultural marriage unfolds.

From the Commodification of Intimacy and Care Chains to Affective Circuits

My analysis builds on work theorizing the role of female migration, care, and the commodification of intimacy in the global economy. Since the 1990s, increasing numbers of women from the global south have sought to earn their livelihoods and sustain their families by migrating to wealthier countries where they take up positions as nannies, maids, entertainers, and, very often, wives (Constable 2009; Ehrenreich and Hochschild 2003; Faier 2009; Parreñas 2001). Pointing to the central role that women's domestic, sexual, and reproductive labor plays in female mobility, one important line of feminist analysis suggests that transnational social reproduction occurs through women's participation in a stratified care economy (Kofman and Raghuram 2015; see also Katz 2001). According to this argument, which was first elaborated through a study of women who migrated to work as nannies and caretakers, transnational social reproduction occurs through the formation of "care chains" (Hochschild 2000) that emerge when middle-class women pay migrant women to do their household labor as they take up better-paid jobs in the workforce.

The migrant women they employ in turn send money to pay a poorer relative to care for their own children back home (Parreñas 2001, 2012). In its original formulation, the care chain is part of an unequal global economy in which love and care are the new surplus value that accrues to developed countries where migrant women go to work and money in the form of remittances trickles back to those who remain at home (see Hochschild 2003). In later studies, scholars have often drawn on a loose interpretation of this model to analyze women who migrate through marriage as well (Palriwala and Uberoi 2008; Piper and Roces 2003; Plambech 2010).

In some ways, this type of argument appears to illuminate how women like Philomène "give life" to their French and Malagasy families and achieve the "considered" (*consideré*) status they desire. After all, they explicitly use their physical charms and the promise of care to find French husbands, which in turn enables them to generate resources they can use to help their kin in Madagascar. The problem, however, is that Malagasy women do not generally see intimate care, love, and monetary transactions as antithetical social domains. Although they expect to receive material gifts and favors in exchange for the domestic work and care they provide their husbands, from their point of view, love and money are entangled, not opposed (Cole 2009; Thomas and Cole 2009; Zelizer 2007). Conseqently, an analysis that places too much weight on the commodification of intimacy not only misrepresents their practice but also inadvertently reproduces and naturalizes state and popular discourses that portray binational marriage as merely an easy way for immigrants to acquire citizenship (see Cole 2014c).

More importantly, this perspective obscures the larger networks of which these women are also a part. As I show in the following discussion, the way *vadimbazaha* regenerate their families entails a far more complicated process than using marriage to migrate to France and then send money back to Madagascar. Rather, to ensure the proper movement of both emotions and various material and symbolic resources between their French and Malagasy families, these women must constantly negotiate competing visions of who they are and what it means to be a wife, mother, or daughter. The way they do so draws attention not only to the importance of gendered labor but also to how different cultural conceptions of kinship and family further mediate transnational social regeneration.

To better capture how Malagasy women regenerate their families in both France and Madagascar, I draw on the notion of *affective circuits*. As Christian Groes and I outline in the introduction to this volume, affective circuits are exchanges of goods, emotions, ideas, and advice through which people negotiate their intimate relationships, sometimes across vast distances. The idea that these circuits are "affective" captures the en-twining of the material and sentimental resources so fundamental to the way Malagasy and many others constitute their intimate relationships. By itself, the circuit metaphor, much like the care chain metaphor, points to the importance of interconnection. Unlike the chain metaphor, however, which simply suggests two or more points along a line, the circuit meta-phor evokes movement back to an original source of relatedness as well as the potential for disconnection. When used to refer to technology, circuits are parts of larger networks through which energy flows; some may con-nect electrical grids that operate at different voltages. The circuit metaphor therefore draws particular attention to the important transforming work required to join different networks without triggering shocks, sparks, or even blackouts.

I focus particularly on how women manage social space and status as they coordinate the different circuits that tie them simultaneously to their French husbands and their Malagasy kin.[3] As I show in this chap-ter, it is by skillfully managing social space and status that *vadimbazaha* negotiate different understandings of their multiple roles as French wife and daughter-in-law and Malagasy mother, sister, and daughter, thereby ensuring the movement of resources through their affective circuits in such a way as to revivify their respective French and Malagasy families. To build my argument, I examine how women manage social space and status while in France. I then draw on a particular case to show the new ways by which they seek to manage space and status when they return with their husbands to Madagascar. To understand the issues relevant to each of these contexts, however, it is useful to start by considering the difficulties Malagasy women encounter when they go to France.

The Dilemmas of Life in France

Although it was fairly easy for Philomène to obtain her resident's card when she arrived in France in the mid-1990s and, later, to receive French citizenship, most Malagasy women who marry Frenchmen today find that this is no longer the case. Since the turn of the millennium, and espe-cially since the presidency of Nicolas Sarkozy (2007–12), the French gov-ernment has increasingly sought to limit migration via marriage (Cette France-là 2010). New laws have extended the probationary period before an in-marrying spouse is eligible either to work or to apply for citizenship. They have also made it harder for a woman to come to France on a tourist visa and then regularize her status, which is what Philomène and others did in the past. Being unable to work and thus having no income of her own makes a woman more dependent on her husband. It also makes it harder for her to accumulate and control the resources that enable her to reposition herself within her social networks. Like the Mozambican women depicted by Groes (this volume), these Malagasy women do not want to be "locked up" in the sense of being unable to work outside the home or earn their own income.

Even those women who manage to marry, establish residency, and get a job often find that that they must negotiate other, less formal obstacles. Over the past few years, the French government has deliberately produced an elaborate discourse demonizing binational marriage as part of its effort to limit family-based migration (Ferran 2009). This discourse draws on the opposition between love and money noted above, but it also folds it together with another set of ideas about the way certain kinds of marriage map onto the dichotomy of modernity and tradition. According to these ideas, romantic love, companionate marriage, and the nuclear family all emerged with—and signify—modernity, while the pragmatic demands of extended families, such as customs and material concerns, are said to characterize more traditional societies (Povinelli 2006; Thomas and Cole 2009; Wardlow and Hirsch 2006). Put simply, "modern" people marry for love and form nuclear families. By contrast, people from so-called traditional countries such as Madagascar marry according to the pragmatic needs of their extended families (see Cole 2014c).

These ideas, which circulate widely in French popular and public discourse, foster suspicion of binational couples in general and foreign spouses in particular (Neveu Kringelbach 2013b; Robledo 2011). Most French people know relatively little about Madagascar beyond the fact that it is a poor African country. They tend to assume that everyone who lives there desperately wants to move to France and is therefore willing to do anything it takes to do so. The result is that they often suspect Malagasy migrant women of contracting sham marriages (*mariage de complaisance*). Madagascar's growing reputation as a destination for sex tourism (Seelow and Hervieu 2013), with its evocation of loose morals and venality, further supports this widespread stereotype, one that can continue to haunt women even after they have lived in France for years.

French ideas about love and intimate relationships are all the more important because the men Malagasy migrants marry are themselves often financially and socially vulnerable; they sometimes worry that they will be taken advantage of. Most French men who seek Malagasy brides work either as farmers, low-level bureaucrats, or artisans. Many are in their fifties and sixties, and like the migrant women they meet, they often have children from prior marriages whom they have to financially support. And while husbands often enjoy the lively social life with other Franco-Malagasy couples that marriage to a Malagasy woman brings, they are not always eager to see their income or that of their wives invested in Madagascar. They may become defensive—or recalcitrant—if their Malagasy wife asks them for things too often or tries to help her family too much.

Malagasy women soon find, however, that if managing their relationships with their French husbands is not easy, managing their relations with their Malagasy kin is equally complicated. An often-cited Malagasy proverb, "The thin cow is not licked by his friends," captures the widespread assumption that wealth draws followers and enables sociality, while poverty leaves one isolated and alone. An important corollary that the proverb does not allude to, however, is that dependents may consume a wealthy person's resources until there is literally nothing left. Unless they have been to France, *vadimbazaha*'s families generally do not know how hard these women work; certainly the women selectively represent their circumstances in France to their kin at home (see Cole 2014b). In some cases, their kin in Madagascar *do* know the difficulties of life in France but feign ignorance because a knowing-not-knowing position (what Malagasy refer to as *fantapantatra*) enables them to ask the women for more than they might otherwise dare. Either way, family demands often far exceed what a woman can give without hurting herself and her ability to build a life in France. *Vadimbazaha* may want to maintain their ties to their kin back home, but they also find it extraordinarily difficult to control the terms by which this happens (see also Fesenmyer, this volume).

To complicate matters further, *vadimbazaha* know that while many of their kin and friends are proud of their success, some are always going to be jealous. Lingering jealousy is particularly common because women generally rely on others for help in finding a *vazaha* (foreigner) to marry in the first place. Even today, no woman goes to an Internet café, common as they now are, or otherwise finds her European husband alone. Rather, she knows someone in town who takes her to someone who happens to own a computer, bought by the person's sister who lives in France so that the two of them can stay in touch, and the woman then uses it to log onto matchmaking websites. Or a friend's sister who has married a Frenchman and settled in France comes home with addresses of bachelors she has culled from a local French newspaper, which she shares—or sells—to a friend who passes them on in turn. Because only a few women succeed in finding French husbands through the densely networked ties of kinship and friendship that bind them to one another, those left behind are frequently jealous. *Vadimbazaha* fear that their rivals, including their former boyfriends or husbands, may sabotage them (Cole 2014b). A woman's marriage to a Frenchman and migration to France repositions her within networks of exchange and creates new opportunities by giving her access to a secure home and regular salary as well as the prestige that most Malagasy associate with life in France. Like most transformations, it also creates new problems.

Regulating Affective Circuits from France: The Uses of Distance and the Necessity of *Copines*

Women's need to enlist their husbands' support for their ongoing commitments to their Malagasy kin prompts them to patch together a variety of strategies to ensure the orderly movement of goods, emotions, and information through affective circuits. Some women address the suspicion that they have only married a Frenchman to gain citizenship or wealth head on. Consider, for example, how Amédée won her husband's trust as a new bride from Madagascar. I had asked her what life had been like when she first came to France, and she exclaimed, "Jennifer, I may not be beautiful, but I'm clever." She then went on to tell me how, not long after her marriage, she overheard her in-laws talking about a bank account into which her husband's godfather had put money since his birth. Curious to learn how much money the account contained, Amédée asked her husband. He named a sum that was far too low given the nature of the conversation Amédée had overheard. Eager to find out the truth, Amédée devised a plan. She said to her husband, "Oh, when we have a child, I'd like to make an investment like that. Can I see the paperwork?" He handed her the papers. Amédée then discovered that her husband had lied to her: the sum in the bank account was far larger than he'd claimed. Bursting into tears, Amédée implored him to immediately buy her a return ticket to Madagascar. Mortified by his wife's sudden change of heart, and fearful that he'd lose his new bride, he asked Amédée what was wrong. She replied that if she had left her ancestral land to travel so far to marry him, it was because she loved him dearly and hoped they would be together for the rest of their lives, but the marriage wouldn't work if he didn't trust her. Terrified that she would leave, her husband apologized, brought out his bank statements, and showed her their assets.

It is possible that Amédée's husband might have taken her interest in his fortune as proof of the gold-digging nature of Malagasy brides. Nevertheless, by cleverly implying that she was more sincere and trusting than her husband and that she'd walk away from the money if the marriage lacked sentimental attachment, Amédée was able to learn about their real household resources. She also established herself as someone who had not migrated simply to acquire French citizenship or to help her family but out of true love. Given the association between love and marriage, the autonomous individual, and proper citizenship in much European thought (Povinelli 2006; Surkis 2006), her capacity for "true love" also signaled her ability to integrate into French society. Because integration might also be taken to mean the adoption of French notions of family, it also arguably helped her prove to her husband that, as an individual with "French" sensibilities, she was capable of managing her relationships with her Malagasy family because, like a "good French wife," she would prioritize the needs of her conjugal household over those of her natal kin.

To further shore up their status as modern and morally deserving and to distinguish themselves from other migrants, women often seek to distance themselves from what they see as negative stereotypes of Malagasy practice. Charlene, whose trip to Madagascar with her French husband I analyze below, emphasized her educated status and often said that she would have continued her studies if her mother had had more money. She also frequently declared that she disapproved of many Malagasy ancestral traditions, saying she thought they were a waste of money. In so doing, she sought to prove to her husband, his parents, and her Malagasy friends that she was a modern woman who came from a good, Christian family and had sound moral judgment. Other women sought to achieve similar ends by claiming that they came from middle-class families in Madagascar, drawing on the widespread but implicit association, well elaborated in urban Madagascar, between middle-class status, education, and modern personhood (Cole 2010). Vola, for example, frequently told her husband that she had grown up with all the modern amenities, including, she often emphasized, a refrigerator. I also often heard her say that she and her family had lived in a modern cement house built for government workers and that if she had known what life was like in France, she might have stayed in Madagascar. Vola hoped that if she could prove herself to be a discerning modern person who had come to France out of choice rather than desperation, she would earn her husband's respect and have a better claim to belonging than the many other poor, unwanted immigrants seeking a more prosperous life there. Earning his trust and respect also made it more likely that she could do as she pleased with the money she earned in France, because he would be less likely to question her judgment.

Even as women sometimes seek to downplay aspects of their Malagasy identity in their self-representations to their husbands, they also deliberately build a network of expatriate Malagasy women on whom they can call for help. Women usually refer to these other *vadimbazaha* as *copines*, using the French word for *friends* (Cole 2014b). Women rely on their *copines* for all kinds of advice about French life, including how to deal with one's papers, where to look for a job, how to manage the conflicts that might arise with one's husband, or where to go to buy the ingredients for Malagasy food. These women also help one another maintain their connections to home by carrying goods, medicine, money, and various documents (land titles, birth certificates) when they travel to and from Madagascar. Sometimes they do so in full view of a woman's husband. At other times they may do so without the French husband knowing. And at still other times a woman may rely on her *copines* to help her hide something from her Malagasy kin.

To regulate these complex relations with their husbands, their kin at home, and their fellow migrants, *vadimbazaha* seek to control communication and the flow of information. To do so, they take advantage of the physical distance that separates Madagascar from France and make strategic use of new communication technologies, particularly cell phones. *Vadimbazaha* cannot invent completely new identities in France, though some might like to, but they can somewhat control what their husbands know about them and where they come from. So too, living in France does not entirely prevent a jealous rival at home from trying to harm them (see also Sargent and Larchanché, this volume). It does, however, offer some protection, at least against more traditional forms of witchcraft and poisoning that require the victim to either come into contact with or ingest medicines. The distance between France and Madagascar also makes it easier for women to ignore demands from kin: fulfilling a kinsperson's request requires that the demand be properly heard. In France, *vadimbazaha* can turn off their cell phones if their kin make demands too frequently or ask for too much. By building relationships with *copines* and by managing social space to control the flow of substances and information so that they can shape their husbands' perceptions, these women regulate the affective circuits that connect them to their kin. They thereby ensure that they maintain those connections without being hurt by jealous rivals or overwhelmed by demands, all the while maintaining their status as French wives.

The Necessity of Returning to Madagascar

Vadimbazaha know, however, that their efforts to regulate the affective circuits that tie them to home from the distance of France can only go so far. They may reassure their husbands that they control what happens to the money or other resources they send home, but they also learn through long and often painful experience that when money and goods pass through many hands, they are liable to end up somewhere other than where the sender intended. Their worries about these practical matters are deeply intertwined with sentimental and cosmological concerns.

These women continue to be drawn back to Madagascar not only by sentimental attachments but also because they believe that it is the locus of ancesetral *hasina*, the generative potential embodied in ancestors and transmitted through ritual blessings that elders bestow on their juniors, which enables them to prosper (see also Bloch 1986). *Hasina*, however, is by nature unstable; without human care and ritual attention, it dwindles and dies (Délivré 1974). Moreover, because *hasina* resides in the ancestors' bones and becomes tied to specific places, it is not portable. Rather, to obtain the blessing of those who have died, descendants must travel to and propitiate their ancestors in the place where they are buried—even when that place is located far in the countryside, perhaps down pitted roads and across muddy rice fields, and may take many days to reach. When a migrant returns home to sponsor a ceremony, it implies that she recognizes the power of her ancestors. These ritual acts in turn perpetuate the ancestors' power and help ensure their continued blessing.

For example, when Pirette, who had grown up in the countryside near Sambava, failed her driver's test for the fourth time, she began to fret that she needed ancestral blessing. Unable to return to Madagascar before the summer harvest was over on her French husband's farm, she waited until her husband and mother-in-law were away at market one afternoon, took out a white plate, put water and coins in it, and begged her ancestors for their help, promising that she would soon return home to conduct a proper ceremony. Her desire to return to her ancestral village grew increasingly intense. Pirette missed her family. She also feared what would befall her if she did not go back; her continued absence from her ancestral land represented a potential source of misfortune. She knew too that her makeshift ritual was just a stopgap measure. She needed to return to Madagascar.

Although Pirette and other women like her want to return to Madagascar to obtain ancestral blessing and attend to family affairs, they know that these trips will bring their French husbands and their extended Malagasy families into close proximity with one another, changing the conditions under which the women usually seek to join their kin networks. As a result, these trips destabilize the different ways of regulating affective circuits that women craft while in France. They pose risks.

Regulating Affective Circuits in Madagascar: Charlene and Roland's Trip

To consider more closely the kinds of challenges women face during trips home and their reliance on a combination of impression management and control of social space as they seek to regulate affective circuits, I examine Charlene and Roland's trip to Madagascar. In her forties when we first met, Charlene had been raised by her mother, who worked as a midwife in the northern coastal town of Sambava. Charlene eventually left Sambava and went to college in Madagascar's capital city of Antananarivo. During the first two years, she did fairly well, but in the third year, she failed her exams. Her mother, who also had to support Charlene's younger siblings, did not have enough money to pay her registration fees, so Charlene started to work, first as a secretary in a government office and, then, when she lost that job, selling snacks by the side of the road. After a while, Charlene amassed enough money to return to school, but she failed the end-of-year exam a second time. By this time, Charlene was thirty years old. Her mother began to worry that as someone who was neither highly educated, and thus could not appeal to a wealthier or more educated Malagasy man, nor particularly young and beautiful, and thus unlikely to be claimed by one of her peers, Charlene might never marry. She begged a cousin who lived in southwestern France to find Charlene a husband. The cousin put an ad in the local paper and found a middle-aged widower eager to marry Charlene. With a three-month tourist visa in hand and a prospective husband supposedly waiting, Charlene went to France.

By the time she arrived there, however, the children of the widower that Charlene's cousin had arranged for her to marry had gotten wind of the project. Fearful that Charlene was coming to steal their father's wealth, they told him they wouldn't tolerate the marriage. The man got cold feet and backed out. By then, Charlene had already told people in Madagascar that she was going to France to get married: she could not bear the humiliation of returning home. Hurt, disappointed, and scared, Charlene turned to a Malagasy migrant friend who encouraged her to persevere, arguing that, until her visa expired, all was not lost. The friend helped her register at a marriage agency, and Charlene began to look for a husband in earnest. She quickly met several candidates. It was Roland, a shy man roughly her age who worked packing vegetables, who stole her heart. Despite her cousin's urging that she should continue to look for someone wealthier and more sophisticated, Charlene had made up her mind. The couple courted for several weeks, and then, when her visa expired, Charlene returned to Madagascar. Several months later, Roland arranged for her return to France, and the couple married. A year after her arrival, Charlene gave birth to a daughter.

In July of 2013, Charlene, Roland, their daughter Lydia, and I took an Air France flight from Paris to Madagascar. That spring had marked the couple's tenth anniversary; Roland had announced that he wanted to visit Madagascar to celebrate. His two elderly bachelor uncles generously offered to pay for the trip as an anniversary gift. Charlene and her husband both requested extra vacation days from their French employers and scheduled the trip for the summer so their daughter would not miss school. It promised to be an exciting trip.

Although Charlene was overjoyed by the prospect of the visit, she worried about what Roland might see and learn. During her time in France, she had worked hard to portray herself as a sophisticated and moral person who had migrated by choice. The modern agentive image she presented depended on her ability to hide what was to her a humiliating fact: that she, like many Malagasy women who seek European husbands abroad, had done so in part because she had failed to make a satisfactory marriage in Madagascar. In short, migration offered Charlene a spatial fix to what might otherwise have been a life of continual humiliation and social diminishment (see also Vigh, this volume).

It was one thing, however, for Charlene to shape Roland's perceptions in France and quite another to do so in Madagascar, where he would have access to much richer and varied kinds of information about who she was and where she came from. Over the course of her visit, it would not have been unthinkable for Charlene to betray herself as the granddaughter of a Malagasy peasant, a one-time college student who had flunked her exams twice, and a woman who, too educated to appeal to most poor Malagasy men yet too old and not educated enough to appeal to a wealthy deputy or doctor, had sought a European husband to better her situation. Nor would it have been surprising for Roland, looking about him and perhaps chatting with her kin, to conclude that Charlene came from a less than modern society and was thus a less than modern kind of person, destroying the image she had carefully constructed while in France. Such a failure to manage her own status would not only be humiliating but might also reduce her ability to make decisions within their household.

At the same time that Charlene sought to manage what Roland saw and did, she also needed to reinvigorate her relationships with her kin and regenerate her ties to home. Both migrants and those who remain at home (locally called "people-in-the-town") know that those who move away must return home either to beg ancestral blessing while they are living or to be buried in the ancestral tomb on their death. People-in-the-town expect those who return, who are often wealthier than they, especially if they have migrated to Europe, to recognize their labor in caring for their families' patrimony. Because giving money or other resources is the best way to show love and care, returning migrants, then, typically must share some of the wealth they have received abroad with their kin back home (see Newell 2012).

Mindful of the need to both maintain the modern persona she had established in France and regenerate her connections to her kin, Charlene organized the trip carefully. During the first few days in Antananarivo, the capital city, the family went to visit a crocodile and wildlife farm as well as the royal palace. Touristic activities continued after the couple returned to Charlene's natal town. The family walked along the beach at low tide, saw Charlene's old school friends, and dined in a local restaurant frequented by tourists and wealthy Malagasy. Toward the end of the visit, Charlene organized an outing to a small town known for the beauty of its deserted beaches. The trip involved an off-road adventure traveling in one of the infamous Malagasy bush taxis, drinking fresh coconut milk, and eating freshly caught lobster. Before returning to France, Charlene arranged for her cousin to ship her several kilos of giant shrimp from the west-coast town where he worked, which she planned to take home as gifts for her in-laws and the bachelor uncles. The setting, the activities, and the gifts for her French family all helped Charlene frame the trip as an exotic vacation, one befitting the persona she had crafted in France.

At the same time that Charlene organized activities for herself, Roland, and their daughter, she also engaged in activities of particular significance to her kin. She distributed the numerous gifts she had brought to her immediate family, made sure to look in on her siblings in her father's second family, and generally made house to house visits, being careful to actually enter each house and sit down and chat with her kin, as is polite. Most importantly, she arranged a cattle sacrifice. To prepare for the sacrifice, the men in the family erected a tent and set up tables in the oldest brother's yard. All the women cooked. The night of the sacrifice, everyone danced until dawn, and each and every one of Charlene's numerous aunts and cousins took particular delight in dancing with Roland. Miraculously, given that cattle sacrifice rituals are often moments when people settle personal scores, no one misbehaved (Cole 2001). The next day, the family feasted and continued dancing. Charlene's mother's older brother, the leader of the family, who was thus responsible for mediating between the ancestors and their descendants, took the microphone and declared how joyous all in the family were that Charlene had returned with her husband and daughter and how happy they were to have met their son-in-law. The photos from the event show Charlene, Roland, and Lydia happy and relaxed. If you look closely, however, you can see Charlene—and her mother, who had encouraged her daughter to seek a husband abroad in the first place—beaming with pride.

Managing Status and Controlling Social Space through Houses

How did Charlene manage her competing networks under the conditions produced by her visit home with Roland? In part, she relied on the spatial organization provided by her house, which she had paid a friend to renovate before her arrival. In Madagascar, as in many parts of the world, houses embody the inhabitants' aspirations and signal their social status (Bloch 1995; Feeley-Harnik 1980; Freeman 2013; Thomas 1998). Not sur-

8.1   Houses made of ravinala palm in the Masoala region of Madagascar, 2010. In villages along the northeast coast, houses are typically one-room rectangular structures made of travelers palm and set on small stilts. Family members usually live in houses clustered together in the same courtyard, like the one shown here. Photo by Eva Keller.

8.2 Creole-style, tin-roofed house, Masoala region, 2006. Since the colonial period, wealthy east coasters have considered it a mark of status to build houses in the style used by creole planters from Mauritius and Reunion. These houses are sometimes divided into several rooms, but the walls are typically made from the ribs of travelers palm, which does not block sound. There are usually no doors between the rooms, affording little privacy. Photo by Eva Keller.

prisingly, then, migrants commonly build new, fancy modern houses in their natal towns both to convey their success abroad and to claim local belonging.[4] By rebuilding and modernizing her mother's house, Charlene proved her success as a migrant, established her rights in the house, and repaid a debt of care to her mother.

But Charlene's new house did more than simply prove her success and establish her continued belonging. It played a third far more ambivalent role. Luke Freeman (2013) argues that the houses left behind by Betsileo migrants in central Madagascar embody tensions intrinsic to the migrant experience: between presence and absence, separation and connection, and individual ambition and collective obligations. To this I would add that as long as they are still inhabited, they also provide a practical means of dealing with those tensions. In Charlene's case, this meant drawing on the spatial layout of the house as she sought to regulate the flow of information, substances, and bodies through the affective circuits that connected her different kin networks.

8.3 A *vadimbazaha*'s modern, cement house, Sambava, Madagascar, 2015. All *vadimbazaha* hope to build a modern, cement house in their natal towns or villages. These houses signal their success as migrants and enable them to claim continued local belonging. They also provide women with a material platform through which they can potentially limit interactions with their kin and negotiate their contending kin networks. Photo by Jennifer Cole.

Before Charlene's remodeling project, her mother's house was a fragile, tin-roofed affair with four rooms organized around a central living room. Rooms were open to one another, which allowed the breeze to blow through in the heat of summer but made privacy nonexistent. The kitchen, shower, outhouse, and bathroom all occupied separate buildings in the courtyard, as is common in the region. Dilapidated and without modern amenities, the house conveyed its owner's straitened circumstances. To make it habitable for Roland and her daughter, Charlene extended the back of the house, creating space for a dining room and kitchen. She added a separate European-style toilet and shower room as well. The most impressive room, however, was the master bedroom: located in the front of the house, off her mother's bedroom, it was the only room with a locking door. Charlene placed an enormous bed in the room and had a large shelf built, on which the family could put their clothes as well as the various French breakfast supplies and foods they'd brought with them.

Charlene took special care in preparing the new master bedroom. Many Malagasy women worry about their ability to create French norms of privacy when they travel to Madagascar with their husbands. I realized this after I returned to France from a trip there with a different woman, when I inadvertently spurred discussion among women who were in the midst of preparing for their own trips home. One young woman who was planning to return with her boyfriend for the first time expressed anxiety to her friend about where she and her boyfriend would sleep. "You don't understand," she said, "my mother is capable of deciding that she wants to come sleep next to us." Her older, more experienced friend advised her, "No no, that isn't right. You are a *vadimbazaha* now. They [your Malagasy kin] need to show you respect." By building a special room for her family, Charlene made sure that Roland was comfortable, as he should be on vacation. She also made the setting one that supported the modern image and sense of domestic tranquility she sought to convey, making it less likely that Roland would perceive her in an unwelcome light.

At the same time that the bedroom with its locked door created an appropriate setting for their vacation, Charlene also used it to keep her kin at bay. In the face of their constant demands for physical and social intimacy, the separate room with the locked door signaled her separation. It also protected her, Roland's, and Lydia's belongings from theft. By shaping people's physical and social intimacy through the layout of the house, Charlene found different ways to separate and connect the affective circuits that simultaneously tied her to her Malagasy kin and to Roland.

Houses also figure centrally in women's efforts to regulate affective circuits by enabling them to limit the flow of resources to their kin. Not taking phone calls, pretending they haven't heard requests, or saying their expenses prevent them from fulfilling requests are all means by which *vadimbazaha* manage the movement of resources through these circuits while they are in France. But they are also keenly aware that distance cuts both ways and that it is hard to control what happens to the money they send home. Often, women send money intended for one project and then learn that their kin use it for something else or share it with others, dividing it into ever-smaller portions that never suffice for any useful purpose, prompting them to ask for more. One woman lamented to me, "My mother, she wants to care for all the world. She tells me God brings her all these people to care for. I yell back, 'Tell God to take them away.'" Having lived in France with French husbands, *vadimbazaha* sometimes grow accustomed to sharing with fewer people, while their mothers who remain in Madagascar retain a far more expansive vision of the kin whom they should help. No wonder relatives who remain in Madagascar often complain that once women have married a *vazaha* and live abroad, "they don't really mix." Their remarks are both tacit critiques of *vadimbazaha*'s behavior and pleas for greater intimacy, which implies material support.

Because houses are the primary units of consumption, women may seek to limit the flow of money and goods through affective circuits by deliberately placing their family members in particular houses to control who consumes what and how much. In doing so, they adopt a strategy similar to that used by Malagasy rulers who placed their dependents in different parts of the kingdom to make claims to particular places and exert control (Esoavelomandroso 1979; Raison-Jourde 1991). Janine, for example, used money she earned in France to buy several plots of land adjacent to her mother's house, where she then proceeded to build two smaller houses. Several of her brothers and nephews also lived in the mother's house. Partly to keep an eye on her brothers, whom she feared would spend the money she sent home on their mistresses (as is common), she asked her maternal cousin, Victor, to live in one of her houses. *Ask*, however, is perhaps too polite a word. As it happened, Victor had been living with his wife's kin in another village. Following his wife and living in her house had made Victor what northern Malagasy refer to as a *jaoloko*, which is considered a subordinate, feminized, position (see also Waast 1980). Victor was aware of his inferior social status and begged Janine to give him money to build his own house on his father's land so that he could regain a more respected position. Instead, Janine told Victor and his wife to live in *her* house. Living in Janine's house meant that Victor lived on his kin's land. Consequently, he no longer occupied an inferior status in relation to his wife. He did, however, become increasingly dependent on his cousin Janine. She even said that she "raised" Victor, using the Malagasy word (*mitarimy*) that refers to the actions of feeding and caring for a child or a domestic animal. And insofar as she had "raised him," he was expected to reciprocate with the appropriate behavior (*mivaly tarimy*). Janine fostered his dependence in part as a managerial strategy. By placing Victor in her house, she made sure that she had someone on hand who would be loyal to her interests. She candidly said as much.

Staging Events: Performing Status and
Controlling Information

Women also seek to regulate affective circuits by carefully staging events to manage people's impressions. At mealtimes during her trip home, for example, Charlene organized the seating so that her French family and her very close kin sat at the table, while the rest of her Malagasy family took their meals, as is traditional in coastal Madagascar, sitting on mats that were spread on the floor. She also drew attention to her French table manners by using only a fork and knife. In Madagascar, people mainly use spoons—forks are seen as quintessentially foreign. As Roland and I sat waiting for dinner to be ready, Charlene criticized her mother for setting a spoon with each place setting, as Malagasy usually do, telling her it was unnecessary because we were not going to be eating soup. She delivered the rebuke in French, to be sure Roland understood, subtly reminding him that she was indeed the person she had claimed to be in France, all while performing her transformed status for her kin.

Even more striking was Charlene's ability to organize her cattle sacrifice in such a way that she could both obtain ancestral blessing and fulfill her kin's expectations without jeopardizing her status as a modern French wife. Any Malagasy knows that a woman who has achieved the trifecta of success—marrying a Frenchman, going overseas, and building a new house in her ancestral land—has relied on her ancestors' power to do so. After all, most women seek their ancestors' blessing and support to overcome the many obstacles that stand in their way. They may make vows to their ancestors, perhaps declaring that if they find a *vazaha* husband and erect a cement house, they will sacrifice a bull in their honor. They may also go to diviners to acquire charms and spells intended to make them luckier and more attractive than their competitors (see also Groes-Green 2013), even if others view such practices, which some liken to witchcraft, ambivalently. Trying to explain why women sometimes sought charms to support their efforts, Charlene's aunt remarked, "It's hard for Malagasy to get to France, very hard." The implicit corollary was that most people used supernatural help to do so. For Charlene to admit that she had relied on either ancestral power or magic to find a husband and get to France, however, would have been to suggest a way of conceiving her place in the world and how power operates at odds with the modern, Christian persona she sought to convey to Roland.

Not only did Charlene complete her ritual responsibilities but she also orchestrated the ceremony to make it seem like a folkloric event performed for Roland's holiday entertainment and to celebrate their ten years of marriage. She did so by concealing certain crucial pieces of information from Roland. When we arrived in Madagascar, Charlene announced that the family would hold a cattle sacrifice. She did not, however, mention that it was intended to fulfill a vow she had made. To do so would have betrayed how deliberately she'd worked to find Roland. It would also have revealed that despite her claims of disbelief in the ancestors, she still feared their retribution should she break her promise to them. Instead, she told Roland a partial truth: that the sacrifice was to celebrate their ten years of marriage and introduce him to her extended family.

Charlene's mother, anxious about her daughter's status, went even further in disavowing the ritual elements of the ceremony. While Charlene was away buying food one day, she told me that she and Charlene had argued about the upcoming sacrifice. According to her, Charlene insisted on holding the sacrifice because Roland, having married a Malagasy girl, wanted to see traditional Malagasy customs. Her mother claimed that she had asked Charlene to forego the ceremony entirely and to give her money rather than spend it on the ritual but that Charlene had refused.

I never asked Charlene whether she had argued with her mother or whether her mother's story about Roland wanting to see "Malagasy customs" was true; I never had any indication from Roland that it wasn't. Nor do I know why Charlene's mother told me she'd asked Charlene not to sponsor the ceremony, though I suspect she was alluding to an ongoing struggle over resources. My point is that although Charlene and her mother gave slightly different reasons for the ceremony, they both sought to explain it in such a way as to distance themselves from its religious dimensions, downplaying its ritual importance and efficacy. Charlene's uncle sacrificed the bull and introduced Roland publicly to Charlene's family. Their ten years of marriage were duly fêted. What Roland didn't know is that after the bull was killed, while everyone was dancing, Charlene's mother and uncles, the family elders, took some of the bull's fat up to their father's tomb on the hill overlooking the village. There they spread the fat on the altar and invoked their father's name, thanking him for his beneficence and asking for his further blessing, thereby fulfilling Charlene's vow. Like Roland, I wouldn't have known about their actions had Charlene's aunt, perhaps frustrated that she had not been invited to the party, not told me what occurred. She explained,

Oh, you *have* to do your customs here. It's very difficult [not to]. Charlene and her mother, they made a vow together, praying that she would get to France one day and finish the house. Once you get to France, you can pray and become as Christian as you like. But before you go, you need the ancestors. Of course the ritual was about fulfilling a vow. What do you think?

By presenting the sacrifice as a simple party rather than a ritually effica- cious event in which she thanked her ancestors for helping her find a *vazaha* husband and complete her house, Charlene simultaneously man- aged to effectively build her connections with her kin, protect herself from the wrath of her ancestors, and maintain her understanding with Roland.

Volatility: Blockages, Short Circuits, and Potential Transformations

The affective circuits that *vadimbazaha* build are subject to change over time. In the last ten years, the French government's efforts to limit im- migration have slowed, and even blocked, these circuits, most often by making it difficult for migrants who do not have their papers to find work or return home. But if the French administration is a particularly powerful "circuit breaker," it is not the only one. In fact, because the affective cir- cuits women build are central to the way they regenerate their families and achieve social value, they, their kin, and other members of the com- munity in both France and Madagascar may all seek to block or even break them at various times.

When women seek to block the flow of resources that tie people to one another, they usually do so by revealing information that destroys the par- ticular impression another woman has worked to build. "Information," after all, is literally "that which informs" in the sense that it enables one to decide between different interpretations of a particular situation. For ex- ample, a *copine* may tell a woman's husband that his wife has done some- thing that she knows he will disapprove of—perhaps she has kept a lover or sent money home behind his back—which in turn may change the husband's understanding of the marital relationship and make him more controlling, potentially blocking the wife's access to essential resources of trust and money. At other times, a *copine* may betray another woman by revealing information about the woman's life in France to her kin in Mada- gascar. Given people-in-the-town's expectation that all women who go to France automatically succeed, this typically means that the *copine* publicly reveals that a woman is poorer and more vulnerable than she claims, per- haps humiliating her and temporarily limiting her ability to expand her social networks (Cole 2014b).

At other times, however, and especially during women's trips to Madagascar with their husbands, kin or other members of the community may try to block or break circuits by taking advantage of women's physical proximity to them. In several cases, widely discussed within the diasporic community at large, men, their wives, or even their children returned to Europe from Madagascar to fall sick or die, misfortunes that *vadimbazaha* attributed to the actions of jealous kin or friends who used witchcraft to harm them. In several other equally notorious cases, women took their husbands to Madagascar only to have them run off with other members of their extended family, leaving the women to return to France alone. The failure to manage physical contact and the flow of information can effectively short-circuit, even destroy, women's networks and perhaps the relationships with their French husbands on which those networks depend.

The destruction of some circuits may enable the growth of others, such that these affective pathways, and with them women's trajectories and the broader social networks of which women are a part, shift and change over time. Sometimes women's efforts to break each other's circuits result in a woman withdrawing from the wider Malagasy diasporic community, perhaps being pushed more deeply into her husband's family (Cole 2014b). When women find that they are unable to control the terms of exchange with their kin and feel themselves unduly taken advantage of, which is especially likely to occur after a trip to Madagascar, they sometimes adopt a commonly repeated French position that, really, "all their families want is welfare." What they mean is that their Malagasy kin take them for granted, treating them and the resources they provide by dint of hard work as a form of support to which they are entitled. French stereotypes of African migrants may hold that these women only come to France to accumulate French resources to send *au pays* (to their country), but in practice, a woman's return trips sometimes reinforce her separation from her Malagasy family and deepen her commitment to her French life and networks.

Alternatively, if women successfully manage to negotiate these visits, as Charlene did, they may solidify their position as mediators by further incorporating their husband into their family. In several cases, men returned from trips to Madagascar distinctly more embedded in their wives' families, perhaps even having agreed to adopt their wives' nieces and nephews as their own. One man came back overwhelmed and moved by a newfound respect for his wife and her Malagasy friends. "I have so much more respect for Vola now," he said, shaking his head as if in wonder, "now that I see where she comes from and how far she's had to go." Generally, when men enjoy their experience, it increases their willingness to invest in Madagascar as well as to welcome other Malagasy—and Malagasy practices—into their homes, solidifying women's position and intensifying positive material and other flows through their affective circuits.

Connect, Disconnect: Social Regeneration in Bicultural Marriage Migration

As I have illustrated, Malagasy women's practices of giving life to their families in France and Madagascar require them to weave together competing understandings of what it means to be a valued wife, mother, sister, and daughter, of how one achieves success in the world, and of the kind of relationship a person should have to kin and to the past. It is precisely because these women bridge French and Malagasy families, with their different understandings of gender, kinship, and female personhood, and because their relations with both their French and Malagasy families are suffused by a complex mix of positive and negative emotions that they have to work so hard to regulate the affective circuits tying them to these different networks. And it is partly because their understandings motivate them to return home to honor their ancestors that Malagasy women illuminate so clearly the importance of controlling social space and status in managing affective circuits. These affective circuits must be forged from noncontinuous, often competing social networks. As a consequence, like magicians working their sleight of hand, *vadimbazaha* rearrange households and manage impressions in order to control the flow of knowledge and the physical proximity that binds them to their French and Malagasy kin. In doing so, they seek to keep their Malagasy and French families both separate and connected in just the right ways, at just the right times, enabling them to shape the affective circuits through which resources, social connections, and emotions flow.

Their efforts show that when it comes to marriage across both national and cultural boundaries, social regeneration entails "making live" multiple different families—French families, Malagasy families, and even French-Malagasy families. They also demonstrate that this undertaking involves the movement through complex circuits of both material and affective resources of various kinds. It is precisely because the circuits relay such resources and because the different parties do not always agree on either what they are or how they should be invested, that they regenerate families in such a dynamic, enlivening fashion. Their example suggests that when it comes to understanding how transnational social regeneration occurs, the coordination of different kinship systems may be just as important a factor to take into account as the appropriation of female reproductive labor by global capitalism. Philomène has built a house with her French husband, filled it with children from three different marriages, brought her younger sisters to France to marry, and helped support her brothers in Madagascar. Her peers admire her ability to both reinvigorate and maintain multiple kin networks. After all, as they all know, and as Charlene's trip home so aptly demonstrates, keeping these competing networks alive is a difficult and sometimes dangerous undertaking.

In part because Malagasy women reveal how difficult it is to regenerate different kinds of families across national, cultural, economic, and even racial divides, their efforts suggest a far more contingent, even fragmentary, model for thinking about transnational social reproduction than is found in much of the contemporary literature on female migration, including marriage migration, and care work. In recent years, several scholars have argued that metaphors of "friction" (Tsing 2005) or "turbulence" (Cresswell and Martin 2012) better capture the dynamics of transnational cultural formations than metaphors of smooth connection. Similarly, I argue that it is more fruitful to conceptualize transnational social reproduction as a process made up of the many moments of microdisconnection and reconnection that allow the resources of life—love, money, care, goods, and information—to move quickly or slowly, smoothly or haltingly, across different networks. With its evocation of slowing, blockage, and intensification, the electrical circuit metaphor does more than enable description of these material and affective flows. It also offers a way of thinking about how social regeneration across different, and incommensurate, kin networks unfolds.

Acknowledgments

This chapter draws from fieldwork conducted in southwestern France from August 2010 to August 2011, with several return visits in 2012, 2013, and 2014 as well as trips to Madagascar in 2012 and 2013. It also builds on several years of research in Madagascar between 1993 and 2007. I thank the National Science Foundation, the Wenner-Gren Foundation for Anthropological Research, and the John Simon Guggenheim Foundation for their generous financial support during the researching and writing of this chapter. Thanks also to Summerson Carr, Julie Chu, Deborah Durham, Christian Groes, Erin Moore, and Costas Nakassis for their helpful comments on drafts.

Notes

1. Though socialist François Hollande replaced Sarkozy as France's president in 2012, the laws regulating immigration have not significantly changed. If anything, the rates of deportation of illegal immigrants have remained steady or increased, although Hollande does not draw rhetorical attention to anti-immigration policies as stridently as his predecessor.

2. Malagasy migration to France began primarily during the First World War, when many men were conscripted into the French colonial army. In addition, Malagasy have long migrated to France to pursue higher education. Historically, those migrating to pursue their studies came from the Merina and Betsileo ethnic groups of Madagascar's high plateau. The practice of marriage and migration I discuss in this chapter has been a largely northern and coastal strategy for social ascension, though in recent years it has spread across the island.

3. I use *social space* to refer to the organization of both physical and social intimacy, as manifested, for instance, in the spatial layout of houses and the giving or withholding of information. *Status*, meanwhile, refers to the way a person is perceived in relation to those around him or her. It captures the idea of rank or social standing, but it may also capture moral qualities— whether, for instance, someone is a good wife or a conniving immigrant. One's status relies in part on impression management (Goffman 1959). Insofar as people often organize physical and social intimacy to shape others' impressions, social space and status are clearly interlinked, mutually reinforcing ideas.

4. For Madagascar, see especially Thomas (1998) and Freeman (2013); for Latin American contexts, see Leinaweaver (2009) and Pauli (2008).

NINE

Life's Trampoline: On Nullification and Cocaine Migration in Bissau

HENRIK VIGH

"It does not allow you to be a man" (*i ka na desjau sedu homi*), Amadu said, when explaining to me what it is like to live in Bissau. "It," the strangely unpersonified entity that he sees as restricting his movement into manhood, refers to the inhospitable social circumstances of his life. "Bissau is fucked [*fudido*]," he continued, "even if you struggle till you tire you will never succeed in being somebody." Amadu's grievance at being unable to reach "proper" manhood is a common complaint among young West African men (see Abdullah 1998; Bayart 1993; Hoffman 2006, 2011; O'Brien 1996; Richards 1995; Utas 2003; Vigh 2006a, 2008). His is a story of poverty and generational stagnation, one whose broad outlines have been encountered by many anthropologists working with youth on the continent. Yet the case of Guinea-Bissau is nonetheless an unusual one. The country has recently become infamous for its role in the movement of cocaine from Latin America into Europe. In fact, Guinea-Bissau is supposedly so central to the transnational flow of cocaine that it has been designated Africa's first narco state (Hanson 2007; Horta 2007; UNODC 2007). The involvement in the trade of the country's leading military and political figures is so profound that civil servants and state structures facilitate, rather than combat, the movement of the illegal drug (*Spiegel Online* 2013; Vigh 2012; West African Commission on Drugs 2014).[1] With a fourth of the cocaine consumed in Europe passing through the region every year (Vulliamy 2008) and the emergence of an economy that has become so influential in the country that it is difficult to imagine its disappearance, the international community worries about the negative effects the drug cartels are having on the already fragile state and economy. "The threat posed by *drug traffickers* is so great that the state is on the verge of collapse. . . . Guinea-Bissau has lost control of its territory and cannot administer justice," a UN official said at a meeting of the Security Council on December 12, 2007 (UNODC 2007).

While outside observers widely perceive the cocaine trade as a problem, it constitutes a space of opportunity for many of the young men I talked to in Bissau, the country's small capital (Vigh 2015). Taking the form of an ethnographic journey, this chapter looks at the way people such as Amadu become caught up in the transnational flow of cocaine and drug trafficking to Europe.[2] It follows the footsteps of the young men who seek to navigate the cocaine trade to gain better lives for themselves and their families. In doing so it falls into two parts. The first part looks at the predicament of youth and their dreams of migration and examines how the flow of cocaine through Bissau has become imbricated in social life, trickling into young men's hopes, fears, and trajectories. Moving from Bissau to Lisbon, the second part dwells on the involvement of young men in the cocaine trade, the migratory dynamics the trade facilitates, and the despair that ensues when a migrant is caught with drugs and deported.

Needless to say, the empirical material does not paint a general picture of life, youth, or migration in Guinea-Bissau. It does, however, shed light on a phenomenon that appears to be of growing significance in the subregion: the emergence of a relatively novel type of transnational criminal trade in West Africa and the effects this trade has on intimate relations and social obligations. As we shall see, the cocaine connection gives hope of positive emplacement within the affective circuits—understood as flows of resources and goods guided by emotion and obligations (see Cole and Groes, introduction to this volume)—that tie close relatives to one another. People are realistic about its dangers. Yet navigating the cocaine trade offers them a potential escape from rampant poverty and a lack of positive prospects, and it affords the possibility of meeting social obligations to provide for and support others (Fesenmyer, this volume), making the pros quickly outweigh the cons. Yusuf explained the trade's attractiveness to me:

Yusuf: You do what is needed [*precisa*]. If you can go as a mule [*ngullidur*], you go. Clearly! Ask all . . . who will not do it? If someone offers who will refuse? If there is a possibility, you go. You must go!

Henrik: And if you do not go. If you do not go what happens?

Yusuf: Nothing [*laughs*]. That is the problem. If I stay here nothing changes. If you do not go, you will become sick with preoccupation. You must go! Like this you will be more. You will be someone good, someone respected. You understand? Here there is nothing, but if you go, if you succeed, you will see it all [*bu na odja tudo*].

Yusuf perceives himself as a young man trapped in a decaying society. Stuck in a city in which he sees no hope of gaining a better future, he is willing to do most anything to get out of Bissau. He consequently approaches the cocaine trade with cautious optimism, as a potential opening toward brighter horizons and an escape from extreme poverty. As such, the trade provides a rare possibility to move on positively in life, making it an opportunity that is hard to pass up. "Who would hide [*tudji*] from opportunity?" he asked later in our interview.

Africa Rising, Polarizing

That cocaine is seen as an avenue of possibility in Bissau testifies to the difficult economic and political situation in the country. Africa is rising, it is currently popular to claim. Yet when seen from Bissau, Africa is not so much rising as *polarizing*, with some regions and social groups becoming increasingly well-off while others continue to suffer hardship and poverty. Certainly, after decades of slow growth and all too frequent downturns, the more resource-rich areas have finally picked up economic speed. With six countries among the world's ten fastest growing economies, the continent is seen to be financially progressing at an unprecedented rate (World Bank 2014). However, the high growth rates do not tell us much about poverty as lived or about the distribution of resources and capital. The dictum takes for granted an extremely low point of departure and is implicitly amplified through contrast to the recession in the United States and Europe.

For those unlucky to be born into societies without the natural resources of the so-called lion economies on the rise, progress, wealth, and growth remain as elusive, distant, and inaccessible as ever. People in Bissau keenly follow the news and debate international developments. They are aware that the economy is picking up in parts of the continent, but they remain skeptical that this trend will have a positive effect on Guinea-Bissau, a country so economically and geopolitically marginal that many locals see it as having been abandoned by the rest of the world. Though it is not in vogue to be an Afro-pessimist, the local skepticism in Bissau makes sense. Rather than presume the economic blessings of trickle-down and knock-on effects, we can challenge the idea of Africa rising by looking at the distribution of wealth in Guinea-Bissau,[3] approaching inequality as a political rather than natural state of affairs. When we do so, we see a country where 87 percent of the population commonly goes hungry, where insecurity is perceived as chronic, and where people experience their lives as persistently difficult at the same time that the country's elite flaunt their wealth and amass fortunes in overseas bank accounts (Shepherd et al. 2014). Although the current government promises to change things for the better, many of the Guinea-Bissauans I talk to do not see their country as a place on the rise but as one caught in a position of poverty, instability, and unbridgeable inequality.

For my interlocutors, the absence of socioeconomic development translates into social vulnerability. Former avenues of mobility and subsistence provided by patrimonial networks, development aid, and remnants of the state have dried up during the last decade of conflict and decline, making positive social movement increasingly difficult (cf. Ferguson 1999; Simone and Abouhani 2005). Patrimonialism defines a sociopolitical configuration in which less-resourceful people commit themselves to a patron to secure access to a flow of resources and power as well as to protection and provision in times of need, offering social and political loyalty and support in return (Eisenstadt 1964; see also Balandier 1970; Bradbury 1969; Eisenstadt and Roninger 1981; Gellner and Waterbury 1977). Yet, currently in Bissau, the networks—kin or patrimonial—that formerly channeled resources between generations have contracted, cutting off the majority of young men and blocking sociogenerational mobility.

Without land to farm or traditional livelihoods at hand, many find themselves dependent on the economic life of the city to generate an income, yet in the current situation of *fallencia*, as generalized insolvency is called in Creole, they are left waiting for an economic improvement that remains distant.

Existential Occlusion

The consequences of decline and polarization are gendered and generational. They affect different social groups in different ways. One result of the above-mentioned processes has been that an extraordinarily large part of Guinea-Bissau's male population, the unconnected and disenfranchised, are caught in a situation of increasing marginality (see Vigh 2006a, 2008; see also Cole 2004; Jensen 2008; Mains 2007; Richards 1996; Utas 2003). Since young men are ideally supposed to be able to fend for themselves, they are often the first to be cut off from patrimonial networks. The resulting lack of resources makes it impossible for them to set up a household, marry, and provide for female relatives, wives, and girlfriends, thus keeping them trapped in the category of youth, that is, those without dependents. Indeed, many of the young men I talk to in Bissau have been stuck in the "social moratorium of youth" for years (Vigh 2006a) and persistently struggle to position themselves positively in social and generational terms.

As in many other cities on the continent, these young men often live the predicament of generational stuckness by hanging out on street corners and squares. Unemployed, they often meet in groups called *collegasons*, where they spend their time chatting, discussing, or just registering the movement of the city that flows by them. *Collegasons* are spaces of solidarity and sociality, full of talk, intrigue, and interpretations of fleeting events and more enduring conditions of life. Yet they are equally spaces of inertia, where hanging out is taken to its literal extreme, as the men slump back in chairs and on low walls in what looks like an intensely lethargic mode of being. The apparent inactivity is, however, involuntary, and the endless relaxation is understood as a sign of existential occlusion (Vigh 2006a; Masquelier 2013). "We have blocked lives (*vida parado*)" or "stagnated lives (*vida stagnado*)," people say when commenting on their "timepass" (see also Jeffrey 2010). The apparent state of ease cloaks the anxiety caused by their inability to meet social norms and expectations.

"I am someone good, I am not someone bad," Bernardinho told me as he was trying to convince me that his social failings were not ascribable to him personally but to the situation at hand. His description of himself as basically "good" addresses the negative stereotype he faces as somebody who not only is finding it difficult to survive but also is unable to constitute himself as a positive participant in the social environment. Another young man, Seku, similarly spoke of what it takes to overcome such stereotyping.

Henrik: What do you have to do to be a respectable man [*homi di respeito*]?
Seku: You must work hard [*pega teso*] so that you can help your family. If you do not help your wife, your children, your mother, people will not respect you. They will say that you have no worth [*ka bali*], that you are a just young.

227

The result of being unable to meet the gendered obligations placed on you is, as Seku points out, an experience of social insubstantiality. The gendered and generational position of being an *homi di respeito*, a respected and "proper" man, is out of reach for my informants as it is defined by the exact capacity that they lack. "If you do not help your family you are nothing," Abdulai told me, as he was explaining the various ways one was expected to provide for one's kin in terms of food, medicine, and clothes (Kea, this volume) and the nullification that haunts men who are unable to do so.

Money for the Market: Being Marginal in the Economy of Affection

The obligation to give is equally important with respect to intimate relationships. Romance is, for example, maintained and communicated via *dinhiero par ferra* (money for the market), a nondescript amount given to a woman after sex. This is not to be confused with payment, which would mark the act as one of prostitution and terminate the relationship. Rather, *dinhiero par ferra* is reciprocal, an exchange that serves to consolidate and continue the connection. Thus, *dinhiero par ferra* does not just point our attention to the transactional nature of sex in Bissau but more generally to the fact that a man's social standing is partly related to his ability to provide, intimately or in terms of patronage (see also Abbink 2005; Hoffman 2006; Hultin 2010). Young men fear their inability to give because it is seen a relational failing, just as giving too little draws ridicule. In general, the inability to provide not only positions a man as poor, *um algin pobre*, but also consigns him to the belittling position of "boy" or "youth," reducing him to a state of juniority (Vigh 2006a). It may also cause him to be stigmatized as someone who is *riso mon* (hard handed): penny pinching and unwilling to share. All of these terms indicate social incapacity. As Bernardinho told me, directly addressing the gendered dimensions of the social obligation to meet expectations of provision:

If she needs a thing, where will he [her boyfriend] see [get] it? If you do not give her, where will she see it? It is the same with marriage. That is why marriage has nearly stopped in Africa. You can know a woman ten years, but you will never have enough money to marry her. To be a respectable man, you need to marry. If you are not married, you will not have respect in society. It is the same thing with work. If you have work, you can organize your life, you can get married, and afterwards you can start a family. But only someone who knows you. Only someone who knows you will give you a job. These days, young people are frustrated. It is this that makes young people want to leave, so you can have a level of life. You go there [abroad] and then you can send money to your family. But it is sad, because you are far from each other. It is difficult. Africans have difficult lives.

Difficulty in marrying, due to their inability to pay bride price and/or support a wife, remains a common complaint among young men, one that reflects how closely tied relational being and worth are to the nature of one's engagement in "the economy of affection." Achieving adulthood and becoming a respected man is directly related to being able to engage constructively in this economy of "support, communication and interaction among structurally defined groups connected by blood, kin, community or other affinities," as Göran Hydén (1983, 8; see also Hydén 1980) has classically defined the concept. While the economy of affection may thus offer a view into the way resources filter through intimate social relations, clarifying the social and emotive embeddedness of economic aspirations and illuminating how resources are affectively bound, it involves more than a redistribution of resources along lines of solidarity, intimacy, and care. It is tied, as Bernardhino makes clear in the above quotation, to gendered and generational expectations and obligations. The youth I talk to have to be able to engage positively in affective circuits vis-à-vis women as well as family members and peers to attain manhood and adulthood (cf. Fesenmyer, this volume). Yet the desire to become a positive presence in an affective circuit also reveals these young men's vulnerability. The weight of the expectations placed on them and their incapacity to deliver patronage clarify the frailty of the masculine position as everyday life becomes a reminder of their impotence (Cohen-Mor 2013, 173).

Walking between Stoves: Nullification and the Struggle for Being

"I walk between stoves [fugon]," Amadu said, as he explained how he survives on a daily basis in Bissau. Walking between stoves is Amadu's way of trying to spread out the burden of his presence. To avoid being too much of a drain on any single household, he moves between his father's, aunts', uncles', and sisters' houses asking for handouts. "Even if you do not want to, you must beg for food [pidi semoula]. You feel shame, but you have to," he said. So although many young men are excluded from the affective

economy of romance and stable relationships, they are still able to survive through affective ties to kin and experience scattered social affiliation by walking between stoves. Despite its connotations of solidarity and
sociability, the economy of affection may, however, pack a nasty social
punch. For young men, being unable to meet expectations and obligations generates an everyday punctuated by nullification, an experience
of being reduced to a body without worth, one characterized by its social
"hollowness" (see also Berman 2006, 20). Nullification is, in this perspective, not to be understood philosophically as an analytical reduction, a
bracketing out of the actual world to arrive at the phenomenological (see
also Husserl [1913] 2012), but rather as an experience of being or becoming socially unsubstantiated. The bracketing out of social expectations is
akin to a neglect of gendered obligations and a suspension of one's social
potential. Being stuck in a situation in which one is dependent on handouts and donations to make it through the day produces a sense of social
insufficiency expressed in ideas of being a "nobody" (*ninguin*), "nothing"
(*ka nada*), and of "no worth" (*ki ka bali*) (cf. Jackson 2002; Mains 2007).

As a person who ought ideally to be able to contribute to the *fugon*
rather than merely feed off it, Amadu encounters his lack of status in
the very practicalities of surviving. When young men in Bissau are asked
about their imagined futures and what they envisage themselves becoming, their answers often start, as examples above show, with a default
"somebody" (*um algin*), a concept that, in all its vagueness, refers merely
to being a valued part of the social body. When further clarifying what
"being somebody" may entail, people often use qualifying terms such as
good or *respected*, which define positive emplacement within a relational
landscape and what one is able to be for one's significant others, such as
mothers, daughters, girlfriends, and close peers. The point may be banal,
but it indicates the aspiration that guides my informants' actions and also
directs our attention to their current experience of being the polar opposite. "Who wants you when you are nothing," Seku asked me rhetorically,
an ironic comment on the endless boasting and description of amorous
adventures that characterized the conversation among the group of young
men we hung out with. The life situations of the young men I talk to in
Bissau often imbue them with a sense of depletion, as their marginality
defines them as socially insubstantial, positioning them as people "whose
words and actions have no place in the life of the collectivity" (Jackson
2012, 174).

It comes as no surprise that these young men attempt to escape their
predicament and move into spaces of possibility from which they may

further their lives in constructive ways. People do not always pilot their lives toward a clearly defined beacon and may not always have a clear idea of where they are going, yet most will probably have very clear ideas of what they wish to escape or avoid. The youth I talk to remain attentive to any change that may allow them to transcend their sociogenerational impasse. I have, in my earlier work, focused on how civil war provided people with exactly such a possibility, as it opened up otherwise closed networks and political structures and enabled them to navigate interpersonal connections and events (Vigh 2006a; cf. Groes-Green 2010, 387). Similarly, today, as conflict has given way to an anxious and insecure period of peace, the intersection between migration and the business of cocaine has replaced military mobilization as an imagined catalyst for momentum and escape for the destitute.

Cocaine as Catalyst

The cocaine connection surfaced in Guinea-Bissau in 2005 as President Nino Vieira returned to office after having been ousted five years earlier. Stepping back into office, Vieira did not seek to rebuild the ruined country. Rather, he sold the services of the state apparatus to Colombian, Bolivian, and Peruvian cocaine cartels to fill his private coffers (Vigh 2012, 2014). As the primary means of payment within the cocaine industry is, unsurprisingly, cocaine, services provided to the cartels to facilitate the large-scale movement of drugs in Bissau are paid in drugs rather than money. In other words, though Guinea-Bissau is merely a transit point in the transcontinental movement of cocaine, not all the cocaine that enters the country leaves it again immediately. The large shipments of cocaine that have been intercepted moving out of Bissau are not controlled by Guineans but belong to the cartels as goods en route. Conversely, the many smaller amounts of cocaine intercepted as mules seek to traffic them through air- and seaports most probably belong to Guinea-Bissauan networks trying to move the rewards gained from working for the cartels into areas where cocaine can actually make a proper profit, because people are too poor to pay for it in Bissau. The large-scale flows of cocaine, then, create smaller secondary flows that travel through local networks and diasporas, as the illicit good moves through a dispersed and complex web of connections, routes, and points of distribution.

If we look more specifically at the movement of cocaine through local connections, we see that it trickles through patrimonial networks in much the same way that resources generally move from "big men" (*homi garandis*) to clients. Cocaine needs to be safeguarded, moved, distributed, and sold—and in doing so, *homi garandis* actualize and reinforce patron-client relationships by providing promises, possibilities, money, or cocaine in return for services. The cocaine trade, then, seems currently to be strengthening existing patrimonial networks in the city by supplying an input of goods into social arrangements that are otherwise running low on resources. Following the distribution of gains from the trade a step further, we see that those that flow to young men are channeled into more intimate networks through affective ties.

Although the trade has caused alarm in the United Nations and various international law enforcement agencies, the people I spend my time with in Bissau regard it with optimism, as a potential avenue to well-being, mobility, and provision (cf. Stoller 2002). As Eliseu explained, the growing cocaine trade in Bissau holds out potentially positive prospects.

Eliseu: People thought that it [the situation in Bissau] would get better. All of us we thought that it would get better, but nothing. Now, if God want, it will rise a bit.
Henrik: What is going to rise?
Eliseu: Since the big man [Nino Vieira] came back, it will rise. Only he can build Bissau.
Henrik: How will he do that? What will he do?
Eliseu: If he puts this thing of cocaine [*ki kussa di cocaina*] . . . if he puts it to use in building the country, we can rise. He can build the land. People think, "This big man he will help people. He will help us. If you do not have, he will give you. Us, we look up to him, so he will help us. If you need a job, he will give you. Even if you want to go abroad, it is possible." You say, "I want to get a job so that I can go abroad," and maybe you see it.

The cocaine trade, as I note above, has not alleviated local poverty but merely led Bissau to become ever more polarized. It has ensured a steady flow of income into the primary positions of the patrimonial networks that make up the political structures in the city. The revenue from the trade primarily stays within the overseas bank accounts of the country's tiny elite. Nevertheless, the cocaine trade has made a few people remarkably wealthy, which has had an interesting effect on the group of people I research. While the trade has not delivered much in the way of actual capital for ordinary people, it creates prospects and energizes imaginaries of better lives (see also Kleinman, this volume). It offers the promise of positive affective emplacement.

"All of those who are building houses. You see them? If you [also] see a brutally big car, then you know that this one went and found his money there [in the cocaine business]," Dario told me. While decay and deterioration generally characterize Bissau's buildings, newly built haciendas have begun to dot the landscape, boldly embodying the profits of the illegal trade. Living in a small annex stuck onto his mother's worndown adobe house, Dario was merely a spectator to the rapid emergence of wealth. In his thirties, he longed to live somewhere other than the shanty-like shelter. For Dario, the new cars being imported and houses being built were not just displays of material wealth but of a move into social being as people became pivotal within social networks and economies of affection. Dario's envy, like that of most people who contrasted their own poverty with the newly found wealth of others, was social as much as material.

Roads and Trampolines

The fact that young men believe that cocaine may enable migration is not completely illusory. As the risks and difficulty of undocumented migration become increasingly clear, including the physical dangers and the loss of lives, people search for alternatives. The ease with which one can potentially move up or on in life by navigating the cocaine trade may be overstated, but, as it has for a limited number of people I know, it does, at times, actually result in a ticket out of Bissau, a fact that consequently spurs a potent mix of information and rumors. Similarly, in local and international news, an array of stories about organized drug trafficking mix truth and fiction, an extreme example being a story about a flight to Amsterdam in December 2006 carrying thirty-two cocaine mules (Vulliamy 2008). Many rumors involving mules are clearly sensationalist, yet couriers are used as is "shotgun" trafficking in which groups of mules are dispatched (Brombacher and Maihold 2009; Hanson 2007; Shaw 2015). These stories have given cocaine an almost mythical status as a purveyor of livelihoods and movement, physical or social. It is seen to embody a chance of obtaining travel documents, airfare, and income that is otherwise inaccessible for most young men in the city. In Iko's words,

Now there is cocaine, everything is possible, everything. If you have cocaine, you bring it to Europe, and you will be rich, rich. You do not even need a lot. Here you can buy a kilo of cocaine for 17,000 euro, 9,000, 8,000. You bring it to Spain, and you see a lot [of money], really, a lot.

Denilson, meanwhile, describes the work of mules, *engulidurs*, who carry cocaine to Europe in more realistic terms:

When this thing of cocaine started to come, many people went to Europe. You swallow [*enguli*] it, you see, and when you come to Europe, you go to the toilet [*laughs*]. If you are lucky, they give you a ticket, passport, and send you to Dakar, then you take the plane again from there.

Denilson generally spoke of cocaine and the possibilities it afforded in pragmatic and factual ways. Indeed, in Guinea-Bissau the trade, and the involvement of senior military and political figures, is broadly accepted and perceived as means to an end: an opportunity rather than an illegality. Cocaine, in other words, stands out as a substance imbued with social potentiality, a tool in the struggle to gain positive presence within affective circuits.

Kadakin na busca si caminho (everyone is looking for his road), people will often say when talking about attempts to smuggle cocaine into Europe. The word *caminho*, "road," in itself indicates a practical rather than a normative evaluation. The road is a metaphor for imaginable connections and trajectories. It implies an opening or possible line of flight out of a difficult situation and, thus, indicates directionality or opportunity. The idea of the road is often paired with the concept of the *trampoline di vida*, life's trampoline, referring to points or positions from which one can gain momentum, that is, pick up the speed necessary to move socially and/or physically. Taken together, the two concepts refer to the direction and momentum needed to escape the negative circumstances that define the present. Denilson spoke about drug trafficking as one *trampoline di vida*.

Denilson: In Bissau there is good weather, women, everything is *fixe* [good], [it is] just that there is no work. If there were work, then everyone would stay here. No one would go anywhere. . . .
Henrik: Where do people go?
Denilson: Mandjakos go to France. Fula, Mandinga go to Spain. They do not have a future here. If you do not have money, who is going to help you? Most young people here wash cars. I wash cars sometimes—I am 36, but I wash cars too. In the beginning you do till seventh [grade], but then you just sit till you get tired, if you do not have someone to bring you. Here there are only two trampoline of life [*trampolina di vida*]. The first trampoline is the drugs thing [*kussa di droga*]. The second trampoline is sports, you see.

Likewise, Kio told me, "This cocaine is just a life trampoline, just a life trampoline." In fact, he said, "it is the biggest trampoline there is [*ki la i trampolina mas garandi ki ten*]. If you know someone who trusts you, you can see a ticket and all [*bu na odja billhete e tudo*]." Because of their difficult social situation, their experience of nullification, and their stigmatization for burdening the affective circuits to which they are expected to contribute, young men value the trade for the chance it gives them to turn latent personhood into recognized being.

To gain value within affective circuits and, thus, social being, young men, as Sarah Pink (2001, 103) so poetically phrases it, "strive to attain what is most treasured in Bissau, namely absence: the empty space left by migration." Cocaine currently provides both the *caminho* and *trampolina* that enable people to achieve this metastate of absent presence. Roads and trampolines do not just refer to physical movement out of Bissau. Rather, they also refer to movement into social place in Bissau through the status acquired by being able to support kin and friends via remittances (see Adams 2003; Taylor 1999). Contrary to popular belief, people strive not merely to generate individual prosperity and attain status by displays of wealth but also to acquire the ability to sustain intimate others and gain worth through the distribution of goods and capital within affective circuits. The desire to migrate is in this respect anchored in a wish to be of value to others rather than in a quest for individual enrichment.

Life in Lisbon: In the Shadow of Deportability

Because of the large-scale involvement of the Guinea-Bissauan state apparatus and military in the cocaine trade, local, regional, and international actors seeking to combat international drug trafficking have intensified their surveillance of the country.[4] As a result, officials increasingly monitor movement in and out of Guinea-Bissau, and Guinea-Bissauans in Europe are increasingly policed. Consequently, the number of deportees returned to Bissau has surged; there are currently so many that they are spoken of as a social category in their own right. The possibility of losing one's newly found positive social emplacement by being forcibly removed and sent back has become a constant source of anxiety for those who have actually made it to Europe (Kleinman, this volume). The fear is of the social *déroute* that lies in being pulled back into a subaltern position and latent personhood. Deportation transforms hope of social becoming into fear of social *un*becoming. To be deported is to become *déclassé*, to experience free fall down the hierarchy of social value. Furthermore, as the deported migrant is often the sole—actual or potential—provider for a group of people, deportation can have dire consequences for the larger circuits in which he or she is involved.

Many Guinea-Bissauan migrants experience the threat of deportation as ever present. As the economic crisis has taken its toll in southern Europe and the level of unemployment has soared, jobs are becoming increasingly hard for irregular or undocumented migrants to find. In other words, not only does the cocaine trade provide a possibility for migration from Bissau but it also provides one of the few ways that Guinea-Bissauans can earn an income once they have migrated. For a few, migration is enabled by smuggling the drug into Europe; for many more, selling cocaine merely makes life abroad possible.

My interviews with Seku took place in a secluded part of Lisbon's Bairro Alto. This part of town quickly fills up in the evening and nights with tourists and students drinking in the bars that line the narrow streets. On the fringes of the area, groups of young, mainly Guinea-Bissauan and Cape Verdean men scan the streets for people partying in the area to whom they can sell pot and cocaine. The small groups of dealers, normally consisting of three to five associated individuals, define both a space of work and a meeting point. Most of the migrants in question live in difficult conditions, sharing small rooms and apartments with as many people as possible to minimize housing costs. Consequently, they spend most of their waking hours on the street.

Having done two periods of fieldwork with pushers in Bairro Alto over the last five years, I have come to know the area well, to enjoy hanging out with the Guinea-Bissauan youth that work there, and to appreciate their slightly sarcastic take on the hordes of drunk people that crowd the alleys. Though they take to the streets to work, the groups also share an element of solidarity and sociality. They may compete for sales, yet they also help each other out in various ways and keep a common eye out for police or danger. At times they feel much like the *collegasons* in Bissau, that is, the peer groups in which youth spend their time together. The internal banter is identical to that in Bissau, and the topics of conversation revolve around the same issues of economic opportunities, football, and romance—with the latter quickly drifting into more carnal areas of interest and endless boasting about individuals' sexual escapades and stamina. Despite its advantages, pushing cocaine is, of course, not what the majority of the people I talk to would do if given a choice. Most of the young men I have followed from Bissau to Lisbon and Paris dream of getting good jobs, gaining recognition and the ability to live a worthy life. Yet the current financial crisis is so severe that selling cocaine is understood as one of the few ways one can survive if not otherwise employed and perhaps even be able to send the occasional remittance home.

"It was the only job I could get," Seku told me as I tried to interview him while he was working hard to sell a few grams of cocaine. In an almost neo-Clausewitzian mode, the trade is seen as a "continuation of business by other means" (Williams 2002, 164). Paul Stoller (2002, xi) describes much the same pragmatic ethic among West African traders he worked with in New York: "We are here in America, trying to make a living," an informant told him; "we have to do this to look after our families. Money has no smell." Similarly, Seku was struggling to make money to send back remittances to his mother in Bissau. "If you are in Europe, everyone who knows you in Bissau will ask you for money," he said. "All the time people call me to ask me, 'Do you know what I want?' They think that if you are in Europe you have made it [saffa], but it is not easy here." Seku would send money to his mother and sister and politely decline the invitation to sponsor most others (Cole, this volume). "I do not put money in his mouth," he remarked, complaining about a distant relative who asked him for help, ending his protest by stating, "Everyone is your cousin." Playing the kinship card when asking for money is of course a way of emphasizing the obligation to give when it comes to who merits help. For those who inhabit the lower echelons of patrimonial networks, relatedness is a major claim on entitlement, yet in a country where cousinhood is not necessarily defined in close family terms but is used to refer to anyone within the same generation from one's kin group, the category can be stretched or contracted as needed—reflecting the flexibility of "parakinship," as Newell terms it (this volume).

Both the distant relative's request and Seku's refusal illuminate the boundaries of the affective economy in question. To acquire positive being, one has to provide a minimum level of support to close female relatives or one's children. The presence made possible by one's absence as a migrant—that is, the social being that one gains in Bissau by being abroad, is constituted by the recognition and respect that comes from having the potential to participate in affective circuits. Even if currently unable to send remittances, migrants talk about their potentiality granting them positive emplacement. Remittances do not just make the recipient happy but equally the giver, as giving generates the eudaemonic contentment of actualizing one's potential and feeling a sense of fulfillment (see also Keyes, Shmotkin, and Ryff 2002; Cole, this volume). The very happiness and relief conveyed in the act illuminate both the obligation and the desire evoked by the affective relations and dynamics at play.

"If you send money home, people say that you are someone serious, that you are someone good," Salifou explained to me. "I have a child in Bissau," he continued; "If I do not send money, he will suffer." For Salifou, pushing coke was, thus, a responsibility. With no other work to be found, he was obliged to do what he could. "I don't force anyone to buy it," Americano said while plying his trade in an alleyway. "I don't put my hand in your pocket, I don't steal, I don't hurt people," he continued, explaining to me that selling cocaine was merely another form of "commerce" (*commercio so*). Equally, Latino, another Bissauan pusher, characterized his line of work by saying, "Go over there (points to a bar) and you can buy beer, go over there and you can buy cigarettes; here you can buy cocaine." In Latino's opinion he was working within the boundaries of the existing order rather than outside it.

The problem, of course, is that the governments of the countries my informants have made their way into do not share their pragmatic attitude toward drugs or toward undocumented migration. As a result, when the Portuguese or French police catch someone selling narcotics, they usually imprison and/or deport them. When I asked him what happens if the Portuguese authorities catch undocumented migrants, Americano outlined the possibilities.

Americano: It depends. They can take you or they let you be.

Henrik: If they take you?

Americano: They take you. You are there—and they ask you questions: "You are from where, you live where, what do you do?" They beat you, they hit you [*dau ku*] with the fist [*suko*], or they slap [*bofado*]. They are bad. It is like this.

Henrik: So they let you go?

Americano: Depends. If you did not do anything, they beat you. But if they catch you, if you are selling things and they catch you, you end up with problems, they deport you. If you go to jail, you will be deported.

Being caught without papers usually lands one in detention while the authorities check the person's identity. It may also lead to being roughed up. But it normally means being released again a few hours or days later. Being caught with cocaine and the intent to distribute usually means going to jail and being deported.

Despite the difficulty of surviving in Lisbon and the constant pressure of the institutional state apparatus weighing on them, my informants speak about deportation as a tragedy. "No one wants to regress" (*ninguin ka misti regressa*), Pape said to me as we were talking about the threat of being sent back home. We were drinking beers in a small café in the outskirts of Reboleira, a suburb of Lisbon, which houses large numbers of Guinea-Bissauan migrants. The café is close to the *baraccas*, a shanty-like area on the boundary of the neighborhood consisting of a mix of derelict and makeshift houses and dwellings, parts of which recall the *bairros* of Bissau in terms of poverty and dilapidation. Much of our conversation that afternoon had focused on the hardship that accompanied migration, on racism, crisis, the struggle to send back remittances, and the lack of possibilities that characterized migrant men's everyday lives. Given the poverty of the *barracas* and the difficulty that pervades men's lives in Portugal, the idea of being sent back home as "regression" was slightly ironic. However, though deportation appears to make little difference in terms of one's immediate well-being, it hurts one's social possibilities and position. Being deported distances one from the eventuality of gaining an income and hence from the ability to contribute to affective circuits. In other words, while the lives of young Guinea-Bissauan pushers may resemble the lives they lived in Bissau in terms of their marginality, they differ in terms of their potentiality and how the men figure in the affective circuits in which they are entangled.

Coming Back with Nothing

The stigma of deportation indexes the centrality of affective circuits to my informants' lives and well-being. These migrants may live lives at a material minimum, constantly shadowed by "a palpable sense of deportability" (De Genova 2002, 439). Still, they see life in Lisbon as preferable to life in Bissau because it holds out the possibility that they can earn enough to be able to help their families and meet their social obligations.

Having followed my informants into Europe since 2005, I am currently following them as they are deported back to Guinea-Bissau. The number of people who are forcefully removed, often because they are caught selling cocaine, has grown rapidly to the point that deportation is seen as a common negative outcome of migratory endeavors. Denilson was one of many *deportados* in Bissau. I interviewed him a couple of months after he had been sent back, and he described a process of migration and deportation that was similar to many other such histories that I was to hear.

I took the plane directly to London. I took a big risk. I went with someone else's passport. He was black, so I just went and I managed, it was another black. God helped me [to have a] life in London. . . . I had money but I did not have documents. I went with someone else's passport, but he is black like me. In England I sold cocaine.

I sold so much cocaine and ecstasy. I had many good customers. If you called me in the night, I would get on my bike and go . . . and one gram [*ngalla*], two grams. No problem. In England there is a lot of cocaine. I was caught. I had cocaine and I had CS-gas in my pocket. They caught me and sent me straight to prison, and I came back to Bissau.

Most deportees I spoke with report being caught with cocaine. As Garandi pointed out,

If they catch you and you have cocaine, then that is certain deportation [*deportason certo*]. You go to the court, and they put you on an airplane. Afterwards you will be in Bissau without anything. You go to build a palace [*kompu paliçio*; build a house back home], and you come back with nothing.

"Coming back with nothing" is deeply stigmatizing, perceived as a sign of having failed to make it despite having been given every advantage in life (Groes, this volume). As Dario told me, "A lot of the deported, they are ashamed. Everyone who migrates wants to come home with a good life. People will say [if someone is deported], 'This one left but came back with nothing.'"

Although both Garandi and Denilson appear somewhat blasé about their deportation, they are in fact struggling to find the money or opportunity that will enable them to leave again. The act of deportation is considered both regressive and embarrassing because it usually means losing the ability to contribute positively to one's affective circuits, and thus it produces an even sharper sense of nullification. Coming back to Bissau is acceptable only if it does not prevent one from providing for others. The stigma that accompanies deportation leads most who are forcibly returned to hide their status. As one recent deportee remarked,

If you are deported, you will tell people, "No, I just came for holidays," or you will say, "No, I came doing business." You say, "I came to look for papers . . . things of the family," but after a while, if you are still here, people will know you are deported. Buba [a friend], he tells people, no [I'm not]! But people know, everyone knows.

The successful pusher or trafficker who is able to send back remittances is seen as a valuable social figure and a resource for his social network in Bissau. The migrant who has been deported, however, is seen as failure and a social burden. The shadow side of the cocaine trade, deportation stands as a fracturing of possibility and a negative social repositioning.

I have known André since I first came to Bissau in 2000. Initially a poor militiaman, he was well connected to key people in ex-president Nino Vieira's network and eventually became a leading figure among a group of inner-city youth. After Vieira's loss in the civil war in 1999, André worked his way into becoming a small patron—a little big man—in his own right, and in 2006 he had managed to amass a kilo of cocaine, *um cabeza*—"a head" as it is called in Creole—by providing services to people higher up in the cocaine trade (see Vigh 2009, 2012). For André the kilo provided a chance of getting out of Bissau. Realizing the potential worth of his cocaine by selling it in Europe would allow him to realize his own potential social worth in Bissau by becoming a pivotal figure in his neighborhood. André boarded a plane with a couple of other men, seeking to smuggle his cocaine into Portugal. Despite his attempts to protect himself, he was caught going through customs and sentenced to jail for a handful of years, of which he served only a few before being deported.

I tried to see him in Lisbon while he was in jail, but he refused to talk to me. When I managed to find him again in Bissau in 2010, he was welcoming but appeared a shadow of his former self. Hanging out with him and the group of people for whom he used to be a minor patron, I was clearly aware that the social standing he had previously enjoyed had all but disappeared. "I am trying to get documents," he told me. "That is the only thing you can do," he reiterated, "just to get new documents." As new identities and personal documents can be bought in Bissau by bribing government officials, he was starting from scratch, literally with a new birth certificate. In many ways, the remaking of his identity through documents is analogous to the way he also had to remake his social position. André's position as a deportee made him a figure of ridicule rather than respect.

Though André's situation was undesirable, he actually managed better than most of the other deportees I have reconnected with in Bissau. Being back in Bissau, he had to live among the ruins of the life he had sought to escape. His way of doing so, however, was by trying to rebuild, which held out some hope. For others it is clear that the estrangement involved in having to reinhabit the remnants of a position they thought they had escaped can be far more destructive.

I first met Justinho in 2000. He was a skinny young man who was constantly sick with a nasty cough. "He has the prostitute's disease" (*douenza di putas*, i.e., AIDS), people said of him then. When I remet him ten years later, he was as frail as when I last saw him, but he was also psychologically troubled and unsettled. During the years between our encounters, we had both traveled to Europe and back again. As we spoke about the last ten years, he conveyed a story of migration and deportation. Eyes lowered, he spoke in a low voice and short sentences.

Justinho: The police took me. I had cocaine and I was caught. It is like this.

Henrik: After [that] what happened?

Justinho: I went to the courtroom and I went to Bissau.

Henrik: What happened?

Justinho: I was cursed. Things from the earth, you know, Africans are powerful. I was
cursed and I did not know what was happening. I did not sleep, nothing. They
gave me medicine and put me on the plane. I did not know what was happening.
When I came to Bissau my friend took me to the church of the Nigerians [Pente-
costal church].

The story of bad luck due to curses and envy runs through a number of the
interviews I conducted as does the sense of estrangement and loss of one's
orientation upon returning home. These points were perhaps most clearly
stated in my interview with a deportee named Tó.

They put me in jail. They caught me and sent me to jail. I was there two years, three
years, and I said, "Send me back, this is no good." When I came back . . . I did not
want to go out. In the evening it was too dark. I was scared. When I ask for people
of my generation, half of them have died. The other half live in Europe. Half of them
have died. Look at this. We live in shit. The place is dirty; people's toilets, rubbish
everywhere, virus, bacteria. I am scared of living here, honestly, I am scared. Hepati-
tis, bacteria. People die, and then when people die they call it things from the earth,
things from the spirits [kussa di iran, problema di terra], and then they start buying
things to make it better for the spirits [iran], but they just make it worse for themselves. Sometimes I smoke to control my nerves. I get nervous. This place it makes
you angry, you understand.

Tó's statement expresses doubt and despair. He communicates an experience of uncertainty in terms of both the causes and the effects of his
misfortune. He also conveys an experience of estrangement crippling in
its magnitude. For Tó, deportation means having become a foreigner in
his own home. Though geographically he has returned home, he experiences a sense of exile. The estrangement that runs through his narrative
does not correspond to the time he was away but rather to the loss of place
created by his forced return. Being deported was an experience of displacement, an act of involuntary mobility with negative social, economic, and
existential implications. Paradoxically, he is exiled at home, socially and
economically uprooted by losing his place within his affective circuits.

Conclusion: Life's Trampoline

This chapter has looked at how young men in Bissau seek to gain better lives for themselves and their families by engaging in the cocaine trade from West Africa into Europe. It has focused on the way masculinity is performed in a field of affection, obligation, and expectation, dwelling on how this context affects the lives of young urban men. Although the story told is perhaps an unusual one, and Bissau a singular case, the social position of the young men I describe illuminates more general issues. Similar to other West African areas that are troubled by prolonged conflict and economic decline, Bissau has become a space of social and existential suffering for many of the city's young men. Many young men in the subregion and beyond are caught in situations in which they are unable to meet social expectations and provide for their families, girlfriends, and friends. Circumstances force them into a position that makes it all but impossible for them to contribute to the social networks and relations that they are emotively bound to. The result of this affective short-circuiting is, I have argued, an experience of social truncation that demonstrates the fragility of the masculine position. Unable to contribute and participate meaningfully in relational flows and affective economies leads these men to feel worthless.

Migration currently stands as the primary antidote to the increasing marginality that many youth suffer. Being abroad grants young men social presence at home. It offers them a way to realize their potential and reposition themselves within affective circuits. From this perspective, migration to Europe does not constitute an end in itself. Rather, it enables young men to gain social worth and value in Bissau and to engage positively in the affective circuits to which they are tied. The illegality of the cocaine trade weighs heavily on these young men's efforts to migrate, as they constantly face the risk and shame that comes with deportation. Although a few lucky ones make it and become big men after retiring from the drug trade, enabling them to be respected family members, husbands, and patrons in Bissau, the great majority are lost in the constant limbo they call "life's trampoline."

Notes

1. Guinea-Bissau's cocaine connection initially drew the attention of antidrug agencies in 2005, and it soon became clear that the small country had

developed into a major drug hub. According to the United Nations Office on Drugs and Crime (UNODC), the value of the drug in Bissau is currently higher than the country's GNP. For an economy in which 80 percent of the official revenue comes from development assistance, however, this probably does not say much. Yet the point is that the cocaine business and the flow of money it feeds into the country have become primary sources of income for groups such as the police, the military, and the navy, who have otherwise been paid irregularly, if at all, and have routinely fed off the country's population.

2. The chapter builds on ethnographic fieldwork conducted between 2000 and 2014.

3. A political rather than spatial perspective. Most of the world's poor do not live in the world's poorest countries, which in itself challenges the taken-for-granted notion of the trickle-down effect in terms of global development (https://www.ids.ac.uk/files/dmfile/AndySumnerGlobalPoverty14May2012 .pdf).

4. They include Interpol, Europol, and the U.S. Drug Enforcement Administration.

TEN

From Little Brother to Big Somebody: Coming of Age at the Gare du Nord

JULIE KLEINMAN

I met Lassana Niaré in September 2009 outside the main entrance of the Gare du Nord railway station in Paris.[1] He ambled over to me and asked for a cigarette. His hair was in cornrows, and he was wearing a hoodie, low-slung jeans, and a backward-pointing Yankees cap. He was not a habitual smoker, but asking for a smoke was a technique he and the West African friends he met at the station each day after work used to start conversations with women. Like many of his comrades at the station, Lassana differentiated himself through his hairstyle and fashion from other West African immigrants, who preferred close-cropped hair and simple, conservative dress. His dress and actions displeased his father and many of his kin in both West Africa and in France, who associated these styles with "hoodlums" who had veered from the path of their strict Muslim upbringing. Lassana's uncle claimed that the station was a place frequented by "delinquents, drug dealers, and junkies." Many West African migrants I spoke to who lived in immigrant dormitories (*foyers*) were suspicious of their compatriots who spent time there.

At first glance it is tempting to interpret Lassana's time at the Gare du Nord in terms of a familiar narrative of cultural loss and assimilation. According to this interpretation, young people who migrate abandon the values and practices derived from their cultures of origin as they are drawn into the modern ways associated with their new home. Indeed, to look at him, one might easily think that Lassana had stepped outside his community to embrace French urban modernity and the cultural styles of global hip-hop (cf. Friedman 1994, 147–66; Newell 2012, this volume). Such an interpretation, however, would be misleading. Far from forsaking his kin and renouncing his belonging in the Soninke community, Lassana remained within the circuits of obligation and exchange that have helped reproduce this society of "willing migrants" across long distances (see Manchuelle 1997). As his family expected, Lassana remitted money home and participated in monthly village council meetings. He took a half day off from work at his construction job on Fridays to pray at the mosque, have lunch at an immigrant dormitory, and visit his relatives in the suburbs of Paris.

How are we to understand the apparent tension between Lassana's sartorial style, his time at the Gare du Nord, and his adherence to what can be clearly seen as traditional commitments? Unlike places where migration appears to disrupt everything from child-rearing to village hierarchies, Lassana and his peers come from West African, Mande-speaking communities in which, as Isaie Dougnon (2013, 40) puts it, "not migrating is not living." That is, migration is synonymous with social reproduction and a key aspect of how men come of age (see also Jónsson 2012; Manchuelle 1997). Becoming a marriageable man means undertaking an initiatory journey during which the migrant is supposed to accumulate wealth before returning home to marry and settle in the village. Lassana and his peers, like many francophone West Africans, refer to this journey in French as *partir en aventure* (to leave on an adventure) and to themselves as *aventuriers* (adventurers), a term that encompasses the idea that emigration is a rite of passage in which one becomes a stranger in a foreign wilderness (cf. Barou 2002; Bredeloup 2014; Canut 2014; Dougnon 2013). In Lassana's native Soninke (as well as in other Mande languages), the space of this journey is called the *tunga*, which translates as a foreign space or a "space of exile" (Whitehouse 2012, 88). The adventurer is *gounikè*, or "the man of vast wilderness" (Dougnon 2013, 40). The phase of adventure is both connected to and outside lineage and social norms, a structural characteristic shared with other "liminal" periods (Turner 1969; van Gennep 1960).[2] Ultimately, through marriage and reinstallation in the village, the adventurer is supposed to convert the wealth he has acquired through this short-term liminal phase into the reproduction of his family.

The ways in which West African men come of age through migration have shifted over time. Before the mid-twentieth century, few migrants went to Europe, and they most frequently returned to their villages. Lassana's father's adventure took him to Senegal to cultivate groundnuts for five years, though he returned to the village during most dry seasons.[3] In the mid-twentieth century, migration destinations began to shift from rural cultivation zones toward urban centers within Africa, and seasonal migration gave way to sojourns lasting several years (Manchuelle 1997). During this time, young men from the Senegal River Valley also began going to France, where they worked on temporary labor contracts and where, until 1974, they did not need special visas or work permits.[4] They lived in dormitories subsidized by the French government, where they often re-created Soninke communities in the French urban environment (Timera 1996).[5] Having amassed wealth in France, they usually returned to their villages in Mali to marry and settle down. At least ideally, the liminal period of young adulthood, the adventure phase, and short-term exchange cycles were to coincide. They were also supposed to be temporary, ultimately transcended when the migrant returned home.

Like his father before him, Lassana too set off on his adventure. Unlike Soninke migrants who entered France in the postwar period, when the state needed laborers and migration policy was permissive, he encountered a restrictive environment: successive reforms beginning in 1974 had made it far more difficult for migrants to obtain legal entry and work, and deportations were increasing dramatically under Nicolas Sarkozy (see Raissiguier 2010).[6] Life without papers led him to precarious, underpaid positions and made it impossible to amass money or return home. He also felt himself constrained by the demands of the wider Malian community that had by then established itself in France (see also Sargent and Larchanché, this volume). As his sojourn extended to over a decade and the signifiers of adulthood—marriage, accumulation of wealth, a permanent job, and founding one's own home in the village—escaped his reach, Lassana turned to the Gare du Nord.

The Gare du Nord is the busiest rail hub in Europe and a node of international, national, and local transportation networks. It is also the center of commuter rail lines that bring young men from their homes in the northern and eastern suburbs of Paris to their jobs in construction, restaurant work, and cleaning. Consequently, the Gare du Nord has become known as a meeting place for West Africans looking for work, cash, papers, potential patrons, and even romance. Young men meet at the station, where they give each other advice on where to find employment, loan money to one another, or exchange information about everything from the latest fashions to how to seduce French girls. They refer to these practices as the "Gare du Nord method."

10.1 Lassana, left, and a friend at a café in the Gare du Nord, 2010. Lassana and his friends
spent their evenings at the entrance to the station and in cafés such as this one. His
sports jersey, long hair, and backward baseball cap drew much criticism from his elders
in Paris, who believed these styles signified a "delinquent" lifestyle. Photo by Julie
Kleinman.

This chapter examines how the "Gare du Nord method" offers young
West African men an alternative way to come of age in the context of the
French state's increased efforts to prevent immigration and make life difficult for migrants in precarious situations. I focus on how coming of age
entails the conjugation of two different but interrelated relational circuits,
each of which, I propose, is characterized by its own "transactional order"
(Parry and Bloch 1989). On the one hand, young men seek to generate "migratory circuits" (see also Newell, this volume), which capture the types of
relationships they form at the station and are largely associated with what
Jonathan Parry and Maurice Bloch (1989) have referred to as short-term
cycles of exchange. These cycles of exchange, aimed at individual accumulation and pleasure, "are allowed only as long as they remain subordinate, over time, to kin-related patronage governed by moralities of social
reproduction and ancestral principles" (Groes-Green 2014, 239). On the
other hand, young men also build affective circuits of "goods, emotions,
ideas, and advice" that tie them to kin both back home and abroad (Cole,
this volume; Cole and Groes, introduction to this volume). It is through
affective circuits that men manage to connect the short-term transactions
conducted in the Gare du Nord to the long-term transactional order as-

sociated with the reproduction of their families back home, potentially achieving new forms of authority and adulthood in the process.

Lassana's own story is proof that the "Gare du Nord method" can be effective. Connections he made through the station helped Lassana while he was undocumented and allowed him to find work and legalize his status in France. Eventually, the Gare du Nord method enabled him to go from a marginalized younger brother beaten up by his older brothers in the village to a patron and source of authority for those older brothers and set him on the path to becoming what he called a *petit patron* (small boss) and, someday, he hoped, a *grand quelqu'un* (a big somebody), a status generally reserved for older, married men who have returned from their journeys abroad.[7] In this sense, Lassana's case reveals how the prolonged occupation of the liminal space of migration can potentially change resource distribution and status relations in home communities, leading to "accelerations and inversions in the normative life course" (Meiu 2015, 474).

Despite his relative success, Lassana's trajectory reveals the ambivalent effects of this new mode of coming of age; as days stretch into months and months into years, the dispositions acquired from their time abroad become increasingly hard for young men to translate into a new life of settlement in the village. Some men claim that their experiences at the Gare du Nord encourage them to delay marriage—and thus, in the view of their village kin, entrée into full adulthood—even once they have the means. Moreover, Lassana and others like him also found that their positions were precarious and that success could easily turn into failure; it took significant toil to maintain their status. Many young men vacillated between what they referred to as *la galère* (struggle) and *le bonheur* (happiness). Lassana's narrative reveals more than the way changing immigration regulations have helped transform paths to adulthood in this migrant community. It also suggests that when short-term exchanges associated with the adventure period occupy an ever-larger portion of the life course, it becomes difficult for migrants to convert what they do on the road into the long-term transactional order associated with life at home. Ultimately, it appears that the provisional status of adulthood attained abroad might well prove temporary.

The structure of this essay follows Lassana's narrative of leaving the village world of lineage for the space of adventure where he is meant to come of age. In that space, he employs the Gare du Nord method as a way to avoid "getting stuck" while reconfiguring his relationship to his siblings. As his time in France extends to over a decade, I first examine how he uses his relative wealth and status to define the movement of his older brothers, and then I turn to the ways that their trajectories throw into question the importance of marriage as a marker of adult status. Finally, I explore how his house-building projects in Mali embody the changes and tensions in familial relations and personhood that prolonged multiple migrations create, caught as they are in the migrant's complex dance of distancing and rapprochement, short- and long-term exchange cycles.

This essay is based primarily on the hundreds of conversations I have had over five years (2009–14) with Lassana Niaré during the time I spent accompanying him and his friends and family in Paris, Bamako, and his home village outside of Diema in Mali. He was part of a group of approximately thirty West African men, aged twenty-four to thirty-three, half of them undocumented, most of them bachelors, who had first met at the Gare du Nord and who then convened there daily for several years. He migrated to France on a short-term merchant visa when he was about nineteen, four years after he had left his village to begin his adventure through West Africa. When we met in late 2009, he had just received a one-year resident permit that legalized his stay in France for the first time since he overstayed his visa nearly a decade earlier, and he had begun to plan his first return trip home since he left his village.

My intensive focus on Lassana's adventure reveals, as Paul Stoller (2002, 179) puts it, "how macrosociological forces twist and turn the economic and emotional lives of real people." Zeroing in on a single story illustrates how an adventurer confronts the precarious realities of contemporary migration while simultaneously negotiating his own coming of age. This approach recalls the life history method, well established in African studies, that privileges narrative depth to show how individuals imagine and build their worlds under a set of historical conditions and structures (see White 2000, 49–50). In following Lassana's adventure, I take my methodological cue from West African perceptions of life trajectories, in particular the way socially embedded life-cycle transformations characterize the migration adventure from departure to return. Following their paths reveals how adventurers combine professional, social, and emotional aspirations with new strategies for confronting precarious conditions.[8] In addition to providing space for analyzing both narrative and political economy (Stoller 2002), by tracking the twists and turns of one adventure, I also highlight the importance of moments of transformation and rites of passage in the migrant's life course as he attempts to succeed in coming of age.[9]

Lassana's path is not, of course, representative of all the varied itineraries that West African migrants take, but when analyzed together, his and his siblings' stories illustrate how immigrant social roles can be transformed through the practice of adventure. These are tales of the trials of social becoming in which the "expected and desired life trajectory" (Vigh 2006b, 33) is impossible to attain. The very desirability of that path is thrown into question as the in-between status of the adventurer prevails at the journey's end. Following Lassana's trajectory as it altered and intersects with those of three of his mobile brothers illustrates how affective circuits are not only constructed and negotiated between those "abroad" and those "at home" but also are the product of the interplay of several migrant trajectories to Europe and within West and Central Africa.

Lassana and His Brothers

Lassana grew up in Yillekunda, ten kilometers from the town of Diema in the region of Kayes. His family was part of the ruling elite of the village, as he often had the "griot of the Gare du Nord" (a Malian immigrant praise singer from a griot family) reiterate through praise songs. He was the first son of his father's second wife, and he had three older half brothers. Nearby there is a public school with instruction in French, but like most of his brothers who were meant to go on their adventure abroad, Lassana attended Koranic school. Koranic school, according to his father, would prepare adventurers for a difficult and disciplined life on the road and help them stay on the right path of Islam while abroad.[10] Lassana's structural position would have several consequences for the trajectory his life took. As the son of a second wife, he had to do the bidding of his half brothers and accept the beatings he got from them without complaint. His mother died when he was ten years old and his older sister left to marry a Malian living in France, leaving him more or less alone to fend for himself against them. By the time he was fifteen, he was already planning his departure.

Unbeknownst to his family, Lassana jumped onto a truck and went from village to village doing odd jobs until he made his way to Mali's bustling capital of Bamako. His dramatic and secretive escape from the clutches of parental and elder sibling authority, as he tells the story, set the stage for his ensuing adventure across West Africa and into France.[11] His father attempted to get him to return, but only halfheartedly, according to Lassana, because he knew that his son's adventure had begun. He also left behind a younger brother, Souleymane, the only other son of his father and mother, who would from then on bear the brunt of his half brothers' abuse and await the moment when he too could depart. His departure was postponed as he watched his other siblings leave: Mohamadou, an older brother (the son of his paternal uncle) who had grown up mostly in Gabon, left for Congo-Brazzaville soon after Lassana; Moussa, the middle brother, went to work as a merchant in a Brazzaville market; the eldest left for a diamond-mining town in Angola.

In this way, the Niaré family diverges from the ideal situation in which the eldest son returns to inherit the family home and take care of his parents as they age. Instead, this obligation fell to Souleymane, who remained in the village. As a younger son, he was unable to inherit, and he had few marriage prospects because of his lack of status and migrant wealth. He was stuck "awaiting the passage to adulthood and economic security that was traditionally secured by migration" (Jónsson 2012, 115) alongside the broader "generation-in-waiting" of urban Malian youth (Schulz 2002) and indeed youth across the continent for whom traditional pathways and markers of adulthood are hard to attain (Cole 2010; Comaroff and Comaroff 1999; De Boeck and Honwana 2005; Groes-Green 2009; Honwana 2012; Mains 2012; Masquelier 2005; Weiss 2004).

Lassana's departure on the truck signified his leaving the world of lineage represented by the village and his entrée into the liminal world of adventure. Far from being outside the bounds of kin reciprocity, however, migrants end up relying on help and financing from family members—usually siblings or uncles—while on the road, and once they are successful, they are also obligated to help kin join them abroad or migrate elsewhere. Leaving has become an expensive business, entailing high fees for identification documents, visas, and travel tickets or large sums paid to traffickers. While some families may save money to help fund migration, Soninke kin abroad more often have the capital to help those on the road.

From the start, Lassana's adventure was intertwined with his siblings' migrations. Once he got to Bamako, Lassana asked his sister, Fanta, who was already living in France with her husband, for help, but she initially refused because his father had not yet given his permission for Lassana's departure. To get out of West Africa, he needed a national ID card, for which he would have to pretend to be over eighteen. Bamako, he intimated, was not sufficiently foreign to be part of a "true adventure," and he knew he had to move on quickly or risk being sent back to his family. As soon as he had made enough to pay for his exit from the capital by working odd jobs for Soninke cousins there, he went to the Ivory Coast. He worked odd jobs in Abidjan, but he did not make enough money to be able to afford a passport and visa fees. By then, his brother Moussa was running a successful clothing store in Brazzaville, and Lassana asked him for help, but Moussa refused. Their older brother, Mohamadou (the son of their paternal uncle) was not faring much better: he had grown up in Gabon but had returned to Yillekunda as a teenager. He left for the Congo at the same time that Lassana left Yillekunda. Lassana stayed in the Ivory Coast (moving from Abidjan to Daloa, a center of the cacao trade) until he had made enough money to get a passport and apply for a merchant visa that would grant him a temporary stay in France. Mohamadou also wanted to leave for Europe but did not have the money. Lassana blamed his brother's lack of success on the fact that he had grown up abroad and thus was missing the Soninke work ethic learned in the village. Success in the period of adventure depended on village hierarchy and upbringing (see Gaibazzi 2013).

These three brothers—Lassana, Moussa, and Mohamadou—were part of the same age group, Lassana being the youngest. By leaving Africa for Europe, he would move up an "imagined hierarchy of global migrant destinations" (Whitehouse 2012, 223). He had proved himself on the road, and when he was eighteen, he achieved his father's blessing for his proposed trip to France. He returned to Bamako to get his papers in order. His father visited him there and shared secret rituals to use once in Europe to avoid deportation. His older brothers were still unable or unwilling to help him pay for a plane ticket to France. Instead, his older sister Fanta came through with the necessary funds, and he left for France without having to return to Yillekunda—a return that, in his eyes, would have signified backward movement and might have gotten him stuck in obligations to kin that would have prevented his adventure from continuing. In 2000, he boarded an Air France flight with a three-month visa. He would not return to Mali for over a decade. In the intervening years, all of his brothers would leave the places where they had been living: Moussa would be forced to leave Brazzaville and would set up shop in Bamako, Souleymane would leave for France, and Mohamadou would return to Yillekunda to marry, only to leave again for Mauritania. Each of these men had to confront the contradictions in and blockages of their contemporary adventures.

Lassana saw his relative success—signaled by his arrival in France—as the story of an underdog brother who usurped his elder brothers' authority. The position he gained through migration would lead him to attempt to control his brothers' movement. In doing so, he would also become a "small patron" with the power to dictate the distribution of affective roles in his family, such as who would be the dutiful brother and return home to care for their father. First, however, he would have to confront the difficulties of African migrant life in France at the turn of the millennium.

Finding True Wilderness: The Changing Forms of Adventure

Like many West African migrants to France, Lassana unrolled his first mattress there in a shared room in a dormitory housing foreign laborers. It was one of about forty-six buildings constructed in Paris beginning in the middle of 1950s for "immigrant workers" presumed to be single men (Bernardot 2006). His roommates were cousins and uncles from his village in the Senegal River Valley; some of them had spent most of their lives in France and in the dormitory, popularly referred to as the *foyer des Maliens* (Malian dorm) after its majority occupants. His sister's husband got him a fake resident and work permit and his first job, cleaning French national railway trains. His brother-in-law also lent him money to get by before his first paycheck, carefully recording the amounts and collecting on the debts as soon as Lassana had a job.

Once Lassana had found employment, he was expected to abide by a well-documented set of obligations that included sending money to his family every month (between one-fifth and one-tenth of the salaries of the men I interviewed were remitted) and extra during holidays and family emergencies (Daum 1998; Timera 1996). He contributed to village burials, repatriation expenses, and weddings. Men from Yillekunda—between thirty and fifty migrants—met every month at the dormitory to discuss village issues, decide on the projects they would contribute to, and pay their dues (usually around ten euros). Through these funds, along with money from migrants' groups in other countries, their village now has a sparkling new mosque and a well, and the men are on their way to collecting enough for a water tower.[12] Financing these projects was part of the community-based "migratory debt," which includes remitting money as well as connecting France to Mali through such activities as helping with marriage agreements, circulating children between home and host country, and aiding other kin to migrate (see Barou 2001; Razy 2007).

While Lassana accepted the obligations to his kin and participated without complaint, they also threatened to stifle his adventure and lead him to "getting stuck," halting his progression to becoming a *grand quelqu'un*. So many of his village friends growing old at the dormitory had fallen into the trap, he said, of believing that their arrival in France signified the attainment of their goal. He blamed this attitude for leading them into situations in which they could not afford to return to Mali or did not have legal status after decades in France. He lamented that many had not learned to speak French well enough to make connections outside their community, which he saw as a requirement of being an adventurer. Although he arrived in France illiterate and with little knowledge of the language, he attended classes at the dormitory, where he learned to read, write, and speak. He then left the *foyer* as soon as he could find an apartment to share with a friend. While he could not break definitively with the village systems of obligation that existed both in Paris and in relation to his family at home, he chose to live farther away from those demands. Once he found a stable job, he requested Friday afternoons off so that he could go to the *foyer*, greet his family and friends, and contribute to the village savings collection.

Lassana maintained traditional networks of obligation while giving himself enough time to dedicate to the requirements of adventure, which he believed had to take him away from the immediate and present kin ties that a large Soninke Malian community in France created. Those ties could act as a "sponge" on his resources; part of the point of migrating was to accumulate the capital that social relations in the village made impossible (Whitehouse 2013). Unless he distanced himself from the migrant community, his heroic departure from his village and from the oppression of his older half siblings (as he tells the story) threatened to terminate in renewed subjugation to elders in France. He sought a new environment that would allow him to circumvent these systems of relations in France while strengthening his status in Mali and heightening his own sense of adventure.

What better site to continue a liminal adventure than a site of transience that was also the busiest railway hub in Europe, uniting local, national, and international networks? The Gare du Nord provided an aesthetic experience, a site for imagining new futures of onward movement, and a sense of hope that despite feeling stuck struggling to get by in France, one still might attain the relative prestige that migration to Europe promised. The station was an ideal site for adventurers because it was suffused with movement, a coming together of various trajectories from various places: here you encountered people who did not belong to the closed world of Parisian sociability or to the world of the immigrant dormitory but those who were on the move, like Lassana. It offered them potential and fodder for imagining futures outside the enclaves created for them in the form of immigrant dormitories, family networks, and housing project neighborhoods where their kin and village friends tended to congregate (Timera 1996). Lassana and some of his peers claimed that the station was a truer wilderness for their adventure precisely because it was outside Malian kin networks in France.

Lassana and other West Africans at the station told me that their reason for being there was not only to find work and meet women or potential patrons but also to learn how to be a successful "adventurer" by listening to the cautionary tales and advice of others. They would spend their time at the entrance of the station, passing on information about potential jobs, greeting old friends, and chatting up women who took the trains in from the regions north of Paris. As Muslims who did not drink alcohol, they preferred this ambiance to the nightclub scene, which they thought frivolous. They were looking for something more durable. The Gare du Nord was serious business, and as improbable as it initially seemed to me, some West Africans found jobs, papers, and even wives through their encounters at the station. Frequenting the station, though, had its risks.

The station's large police presence represented the risk of arrest and deportation, while the temptation to make easy money in illegal activities that took place there could easily lead a less-disciplined adventurer down the "wrong path" of delinquency. While I was at the station, several men were arrested for not having resident permits, and one was sent back to Mali. Lassana called such an occurrence a small problem, not the end of an adventure. I heard many stories of men who had been deported back to Mali several times, each time persistently finding a new way to reenter France only to be arrested and deported again. Despite their apparent failure, Lassana and his peers talked about them admiringly, agreeing that they were right to continue the "work of adventure" (*l'aventure, c'est du travail!*) instead of getting stuck.

This hard work, enacted through the Gare du Nord method, enabled these migrants to find work, transfer money, and meet both women and potential patrons in France outside their kin and village communities (Kleinman 2014). As the "true wilderness," the Gare du Nord method offers resources, tactics, and an arena for masculine self-performance in the absence of traditional coming-of-age markers. The station would lead Lassana away from his Soninke elders in France, but the success gained in short-term exchanges there would be invested in strengthening his ties to his village and asserting power over his elder brothers abroad.

Moving Brothers: New Expressions of Authority

In 2009, Lassana formalized his status in France thanks to his employer, who petitioned for a resident permit on his behalf and awarded him a coveted long-term contract (CDI; *contrat à durée indéterminée*). His papers not only signified his legal status in France but they also required new engagement with kin at home. Once he was no longer undocumented, his father expected him to return home for a visit and to marry, to follow the normative trajectory of the Soninke adventure even if he then returned to France to continue accumulating.

Lassana's precarious situation led to strained relationships with his father and elder kin in France. Although it was an improvement, a one-year resident permit (*carte de séjour*) did not allow Lassana to leave and reenter France as he wished. He waited over six months with a temporary receipt before he received the permit. By the time he received the actual permit, he only had a few months left before he had to renew again, and he did not want to risk leaving and being refused reentry after almost a decade of trying to obtain legal status. Even though he had a resident card, this uncertainty caused him significant anxiety, as his family members in the dormitory put increasing pressure on him to pay a visit home and his father berated him for not returning. His unwillingness to observe Ramadan and his hip-hop "delinquent style" clothes (as he called them) were cited as further markers of poor judgment. His father accepted his remittances but did not hide his distaste for Lassana's style and activities.

Through the Gare du Nord, Lassana had already begun to carve his own path toward success. Nonetheless, he was still concerned about his elders' perceptions, for they could undermine his authority in his village association. He thus poured his energy and resources into maintaining the affective circuits that tied him to his siblings and their families. He started emphasizing his social role as maternal uncle to his sister's nine children growing up in the suburbs of Paris. Lamenting that they all seemed to be "lost like the many Soninke children growing up in France instead of in the village," he began to visit his sister more frequently and devise ways to help his nieces and nephews "find their pathway." Against his sister's wishes, he succeeded in having her middle-school-age daughter return to Yillekunda because of her frequent suspensions from school. He threw himself into helping her older sister, his eighteen-year-old niece, find a job because she shared the same first name as his mother. He also started monitoring what his other older half brothers were up to, offering to send money to them if they agreed to return to the village to be with his aging father. While he did not follow his father's pathway, he was able to manipulate the affective circuits that relate migrant siblings to each other and to their village.

While Lassana was dealing with the pressure to follow a path that precarious conditions in France precluded, his younger brother Souleymane was disobeying his father's mandate that he remain in Yillekunda. Lassana agreed to help him come to France if he could attain a visa, but Souleymane's application was denied. When Lassana left for France in the late 1990s, despite increasing deportations from that country, it was still possible for a village boy without much property or a big bank account to get a short-term merchant visa to allow his initial entry. By the time Souleymane was old enough to leave home, increasing restrictions on immigration meant that visas were granted only to those with significant capital and property in Mali. He got restless. He went to Bamako to apply for a merchant visa to sell jewelry, the same kind of visa that had allowed Lassana to journey to France almost a decade earlier. When he was denied, he started to look into "the boat method" as an alternative. Lassana said he told him not to look for clandestine passage, that it was too dangerous. He tried to get their father to bar Souleymane from leaving. "You yourself left without my permission," his father responded. "If he wants to leave, he will."

While Lassana was negotiating with his family about his own return visit, he learned that his brother had traveled overland to the Mauritanian coast, where he made it onto a boat headed for the Canary Islands with some other men from their village. Several weeks later, the other men returned to the village without Souleymane. They told his father that when the boat hit rough waters, his son fell into the sea and did not make it out. "He was too weak, he couldn't make it, he failed," Lassana said to me. He used the word *échouer*, meaning "to fail," but also, concerning boats, to run aground, or sink.

When Lassana retold his brother's "failure" at sea, he emphasized the stopped trajectory and the wreckage, thereby constructing Souleymane's story as a foil to his own narrative of success. He fashioned his own "destiny" as the opposite of "God's will" for his brother. "What is my own path?" Lassana would often asked rhetorically, before telling me what "Lassana's path" would be and how it would differ from those who saw their path already set in advance.

You think you arrived because you made it to France. France is not the end. It's not even the goal. You think you arrived because you got papers? Papers are not the end. You think you arrived because you got a CDI? Well then you're stuck. You think if you get sent back [*refoulé*, deported] that's the end of your path? Then you're going to fail. Me, I have papers. I'm in France. I have a CDI. But have I found my happiness? No, my path is not done. I'm not satisfied with my boss, I'm going to find a better one. I'm going to get a better salary. Maybe I'll go back to temporary work if I can get good pay. The problem with French people and some of these Africans is that they think if they have these things they are *done.* They're content. Not me. That's why I'm at this station . . . it's an international station. Maybe I'll meet a girl from Germany and go there. And then somewhere else. And then who knows.

He sought incremental progress, made through constant movement and strategizing. The pathway did not have an endpoint of village prestige, marriage, and return. In the wake of his brother's death at sea, Lassana reimagined his becoming as a continuation of social and physical mobility.

Lassana negotiated his social position in relation to his brothers through the affective circuits created by migration. While remitting money home to his father satisfied an obligation, sending money to his brothers who had left on their own adventures signaled that he had surpassed their status. The older brothers who had once domineered and teased him now relied on him for support. In return for money, Lassana tried and sometimes succeeded in dictating where they would go and when. After a resurgence of conflict in Brazzaville and the threat of sudden deportation, his brother Moussa decided to return to Mali in 2009. Lassana remembers Moussa calling him from Brazzaville to ask him for money for the trip. Citing the exact amount he wired his brother, €330, Lassana reminds me that Moussa had done nothing to help him get to France. By helping him return, Lassana performed his role as a giver and not a receiver, while Moussa had to take the subservient role of accepting money when he should also have been remitting it. Instead of going back to the village where he had a wife and two children, Moussa set up a new shop in Bamako next door to some Soninke friends. His store, which sold used clothing and electronics from the United States, however, was unsuccessful. He went to the village every few months but cited his store as a reason to make a quick exit. Lassana began sending money directly to Moussa, but only on the condition that he use some of it to return to the village for longer stretches of time.

The adventure pathway also changed for Mohamadou, who, instead of returning to marry and settle, attempted to negotiate between his taste for the road and his obligations at home. In 1997, Mohamadou went to Gabon and then to the Congo, but in both places he failed to make any money. "Now it should be finished," said Lassana, explaining that Mohamadou was not cut out for success on the road because he "aime trop l'ambiance," that is, he liked to go dancing and drinking. After an unsuccessful attempt to make enough money to get to Europe, Mohamadou returned to Yillekunda in 2003. He agreed to marry, but after only one year he sought to leave again. Lassana sent him money for a motorbike, which would enable him to make money in the nearby town of Diema instead of leaving altogether.

In early 2011, after he had received a brand new one-year resident card, which enabled him to leave without fearing that he'd be blocked from reentering France, Lassana made the journey home. He spent almost a month in Bamako before he returned to Yillekunda for the first time since he had left as a teenager, bearing suitcases full of gifts from Paris. He was celebrated as the successful "adventurer." Lassana's father was still unhappy with his decision not to marry. More than remittances, traditional marriage to a woman from Yillekunda or from a nearby village would have cemented Lassana's place in these familial circles of exchange. He could have then returned to France and even remained in Europe. But Lassana continued to refuse the clearest marker of his entrée into adulthood.

Contested Adulthoods: Bachelor Big Somebodies and Married Bandit Boys

The Gare du Nord method allowed Lassana to become a breadwinner and patron in relationship to his kin, but in their eyes his bachelorhood confined him to the realm of someone who had not attained full adult status. Attitudes about the place of marriage in migration among Lassana's peers abroad, on the one hand, and their families in the village, on the other, often create significant tensions. In Mali, people often cite "marriage to a suitable woman" as a primary reason for young bachelors to migrate. Marriage required some capital accumulation, and as Souleymane found out, the most eligible bachelors were migrants on return trips from abroad. Adventurers at the Gare du Nord, however, rarely spoke of marriage and did not emphasize its role in their trajectory. "Malian women don't interest me," Lassana often would say, "I prefer a European woman who wants to work and contribute. Malian women just want to be supported, and they don't think of the future. I need someone who thinks always of the future." After ten years in France, he had begun to refuse what he saw as the traditional gender roles that he believed would come with a village marriage. Likewise, his peers insisted that they were only interested in meeting "Frenchwomen," by which they meant white women—they were uninterested when their uncles in Paris proposed setting them up with Malian-French women born in France even if those relationships would also lead to papers.

In addition to providing opportunities to accumulate money, the Gare du Nord provided a space where men could perform an alternative acquisition of masculine status by entering into relationships with white women. As an international train station filled with travelers from around the world, the Gare du Nord seemed to offer the possibility to meet women who "think of the future," and Lassana often cited "hitting on women" as a main reason for hanging out at the station. I met four couples in long-term relationships (three of them had children together but were not married) that had resulted from encounters at the Gare du Nord. The men I spoke to in these couples avoided marriage to their partners and received long-term resident permits because they had children born in France (or in one case, as a partner in a civil union). I also heard secondhand of seven other such cases, most of which involved West African immigrant men and white French women from working-class families in the north of France. Relationships with women they meet at the station also enable these men to pursue their coming of age as men even if these unions do not fulfill their becoming in relation to their communities' standards. Negotiating relationships with French women, including parenting and in-laws, often proved difficult and fraught with misunderstanding (Cole 2014c). In some ways, the difficulty was part of the point: there was no happiness without struggle, as Lassana frequently said, and these intimate social relations provided the real wilderness of adventure. Given the adventure's extension in time and the novel reproductions (including French-African children) that resulted from these relations, they could also compromise reintegration into the natal community at the moment of return.

While Lassana continued to find ways to obtain authority while remaining in the space of adventure, Mohamadou was a good example of how *not* to succeed. He returned to the village to marry too soon and ended up with failed marriages. "He didn't become a man yet," lamented Lassana, "He's still a bandit." When I met Mohamadou in 2012 in Yillekunda, he had recently married a second wife after a divorce, though I initially assumed he was single because he spent his days hanging out with young bachelors in the village. He told me he did not want to marry because he had fallen in love with a "*métisse*" (a woman of mixed European and African ancestry) whom he had met on a bus in Senegal. Like Lassana, he wanted to marry outside the community, in keeping with his hopes to construct a future for himself. Once he returned to the village, he used the motorbike that Lassana paid for to make connections in the nearby town of Diema and start a small phone repair business. When the business failed, he decided to leave again. He went to Mauritania to find work with the hope of eventually securing passage to Europe. His back-and-forth movement diverges from the ideal trajectory and his unsuccessful adventures meant that even after marriage he had not fully come of age (cf. Meiu 2015). Lassana, meanwhile, had begun to change his style; he grew a beard and got rid of the braids, wearing his hair somewhat long and natural. He was acquiring the trappings of adulthood and the status it entailed without either returning to the village or marrying. Yet he still needed to cement these acquisitions by buying land and beginning his house-building project. Lassana's imminent return posed a further predicament: how could he translate the adventurer's mobility into the elder's stasis, of which founding a family and constructing a village house are emblematic?

The Place of Diala Trees and Hard Earth: Building Houses without Going Home

While house building often helps migrants maintain social ties and status from afar, it also allows them to maintain distance from home and defer return (Freeman 2013). In Lassana's case, building a house in the capital while bypassing village networks carved out a space for him to imagine return without forsaking his adventure. After he received his resident permit, Lassana started planning to construct a house in Bamako. Unlike his sister's unfinished house, undertaken through a cousin contractor, Lassana's project took shape through the connections he had made at the Gare du Nord. In 2011, he got a loan from an African bank with a Paris office. He then bought land outside the city through a Malian cooperative, ignoring his brother Moussa's advice to buy in a more central neighborhood. The house planning and building was a source of constant anxiety: since he could only watch over the process from afar, he worried about getting ripped off. Lassana spent hours poring over the possible architectural plans, furnished by a Senegalese contractor he met at the Gare du Nord. He planned to include small stores on the ground floor, one of which he would run while renting out the others.

When I went to Mali in 2012, he sent me to visit the land he had bought, sign the deed as his proxy, and bring it back to him in Paris. The entire transaction became part of a larger performance of his status: he made his older brother Moussa take a day off from work to accompany me on my visit to the land almost an hour outside the capital. The as yet nonexistent housing development has a name, roughly translated as "The Place of Diala Trees and Hard Earth." Millet fields surround demarcated plots on which nothing has been built; most of them are owned by migrants abroad like the young man from Kayes who accompanied us on the visit. While we were there, Moussa disparaged the site for being too remote but was reassured when he found out that "the Chinese" will be building a highway from Bamako to another city that will run right by it. "It's hard! Hard, hard!" Moussa repeated as we surveyed the land. Moussa watched me sign the deed, and as the clerk handed it to me, he said, "The buyer insists that you and only you may sign in his place." In this case, we see how Lassana's encounter with me allowed him to circumvent kin networks throughout his house-building process and thus maintain his status as a patron who did not depend on his older brothers.

The conversion of social relations from the fluidity that characterized the adventure period to their fixity upon return often remains incomplete (see Lubkemann 2005). More than four years after I signed the deed, ground had still not been broken on Lassana's house, just as Moussa's shop in Bamako remained unfinished concrete, and the village house the brothers began for their father was only a shell. In theory, the adventure process involves a translation from the mobile to the stable, from the network to the dwelling. In reality, however, the fixed abode remains incomplete and empty and plays a role less as a space for living than as a space for imagining a return that does not forsake adventure. The process of building helps maintain the channels that connect the adventurer to the country but does so as a future prospect, as part of their becoming while on the road.

Those in the middle of the rite of passage are trying to secure what will happen after it, using relationships that preceded it while nonetheless attempting to maintain the freedom provided by the space-time of adventure. In addition to building houses in Bamako, many of these adventurers plan and implement a village project as a replacement for physical return (cf. Freeman 2013). Through these projects, which included mosques, water towers, and wells, they maintain a connection to the village and gain prestige for their families (see Daum 1998 for further examples). The most prestigious villages near Lassana's hometown were two that had sent many sons to the United States. Unlike most of the other villages, these two had electricity, the infrastructural display of their modernity as well as a source of local stature (cf. Larkin 2008).

Lassana's three-month return in early 2014 was a further display of his new status. He split his time between Bamako and Yillekunda, working on his father's house and evaluating the land he had bought. He had recently received a ten-year resident and work permit. I visited him at Moussa's shop, which, two years after I had first seen it, was still exposed concrete with clothes for sale hanging from wires strung on the walls. Moussa was outside sweeping the front porch and looking for potential customers when I arrived. Lassana was inside reclining on the store's only chair, surveying the street from behind his shaded glasses. Despite the 95-degree heat, he was wearing heavy, shiny jeans, a polo shirt, and a black corduroy blazer, a contrast to his French wardrobe, which consisted of a few T-shirts and hoodies and a couple of old pairs of low-slung jeans. He kept his big earphones on as I approached, nodding his head to the music, and looked up to shake my hand before returning his gaze to the street. He was now the patron to his older, married brother, who was sweeping the sidewalk.

Return and marriage are meant to end the phase of adventure as society reintegrates the adventurer as a man. Yet this phase—meant to be liminal—has become more permanent, sometimes encompassing most of migrants' adult lives. This permanence has made dispositions formed

10.2 Lassana sitting in his elder brother Moussa's store in Bamako, 2014. After receiving his French ten-year resident permit, Lassana returned to Mali for several months. His clothing and electronics display his newfound status as a successful adventurer, a point that is further reinforced by his sitting down in the only available chair while his elder brother stands nearby. Photo by Julie Kleinman.

during the migratory journey more difficult to shed once migrants return to the village. Returnees in Yillekunda who had spent more than five years abroad confronted the rigidity of local hierarchies stoically while finding ways to reconfigure their trajectories through continued movement, as if adventure still guided their strategies. Moussa, for instance, spent minimal time in the village, returning infrequently to see his wife and children, and was trying to find ways to leave for the United States while Lassana insisted he stay in Mali.

Yillekunda was full of long-term adventurers. One was an older man named Ousmane, who had spent his adventure years in Zambia but was living with his family in the village when I visited in 2012. Other village residents were wary of the succession of "schemes" he got himself into, and a few called him "crazy." These schemes included an American NGO education project for which he was running satellite activities in the village from a folding table near the main square. He was looking for more projects, his attention having shifted from trade in precious metals to the potential futures that development projects offered.

Long-Term Adventure and Precarious Adulthood

The way people imagine their future and try to achieve status have significant effects on communal social relations as much as on individual trajectories, making the negotiation of transitional moments such as coming of age a key site in social reproduction and social change (Cole 2010, 19). As political economic transformations alter, block, or frustrate the pathways for coming of age in Africa, young people seek new ways, transforming relations between generations and among peers (Cole 2010; Meiu 2015).

Born of the legal restrictions on migration, collapsing labor markets, and increasing deportations that have all made migration more precarious, the Gare du Nord method provides some West African young men with a way of confronting their "ambiguous adventures" (Kane 1961). It has parallels in other places Soninke emigrate to, where well-developed communities exist; some adventurers may build their networks outside these circuits to avoid the "burdens" of "negative social capital" that made them leave home in the first place (Whitehouse 2013, 25). But as more members of families spend longer and longer periods of their lives abroad, the temporality of adventure may overtake the long-term social reproduction of home communities. Migrants adapt to the new requirements of contemporary journeys of migration and fashion new ways to become adults even as the men in Lassana's village often remain adventurers when they return home, creating channels that take them outside village circuits of accumulation and relation only to reinvest in those circuits in new ways. When migrants enact these new forms of investment, they reshape the affective circuits among siblings, restructuring adventurers' relationships with each other. They also transform their relationships to the places they leave and reenter.

While Lassana's experience suggests that some men are able to convert short-term exchanges at a rail hub into long-term social ties, creating new ways to become a Soninke man, it also reveals how the legal and economic precariousness experienced by African migrants in France make this conversion more fragile and subject to reversal. Despite Lassana's display of success and embodiment of *grand quelqu'un* dispositions, when he returned to France he had to go back to a life on the margins that was less secure than before. Having lost his job, he led a precarious existence, despite his legalization. For a few months he could not pay his rent and almost had to go back to living at the *foyer*. He performs his arrival as a big somebody in Mali but returns to France to find he has no job to maintain that status and no wife or finished house to confirm to his kin that he has become a man. Even as young men attempt to leave the constraints of village hierarchy and depart from their communities to come of age abroad, their becoming remains a collective affair constituted through their negotiation of affective circuits that tie them to kin both near and far. When many siblings migrate—which is increasingly the case across sub-Saharan Africa—this renegotiation occurs not only between home and abroad but also among several relatives attempting to find success through migration.

When I met him at the Gare du Nord in the summer of 2014, Lassana had given up the "delinquent style" in favor of polo shirts and corduroys. He kept the shaved head he had in Mali and had grown a more prominent beard. For the first time since he arrived in France, he was fasting for the month of Ramadan. When I asked him what made him fast this year in particular, he said it was to satisfy his father's wishes. His father had always wanted him to fast, he said, but he had never bothered him about it because Lassana braided his hair, a sign that he was still an errant youth for whom observing Ramadan would have been an incongruous practice. Now that he had become, however temporarily, a *petit patron*, he said, he had to dress and act accordingly. The braids and the hip-hop clothes had simply been part of the Gare du Nord method when he was undocumented. They were not part of his identity but rather a strategy among others, one that represented the provisional performance of the adventurer self, which transforms over time. Yet the endpoint remains uncertain. When I saw him in 2014, he said he had not yet found happiness and was still searching for the alternative pathways that would take him there. The adventure will continue.

Acknowledgments

I would like to thank Lassana Niaré, his brothers, and their extended family for their hospitality and generosity during my fieldwork in Paris, Bamako, and Diema. Thanks to Jennifer Cole and Christian Groes for providing useful feedback on several drafts, to Isaie Dougnon for his comments, and to the two anonymous reviewers for the University of Chicago Press. The field research for this chapter was carried out in France and Mali between September 2009 and January 2015 thanks to support from the

Social Science Research Council's International Dissertation Research Fellowship and the Harvard Center for African Studies. Supplemental research was carried out in January 2014 and May–June 2014 with funding from the Oberlin College H. H. Powers travel grant and the Mellon Postdoctoral Fellowship in the Humanities.

Notes

1. All research participants' names have been replaced with pseudonyms.
2. The structure of Mande migration as departing for the "true wilderness" finds similarities in other coming-of-age practices that connect migration to the wilderness, such as Cameroonian "bushfalling" (see Nyamnjoh 2011).
3. The pattern of Lassana's father's adventure corresponded to the *navétanat*, or rainy-season labor migration to cultivate groundnuts, that developed in colonial Senegal and Gambia in the nineteenth century and continued until the 1970s (see Manchuelle 1997, 53).
4. While immigration to France from the Senegal River Valley increased after the Second World War, the vast majority (between 85 and 90 percent) of migrants continue to leave for destinations within Africa (see Whitehouse 2012, 4; World Bank 2011).
5. In 2006, there were approximately 614,000 sub-Saharan Africans (without French nationality) living in France (18.6 percent of all immigrants); more than half lived in Paris and the surrounding region. According to the 2007 census, there were sixty thousand immigrant Malians in France, but undocumented entries not accounted for in a census would increase this number, and the Malian embassy estimated that 120,000 Malians lived in France in the early 2000s (Gonin and Kotlok 2012). Many of these immigrants came from the Senegal River Valley of eastern Mali (the Kayes region) and western Senegal. Many were part of the Soninke (Sarakhole) ethnic group, a minority language group in both Mali and Senegal.
6. The first restrictions on this African migration came into effect in the 1970s during the economic crisis, when, for the first time, Malians were required to have a visa and passport to enter France. While the more extreme policies that emerged during this period were defeated or repealed after massive strikes and protests among immigrant and French workers, by the 1990s the government had succeeded in implementing restrictions aimed at stopping the flows of migration from Africa (see Hargreaves 1995).
7. The term *un grand quelqu'un* is most often used in Ivorian French to refer to someone who has achieved a high social status (Kouame 2012); Lassana probably picked it up during his time in Abidjan. Given extensive migration and shared media in French West Africa, this phrase, like other Ivorian French expressions, is increasingly used throughout the region.
8. The Nigerien merchants in Paul Stoller's *Money Has No Smell* (2002) have a

similar notion of a "path" that structures experiential as well as professional orientations toward migration: "Life is seen as a series of winding paths, all of which end by branching off in different directions. These ends and beginnings are seen as points of misfortune. Men are said to have thirty points of misfortune, women forty. If one chooses the wrong path and walks off in a dangerous direction, one will invariably suffer the consequences: a poor millet harvest, a streak of commercial losses, a series of thefts, a truck accident resulting in injury, a lingering illness, the premature death of a child, or perhaps, one's own death. . . . In West Africa, the path is also a metaphor that extends beyond existential practice to more professional pursuits: learning to fish or weave, cook or farm; understanding how to husband livestock or butcher meat; recognizing when and where to buy low and sell high" (Stoller 2002, 176).

9. Isaie Dougnon (*Cycle de vie, carriere e rites: Étude de cas des employés de la fonction publique au Mali*, book manuscript in prep.) highlights the importance of following life cycles and rites of passage to understanding the careers of Malian public servants; I use a similar approach here to understand the coming of age of migrants.

10. While immigration abroad remains the most prevalent form of adventure, since Malian decentralization in the 1970s, families have also diversified their strategies by sending some sons to "French schools" (public schools with instruction in French) so that they can enter government positions, a kind of interior adventure into a different sort of wilderness—a bureaucratic one (see Dougnon 2010).

11. Lassana is not alone in representing his departure in these heroic terms; my own fieldwork as well as other ethnographic work in the region confirms the widespread existence of the trope in West African migrant narratives of the individual's heroic departure from the highly collectivist world of the village (see Bredeloup 1994; Bredeloup and Pliez 2005; Dougnon 2013).

12. These projects and practices were similar to those of other Malian village associations in France (see Daum 1998).

ELEVEN

Circuitously Parisian: *Sapeur* Parakinship and the Affective Circuitry of Congolese Style

SASHA NEWELL

The Sape, it's . . . How to explain it? It is like nuclear technology. It's useful, but it's cruel. It is the thing and its reverse. It is like oil or diamonds. Just that! Double-sided. Having oil wells, that's something, but driving a car, that's another thing. Having a mountain of diamonds up your ass, it's good in the ass. But to have them around your neck, that's better . . . To possess the clothing industry, that's like owning the car, but to master the code of clothing, that's like mastering the rules of the road, it is more secure and the *sapeur* possesses the code.

JULIEN BISSILA, *AU NOM DU PÈRE ET DU FILS ET DU J. M. WESTON* (2013)

The title of Bissila's recent play about *la sape* in postwar Congo translates deliciously as "In the Name of the Father, the Son, and J. M. Weston," concisely implicating European clothing within Congolese religion and kinship.[1] The play follows the story of two brothers exploring the ravaged and unrecognizable city of Brazzaville after fighting in the civil war has stopped; they are haunted by the specter of their deceased father as they search for a single pair of J. M. Weston shoes (worth several thousand dollars) they had buried in his yard when fleeing the violence. They discuss the Congolese reverence for J. M. Weston shoes as a religion more popular than Catholicism or Islam, critical of their culture's obsessive relationship to clothing even as they feverishly continue their pursuit of the lost shoes. When Bissila compares *la sape* to "mastering the rules of the road," opposing *sapeurs* to those who merely "own the car," he points toward the central importance of mobility within the values of *la sape*, an identity that has placed migratory flow at the center of their economic life as well as a driving factor in their cosmological model for social and personal success.

For the uninitiated reader, the SAPE, a somewhat tongue-in-cheek acronym that stands for the "Société des ambianceurs et personnes élégantes," is a Congolese movement organized around a liminal passage to Paris. There, migrants would acquire (through a variety of not always legal means) a collection (*une gamme*) of authentic high-end suits and accessories, always including several pairs of the all-important J. M. Weston shoes (Devisch 1995; Friedman 1990; Gandoulou 1984, 1989; Gondola 1999, 2010; MacGaffey and Bazenguissa-Ganga 2000; D. Thomas 2003; Trapido 2011). Through a variety of ingenious informal economic practices and access to what *sapeurs* refer to as *kula* networks of stolen designer clothes (Trapido 2011, 210),[2] the early *sapeurs* were able to accumulate unprecedented arrays of clothing—typically of top-end brands such as Dolce and Gabbana, Armani, Yves St. Laurent, KENZO, Smalto, Weston, Marithé et François Girbaud, Dior—and return heroically transformed to Brazzaville. The verb *se saper* is old French slang for dressing well; with a curious etymology linked to concepts of "undermining" and "degrading," in contemporary parlance it is more typically used across francophone Africa to indicate sartorial style, in noun, adjective, and verb forms. Thus, *la sape*, as used throughout this chapter, refers to the Congolese art of dress.

This chapter explores Congolese affective circuits (see Cole and Groes, introduction to this volume) between France and the Congo as well as within France to highlight the productivity of circulation and the dislocated mobility of culture even when that mobility is itself under attack. Affective circuits fold together the concept of social network with the circulatory movement that takes place across widely dispersed spatial locations. As people, goods, money, ideas, love, and words circulate across space and time, people channel those flows in socially productive, often hierarchizing ways. The concept of affective circuits helps us to think past the boundedness of culture without losing the idea of pattern, for a circuit channels energy in motion, forging pathways that are continually being blocked, edited, slowed, detoured, or split but that must reconnect to their origins to reproduce the continuous flow. Rather than considering migratory pathways as subcultural or hybrid offshoots of more established social groupings, I examine circulation itself *as* a form of culture, understood

11.1 *Sapeurs* "friment" (pose) at a funeral in Paris, 2000. *Sapeurs* are always in search of a public, and so funerals, baptisms, and weddings are among their favorite haunts. They often pay professional photographers at these events to document their look. Photo by Sasha Newell.

as the fractal flow of people, goods, and cosmological perspectives across spatial and temporal trajectories. In this sense, affective circuits can be central, even normative forms of cultural production and reproduction, building up new patterns of their own with enduring power, as demonstrated by the supposedly ephemeral youth movement of *la sape*, now over forty years old. At the same time, I consider how blockages in affective circuits caused by efforts at policing frontiers and expelling *étrangers* (immigrants) can produce creative social distortions by shunting affective labor into more easily accessible social circuitry. The way in which *sapeur* society has increasingly taken on the form of an alternative kinship network (or what I call here *parakinship*) is one example of such a social distortion. The new *sapeur* style inspired by the philosophy of *sapelogie* I describe in the conclusion is another.

The final border crossing to Europe was often just as desperate as imagined by our media-fueled portraits of capsizing boats and razor-wire fences, but their motivations for migration and their pathways after arrival diverged sharply from this image. During my fieldwork in 2000, the primary goal of the *sapeurs* was still to put together a sufficiently complete collection of European clothing and make a *descente* to the Congo, earning themselves the title of *Grand*. They were often met at the airport in

Brazzaville by supporters, and as the movement gathered steam, by video cameras and even television reporters. They paraded through the streets and gathered in outdoor bars and even formal ballrooms in Brazzaville, where they performed *la danse des griffes* (the dance of labels), slowly and elegantly demonstrating the quality of their accoutrements, their mouths fixed all the while in a grimace of disdain. Indeed, facial expressions, mannerisms, gestures, and walk were studied and carefully executed when *sapeurs* became aware of the public gaze, even in Paris. A commonly repeated Lingala phrase, often attributed to the Kinshasan musician King Kester Emeneya, suggests, "The Europeans may have invented clothing, but it is we who created the art of dress."

Games of one-upmanship were accomplished through public clothing duels,[3] and the relative value of brands, clubs, and individual *sapeurs* themselves was in constant contestation. In addition to the prestige accumulated on journeys to Europe, the *sapeur* was often able to sell items from his or her collection at a considerable markup and thereby fund part of the next leg of a sojourn in Paris.[4] The migratory affective circuit between Paris and Congo-Brazzaville was thus a central mode of initiation into the upper hierarchy of *sapeur* society as well as an important part of the *sapeur* economy. The mythology of *la sape* emphasized a triumphant and redemptive return rather than the possibility of staying in Europe. But this kind of passage between Paris and the Congo was endlessly repeated, as the *sapeurs* could not maintain their luxurious lifestyle and generous material distributions to kin and close friends in Brazzaville and typically headed back to Paris to begin the cycle of accumulation all over again. Out of close to fifty Congolese contacts I made in Paris, most of the established *sapeurs* I spoke with had made *descentes* to the Congo between four and eight times. However, as the journey became increasingly hazardous, more and more had begrudgingly come to recognize France as their permanent location if not their home or community of reference, and the importance of owning authentic designer labels was diminishing relative to a more abstract display of refined sartorial sensibilities in the new philosophy of *sapelogie* that sprang up in 2000.

I highlight the normative power of this affective circuit of migration by investigating the way in which *sapeur* sociality is loosely modeled on kin relations, at once compensating for the lack of strong kin support in France and in competition with the demands of kin at home. When European anti-immigration policies and policing short-circuit the long-standing affective bonds with home, local informal ties take on increased social, economic, and affective importance. However, while the *sapeur* network is essential to survival and accumulation in Europe, it also siphons funds from the wealth that would otherwise be sent home in remittances, leaving actors negotiating conflicting social obligations. Primarily from the matrilineal Bakongo ethnicity, *sapeurs* create metaphorical patrifilial bonds to produce both connectivity and social hierarchy. Relations of fatherhood once had great political significance in this region, because in the sixteenth-and-seventeenth-century Kingdom of Kongo, matrilineages were linked and ranked through classificatory father-child relationships. These hierarchical relationships formed the skeletal structure of an empire by organizing affective circuits of trade through which wealth, slaves, and political titles circulated between the Atlantic and the interior. Since elites channeled the flow of European commodities through these patrifilial links, foreign goods became precise signifiers of one's proximity to the king. In a looser, metaphorical way, in the 1970s young Bakongo men organized themselves as a series of social clubs oriented around the aesthetics of European elegance (Friedman 1990), activities that are often interpreted as a form of political resistance to control of the Congo-Brazza state by the minority Mbochi ethnic group (Bazenguissa-Ganga 1992). What is perhaps most surprising is that over time, *sapeurs* have traced these patrifilial-like ties to create ancestral lineages of *la sape*, building a heritage of aesthetic mastery that has become increasingly explicit and self-conscious over the last decade. Described by increasing numbers of Congolese as a part of their national and ethnic heritage, *la sape* demonstrates that migration is not merely a force of sociocultural transformation but also works to reinforce identity and reinvent the past. Migration becomes a means through which to build and stabilize social networks, folding older modes of sociality into new affective circuitry. Indeed, as Vigh writes (this volume), a central motivation of involvement in migration and illicit economies is the "hope of positive emplacement within the affective circuits" back home, where the option of staying home implies blockage and stagnation and relative social isolation.

Marshall Sahlins, drawing on Viveiros de Castro's (2009) magnificent synthesis of gift, kin, and magic, has recently argued that all kinship is a form of magical thinking that connects people in a culturally produced "mutuality of being" (Sahlins 2013, 19–20, 58–61), once again relegating biology to its symbolic incorporations. Nevertheless, societies go on differentiating between kin relationships they consider "real" and those that are in some way "less than" real. I use the word *parakinship* here as shorthand for the kinds of complex socialities that exist the world over, modeled on ascribed kinship relations, often entangled with them, metaphorically drawing on their strength, but not quite recognized by their own public as kinship itself. Examples include ritual adoptions and god-

parents, Kath Weston's "chosen families" (1997), fraternities and sorori-
ties, the "brotherhood" of gangs, the mafia "family," or more generally
the way slaves were incorporated into flexible African kinship systems
(Kopytoff and Miers 1977). Drawing on the labile usage of the prefix *para-*,
I employ it here to indicate at once a sociality that stands alongside kin
networks (para-llel), that goes beyond kinship (para-normal), that works
as an auxiliary to kinship (para-legal), but that also can work to protect
from kinship obligations (para-sol, para-chute). While parakinship is typically not recognized as "true kinship" by members of one's larger society,
from an anthropological perspective that emphasizes the constructedness
of "biological" kinship, parakin relationships often constitute as valid and
full-fledged a "mutuality of being" as any kinship constituted by metaphors of "blood" or "nourishment" (Sahlins 2013).[5]

In the case of the *sapeurs* we find "mutuality of being" being forged
between *Grand* and *petit*, that is, an established *sapeur* who returns from
Europe transformed and someone from his circle who has not yet made
the voyage. The *petit* acts as an assistant and promoter of his *Grand* (a father
figure) in exchange for loans and gifts of clothing the *Grand* has brought
with him. Economically, these exchanges are essential to both actors'
ability to access the expensive clothing they need to *sape*. But as Jonathan Friedman (1990, 1991) suggested long ago, *sapeur* clothing contains
ngolo, a Bakongo concept of spiritual force or power that promiscuously
flows through contact between people, objects, and space (Ekholm Friedman 1991).[6] Jonathan Friedman (1991, 157) argues, "[Clothing] is not a
symbol of wealth or status as we understand the terms, nor is it power of
life-force in itself. Rather it is the vehicle or embodiment of the flow of life-
force from its cosmic sources." I suggest that it is in the passage of *ngolo*, or
"life force," between *sapeurs* through clothing exchanges that a kin-like
relationship of interconnected being is established. As bonds of actual
kinship have been strained by the increasing difficulty of maintaining
patterns of circular migration over the last twenty years, new affective circuitry of parakinship has become increasingly established in their place.

Migratory Socialities and Cosmologies of Movement

If the *sapeur* economy depends on migration to produce value, the concept of movement is also cosmologically conceived of as value in itself,
condensed in the figure of *ngolo* mentioned above. The Swedish missionary Laman described *ngolo* in his Kongo lexicon as "violence, force, energy,
power, vigor, resistance, durability, firmness, health" (Ekholm Friedman

1991, 127). Similar to cousin concepts from elsewhere—such as *mana* in Polynesia, *hasina* in Madagascar, and *baraka* in the Muslim world—*ngolo* is best conceived of in terms of a flow that circulates through objects and people, often transferring through physical contact and endowing those places, things, and people in which it accumulates above all with a kind of "potentiality." To return to the concept of circuit, *ngolo* is, therefore, a local conceptualization of "current" or flow of force that can be channeled through affective circuits, a cosmological mirror of a society built on harnessing transnational flow—"the rules of the road," as Bissila put it in the opening epigraph.

The *sapeurs* thus present a wonderful case for moving beyond the typical frames of research on migration: neither the assumption that migrants naturally seek the greater wealth and creature comfort of the "Western World" nor the common frame of investigating the "governmentality" of immigration in Europe captures the modality of the *sapeur* affective circuit, which builds identity and value out of the circulatory movement in between rather than at the spatial poles migration connects (Cole and Groes, introduction to this volume). While the dominant social science model of migration continues to imagine it as a one-way street bringing poor migrants to a wealthy Europe where they struggle to survive and accumulate remittance money for their needy kin at home, this chapter argues that African migration is often imagined by its sending community as a circular pattern in which passage to the "external" allows for the accumulation of wealth and personal force that is carried back to the community, much as the neophyte travels to the world of the dead in initiation and comes back transformed. Migration is not only an economic product of disparate financial spheres; cosmological perspectives that value mobility are often central motivations for migrant laborers (Mains 2007; Whitehouse 2013), and migration has been described as "customary" in many West African cultures, where the youth's "adventure" is seen as a fundamental link to his or her developmental maturity as well as economic development (Boesen 2007; Kleinman, this volume; Whitehouse 2012). "You don't get civilized if you don't travel," run the lyrics of an old Akan song (Koenig 2005). Similarly, Manchester School ethnographers documenting the repeated flows between cities and villages during the colonial period emphasized the fluid nature of migrant identities (Ferguson 1999; Gluckman 1961; Mayer 1962). Their innovative use of social network and role theories revealed ways in which actors were affected by sets of social ties that stretched across multiple locations and often produced conflicting normative expectations depending on context. These networks were in effect affective circuits that created new cultural forms through the connective tissue they generated via migratory circulation between village and city.

Anthropological attention to African migration has increasingly examined the circularity of migration patterns and the importance of reputation in the sending country to the actions and motivations of migrants in the transnational sphere (Cole 2014b; Hahn and Klute 2007; Mains 2007; Newell 2005), but there has been little theorization of circulatory mobility as a force of cultural production. I see migration as constitutive of its own socialities rather than merely complementary to or even disruptive of those it connects. Such affective circuits produce their own worlds of meaning: "migratory processes may actually generate *cultures of migration* that include migrants and returnees, as well as those left behind" (Hahn and Klute 2007, 16). Such a perspective sharpens the focus on how circulatory movement produces affective circuits that become their own cultural fields. I am inspired here by AbdouMaliq Simone's observations on African mobility drawn from a border-town Nigerian market:

Movement was not simply a matter of running away or running toward, of vacating or re-inhabiting. Rather, it was a stepping into a fold created in the moments where the unstable and the sedentary assume an intense contiguity. . . . [What is most significant is] their recognition that movement is not simply a reaction to conditions and forces, nor the instigator of still others, but its own "world," and a world that need not make sense in order to exert value. (Simone 2011, 380–81)

Seeking to delineate such a world, I trace the dialectical relationships between a cosmology of energy flow that drives migration and the transformative socialities of migration through an in-depth exploration of *sapeur* parakinship.

Social Circulation in the Fluid Markets of La Paname

Arriving in Paris in December of 1999 to work as *lecteur* at a local university, I found an apartment only blocks from the heart of the Congolese community in Chateau Rouge and began to frequent a bar fittingly called Café Mboka ("our place" or "place of origin").[7] Because such a high percentage of those in the community were *sans papiers* (literally, no documents or without formal papers), my presence was often met with suspicion, but I gained trust through my knowledge of Congolese history and *sapeur* culture. I often used my own (comparatively pathetic) efforts to dress as a means of learning the mysterious principles of *reglage* through

11.2 The author crashes a wedding reception with some *sapeur* friends, Paris 2000. My efforts at sartorial participant-observation were received with tolerance and patient encouragement. Note that the woman on the left side of the photo is a *sapeuse* "a la garçonette." Women who wanted to gain respect as *sapeuses* often had to compete on male terrain by wearing men's clothing, though in recent years *la sape* is increasingly open to feminine style as well. Photo by unknown *sapeur*.

which *sapeurs* combined elements of clothing. As a regular among the *ngandas* (clandestine, often not-quite-legal bars, the gathering points par excellence of urban Congolese) and streets of Chateau Rouge, I was soon adopted into several social networks and increasingly invited to the funerals, wedding receptions, concerts, and underground African nightclub outings that made up the most important part of a *sapeur*'s social itinerary.

The Congolese community in Paris has been shaped by the increasing efforts of "Fortress Europe" to control movement across and within its borders. After France passed the Pasqua laws in 1993–1994 (Schain 2008), migrants faced stricter border policing and detention zones (especially at airports), far greater chances of arrest and expulsion after entering because of stop-and-frisk procedures targeting illegal immigrants, and no clear avenue for regularization among an increasing xenophobic population (Schuerkens 2007). At the end of the twentieth century, the Congolese migratory circuit became caught in a double bind: just as European immigration laws were increasingly tightening and delimiting their movement from the home country to Europe, it became increasingly dangerous to return to the Congo, which was ravaged by a series of civil wars (in 1993, 1997, 1998, and 2002) during which oppositional ethnic politics led to increasingly genocidal attacks on civilians. In particular, during the conflicts at the end of the 1990s, the Bakongo ethnic group (among whom *la sape* originated) claimed they were being indiscriminately targeted by the Sassou-Nguessou regime. For the Congolese of Bakongo ethnicity, deportation from Europe increasingly represented death: the return home was to a war zone in which they were the targets of helicopter attacks, bombardment, and roving Mbochi militias. André had seen his father killed and his mother flee to the forest before losing track of his wife and kids and making his way to Europe. Having spent only six months in France, he told me, "I am always afraid, even when walking down the street, even when buying a subway ticket." Ironically, however, it was precisely the inability of illegal immigrants to work that drove them to profit from borders by smuggling merchandise, and police efforts to stop illegal migrants on the street pushed immigrant sociality toward covert and fluid forms of social engagement. In other words, the "circuit breakers" of policing boundaries and stopping immigrant traffic in the street often only served to increase the pace of circulation through alternative channels.

Thus, the very basis of Congolese community in Paris was an unceasing circulation. Not only was the population itself in steady flux through movement in and out of France despite the increased policing of border crossings, but also there were no fixed spaces of public life in which people could gather. A large portion of migrants were *sans papiers*, whose undocumented status made it difficult for them to establish a legal business. Even with correct paperwork, one's clientele became a target for regular police raids, something I witnessed frequently during my fieldwork. Not only did a great deal of Congolese transactional life take place on the street itself, but even the many shops, restaurants, and *ngandas* rarely stayed open in the same space for long. This was a community of densely interwoven networks maintained by word of mouth but almost completely deterritorialized. Although the 18ième arrondissement was already in those days known as an immigrant district, very few Congolese actually lived nearby—many lived in nearby *banlieues* (suburbs) and took buses or commuter trains in on a daily basis to wander the streets in search of a deal or something to do. While maintaining a public life of luxury and elegance, *sapeurs* sought out the cheapest possible means of satisfying private necessities. Thus, in the 1980s *sapeurs* inhabited the Maison des Élèves Congolais, an unsupervised and unmaintained state-owned building on the Place de la République (Gandoulou 1984), and when that was closed they resorted to breaking in and occupying uninhabited apartments (Mac-Gaffey and Bazenguissa-Ganga 2000) or couch surfing between various members of their kin and club networks. One Congolese friend complained to me about another *sapeur* who had been sleeping on his floor for a month and paid no bills even though he never appeared in public without his *Crocos* (crocodile-skin Westons). When he couldn't find anywhere to crash at night, the gentleman was said to sleep underneath beds in the hospital.

The network of small streets between Chateau Rouge and Marx Dormoy were lined with African grocery stores, wax-print cloth shops, and restaurants and bars of a variety of African nationalities. But these stores were in a perpetual state of flux, opening and closing without warning. When I returned to Paris in 2009, I was unable to locate a single *nganda* or restaurant from my list of former haunts. Many French businesses continued to eke out a living, and Africans often frequented them; one witnessed an antagonistic joking relationship between bartenders and this new clientele. Often, legitimate businesses rented out a back room or basement space to African migrants, and many *ngandas* went completely unmarked, sometimes even occupying private residences until police were alerted. *Ngandas* were not only key spaces of masculine display and consumption but an important source of income in the community, especially for women, who often worked in them either as owners, cooks, bartenders, or simply as lures to draw in customers (see note 4).

Congolese migrants commonly refer to Paris as "Paname." An old nickname for Paris, it had particular resonance for them because the beating heart of the Congolese informal economy was on Rue Panama. This one-block-long, ragged, nondescript street near the Chateau Rouge metro stop was a daily marketplace as well as battleground between Congolese street merchants and the police, and not infrequently a panicked whistle would send everyone scrambling to escape before both ends of the street were blocked. While women sold African produce from cardboard boxes on some nearby streets, Rue Panama was the domain of men carrying shopping bags filled with clothing, perfumes, belts, sunglasses, and other accessories. A few sold DVDs and CDs as well. Most of the exchanges actually took place in the darkened interiors of several small bar/restaurants that lined the street. This informal economy of apparel, whose transactions were almost entirely between people already connected in social networks, was at once a principal source of income and a discounted mode of acquiring the expensive prestige items through which the *sapeurs* constructed their public appearance. When I returned to this *quartier* in 2009, street merchants had abandoned Rue Panama and spread out to surrounding side streets, presumably to avoid constant police harassment, but this only made the market larger and more diverse. In other words, a rich and textured public social life was maintained day and night in various terrains colonized by the Congolese community even though the specific locations shifted unpredictably and mysteriously and there were few public markers to indicate their presence.

Furthermore, migratory circulations within Europe enabled *sapeurs* to procure (and profit from) many of the luxury goods sold in the *quartier*. Sitting in one of the bars on Rue Panama, Delphin leaned in and said,

This is where all the people that make a living by selling shirts and ties hang out. That is how I make a living. None of what you see in France could exist without Italy. Clothing is much cheaper there. You can buy something for 10,000 lire and sell it here for 100 francs.

Ntéka likewise explained,

A lot of people go to Italy too and buy in bulk. They buy one there for 1,000 [francs] and sell it here for 2,500.[8] If you go there with 8,000 *balles* [francs] you can probably get ten suits. It's very easy there if you know where to go.

In addition to bringing goods from Italy to France, many described the *descente* to Brazzaville as a lucrative economic activity. Blaise, a recent refugee from the war who worked as a bouncer in an *nganda*, said,

People make money here by many means. For one thing, in the Congo everything is more expensive. The Congo is the second most expensive country in the world. A suit that costs 1,000 [francs] here costs 3,000 or 4,000 there. And people buy them there. People even buy Westons *en croco* [the most expensive] there, which cost 8,000 here, so you can only imagine.

Thus, movement through migratory circuits becomes itself the principal source of profit. As Janet MacGaffey and Rémy Bazenguissa-Ganga (2000, 95) argue, frontiers create value differentials that can be exploited by smuggling things across them.

But there were other kinds of thresholds that could be passed through the right contacts or techniques; in other words, the affective circuits of parakinship were key to forms of economic production. Blaise continued.

One very common way [to get clothes] is through the networks. The store managers share 50/50 with the thief and pretend they are blind to the thief's activities. I know someone who once stole 100 suits. You can sell one suit for 800 francs, so that is 80,000 francs right there, and you can live off that for a year without doing anything. There are also many "antidotes" for security systems, like bags specially lined to protect against the alarm, and counterfeit money. People also steal perfumes and other accessories. The Congolese live through stealing.

One enterprising man I knew had targeted specific bulk vendors in flea markets around Paris and scoured piles of clothes for used name brands that he would sell on the street without divulging their less than glorious origins. Others who frequented the same bars had more diversified and established transnational business. One heavyset man (physical bulk is typically understood as a sign of financial success among Congolese) bought cars in Germany, cloth in Italy, peanuts in Congo, and telephones in Switzerland, and he sold each elsewhere for a profit. He told me secretively that he knew people who sold diamonds. He said he no longer bothered with *la sape*, perhaps because his success was already physically visible.

In this way, the very efforts of European states to impose barriers on migration produced financial opportunities through which *sapeurs* maintained their way of life (see also Vigh, this volume). Nevertheless, as Joseph Trapido (2011) has recently documented, police controls and raids have gradually extinguished many lucrative illicit sources of income that *sapeurs* depended on, and for a time at least, the Kinshasan *mikilistes* he studied were disappearing under the pressure.[9] The ability to procure as well as sell the goods that sustained the Congolese community thus depended on informal interpersonal contacts spread across a vast transnational space. In this sense, reputation and bonds of trust became crucial factors in economic success, and it was precisely through the development of *références* in the *sapeur* affective circuit that one could increase economic potential in Europe. It is no coincidence that this dialectic between a reputation based on spectacular consumption and financial success within informal social networks was at the basis of the *bluffeur* lifestyle I have described in Côte d'Ivoire as well (Newell 2012). In both cases, we find a system based on "wealth in people" in which display is used to seduce new clients into the patron-client chains on which real profits depend. Status had to be negotiated through continuous persuasion carried out in the performative mode: "I am a *Grand*."

Style Lineages: *Sapeur* Networks as Parakinship

Sapeur society was organized primarily around an elaborate hierarchy of crosscutting peer-to-peer networks. These relationships were most often framed through the idiom of kinship, but more importantly, in the alienating space of Paris, they also fulfilled many of the roles of kinship groups. These affective circuits transcended mere webs of solidarity or exchange networks—they constituted a form of relatedness that provided emotional comfort as well as financial support. But membership within these networks also determined legitimacy within the competitive prestige system and gave one a place within the ancestry of *la sape*. Through the medium of hierarchical but affective ties, *sapeurs* loaned their valuable clothing and accessories, such as Yves St. Laurent glasses or Weston shoes, to one another. Others provided temporary housing to their friends or provided lodging at discounted rates. Many sold items of clothing on credit or loaned money when bills were due despite the difficulties of collecting one's debts, and these networks were riddled with a secretive and shameful indebtedness, as *sapeurs* loathed to be caught short of money in public. These services became especially important in Paris, where most arrived without a relative in sight. Justin Gandoulou writes,

It is not unusual for certain *sapeurs* to speak of "family" when alluding to the club; they have the tendency to perceive the other members as true kin. This could be explained by the fact that the club plays, in these conditions, the role of the family. (Gandoulou 1989, 90)

Youth needed such "club" membership to succeed and even to survive, but the clubs also pulled them away from family networks of support, requiring devotion and loyalty.

Even though many of those I met in Paris had kin in France and occasionally turned to them for economic support, scattered kin members did not provide the same kind of safety net as a full-fledged kinship group at home. As Rogé told me,

Kandas [matrilineages] are less powerful here because they don't really exist. I for example am alone in Paris. Sometimes people have as many as ten [family members], but even then it's not really the same because everyone lives in their own house, not together in the same compound. Rather they are dispersed over the whole city.

At the same time that they were largely cut off from the support of their kin, migrants were expected to help support their kin in the Congo—they could not display individual success and neglect the needs of their family. *Sapeurs* thus found themselves teetering between the demands of their kin in the Congo (often including spouses and children left at home) and the social groups in Paris on which they depended. Most *sapeurs* prioritized their face-to-face networks, sending what they could manage to kin in the Congo through informal money-sending operations modeled on Western Union, another way Congolese made money from transnational affective circuits (themselves employing transnational kinship relationships to secure funds). Those who were still putting together their *gammes* (collections of suits) could not afford to send much money home and fended off family requests with promises of what they would bring on a *descente*. However, during the civil wars, the demands of families at home intensified along with the obligatory costs of funerals, and *sapeurs* found the value of their "religion of *kitendi* (clothing)" decreasing in comparison to the misery of loved ones at home. The following examples are meant to highlight the balancing act *sapeurs* were faced with in their social relationships stretching between the Congo and Paris.

Didier was a good example of someone who struggled to uphold the affective circuits of transnational kin most often explored in this book, all the while maintaining his own livelihood and reputation in Paris. Because his sister in the Congo was extremely sick, he was constantly sacrificing his Parisian contacts (some of whom he owed money) while prioritizing family in the Congo, and I once spent an entire afternoon with him trying to send money through the informal money networks. But this made for precarious navigation because he relied much more on a day-to-day basis on his Parisian connections. Didier made a name for himself in the 1980s, making *descentes* in 1983, 1984, 1986, and 1990, and so he felt comfortable withdrawing from the fierce competition of *la sape*. But he still kept up appearances and daily elegance, sometimes wearing a shirt and tie (protected by a T-shirt) even when working as a cook at the *nganda*. Didier had four children, all from different mothers, two in France and two in the Congo.

By contrast, his younger brother Ntéka (age twenty-seven) was far more invested in his reputation as a *sapeur* than in his kin and made money almost entirely through the clothing and drug trades. As he said, he simply "did not feel right" if he went more than three days without wearing a suit. He lived in a seventh-floor, one-room walk-up with a hot plate, sink, and shared bathroom in the hall, but the walls were lined with his beautiful suits hung on nails in the place of paintings. I never heard Ntéka mention his sick sister, and Didier was often bitter about the irresponsibility of his younger brother, whom he rarely spent time with. Still, to buy a pair of roller blades for a son who lived in France, Ntéka sold off a bunch of clothing at low prices and skipped a wake (an important but expensive opportunity to *sape*). Ntéka also had a wife and children in the Congo, and one of his grand strategies was to bring them to France, even though he had already been imprisoned as a *sans papier* twice for periods of three months. The prison time threw off another set of plans with his live-in girlfriend in Paris, with whom he had agreed to be monogamous. While he was in prison, the latter woman found that she could not make rent without inviting men to Ntéka's apartment, and he kicked her out when he heard about it. By the time I left France, they were back together again and had plans to have a baby in France in hopes of getting residency status. Ntéka provides an example of the way blockages in transnational affective circuits can lead to the strengthening of local circuits and further social investment in Europe.

Sapeur parakinship circuits not only enabled survival in the unpredictable economy of underground Paris but also were crucial to the legitimacy of the *sapeurs*, who could only succeed in building recognition if they descended from an established "clan" of *la sape*. Groups were organized around particular styles influenced by famous *sapeurs*. Mustapha—or Le Roi du Soleil, as he was known—was an elderly *sapeur* who needed crutches to walk yet still wore an eye-catching blue-and-green-plaid jacket with a red-and-yellow-plaid tie and J. M. Westons the first time I met him. He explained, "People follow particular men who they think were the greatest *sapeurs*. They are the inspiration for the group. And one must recognize who came before you. *It is like a kinship system*" (my emphasis). Notice that Mustapha is not only drawing on kinship to denote close affective membership but also describing a system of stylistic *descent*. These lines of descent are crucial to determining the legitimacy of a *sapeur*'s claims to grandiosity.

The *sapeur*/scholar Elvis Makouezi lists six generations of *sapeurs* in his *Dictionnaire de la SAPE* (2013, 57–65), though through my own efforts at compiling such lists, I learned that they were always subjects of debate, because they were essentially maps of social hierarchy and thus highly politicized. Mustapha continued,

Most people who come to Paris were already *sapeurs* in the Congo, and so they were part of a "clan." But there are some who didn't start until after they got to Paris. They became interested here and bought clothes and went back. But when they got there, they were ignored, rejected, because they were not part of the system, they were not a member of a clan. Djo Ballard is an example. He became interested in *la sape*, and he managed to get interviewed a few times by French people so that he became quite well known. But in these interviews he never mentioned the greats who came before him. He pretended that he was the one who created [*la sape*]. And so he could not have success in the Congo. He was rejected.

Djo Ballard had built personal fame by harnessing the curiosity of French media in the late 1980s about the African dandies increasingly present in their midst. The reportage circulated widely enough that most young French people had heard of *la sape*. Djo Ballard was excellent at self-marketing and profited significantly from convincing Africans of other nationalities (especially Ivoirians and Congo-Kinshasans) to adopt his stylistic innovations, and he continues to be cited by many as one of the great *sapeurs*. However, most Congo-Brazzaville men I spoke with scorned Djo Ballard because of his lack of affiliation with a lineage of *la sape*. Magré told me Djo Ballard could never attain the title of *un Grand*.[10] Just as in most kinship systems, not only did these parakin groups support each other, but, in addition, one's identity vis-à-vis the larger *sapeur* society was produced by one's position within their affective circuitry.

The most important relationship among *sapeurs* was that between the *Grands* and the *petits*, organized hierarchically according to the year in which a *sapeur* made his first *descente*. Thus, although *sapeurs* speak of elders and ancestors when referring to hierarchy in *la sape*, it is not strictly age but rather how long one has been a *sapeur* that marks hierarchical generation between *sapeurs*. Magré told me that he might not be the greatest *sapeur*, but he was still at the top simply because he had been around for so long: "All of these here are my cadets," he said, gesturing so as to encompass the room. To be become a *Grand* required "confirmation," attained by making *descentes* and publically demonstrating one's success in the Congo. Those who descended in the same year thus attained the same rank, their longevity as *sapeurs* counted from the moment of the first descent. They employed the language of "promotion," used in French for those who share the same year in school or same initiation experience, cementing the association Gandoulou (1984, 170) makes between *la sape* and an initiation ritual.

Although members of the same promotion were on equal footing initially, this did not diminish competition between them for dominance. *Sapeurs* were always in search of a moment to boast of their success and build *références*, but they had to be careful not to do so too loudly in the presence of their superiors, who could challenge them with a mere look. One evening in Moukasha's new restaurant, a mixed gathering of mostly young *sapeurs* was drinking, and Delphin invited me to their table. Ferhal, the most charismatic of the "British" group,[11] dominated the table and was expounding on his virtues in the classic prestige-building oratory through which *sapeurs* sow the seeds of their own legends. The performance was framed as a conversation with me, but the tone and decibel level of his speech were aimed at the entire room: "I have the entire collection of Westons, *les crocos*, I have them all. But I never talk about it. I keep them in my house in a locked box. I have a one-year-old baby that wears Westons to bed at night!" The very ostentatiousness of his discourse drew an older man from across the room to begin yelling at Ferhal. The latter tried to calm the man by telling him he was just providing me with information for a book. "You are still solid. You are still a *Grand*." With enough repetition this seemed to satisfy the gentlemen, who returned to his seat. Not to be deterred, Ferhal continued: "Now look at Delphin. He doesn't follow the rules of *la sape*. He puts on a Ferre shirt and thinks he's all set. He only thinks of labels, not the *reglage*, so he is *petit* compared to me." Ferhal's tone was jesting, but he was abusing the "play" frame of addressing me to threaten Delphin's position. Delphin responded, "Anyway, to be *un Grand* you have to go back home and do a *descente* to be confirmed. I have gone back four times already." It was a powerful retort, because Ferhal was still on his initiatory voyage in Paris and, like many, unable to return because of the war. While he had a reputation in France already, he was not yet "confirmed." Another *Grand* who felt his authority had been threatened then interrupted, saying, "Maintenant, l'ambience est dangereuse" (Now the atmosphere is dangerous). Both Delphin and Ferhal dropped their conflict immediately to assuage the superior's complaint, and Ferhal launched in with more hyperbole: "You, you are strong, strong since long ago. Even if you plunge to the bottom of the sea, you will not get wet. Even if you swam underwater from Marcadet to the Gare du Nord, you will come out. You are solid." These kinds of public alternations between claims of superiority and recognition of inferiority constituted the very mode through which hierarchy was produced, policed, and maintained—and the very activity through which affective circuits were channeled and institutionalized.

Grands and *Petits*: The Patrifilial Transmission of *La Sape*

La sape is in our blood; it is our folly
JAKE, WHO ARRIVED IN FRANCE IN 1989

Sapeur networks not only fulfilled many of the roles of a kin group but also transmitted identity, clothing, and *ngolo* along socially constructed patrifilial lines. When *sapeurs* speak of *la sape*, they refer to it as something beyond their personal control, something that comes from their body, that they have inherited from their father and grandfather. Thus, when Jake said that *la sape* "is in our blood," he meant that it is quite literally passed down physically, inherited collectively within the Bakongo ethnicity. But individual aptitude was also thought to be transmitted directly from fathers as well as inherited through objects and lessons earned through father-like relationships with particular *Grands* who became patrons.

Sapeur hierarchy was built out of intimate personal relationships with both economic and affective impact. Gandoulou describes the pressure placed on migrants by their *petits* at home:

In leaving for Paris, the *sapeur* assures his friends "you will not be disappointed." He becomes a sort of ambassador of the *quartier*, especially for his small circle of friends. So he does not have the right to fail, nor to suffer defeat. From that moment, he carries the heavy psychological charge from which he cannot escape until his *descente*, when he can satisfy his friends. (Gandoulou 1989, 69)

Typically, the newly arrived "Parisien" will parade through the streets attended by a *mazarin*,[12] who works as his frontrunner and assistant, sometimes carrying a briefcase or umbrella for him in colonial style, thus performing the hierarchy produced between former friends and equals.

Such loyal *petits* receive preferential treatment in the form of loans and gifts of prized articles of clothing from the collection of the *Grand* before he returns to Paris. Le Roi du Soleil told me,

You know, it is possible to become very well known without any money at all. You can go and borrow everything. A tie from one person, a jacket from another, etc. But they have to all go together very well. But if you look really good in borrowed clothes, even if everyone knows you borrowed them, you can become very important just from that.

Loaning relationships typically take place between the *petits* and the *Grands* who have full wardrobes and with returned "Parisiens" on their *descentes*. In other words, simply by loaning his clothes, the *Grand* asserts his superiority while simultaneously forging a lasting social bond. It is in part through this hierarchy of mutual aid that *les Grands* are able to achieve their success in the first place, including obtaining the funds necessary to get to Paris. As one older man assured me, "If there are no *petits*, there is no way." Note that the exchanges that produce the relationship between *Grands* and *petits* typically involve both a transnational relationship between a new "Parisien" and a still-Congo-bound neophyte as well as the passage of clothing brought back across this spatial divide, carrying with it the mystique of the external space of the imaginary. The productive social relationship is built out of the juxtapositions made possible by mobility.

This more affective hierarchy between *Grands* and *petits* is modeled on the father-child relationship (*tata-mwana*), a structure with important historical precedents for producing hierarchy in Bakongo kinship patterns (Hilton 1985; MacGaffey 1986). One younger man approached my friend Hervé, a man in his fifties, and they exchanged the Congolese male greeting of intimacy, rubbing their foreheads together on each temple. Opening his overcoat widely to display his suit and tie, the man told me, "Hervé raised me, he is the one who made me *grandir* [grow up]. *C'est un Grand, un Grand!*" seemingly indicating with his gesture the sartorial effects of this relationship.

Fathers are frequently cited by *sapeurs* as the origin of their need to *sape*. As one *sapeur* interviewed on French radio in 1984 said, "It is a tradition, Madame, we are born like this. My father was like this, my grandfather too. We cannot help but be like them" (Gandoulou 1989, 11). I heard this echoed almost verbatim sixteen years later in my own research, when Raoul said that *la sape* "cannot be reduced to colonialism. It is rooted in Congolese values and tradition. It started with the first Congolese to go to France and has been passed down from fathers and grandfathers and great-grandfathers." On multiple occasions when asking about kinship and Bakongo matrilineality, I was told that "no one is more important in the family than the father." The Bakongo have a cosmology of maternal blood as connective substance linking those of the same lineage to one another. However, the father was thought to pass individual differentiation and the capacity for prestige and power through his own paternal "blood."[13] The father, as well as, to a lesser extent, all members of his clan, is "mystically or spiritually responsible for the child's success in life" (MacGaffey 1986). Much as Annette Weiner (1988) has described Trobriand fathers as responsible for giving children their first adornments as well as their first prestige objects (and physical appearance), Bakongo fathers were understood to pass to their children both the cultural skills as well as immanent bodily capacity to *sape*. Belonging and corporate ownership were linked to the mother and the authority of the mother's brother, but it was the father who provided the differentiation of the individual social persona.

Moreover, at the historical height of power before the Kingdom of the Kongo crumbled, patrifiliation worked as a political hierarchical mechanism linking lineages to each other in a stratified exchange pattern such that a lineage with descendants of male members of another matrilineage looked to both male and female members of that entire lineage as "fathers" (Hilton 1985). A pattern of matrilateral cross-cousin marriage thus centralized power and wealth, strategically linking lineages together in hierarchical relations of exchange in which tribute and women were passed upward while titles and prestige objects were passed down from fathers to the children in their wives' lineages. According to Ekholm-Friedman's account (1991), the Kongolese ontology of power focused on the transmission of the spiritual force *ngolo*, which passed from the ancestors in the world of the dead through the king and downward from father to son.

As Friedman (1990) suggested, there was a loose correspondence between the club structures of *sapeur* hierarchy and the Kongo politico-kinship system that worked similarly to channel the force of *ngolo*. The flow of *la sape* was conceived of as a kind of force circulated through exchanges of objects and channeled by parakin networks and generational hierarchy. *Sapeurs* were understandably skeptical about discussing questions of spiritual force with a white ethnographer in Paris, and they rarely spoke directly about such matters in my presence without my asking. However, when I did start asking people about *ngolo*, no one ever denied believing in it. Nkounkou, an older man who frequented Café Mboka and carried a reputation as a *feticheur*, said of *ngolo*,

Yes, yes. The force. If you take a meter and compare it with a centimeter of *ngolo,* the *ngolo* is still bigger. It is in everything. It is in the hearts of Congolese and it cannot be stolen, not by colonialism, not by the war. . . . It is also in *la sape.*

The concept also makes a recent appearance in the new *Dictionnaire de la SAPE* (Makouezi 2013), translated simply as "la force." To understand the connection between *ngolo* and kinship, it is useful to turn to Wyatt MacGaffey's description of Bakongo understanding of hierarchy, which confirms how power was once channeled metonymically through kin networks:

The transmission of power from above to persons lower in the hierarchy is expressed metonymically: It is brought about, as the ancestors understand it, by contact with the higher power, by ingestion with substances associated with it, and by other modes of participation and incorporation. Patrifiliation (*se/mwana*) provides the social model for this relationship. (MacGaffey 1986, 12)

Ngolo thus becomes the mediating force connecting the power of externality to the body of the person, a product of the circulation of impregnated substances and objects. It is also the substance of the connective bond between father and son, and transmission of potency is thus imagined in the patrifilial mode, a male appropriation of the female capacity for reproduction. Both kinship and parakinship can thus be understood as forms of slow circulation through which things such as identity, force, blood, prestige goods, and status flow through social channels. Patrifiliation produces an affective circuit that overcomes the blockage of transmission between fathers and sons in a matrilineal system.

Contemporary *sapeurs* channel the movement of goods, spiritual force, and people through new affective circuits to produce stratified rankings and build social recognition by mediating externality. *Sapeur* social organization seems to redeploy an ancient patrifilial political model once used to control the flow of wealth and power throughout West Central Africa in the glory days of the Kingdom of the Kongo. The *tata-mwana* links that bound together generational levels and stylistic groupings of *la sape* not only produced a "wealth in people" that facilitated the accumulation of incredibly expensive luxury goods but they also enabled a mode of political resistance that allowed contemporary claims to ethnic and aesthetic superiority against the ruling Mbochi ethnic group.

Sapeur parakinship exists in constant tension with kinship, just as the patrifilial hierarchy of the Kingdom of the Kongo was itself tensely conjoined with matrilineality, easily disrupted by more egalitarian patrilateral marriages and the decentralization of trade that accompanied such changes (Hilton 1985; MacGaffey 1986). In the midst of building a reputation and consolidating the wealth necessary for a *descente*, a *sapeur* must often sacrifice his own matrilineal kin ties. But *sapeur* parakinship is also a way to support Bakongo migrants in Paris when they are too far removed from kin to be helped by them, and when the *sapeur* completes a *descente* successfully, the family benefits both directly in the form of material wealth distributed as proof of the *sapeur*'s success and indirectly from the prestige of association with a confirmed *Parisien*. In this sense, just as patrifiliation (a kind of parakinship even in its original historical form) created a hierarchical spine joining together matrilineal corporate groups, *la sape* exists as a parakin network overlaid on official channels, at once complementing and competing with kin values.

The Spiritual Father Matsoua and the Ancestry of the *Sapeur* Affective Circuit

The ancestors are very important to *la sape*, and we always give them their respect.
MUSTAPHA, LE ROI DU SOLEIL

Far from being a youth movement oriented against elders, "tradition," and historical origins, *sapeurs* (some of whom are still active even as they approach eighty years of age) turned to their ancestors to prove the autochthony of their modernity and sought their origins within an ancient appropriation of Europeanness. Just as the *sapeur* culture of mobility produced what I have called parakinship, this alternative connectivity increasingly emphasizes its own historicity and seeks legitimacy in connections to particular historical figures as well as references to the glorious cosmopolitan empire once controlled by the Bakongo. In other words, even as it is a sociality built out of mobility, it is nonetheless wrapped up in its own historicity and origin story, which *sapeurs* increasingly turned to for legitimacy and claims to ownership of the movement vis-à-vis its imitators. As the mounting ramparts of Fortress Europe made it increasingly difficult to support the exuberant spending habits of the original *sapeur* style, *sapeurs* increasingly turned to knowledge of cultural heritage and ancestry to distinguish themselves.

The origin of *la sape* is a matter of debate among *sapeurs* themselves and an important topic within *sapelogie*, which includes the practice of outperforming other *sapeurs* by demonstrating one's knowledge of the history, meaning, and philosophy of *la sape*. Many *sapeurs* pride themselves on knowledge of the Kingdom of the Kongo, drawing from readings of key historians, such as John Thornton (1988) and Georges Balandier (1968), or even (on more than one occasion) explaining elaborate theories about how the Bakongo were in fact ancient Jews (for which they cited genetic and linguistic evidence as well as comparison of shared customs concerning twelve tribes and circumcision). A now defunct website run by Elvis G. Makouezi, author of *Dictionnaire de la SAPE* (2013), cited the seventeenth-century Dutch geographer Olfert Dapper on the Kingdom of the Kongo: "The art of cloth and of clothing rests intimately linked to royalty for reasons at once mystical—associating dress with personality—and economic: pieces of cloth comprise taxation and play the role of money." Indeed, not only was handmade raffia cloth formerly a currency and mark of status in this region, but rich historical materials document the appropriation of European clothing as early as the fifteenth century and its continuing importance up through the colonial period (Martin 1994). At the top of Makouezi's website is an etching of the Kongolese ambassador Né Vunda in 1608, the year that he presented himself at the Vatican to plead for a Kongolese bishop, dressed in indigenous regalia (another portrait in the Vatican shows him in European finery), marking the historical importance of migration to Europe in the beginning of the seventeenth century. Thus *sapeurs* I met during the crisis period of civil war used implicit and explicit references to their connection to the Kingdom of the Kongo as masked political statements implying that the Mbochi (the ruling ethnic group) could never match the innate superiority and ancient cosmopolitanism of the Bakongo (Bazenguissa-Ganga 1992).

Sapeurs more commonly cite the *anciens combattants* as the inspiration for *la sape*, Congolese soldiers who came back from fighting for France in World War II with tales of Europe and lots of new clothes. Thus, a favorite song played in the *ngandas* of Paris in 2000, and sometimes referred to as the "hymn" of *sapeurs*, was "Un vrai histoire de la sape" (A true history of *la sape*) by Rapha Bounzeki and Papa Wemba:

The origin of *la sape* begins with the return of the *anciens combattants*,
The *anciens combattants* in the Congo
At the time of the end of the Second World War,
The life they led, the harmony,
Made their *fiertés* [dignity, pride, arrogance]
The soldiers were coming back from the country of *la sape*.

The song proceeds to list seventeen names, none of them those of the World War II soldiers the song purports to be about but rather those of the first generation of *sapeurs* who traveled to France specifically in search of high fashion.[14] Contemporary *sapeurs* thus emphasize their heritage and direct parakin connection to figures on this list to claim their connection to the true tradition of *la sape* and exclude others they see as "false" *sapeurs*. Moreover, the ability to list these important figures and describe their generational placement and interrelation was itself a performance of legitimacy and placement within the movement.

The first and most important name on the list in the song, however, is "the spiritual father André Grenard Matsoua." *Sapeurs* almost always describe Matsoua with this reverential language, and it is not uncommon for them to keep a framed image of him in their apartment like an icon. I want to emphasize the curious phrase "spiritual father," which points to the importance of patrifiliation as a kind of spiritual kinship organizing the movement. In Tamagni's gorgeous photo essay on *la sape*, the *sapeur* KVV Mouzieto says that "I feel like a missionary, a spokesman for the spiritual inheritance of André Granard Matsoua, who wore a white suit with a three-button blazer when he was arrested in 1933" (Tamagni 2009).[15] Matsoua is often spoken of by *sapeurs* as an ancestor figure and an originating source for the movement, and so it is worth investigating his resonance within Congolese culture more generally.

Matsoua was an intellectual and early *ancien combattant* who fought in the Rif war of 1924–1925 before starting the Association amicale des originaires de l'AEF in Paris, an organization for expats from French Equatorial Africa, which by 1929 had transformed into an anticolonial pacifist pan-African political movement with thirteen thousand members (Bernault 1996, 72; Gondola 2010, 160–64; Mantot 2007, 46). Matsoua soon had the French scared enough to arrest him for insurrection. He later died in French custody, and his body was never returned to his kin, turning him into an instant martyr. Without the body to verify, many refused to accept his death and awaited his return. For fifteen years following his death, at every election, over a third of the voting populace wrote in *bi-hisi* (bones) on their ballot, "like a magic spell" (Bazenguissa-Ganga 2011, 447). Shortly after Matsoua's death, a prophetic church sprang up called Ngunza, which channeled his spirit and awaited his messianic return.[16] This very church was an often-mentioned part of Congolese life in Paris in 2000 and included *sapeurs* in its congregation. The branch of the church I attended rented out a small room in the basement of a public building apparently devoted to housing immigrant religions. It was typically crowded with between thirty and forty people all dressed in white and dancing ecstatically to drums in sessions lasting several hours. Ngunza was a source of community as well as material and spiritual support, regularly healing the sick while providing moral and practical guidance for migrants navigating the hostile and coldly alienating space of Paris. The church framed the bonds of community through the idiom of kinship, the category most lacking in the lives of migrants, and attendants referred to each other entirely in kinship terms. Unlike Pentecostalism, which, as Leslie Fesenmyer describes (this volume), has the ability to reconfigure affective circuits, Ngunza seemed to reinforce moral connections with both kin and parakin relations. Hymns were sung to Matsoua and the Holy Spirit. Congregants took turns shaking the pastor's hand, which caused them to jump into the air in sync with his arm motion as though electrified. Both these rites of contact and the sermons focused on absorbing power from *Nzambi* (a Congolese concept of all-encompassing God). Thus, the pastor intoned, "Father *Nzambi* give *ngolo* [spiritual force] to live to all the Congo, all who are in prison and all the *sans papiers.*"

Matsoua is an important political figure in Congo history, and he has also inspired a powerful religious movement that has itself become part of the migratory affective circuit. But why is Matsoua considered the "father" of *la sape*? *Sapeurs* who revere Matsoua often speak (as Mouzieto above) of how he came back from France fully transformed in European attire, and even at the moment of his arrest by French authorities, he famously wore a white three-button suit. Matsoua forged the pathway of the affective circuit of *sapeur* migration by living in Paris and making the first *descente*, returning transformed in elegant suits and military uniforms, and just as frequently occurs with contemporary *sapeurs*, his self-transformation ran afoul of French police.

Ngolo, the Body, and the Religion of *La Sape*

Ngunza appeared to be the antithesis of *la sape* in that everyone was sup-posed to wear white robes and remove all metal from their body, but these were in fact two loosely interwoven worlds. Holding the fabric of his robe, the pastor cajoled his church to give more money: "Both God and *la sape* are good things, but one cannot zigzag between them; one must be steady in the church." The introduction to Makouezi's *Dictionnaire de la SAPE*, as much manifesto as lexicon, lays bare an underlying religious dimension to *la sape* while highlighting the connective tissue between the *sapeur* move-ment and the church of Ngunza. He writes somewhat coyly,

> We are not saying that all *sapeurs* are *ngunza* or that all *ngunza* are *sapeurs*. What we are saying is that the first disciples of Matsoua (the Matsouanistes called "les Cor-beaux") were the first *sapeurs* of modern times. . . . There is a link between *ngunza* and the *sapeur* and anyone is free to research it. Even today, it is not unusual to see *sapeurs* go towards the spirituality of *ngunza* and find completion and the universality of certain things. (Makouezi 2013, 19)

Ngunza was thus a Congolese movement that paralleled *la sape* and was focused on similar motivations of absorbing *ngolo*, combining European and Congolese symbolic principles of value, and supplementing the mea-ger communal life of the migrant in Paris. Both Ngunza and *la sape* use techniques of metonymic contact to absorb and embody forces of exter-nality, and they both turn to Matsoua as a figure that inspires and guides that activity, especially in terms of external forces of the metropole. But by making Rapha's song about the history of *la sape* and Matsoua's role in it their "hymn," the *sapeurs* demonstrated their inward turn, tracing the flow of ancestry itself through lineages of "soldiers" who had made the difficult passage to Europe and back. It marked a turn to the *spirit* of *la sape*.

The *sapeur*'s migratory journey and competitive collection of clothes were not simply a matter of prestige accumulation, for such a perspec-tive cannot account for the awe-invoking reverence *sapeurs* have for clothes—the "religion of *kitendi* [clothes]," as it is often referred to. Ma-kouezi (2013, 15) claims that there is a spirituality to *la sape* that has gone largely overlooked in scholarly explanation. Kennedy, a Congolese man in his midthirties who ran a clothing store in Paris and organized a Con-golese basketball league, told me in no uncertain terms that "*la sape* is a religion. We do not believe in one overarching God, but in a sense we are

11.3 *Sapeurs* often glower at the camera as part of the physical comportment of *la sape*, Paris 2000. The performance of nonchalance and even disdain for one's surroundings is an essential aspect of how *sapeurs* embody and convey their stylistic superiority. Photo by Sasha Newell.

all gods, gods of *la sape*." This focus on the individual as an incarnation of spiritual force corresponds to the role of the body as the site of accumulation. Filip De Boeck and Marie-Françoise Plissart (2006, 238–43) have eloquently described the body as a fundamental infrastructural "building block" of cities like Kinshasa as well as the principal site of accumulation, finally expressed and publically confirmed through exuberant "excretion" of wealth.

When I told Kennedy I had heard that it was the body that made people *sape*, he responded without hesitation.

Just as my body demands food, it makes me hungry, but my tongue demands particular food, so it is with *la sape*. My body demands that I dress well. It has demands, like the belly. When I leave the house I can't just put on clothes, I often have to try on three or four suits to feel at ease. My body demands that I find clothing that is suitable—that is *bien sapé.*

The body is often invoked by the *sapeur* as being sustained by *la sape,* or as itself exigent of elegance. Djo Ballard similarly told the television cameras, "Je me sape pour mon corps. Je fait vivre mon corps à moi" (I *sape* for my body. I give life to my body of mine). Patrick told me *la sape* was a sickness: "All of my money goes to clothing—it's normal for Congolese." Why? "Because it comes from the body. The body demands it. One must satisfy the body and it will reciprocate." This conceptualization of the body demanding satisfaction speaks to the act of dress as a kind of nourishment, as though clothing is a medium containing the spiritual sustenance or energy required of the body. Florence Bernault (2006, 215) writes that in the West Central African region, "the relationship between power/force and its material support was complicated by the metonymic quality of the body. . . . All living things, including people, possessed a force that remained in each fragment of the living entity, even if detached from it."[17]

Indeed, Wyatt MacGaffey's (1986, 182) classic Africanist take on the fetish suggests that for the Congolese, bodies and objects are really varying kinds of containers for spirits. The conceptualization of clothing as a container for spirit rather than mere appearance or "status symbol" is reflected in the way people mourned the clothes they lost during the civil wars. It was very common for *sapeurs* fleeing the war to bury some of their most valued clothes in a hidden location in hopes of retrieving them later, as in Bissila's play. In a curious five-minute documentary funded by Guinness and aired on YouTube in 2014,[18] a *sapeur* named Severin dolefully stands over the site where he had hidden his most valued possessions. He had tried to retrieve his cherished clothing when he returned after the fighting ceased and found it had all disintegrated. Solemnly, he explains, "It is like a cemetery, as though there was really someone buried there." Severin's comparison of his lost possessions to "someone" buried indicates that they are mourned not only as lost objects but also as extensions of the dividual self. Severin's collection of clothes was an integral part of his being and connection to *la sape*—a material manifestation of his sociality.

Thus, the act of clothing the body is to nourish it with *ngolo,* to draw indexically through contact with clothing that *belongs* to Europe on the strength and force of Europe itself. Through the local ontology of consumption as the absorption of *ngolo,* the circulatory migration of *sapeurs* is also a contagious flow of qualitative properties through contact. Or to put it another way, drawing on Sahlins's (2013) insight that kinship is a form of magical Lévy-Bruhlian participation, it creates a *mutuality of being* and a shared substance between the place of Europe and the Bakongo who appropriate the best of European attire while forging intense affective circuits among those who share this spirit between them.

Conclusion: Affective Circuits and Cosmologies of Flow

The migratory journey is thus confirmation of an extraworldly worldliness, a cosmopolitanism projected and now incorporated through literal contact with the external world. It is externality internalized. The ideal form of Congolese migration is a continuous circulation of people, goods, and culture, producing (and absorbing) a "culture of migration" (Hahn and Klute 2007). *Sapeur* sociality exists in a deterritorialized affective circuit born of the interstitial productivity of mobility itself. This sociality of movement is mirrored in the collective representation of *ngolo*, an image of life as the perpetual circulation of vital force through people, objects, and space. *La sape* as religion thus dialectically motivates the very mobility Bakongo sociality thrives on. At the same time, the SAPE as parakinship channels wealth, excludes illegitimate imitators, and builds a normative institutional social life that extends throughout the affective circuit, at once replacing the support system of the ascribed kin network in its absence and protecting against its exigencies in a remittance-driven Congolese economy. Thinking of *sapeur* movement as an affective circuit directs attention to the channeling of sociospatial flows and how new socialities are produced in the movements between places rather than the spaces of culture. At the same time we can see that movement can be considered a heritage, a belonging, a cultural resource such that migration becomes a way of claiming rightful membership in a realm of social registers.

And yet, it is also apparent that these affective circuits are regularly blocked, chopped, and rerouted by anti-immigration politics in contemporary Europe. Although I did not realize it until much later, my Parisian fieldwork took place at the nadir of Brazzaville *sapeur* style, at a moment of existential crisis in the movement. Indeed, quite a few Congolese I met in Paris told me that *la sape* was over. Others, however, were quick to question the knowledge and identity of those who made such claims, typically implying that anyone who questioned the vitality of *la sape* was not of true Brazzaville extraction. What I experienced in 2000 was a moment of inward withdrawal and reflection that actually led to a critical transformation in *sapeur* style and identity. Unable to afford the expensive labels that had been the mainstay of the movement, *sapeurs* developed a new aesthetic of artistic mastery and ethnic heritage. Ben Moukasha was that very year creating his theory of *sapelogie*, emphasizing a new spirit of *la sape* that de-emphasized excess and expense and instead favored the art of color combination and an ethics of respectful and peaceful demeanor, including his proclamation of the "ten commandments" of *sapelogie*. Moukasha's new philosophy of *la sape* became linked to the design aesthetic of another *sapeur* named Le Bachelor who opened his own design shop in Chateau Rouge selling brightly colored suits that gave the *sapeurs* a new unique look that attracted the attention of the international media. *Sapelogie* was not merely about a style transformation, however; in a more subtle way it drew on knowledge of the history of *la sape* to emphasize the importance of *sapeur* lineages and ancestral figures. In drawing more explicitly on a form of parallel kinship organizing *sapeur* membership to build legitimacy, the new *sapelogues* created exclusivity through delimited social circuits rather than brand authenticity per se, effectively proclaiming their superiority to any African imitators as well as the Mbochi political oppressors in their homeland. Finally, *sapelogie* embraces digital technology as a new mode of transnational circulation through which to circumvent the blockages surrounding border crossings.[19]

The original vision of the *sapeur* was that of a pure consumer, absorbing the space and materiality of Paris into his very body to make the transformation into "Parisien" and return to the Congo. Even during my fieldwork in 2000, most *sapeurs* snickered at the idea of purchasing clothes made by an African designer. But that very year Jocelyn "le Bachelor" opened his store *Connivences*, revolutionizing the look of the *sapeur* by emphasizing principles of *reglage* and the harmony of colors that many spoke of as the true art of *la sape* (De Block 2010). In so doing he demonstrated that *sapeurs* were not simply absorbers of "Europeanness" but Parisian designers with the ability to create fashion in their own right. These "New Sapeurs" have reinvented the movement, creating a bold new look that captures cameras and headlines while channeling their affective circuits ever more closely, both protecting themselves from the exigencies of Fortress Europe and ensuring their exclusivity even in the midst of imitation.

Notes

1. This chapter primarily discusses people from the Republic of the Congo, or Congo-Brazzaville, as it is frequently called to differentiate it from the Democratic Republic of the Congo (Congo-Kinshasa). Congo in the unmarked form appearing in this chapter thus refers to the former French colony.

Kongo refers to the historical kingdom that once ruled over significant terrain in both countries (as well as northern Angola) and whose descendants, the Bakongo, have shaped the movement of *la sape* in both countries.

2. According to Trapido, *kula* derives from the KiKongo word for red, a color that symbolizes power and mediation in Kongo cosmology. Trapido discounts the testimony of a Congolese friend who says the word is derived from Malinowski, but given the propensity for *sapeurs* to read academic and sociological texts, it is not impossible that it also references the famed Melanesian trade circuits, forming a quite lovely multicultural pun.

3. These are talked about more than they are actually practiced, and I have never personally witnessed one take place, though it is relatively easy to find examples in the burgeoning DVD/YouTube genre of *sapeur* performance.

4. Although *sapeur* culture is male oriented, it is not exclusively so. Though rare, female *sapeuses* have typically dressed *à la garconette*, in male clothing, and participated in competitive display with men. In part because of family reunification laws, African women have been increasingly present in European public space. Indeed, their participation seems to have opened a space for a more feminine version of *la sape*, as women make up an increasingly important part of the *sapeur* videos circulating online. This is a further demonstration of the way cultures of mobility adjust to the changing "circuitry" of migration.

5. The word *parakinship* has been used as a synonym for "fictive" kinship and sometimes implies "less than" real kin. In contrast, I do not oppose parakinship to a biological understanding of kinship; it references the way that communities themselves distinguish between "real" kin and "made" kin.

6. This cosmological perspective on *la sape* has largely been ignored or rejected in favor of emphasizing themes of political resistance or class transcendence, but I try to demonstrate here the complementarity of these perspectives while building an ethnographic case for the relevance of a spiritual dimension to *la sape*.

7. I had spent several years researching *sapeurs* as a graduate student, but just as I sought funding to head to the field, the Republic of the Congo disintegrated into civil war. I responded by applying for funding to research Congolese in Paris or to work in the Côte d'Ivoire, where, I had learned, Ivoirians were imitating the *sapeurs*. As it turned out, I spent eight productive months in Paris before a grant from the Wenner-Gren Foundation for Anthropological Research enabled me to begin my fieldwork on *bluffeurs* in Côte d'Ivoire. I did have a chance to visit Chateau Rouge again in 2003 and 2009, though my focus was on Ivoirians.

8. In early 2000, a U.S. dollar was worth 5.83 francs, so 1,000 francs was approximately US$170.

9. *Mikiliste* is a Lingala word that originated in Kinshasa to described *sapeurs*. Trapido (2011, 205) writes "*mikiliste* relates to *mikili*, a term which denotes not the entire world but rather the collection of *vrai mboka*—'real

countries'—that constitute the rich and, to the Kinois, desirable part of the world."

10. However, Djo Ballard does show up in Makouezi's list.

11. The "British" *sapeurs* wore exclusively British labels and specialized in plaids and apparently even kilts. I did not see any kilts during my fieldwork in Paris, so this may have been a later development. However, the connection to the "British" identity is clear in Daniele Tamagni's work (2009). One *sapeur* told me that women who adopted this style were called Margaret Thatchers.

12. The reference would seem to be to the historical figure Mazarin, who began his career as a military aide to Cardinal Richelieu and eventually became chief minister of France and cardinal himself. The label thus emphasizes the aspirant status of the *petit* serving the "Parisian."

13. There is a comparison here to the concept of *lusolo* as described by MacGaffey and Bazenguissa-Ganga (2000, 127). Many of the Congo traders they spoke with described a kind of gift for commerce and financial success that was passed down through their family, often skipping over some and landing on others. While the idea of a capacity for success seems quite related, it is clear in their description that the force they describe is passed matrilineally and is far more associated with the ability to accrue wealth than titles, prestige, and internal force.

14. After a repetition of the list, Papa Wemba added the names of two people who introduced him to *la sape* but who do not typically figure in Congo-Brazza lineages. The addition is quite significant, for Congo-Brazzaville *sapeurs* question the role of Papa Wemba in the history of *la sape*, while Kinshasans tend to consider him the key origin point of the movement.

15. Matsoua's name has various spellings—another quite common one is "Matswa," and his middle name is sometimes spelled "Granard," as in the quotation found here.

16. The church is closely related to several other prophetic movements, including Kimbanguism and Kakism (in which all members wear khaki). Another popular youth movement against tribal elders was called *Ngol*, combining the word *ngolo* with the name of De Gaulle, whom youth revered as a figure of extraworldly powers (Le Vine 2004, 189). Matsouanism was also later appropriated by Pastor Ntumi, who became the "spiritual" leader of the Bakongo or "Ninja" rebel forces in the civil war of 2002–2003, spearheading another wave of violence.

17. An uncanny ethnographic parallel can be found in Jennifer Cole's (2001) writing on *hasina* among the Malagasy, who similarly locate force within the ancestors but also the world at large such that families constantly work to channel and maintain the force they inherit ancestrally while absorbing new influence from beyond.

18. The documentary accompanied a Guinness beer commercial featuring the *sapeurs*. Funded by Guinness, both videos were shot by Spanish photogra-

pher Hector Mediavillea, who has spent years in Paris and the Congo documenting *sapeur* lives. https://www.youtube.com/watch?v=CScqFDtelrQ.

19. This transformation began with DVDs produced by Max Toundé such as the one accessible at the following link: https://www.youtube.com/watch?v=-sDXSw5ISb8. YouTube and Facebook are now becoming primary media for building transnational reputation.

References

Abbink, Jon. 2005. *Being Young in Africa: The Politics of Despair and Renewal*. Leiden: Brill.

Abdallah, Mogniss H., and Le Réseau No Pasaran. 2000. J'y suis, j'y reste! Les luttes de l'immigration en France depuis les années soixante. Paris: Éditions Reflex.

Abdullah, Ibrahim. 1998. "Bush Path to Destruction: The Origin and Character of the Revolutionary United Front/Sierra Leone." *Journal of Modern African Studies* 36 (2): 203–35.

Abranches, Maria. 2014. "Remitting Wealth, Reciprocating Health? The 'Travel' of the Land from Guinea-Bissau to Portugal." *American Ethnologist* 41 (2): 261–75.

Adams, Richard. 2003. "International Migration, Remittances, and the Brain Drain: A Study of 24 Labor-Exporting Countries." World Bank Policy Research Working Paper 3069, June. https://openknowledge.worldbank.org/handle/10986/18161.

Adeku, J. 1995. "Ghanaians Outside the Country." In *Migration Research Study in Ghana*, vol. 2 of *International Migration*, edited by K. A. Twum-Baah, J. S. Nabila, and A. F. Aryee, 1–18. Accra: Ghana Statistical Service.

Adésínà, Jìmí. 2010. "Re-appropriating Matrifocality: Endogeneity and African Gender Scholarship." *African Sociological Review* 14 (1): 2–19.

Adogame, Afe. 2009. "African Christians in a Secularizing Europe." *Religion Compass* 3 (4): 488–501.

———. 2010. "From House Cells to Warehouse Churches? Christian Church Outreach Mission International in Translocal Contexts." In *Traveling Spirits: Migrants, Markets and Mobilities*, edited by Gertrud Hüwelmeier and Kristine Krause, 165–85. New York: Routledge.

Agadjanian, Victor. 2005. "Men Doing 'Women's Work': Masculinity and Gender Relations among Street Vendors in Maputo,

Mozambique." In *African Masculinities*, edited by Lahouzine Ouzgane and Robert Morrell, 257–70. New York: Palgrave Macmillan.

Ahmed, Sara. 2004. "Affective Economies." *Social Text* 22 (2): 117–39.

Åkesson, Lisa. 2004. "Making a Life: Meanings of Migration in Cape Verde." PhD diss., Göteborg University.

———. 2011. "Remittances and Relationships: Exchange in Cape Verdean Transnational Families." *Ethnos* 76 (3): 326–47.

Alber, Erdmute. 2003. "Denying Biological Parenthood: Fosterage in Northern Benin." *Ethnos* 68 (4): 487–506.

Alber, Erdmute, Jeannett Martin, and Catrien Notermans, eds. 2013. *Child Fostering in West Africa: New Perspectives on Theory and Practices.* Leiden: Brill.

Alpes, Maybritt Jill. 2011. "Bushfalling: How Young Cameroonians Dare to Migrate." PhD diss., University of Amsterdam.

Amadiume, Ifi. 1987. *Male Daughters, Female Husbands: Gender and Sex in an African Society.* London: Zed Books.

Ames, David W. 1955. "The Economic Base of Wolof Polygyny." *Southwestern Journal of Anthropology* 11 (4): 391–403.

Amt für Statistik Berlin-Brandenburg. 2013. *Einwohnerinnen und Einwohner im Land Berlin am 30. Juni 2013.* Statistischer Bericht A|5-hj 1/13. https://www.statistik-berlin-brandenburg.de/Publikationen/Stat_Berichte/2013/SB_A01-05-00_2013h01_BE.pdf.

Anarfi, John, Stephen Kwankye, Ofuso-Mensah Ababio, and Richmond Tiemoko. 2003. "Migration from and to Ghana: A Background Paper." Development Research Centre on Migration, Globalisation, and Poverty Working Paper C4. Accessed September 26, 2013. http://www.migrationdrc.org/publications/working_papers/WP-C4.pdf.

Andersen, Signe Hald, and Peter Fallesen. 2010. "A Question of Class: On the Heterogeneous Relationship between Background Characteristics and a Child's Placement Risk." *Children and Youth Services Review* 32 (6): 783–89.

Anderson, Bridget. 2013. *Us and Them: The Dangerous Politics of Immigration Control.* Oxford: Oxford University Press.

ANSD (Agence nationale de la statistique et de la démographie). 2012. *Enquête démographique et de santé à indicateurs multiples Sénégal (EDS-MICS) 2010–11.* Dakar: ANSD.

Antoine, Philippe, and Jeanne Nanitelamio. 1995. "Peut-on échapper à la polygamie à Dakar?" *Chronique du CEPED* 32. http://grab.site.ined.fr/fichier/s_rubrique/20430/polygamie.dakar.fr.pdf.

Antoine, Philippe, Mireille Razafindrakoto, and François Roubaud. 2001. "Contraints de rester jeunes? Évolution de l'insertion dans trois capitales africaines: Dakar, Yaoundé, Antananarivo." *Autrepart* 18: 17–36.

Appadurai, Arjun. 1996. *Modernity at Large: Cultural Dimensions of Globalization.* Minneapolis: University of Minnesota Press.

Apt, Nana Araba. 1993. "Care of the Elderly in Ghana: An Emerging Issue." *Journal of Cross-Cultural Gerontology* 8 (4): 301–12.

Arnfred, Signe. 2011. *Sexuality and Gender Politics in Mozambique: Rethinking Gender in Africa*. Woodbridge, UK: James Currey.

Astone, Nan Marie, Constance A. Nathanson, Robert Schoen, and Young J. Kim. 1999. "Family Demography, Social Theory, and Investment in Social Capital." *Population and Development Review* 25 (1): 1–31.

Bâ, Mariama. 1984. *Un chant écarlate*. Dakar: Nouvelles Editions Africaines.

Bacigalupe, Gonzalo, and María Cámara. 2012. "Transnational Families and Social Technologies: Reassessing Immigration Psychology." *Journal of Ethnic and Migration Studies* 38 (9): 1425–38.

Bailkin, Jordanna. 2012. *The Afterlife of Empire*. Berkeley: University of California Press.

Bal, Meike. 2003. "Visual Essentialism and the Object of Visual Culture." *Journal of Visual Culture* 2 (1): 5–32.

Balandier, Georges. 1968. *Daily Life in the Kingdom of the Kongo from the 16th to the 19th Century*. Translated by Helen Weaver. London: Allen and Unwin.

———. 1970. *Political Anthropology*. London: Penguin.

Baldassar, Loretta. 2007. "Transnational Families and the Provision of Moral and Emotional Support: The Relationship between Truth and Distance." *Identities: Global Studies in Culture and Power* 14 (4): 385–409.

———. 2008. "Debating Culture across Distance: Transnational Families and the Obligation to Care." In *The Family in Question: Immigrant and Ethnic Minorities in Multicultural Europe*, edited by Ralph Grillo, 269–91. Amsterdam: Amsterdam University Press.

Balibar, Etienne. 2004. *We, the People of Europe: Reflections on Transnational Citizenship*. Princeton, NJ: Princeton University Press.

Balibar, Etienne, Monique Chemillier-Gendreau, Jacqueline Costa-Lasoux, and Emmanuel Terray, eds. 1999. *Sans-papiers: L'archaisme fatal*. Paris: La Découverte.

Ballard, Roger. 1990. "Migration and Kinship: The Differential Effect of Marriage Rules on the Process of Punjabi Migration to Britain." In *South Asians Overseas: Contexts and Communities*, edited by Colin G. Clarke, Ceri Peach, and Steven Vertovec, 219–49. Cambridge: Cambridge University Press.

Barou, Jacques. 2001. "La famille à distance: Nouvelles stratégies familiales chez les immigrés d'Afrique Sahélienne." *Hommes et Migrations* 1232: 16–25.

———. 2002. "Les immigrations africaines en France au tournant du siècle." *Hommes et Migrations* 1239: 6–18.

Barthes, Roland. 1981. *Camera Lucida: Reflections on Photography*. New York: Hill and Wang.

Bauman, Zygmunt. 1998. *Globalization: The Human Consequences*. Oxford: Polity.

Bayart, Jean-François. 1993. *The State in Africa: The Politics of the Belly*. London: Longman.

Bazenguissa-Ganga, Rémy. 1992. "La sape et la politique au Congo." *Journal des Africanistes* 62 (1): 151–57.

———. 2011. "The Bones of the Body Politic: Thoughts on the Savorgnan De

Brazza Mausoleum." *International Journal of Urban and Regional Research* 35 (2): 445–52.

Beauchemin, Cris, Kim Caarls, and Valentina Mazzucato. 2013. "Senegalese Migrants between Here and There: An Overview of Family Patterns." MAFE Working Paper 33. https://www.ined.fr/fichier/s_rubrique/351/wp33_senegal _family.fr.pdf.

Beck, Ulrich, and Elisabeth Beck-Gernsheim. 2010. "Passage to Hope: Marriage, Migration, and the Need for a Cosmopolitan Turn in Family Research." *Journal of Family Theory and Review* 2 (4): 401–14.

———. 2014. *Distant Love: Personal Life in the Global Age.* Cambridge: Polity.

Beck-Gernsheim, Elisabeth. 2007. "Transnational Lives, Transnational Marriages: A Review of the Evidence from Migrant Communities in Europe." *Global Networks* 7 (3): 271–88.

———. 2011. "The Marriage Route to Migration: Of Border Artistes, Transnational Matchmaking and Imported Spouses." *Nordic Journal of Migration Research* 1 (2): 60–68.

Bello, Patrizia Di. 2007. *Women's Albums and Photography in Victorian England: Ladies, Mothers and Flirts.* Aldershot, UK: Ashgate.

Benjamin, Walter. 1979. "A Small History of Photography." In *One-Way Street and Other Writings*, translated by Edmund Jephcott and Kingsley Shorter, 243–57. London: Verso.

Benneh, E. Yaw. 2004. "The International Legal Regime and Migration Policies of Ghana, the ECOWAS Sub-Region and Recipient Countries." In *At Home in the World? International Migration and Development in Contemporary Ghana and West Africa*, edited by Takyiwaa Manuh, 103–17. Legon: Sub-Saharan Publishers.

Berlant, Lauren. 2011. *Cruel Optimism.* Durham, NC: Duke University Press.

Berman, Morris. 2006. "Coming to Our Senses." In *Global Aesthetics*, edited by J. E. Jacobs. Decatur, IL: Millikin University.

Bernardot, Marc. 2006. "Les foyers de travailleurs migrants à Paris: Voyage dans la chambre noire." *Hommes et Migrations* 1264: 57–67.

Bernault, Florence. 1996. *Democratie ambiguës en Afrique centrale, Congo-Brazzaville, Gabon, 1940–1965.* Paris: Karthala.

———. 2006. "Body, Power and Sacrifice in Equatorial Africa." *Journal of African History* 47 (2): 207–39.

Berry, Sara. 2002. "Debating the Land Question in Africa." *Comparative Studies in Society and History* 44 (4): 638–68.

Bird, Charles, and Martha Kendall. 1980. "The Mande Hero: Text and Context." In *Explorations in African Systems of Thought*, edited by Ivan Karp and Charles Bird, 13–26. Bloomington: Indiana University Press.

Bissila, Julien Mabiala. 2013. *Au nom du père et du fils et du J. M. Weston.* Châtenay-Malabry: Acoria.

Bledsoe, Caroline H. 1990. "'No Success without Struggle': Social Mobility and Hardship for Foster Children in Sierra Leone." *Man* 25 (1): 70–88.

Bledsoe, Caroline H., and Papa Sow. 2011. "Family Reunification Ideals and the Practice of Transnational Reproductive Life among Africans in Europe." In *Reproduction, Globalization, and the State: New Theoretical and Ethnographic Perspectives*, edited by Carole H. Browner and Carolyn F. Sargent, 175–90. Durham, NC: Duke University Press.

Bloch, Alexia. 2011. "Intimate Circuits: Modernity, Migration and Marriage among Post-Soviet Women in Turkey." *Global Networks* 11 (4): 502–21.

Bloch, Maurice. 1986. *From Blessing to Violence: History and Ideology in the Circumcision Ritual of the Merina of Madagascar.* Cambridge: Cambridge University Press.

———. 1995. "The Resurrection of the House among the Zafimaniry of Madagascar." In *About the House: Lévi-Strauss and Beyond*, edited by Janet Carsten and Stephen Hugh-Jones, 69–83. Cambridge: Cambridge University Press.

Bloch, Maurice, and Jonathan Parry. 1989. "Introduction: Money and the Morality of Exchange." In *Money and the Morality of Exchange*, edited by Maurice Bloch and Jonathan Parry, 1–32. Cambridge: Cambridge University Press.

Bochow, Astrid, and Rijk van Dijk, eds. 2012. "Christian Creations of New Spaces of Sexuality, Reproduction, and Relationships in Africa: Exploring Faith and Religious Heterotopia." Special issue, *Journal of Religion in Africa* 42 (4): 325–44.

Bocquier, Philippe, and Jeanne Nanitelamio. 1991. "Les déterminants socio-économiques des changements matrimoniaux des femmes de Dakar." In *Conférence "Femme, famille et population": Ouagadougou, Burkina Faso, 24–29 avril 1991*, 369–86. Dakar: Union pour l'étude de la population africaine.

Boehm, Deborah A. 2012. *Intimate Migrations: Gender, Family, and Illegality among Transnational Mexicans.* New York: New York University Press.

Boesen, Elisabeth. 2007. "Pastoral Nomadism and Urban Migration: Mobility among the Fulbe Wodaabe of Central Niger." In *Cultures of Migration: African Perspectives*, edited by Hans Peter Hahn and Georg Klute, 31–60. Berlin: LIT.

Bois, Dominique. 1997. "Tamatave, la cité des femmes." *CLIO* 6: 61–86.

Bop, Codou. 1996. "Les femmes chefs de famille à Dakar." In *Femmes du sud, chefs de famille*, edited by Jeanne Bisilliat, 129–50. Paris: Karthala.

Bourdieu, Pierre. 1990. *The Logic of Practice.* Translated by Richard Nice. Cambridge: Cambridge University Press.

Bourdieu, Pierre, and Marie-Claire Bourdieu. 2004. "The Peasant and Photography." *Ethnography* 5 (4): 601–16.

Bowie, Fiona. 2004. "Adoption and the Circulation of Children: A Comparative Perspective." In *Cross-Cultural Approaches to Adoption*, edited by Fiona Bowie, 3–20. New York: Routledge.

Boyd, Monica. 1989. "Family Networks in International Migration: Recent Developments and New Agendas." *International Migration Review* 23 (3): 638–70.

Bradbury, Robert E. 1969. "Patrimonialism and Gerontocracy in Benin Political Culture." In *Man in Africa*, edited by Mary Douglas and Phyllis H. Kaberry, 17–37. London: Tavistock.

Bredeloup, Sylvie. 1994. "L'aventure des diamantaires sénégalais." *Politique Africaine* (56): 77–93.

———. 2014. *Migrations d'aventures: Terrains africains.* Paris: Comité des travaux historiques et scientifiques.

Bredeloup, Sylvie, and Olivier Pliez. 2005. "Migrations entre les deux rives du Sahara." *Autrepart* 36: 3–20.

Brennan, Denise. 2004. *What's Love Got to Do with It?* Durham, NC: Duke University Press.

Brenthurst Foundation. 2011. *Putting Young Africans to Work.* Johannesburg: Brenthurst Foundation.

Briggs, Laura, and Diana Marre. 2009. "Introduction: The Circulation of Children." In *International Adoption: Global Inequalities and the Circulation of Children*, edited by Diana Marre and Laura Briggs, 1–28. New York: New York University Press.

Brombacher, Daniel, and Gunther Maihold. 2009. *Cocaine Trafficking to Europe: Options of Supply Control.* Berlin: Stiftung Wissenschaft und Politik.

Brown, Wendy. 2010. *Walled States, Waning Sovereignty.* Cambridge, MA: MIT Press.

Brubaker, Rogers. 1992. *Citizenship and Nationhood in France and Germany.* Cambridge, MA: Harvard University Press.

Brummel, Elizabeth. 2015. "'Youth for Life': Language, Narrative, and the Quality of Youth in Urban Kenya." PhD diss., University of Chicago.

Bryceson, Deborah. 2002. "The Scramble in Africa: Reorienting Rural Livelihoods." *World Development* 30 (5): 725–39.

Brydon, Lynne. 1979. "Women at Work: Some Changes in Family Structure in Amedzofe-Avatime, Ghana." *Africa* 49 (2): 97–111.

Buggenhagen, Beth A. 2012. *Muslim Families in Global Senegal: Money Takes Care of Shame.* Bloomington: Indiana University Press.

Bundesministerium für Justiz und Verbraucherschutz. 2014. "Staatsangehörigkeitsgesetz in der im Bundesgesetzblatt Teil III, Gliederungsnummer 102-1, veröffentlichten bereinigten Fassung, das zuletzt durch Artikel 1 des Gesetzes vom 13. November 2014 (BGBl. I S. 1714) geändert worden ist." http://www.gesetze-im-internet.de/rustag/BJNR005830913.html.

Cabezas, Amalia L. 2009. *Economies of Desire: Sex and Tourism in Cuba and the Dominican Republic.* Philadelphia: Temple University Press.

Caldwell, John C. 2005. "On Net Intergenerational Wealth Flows: An Update." *Population and Development Review* 31 (4): 721–40.

Canut, Cécile. 2014. "On m'appelle le voyageur . . ." In *La migration prise aux mots: Mise en récits et en images des migrations transafricaines*, edited by Cécile Canut and Catherine Mazauric, 261–78. Paris: Le Cavalier Bleu.

Carling, Jørgen R. 2002. "Migration in the Age of Involuntary Immobility: Theoretical Reflections and Cape Verdean Experiences." *Journal of Ethnic and Migration Studies* 28 (1): 5–42.

———. 2006. *Migration, Human Smuggling and Trafficking from Nigeria to Europe.* Geneva: International Organization for Migration.

———. 2008. "The Human Dynamics of Migrant Transnationalism." *Ethnic and Racial Studies* 31 (8): 1452–77.

Carling, Jørgen, Cecilia Menjivar, and Leah Schmalzbauer. 2012. "Central Themes in the Study of Transnational Parenthood." *Journal of Ethnic and Migration Studies* 38 (2): 191–217.

Carney, Judith, and Michael Watts. 1991. "Disciplining Women? Rice, Mechanization and the Evolution of Gender Relations in Senegambia." *Signs* 16 (4): 651–81.

Carsten, Janet. 1995. "The Substance of Kinship and the Heat of the Hearth: Feeding, Personhood, and Relatedness among Malays in Pulau Langkawi." *American Ethnologist* 22 (2): 223–41.

———. 1997. *The Heat of the Hearth: The Process of Kinship in a Malay Fishing Community.* Oxford: Clarendon Press.

———. 2000. "Introduction: Cultures of Relatedness." In *Cultures of Relatedness: New Approaches to the Study of Kinship*, edited by Janet Carsten, 1–36. Cambridge: Cambridge University Press.

Castañeda, Heide. 2008. "Paternity for Sale: Anxieties over 'Demographic Theft' and Undocumented Migrant Reproduction in Germany." *Medical Anthropology Quarterly* 22 (4): 340–59.

———. 2013. "Medical Aid as Protest: Acts of Citizenship for Unauthorized Im/migrants and Refugees." *Citizenship Studies* 17 (2): 227–40.

Castle, Sarah E. 1994. "(Re)Negotiation of Illness Diagnoses and Responsibility for Child Death in Rural Mali." *Medical Anthropology Quarterly* 8 (3): 314–35.

Cette France-là. 2010. *Sans papiers et préfets.* Paris: Association Cette France-là.

Chant, Sylvia, and Alice Evans. 2010. "Looking for the One(s): Young Love and Urban Poverty in The Gambia." *Environment and Urbanization* 22 (2): 353–69.

Charsley, Katharine. 2005. "Unhappy Husbands: Masculinity and Migration in Transnational Pakistani Marriages." *Journal of the Royal Anthropological Institute* 11 (1): 85–105.

———. 2006. "Risk and Ritual: The Protection of British Pakistani Women in Transnational Marriage." *Journal of Ethnic and Migration Studies* 32 (7): 1169–88.

———, ed. 2012. *Transnational Marriage: New Perspectives from Europe and Beyond.* London: Routledge.

———. 2013. *Transnational Pakistani Connections: Marrying "Back Home."* London: Routledge.

Charsley, Katharine, and Anika Liversage. 2012. "Transforming Polygamy: Migration, Transnationalism and Multiple Marriages among Muslim Minorities." *Global Networks* 13 (1): 60–78.

Chauvin, Pierre, and Isabelle Parizot. 2005. *Santé et recours aux soins des populations vulnérables.* Paris: Inserm.

Chouliaraki, Lilie. 2006. *The Spectatorship of Suffering.* London: Sage.

Christiansen, Catrine, Mats Utas, and Henrik E. Vigh, eds. 2006. *Navigating Youth, Generating Adulthood: Social Becoming in an African Context.* Uppsala: Nordiska Afrikainstitutet.

Chu, Julie. 2010. *Cosmologies of Credit: Transnational Mobility and the Politics of Destination in China.* Durham, NC: Duke University Press.

Clarke, Kamari Maxine. 2009. *Fictions of Justice: The International Criminal Court and the Challenge of Legal Pluralism in Sub-Saharan Africa.* Cambridge: Cambridge University Press.

Clignet, Rémi. 1987. "On dit que la polygamie est morte: Vive la polygamie." In *Transformations of African Marriage,* edited by David Parkin and David Nyamwaya, 199–209. Manchester: Manchester University Press.

Coe, Cati. 2008. "The Structuring of Feeling in Ghanaian Transnational Families." *City and Society* 20 (2): 222–50.

———. 2011. "What Is Love? The Materiality of Care in Ghanaian Transnational Families." *International Migration* 49 (6): 7–24.

———. 2013. *The Scattered Family: Parenting, African Migrants, and Global Inequality.* Chicago: University of Chicago Press.

———. 2014. "'Posted Babies': The Fosterage of Transnational Migrants' Young Children in Ghana." Paper presented at the annual meeting of the American Anthropological Association, Washington, DC, December 3.

Cohen-Mor, Dalya. 2013. *Fathers and Sons in the Arab Middle East.* New York: Palgrave Macmillan.

Cole, Jennifer. 2001. *Forget Colonialism? Sacrifice and the Art of Memory in Madagascar.* Berkeley: University of California Press.

———. 2004. "Fresh Contact in Tamatave, Madagascar: Sex, Money, and Intergenerational Transformation." *American Ethnologist* 31 (4): 573–88.

———. 2009. "Love, Money, and Economies of Intimacy in Tamatave, Madagascar." In *Love in Africa,* edited by Jennifer Cole and Lynn M. Thomas, 109–34. Chicago: University of Chicago Press.

———. 2010. *Sex and Salvation: Imagining the Future in Madagascar.* Chicago: University of Chicago Press.

———. 2012. "The Love of Jesus Never Disappoints: Reconstituting Female Personhood in Urban Madagascar." *Journal of Religion in Africa* 42 (4): 384–407.

———. 2014a. "Producing Value among Malagasy Marriage Migrants in France: Managing Horizons of Expectation." In "Crisis, Value and Hope: Rethinking the Economy," supplement, *Current Anthropology* 55 (S9): S85–S94.

———. 2014b. "The Télèphone Malgache: Transnational Gossip and Social Transformation among Malagasy Marriage Migrants in France." *American Ethnologist* 41 (2): 276–89.

———. 2014c. "Working Mis/Understandings: The Tangled Relationship between Kinship, Franco-Malagasy Binational Marriage, and the French State." *Cultural Anthropology* 29 (3): 527–51.

Cole, Jennifer, and Deborah L. Durham. 2007. "Age, Regeneration, and the Intimate Politics of Globalization." In *Generations and Globalization: Youth, Age, and Family in the New World Economy*, edited by Jennifer Cole and Deborah Durham, 1–28. Bloomington: Indiana University Press.

Cole, Jennifer, and Lynn M. Thomas, eds. 2009. *Love in Africa.* Chicago: University of Chicago Press.

Collard, Chantal. 2009. "The Transnational Adoption of a Related Child in Québec, Canada." In *International Adoption: Global Inequalities and the Circulation of Children*, edited by Diana Marre and Laura Briggs, 119–34. New York: New York University Press.

Comaroff, Jean, and John L. Comaroff. 1999. "Occult Economies and the Violence of Abstraction: Notes from the South African Postcolony." *American Ethnologist* 26 (2): 279–303.

———. 2001. On Personhood: An Anthropological Perspective from Africa. *Social Identity* 7 (2): 267–83.

———. 2005. "Reflections on Youth from the Past to the Postcolony." In *Makers and Breakers: Children and Youth in Postcolonial Africa*, edited by Filip de Boeck and Alcinda Honwana, 19–29. Trenton, NJ: Africa World Press.

———. 2011. *Theory from the South; or, How Euro-America Is Evolving Toward Africa.* Boulder, CO: Paradigm.

Comité interministériel de contrôle de l'immigration. 2012. Les chiffres de la politique de l'immigration et de l'intégration. Paris: La Documentation française.

Constable, Nicole. 2003. *Romance on a Global Stage.* Berkeley: University of California Press.

———, ed. 2005. *Cross-Border Marriages: Gender and Mobility in Transnational Asia.* Philadelphia: University of Pennsylvania Press.

———. 2009. "The Commodification of Intimacy: Marriage, Sex and Reproductive Labor." *Annual Review of Anthropology* 38: 49–64.

Cooper, Frederick. 1997. *From Slaves to Squatters: Plantation Labor and Agriculture in Coastal Kenya, 1890–1925.* Portsmouth, NH: Heinemann.

Cordell, Dennis D., Joel W. Gregory, and Victor Piché. 1996. *Hoe and Wage: A Social History of a Circular Migration System in West Africa, 1900–1975.* Boulder, CO: Westview Press.

Cornuau, Frédérique, and Xavier Dunezat. 2008. "L'immigration en France: Concepts, contours et politiques." *Espace Populations Sociétés* 2008 (2): 331–52.

Cornwall, Andrea. 2002. "Spending Power: Love, Money, and the Reconfiguration of Gender Relations in Ago-Odo, Southwestern Nigeria." *American Ethnologist* 29 (4): 963–80.

Couldry, Nick. 2008. "Mediatization or Mediation: Alternative Understandings of the Emergent Space of Digital Storytelling." *New Media and Society* 10 (3): 373–91.

Coutin, Susan Bibler. 2003. "Illegality, Borderlands, and the Space of Nonexistence." In *Globalization under Construction: Governmentality, Law, and Identity*, edited by Richard Warren Perry and Bill Maurer, 171–202. Minneapolis: University of Minnesota Press.

Covell, Maureen. 1989. *Madagascar: Politics, Economics, Society.* London: Pinter.

Cresswell, Tim, and Craig Martin. 2012. "On Turbulence: Entanglements of Disorder and Order on a Devon Beach." *Tijdschrift voor Economische en Sociale Geografie* 103 (5): 516–29.

DAAD (Deutscher Akademischer Austauschdienst). 2016. *Proof of Financial Resources: 8,000 Euros for One Year.* https://www.study-in.de/en/plan-your -studies/requirements/8000-euros-for-one-year_27533.php.

Daily Graphic. 2008. "Balotelli's Story Takes a New Twist." *Daily Graphic*, October 14.

Danmarks Statistik. 2014. Statistikbanken. http://www.statistikbanken.dk.

Daswani, Girish. 2010. "Transformation and Migration among Members of a Pentecostal Church in Ghana and London." *Journal of Religion in Africa* 40 (4): 442–74.

Davies, Christopher. 2008. "Now I'm a Serie A Star They Want to Come and Find Me—Inter Star Balotelli Accuses Biological Parents of Glory Hunting." *Daily Mail,* November 6. http://www.dailymail.co.uk/sport/football/article -1083620/Inter-star-Balotelli-accuses-parents-glory-hunting.html.

Daum, Christophe. 1998. *Les associations de Maliens en France: Migrations, développement et citoyenneté.* Paris: Karthala.

De Block, Sédar. 2010. "De la sape à la sapelogie: L'histoire des dandys congolais." *Star Du Congo*, April 19. http://www.starducongo.com/De-la-Sape-a-la -Sapelogie-l-histoire-des-dandys-congolais_a2142.html.

De Boeck, Filip, and Alcinda Honwana, eds. 2005. *Makers and Breakers: Children and Youth in Postcolonial Africa.* Trenton, NJ: Africa World Press.

De Boeck, Filip, and Marie-Françoise Plissart. 2006. *Kinshasa: Tales of the Invisible City.* Ghent: Ludion.

De Genova, Nicholas. 2002. "'Migrant Illegality' and Deportability in Everyday Life." *Annual Review of Anthropology* 31: 419–47.

———. 2013. "Spectacles of Migrant 'Illegality': The Scene of Exclusion, the Obscene of Inclusion." *Ethnic and Racial Studies* 36 (7): 1180–98.

De Haas, Hein. 2008. "The Myth of Invasion: The Inconvenient Realities of African Migration to Europe." *Third World Quarterly* 29 (7): 1305–22.

Deleuze, Gilles, and Felix Guattari. 1987. *A Thousand Plateaus: Capitalism and Schizophrenia.* Minneapolis: University of Minnesota Press.

Délivré, Alain. 1974. *L'histoire des rois d'Imerina: Interprétation d'une tradition orale.* Paris: Klincksieck.

Despres, Altaïr. 2015. "Et la femme créa l'homme: Les transactions culturelles intimes dans la danse contemporaine Africaine." *Sociologie* 3 (6): 263–78.

Devisch, René. 1995. "Frenzy, Violence, and Ethical Renewal in Kinshasa." *Public Culture* 7 (3): 593–629.

Dial, Fatou B. 2008. *Mariage et divorce à Dakar.* Paris: Karthala.

Diop, Abdoulaye-Bara. 1985. *La famille Wolof.* Paris: Karthala.

Diouf, Mamadou. 2001. *Histoire du Sénégal.* Paris: Maisonneuve and Larose.

Dougnon, Isaie. 2010. "Life Cycle, Career, and Rites in Modern Work: A Case Study of Public Sector Employees in Mali." Working Papers of the IGK (International Centre on Work and Human Life Cycle in Global History). Berlin: Humboldt University.

———. 2013."Migration as Coping with Risk: African Migrants' Conception of Being Far from Home and States' Policy of Barriers." In *African Migrations: Patterns and Perspectives,* edited by Abdoulaye Kane and Todd H. Leedy, 35–58. Bloomington: Indiana University Press.

Drazin, Adam, and David Frohlich. 2007. "Good Intentions: Remembering through Framing Photographs in English Homes." *Ethnos* 72 (1): 51–76.

Dreby, Joanna. 2010. *Divided by Borders: Mexican Migrants and Their Children.* Berkeley: University of California Press.

Durand, Béatrice. 2004. *Die Legende vom typisch Deutschen: Eine Kultur im Spiegel der Franzosen.* Leipzig: Militzke.

Durham, Deborah. 2004. "Disappearing Youth: Youth as a Social Shifter in Botswana." *American Ethnologist* 31 (4): 589–605.

Durpaire, François. 2006. *France blanche, colère noire.* Paris: Odile Jacob.

Ebron, Paulla. 1997. "Traffic in Men." In *Gendered Encounters: Challenging Cultural Boundaries and Social Hierarchies in Africa,* edited by Maria Grosz-Ngate and Omari H. Kokole, 223–44. New York: Routledge.

Edwards, Elizabeth. 2012. "Objects of Affect: Photography beyond the Image." *Annual Review of Anthropology* 41: 221–34.

Edwards, Elizabeth, Chris Gosden, and Ruth Philips. 2006. "Introduction." In *Sensible Objects: Colonialism, Museums and Material Culture,* edited by Elizabeth Edwards, Chris Gosden, and Ruth Philips, 1–31. Oxford: Berg.

Edwards, Elizabeth, and Janet Hart. 2004. "Introduction: Photographs as Objects." In *Photographs Objects Histories: On the Materiality of Images,* edited by Elizabeth Edwards and Janet Hart, 1–14. London: Routledge.

Ehrenreich, Barbara, and Arlie Russell Hochschild. 2003. *Global Woman: Nannies, Maids, and Sex Workers in the New Economy.* New York: Holt.

Eisenstadt, Shmuel N. 1964. *From Generation to Generation: Age Groups and Social Structure.* New York: Free Press.

Eisenstadt, Shmuel N., and Leo Roniger. 1981. "The Study of Patron-Client Relations and Recent Development in Sociological Theory." In *Political Clientelism, Patronage and Development,* edited by S. N. Eisenstadt and René Lemarchand, 271–96. London: Sage.

Ekholm Friedman, Kajsa. 1991. *Catastrophe and Creation: The Transformation of an African Culture.* Chur, Switzerland: Harwood Academic.

Engelke, Matthew. 2004. "Discontinuity and the Discourse of Conversion." *Journal of Religion in Africa* 34 (2): 82–109.

———. 2010. "Past Pentecostalism: Notes on Rupture, Realignment, and Everyday Life in Pentecostal and African Independent Churches." *Africa* 80 (2): 177–99.

Englund, Harri. 2004. "Cosmopolitanism and the Devil in Malawi." *Ethnos* 69 (3): 293–316.

———. 2007. "Pentecostalism beyond Belief: Trust and Democracy in a Malawian Township." *Africa* 77 (4): 477–99.

Esoavelomandroso, Manassé. 1979. *La province maritime orientale du royaume de Madagascar à la fin du XIXe siècle (1882–1895)*. Antananarivo: FTM.

Etienne, Mona. 1979. "Maternité sociale, rapports d'adoption et pouvoir des femmes chez les Baoulé (Côte d'Ivoire)." *L'Homme* 19 (3/4): 63–107.

Faier, Leiba. 2009. *Intimate Encounters: Filipina Migrants and the Remaking of Rural Japan*. Berkeley: University of California Press.

Fainzang, Sylvie, and Odile Journet. 1988. *La femme de mon mari*. Paris: L'Harmattan.

Fassin, Didier. 2000. "Repenser les enjeux de santé autour de l'immigration." In "Santé: Le traitement de la différence," edited by Didier Fassin, special issue, *Hommes et Migrations* 1225: 5–12.

———. 2005. "Compassion and Repression: The Moral Economy of Immigration Policies in France." *Cultural Anthropology* 20 (3): 362–87.

———. 2010. "Frontières extérieures, frontières intérieures." In *Les nouvelles frontières de la société française*, edited by Didier Fassin, 5–24. Paris: La Découverte.

———. 2011. *Humanitarian Reason: A Moral History of the Present*. Berkeley: University of California Press.

Fassin, Didier, Alain Morice, and Catherine Quiminal. 1997. *Les lois de l'inhospitalité: Les politiques de l'immigration à l'épreuve des sans-papiers*. Paris: La Découverte.

Fassin, Eric. 2009. Entre famille et nation: La filiation naturalisée. *Droit et Société* 2009/2 (72): 373–82.

———. 2010. "National Identities and Transnational Intimacies: Sexual Democracy and the Politics of Immigration in Europe." *Public Culture* 22 (3): 507–29.

Fedyuk, Olena. 2012. "Images of Transnational Motherhood: The Role of Photographs in Measuring Time and Maintaining Connections between Ukraine and Italy." *Journal of Ethnic and Migration Studies* 38 (2): 279–300.

Feeley-Harnik, Gillian. 1980. "The Sakalava House (Madagascar)." *Anthropos* 75 (3/4): 559–85.

Feierman, Steven, and John M. Janzen, eds. 1992. *The Social Basis of Health and Healing in Africa*. Berkeley: University of California Press.

Feldman-Savelsberg, Pamela. 1999. *Plundered Kitchens, Empty Wombs: Threatened Reproduction and Identity in the Cameroon Grassfields*. Ann Arbor: University of Michigan Press.

———. 2011 "Fleeting Trust and Braided Socialities: Temporality and Belonging in African Migrants' Reproductive Practices." Paper presented at the annual meeting for the American Anthropological Association, Montreal, Quebec, November 19.

Feldman-Savelsberg, Pamela, Flavien T. Ndonko, and Bergis Schmidt-Ehry. 2000.

"Sterilizing Vaccines or the Politics of the Womb: Retrospective Study of a Rumor in Cameroon." *Medical Anthropology Quarterly* 14 (2): 159–79.

Feldman-Savelsberg, Pamela, Flavien T. Ndonko, and Song Yang. 2005. "Remembering 'the Troubles': Reproductive Insecurity and the Management of Memory in Cameroon." *Africa* 75 (1): 10–29.

Ferguson, James. 1999. *Expectations of Modernity: Myths and Meanings of Urban Life on the Zambian Copperbelt.* Berkeley: University of California Press.

———. 2006. *Global Shadows: Africa in the Neoliberal World Order.* Durham, NC: Duke University Press.

———. 2013. "Declarations of Dependence: Labour, Personhood, and Welfare in South Africa." *Journal of the Royal Anthropological Institute* 19 (2): 223–42.

Fernandez, Nadine. 2013. "Moral Boundaries and National Borders: Cuban Marriage Migration to Denmark." *Identities* 20(3): 270–87.

Fernandez, Nadine, and Tina Jensen. 2014. "Intimate Contradictions: Comparing the Impact of Danish Family Unification Laws on Pakistani and Cuban Migrants." *Journal of Ethnic and Migration Studies* 40 (7): 1136–53.

Fernando, Mayanthi. 2013. "Save the Muslim Woman, Save the Republic: Ni Putes Ni Soumises and the Ruse of Neoliberal Sovereignty." *Modern and Contemporary France* 21 (2): 147–65.

Ferran, Nicolas. 2008. "L'intégration des étrangers saisie par le droit: Contribution à l'analyse du droit des étrangers 1981–2006." PhD diss., L'Université de Montpellier 1.

———. 2009. "La politique de l'immigration contre les couples mixtes." In *Douce France: Rafles, rétentions, expulsions,* edited by d'Olivier Le Cour Grandmaison, 151–72. Paris: Seuil.

Fesenmyer, Leslie E. 2013. "Relative Distance: Practices of Relatedness among Transnational Kenyan Families." PhD thesis, University of Oxford.

———. 2014. "'Do I Turn Up and Help Others?': Weddings and the Making of a Moral Community among Kenyan Pentecostals in London." Paper presented at the Association of Social Anthropologists of the UK and Commonwealth, University of Edinburgh, June 19–22.

———. 2016. "Deferring the Inevitable Return 'Home': Contingency and Temporality in the Transnational Home-Making Practices of Older Kenyan Women Migrants in London." In *Transnational Migration and Home in Older Age,* edited by Katie Walsh and Lena Näre. London: Routledge.

Fikes, Kesha, and Elena Lemon. 2002. "African Presence in Former Soviet Spaces." *Annual Review of Anthropology* 31: 497–524.

Fink-Nielsen, Mette, Peter Hansen, and Nauja Kleist. 2004. "Roots, Rights and Responsibilities: Place-Making and Repatriation among Somalis in Denmark and Somaliland." *Stichproben* 7: 26–47.

Fioratta, Susanna. 2015. "Beyond Remittance: Evading Uselessness and Seeking Personhood in Fouta Djallon, Guinea." *American Ethnologist* 42 (2): 295–308.

Fleischer, Annett. 2012. *Migration, Marriage, and the Law: Making Families among Cameroonian "Bush Fallers" in Germany.* Berlin: RegioSpectra.

Flynn, Don. 2005. "New Borders, New Management: The Dilemmas of Modern Immigration Policies." *Ethnic and Racial Studies* 28 (3): 463–90.

Fonseca, Claudia. 2009. "Transnational Connections and Dissenting Views: The Evolution of Child Placement Policies in Brazil." In *International Adoption: Global Inequalities and the Circulation of Children*, edited by Diana Marre and Laura Briggs, 154–73. New York: New York University Press.

Forna, Aminatta. 2002. *The Devil That Danced on the Water: A Daughter's Memoir.* London: Harper Collins.

Fortes, Meyer. 1969. *Kinship and the Social Order: The Legacy of Lewis Henry Morgan.* Chicago: Aldine.

Foucault, Michel. 1997. "Polemics, Politics and Problematizations." In *Ethics: Subjectivity and Truth*, vol. 1 of *Essential Works of Foucault, 1954–1984*, edited by Paul Rabinow, 111–19. New York: New Press.

Fouquet, Thomas. 2007a. "De la prostitution clandestine aux désirs de l'ailleurs: Une 'ethnographie de l'extraversion' à Dakar." *Politique Africaine* 3 (107): 102–23.

———. 2007b. "Imaginaires migratoires et expériences multiples de l'altérité: Une dialectique actuelle du proche et du lointain." *Autrepart* 41 (1): 83–98.

Fouron, Georges E., and Nina Glick Schiller. 2002. "The Generation of Identity: Redefining the Second Generation within a Transnational Social Field." In *The Changing Face of Home: The Transnational Lives of the Second Generation*, edited by Georges E. Fouron and Mary C. Waters, 168–208. New York: Russell Sage Foundation.

Francis, Elizabeth. 2002. "Gender, Migration and Multiple Livelihoods: Cases from Eastern and Southern Africa." *Journal of Development Studies* 38 (5): 167–90.

Frederiksen, Bodil F. 2000. "Popular Culture, Gender Relations and the Democratization of Everyday Life in Kenya." *Journal of Southern African Studies* 26 (2): 209–22.

———. 2001. "African Women and Their Colonisation of Nairobi: Representations and Realities." *Azania: Archaeological Research in Africa* 36 (1): 223–34.

———. 2002. "Mobile Minds and Socio-economic Barriers: Livelihoods and African-American Identifications among Youth in Nairobi." In *Work and Migration: Life and Livelihoods in a Globalizing World*, edited by Ninna N. Sørenson and Karin Fog Olwig. London: Routledge.

Freeman, Caren. 2011. *Making and Faking Kinship: Marriage and Labor Migration between China and South Korea.* Ithaca, NY: Cornell University Press.

Freeman, Luke. 2013. "Separation, Connection, and the Ambiguous Nature of Émigré Houses in Rural Highland Madagascar." *Home Cultures* 10 (2): 93–110.

Friedman, Jonathan. 1990. "The Political Economy of Elegance: An African Cult of Beauty." *Culture and History* 7 (1): 101–25.

———. 1991. "Consuming Desires: Strategies of Selfhood and Appropriation." *Cultural Anthropology* 6 (2): 154–63.

———. 1994. *Cultural Identity and Global Process*. London: Sage.

Fumanti, Mattia. 2010. "'Virtuous Citizenship': Ethnicity and Encapsulation among Akan-speaking Ghanaian Methodists in London." *African Diaspora* 3: 13–42.

———. 2013. "'Showing-Off Aesthetics': Looking Good, Making Relations and 'Being in the World' in the London Akan Diaspora." *Ethnos* 78 (2): 200–25.

Gaibazzi, Paolo. 2013. "Cultivating Hustlers: The Agrarian Ethos of Soninke Migration." *Journal of Ethnic and Migration Studies* 39 (2): 259–75.

———. 2015. *Young Men and Rural Permanence in Migrant West Africa*. New York: Berghahn.

Gandoulou, Justin. 1984. *Au coeur de la Sape: Moeurs et aventures de congolais à Paris*. Paris: L'Harmattan.

———. 1989. *Dandies à Bacongo: Le culte de l'élégance dans la société congolaise contemporaine*. Paris: L'Harmattan.

Garcia, Antonio. 2006. "Combien d'immigrés clandestins en France?" Radio France Internationale, April 13. Accessed August 6, 2015. http://www1.rfi.fr/actufr/articles/076/article_43041.asp.

García, Dan Rodríguez. 2006. "Mixed Marriages and Transnational Families in the Intercultural Context: A Case Study of African Spanish Couples in Catalonia." *Journal of Ethnic and Migration Studies* 32 (3): 403–33.

Gardner, Katy. 1993. "Desh-Bidesh: Sylheti Images of Home and Away." *Man*, n.s., 28 (1): 1–15.

———. 1995. *Global Migrants, Local Lives: Travel and Transformation in Rural Bangladesh*. Oxford: Oxford University Press.

Gasparetti, Fedora. 2011. "Relying on Teranga: Senegalese Migrants to Italy and Their Children Left Behind." *Autrepart* 1 (57/58): 215–32.

Gell, Alfred. 1998. *Art and Agency: An Anthropological Theory*. Oxford: Clarendon Press.

Gellner, Ernest, and John Waterbury. 1977. *Patrons and Clients in Mediterranean Societies*. London: Duckworth.

Geschiere, Peter. 2007. "Regional Shifts: Marginal Gains and Ethnic Stereotypes." *African Studies Review* 50 (2): 43–56.

———. 2009. *The Perils of Belonging: Autochthony, Citizenship, and Exclusion in Africa and Europe*. Chicago: University of Chicago Press.

Geschiere, Peter, and Francis Nyamnjoh. 2000. "Capitalism and Autochthony: The Seesaw of Mobility and Belonging." *Public Culture* 12 (2): 423–53.

Ghana Soccernet. 2013. "Mario Balotelli Doesn't Like Talking about His Real Ghanaian Parents." Ghana Soccernet, August 21. http://www.ghanasoccernet.com/mario-balotelli-doesnt-like-talking-about-his-real-ghanaian-parents/.

Gibney, Mathew. 2004. *The Ethics and Politics of Asylum: Liberal Democracy and the Response to Refugees*. Cambridge: Cambridge University Press.

Gifford, Paul. 2004. *Ghana's New Christianity: Pentecostalism in a Globalizing African Economy*. Bloomington: Indiana University Press.

———. 2009. *Christianity, Politics and Public Life in Kenya*. London: Hurst.

Gingrich, Andre, and Marcus Banks, eds. 2006. *Neo-Nationalism in Europe and Beyond: Perspectives from Social Anthropology.* Oxford: Berghahn.

Ginsburg, Faye D., and Rayna Rapp, eds. 1995. *Conceiving the New World Order: The Global Politics of Reproduction.* Berkeley: University of California Press.

Glick Schiller, Nina, Linda Basch, and Christina Blanc-Szanton. 1992. "Transnationalism: A New Analytic Framework for Understanding Migration." In *Toward a Transnational Perspective on Migration: Race, Class, Ethnicity, and Nationalism Reconsidered*, edited by Nina Glick Schiller, Linda Basch, and Christina Blanc-Szanton, 1–24. New York: New York Academy of Sciences.

Gluckman, Max. 1961. "Anthropological Problems Arising from the African Industrial Revolution." In *Social Change in Modern Africa*, edited by Aidan Southall, 67–82. Oxford: Oxford University Press.

Gocking, Roger. 1997. "Colonial Rule and the 'Legal Factor' in Ghana and Lesotho." *Africa* 67 (1): 61–85.

Goffman, Erving. 1959. *The Presentation of Self in Everyday Life.* New York: Anchor.

Gondola, Didier. 1999. "Dream and Drama: The Search for Elegance among Congolese Youth." *African Studies Review* 42 (1): 23–48.

———. 2010. "La Sape Exposed! High Fashion among Lower-Class Congolese Youth: From Colonial Modernity to Global Cosmopolitanism." In *Contemporary African Fashion*, edited by Suzanne Gott and Kristyne Loughran, 157–74. Bloomington: Indiana University Press.

Gonin, Patrick, and Nathalie Kotlok. 2012. "Migrations et pauvreté: Essai sur la situation malienne." *CERISCOPE Pauvrete.* http://ceriscope.sciences-po.fr/pauvrete/content/part2/migrations-et-pauvrete-essai-sur-la-situation-malienne.

Goody, Esther N. 1982. *Parenthood and Social Reproduction: Fostering and Occupational Roles in West Africa.* Cambridge: Cambridge University Press.

Goody, Esther N., and Christine Muir Groothues. 1982. "The Quest for Education." In *Parenthood and Social Reproduction: Fostering and Occupational Roles in West Africa*, by Esther N. Goody, 217–33. Cambridge: Cambridge University Press.

Goody, Jack. 1969. "Adoption in Cross-Cultural Perspective." *Comparative Studies in Society and History* 11 (1): 55–78.

Gordon, April. 1995. "Gender, Ethnicity, and Class in Kenya: 'Burying Otieno' Revisited." *Signs* 20 (4): 883–912.

Gottlieb, Alma. 2004. *The Afterlife Is Where We Come From: The Culture of Infancy in West Africa.* Chicago: University of Chicago Press.

Granjo, Paulo. 2005. *Lobolo em Maputo.* Maputo: Campo das Letras.

Graw, Knut, and Samuli Schielke. 2012. "Introduction: Reflections on Migratory Expectations in Africa and Beyond." In *The Global Horizon: Expectations of Migration in Africa and the Middle East*, edited by Knut Graw and Samuli Schielke, 7–22. Leuven: Leuven University Press.

Grillo, Ralph. 2008. *The Family in Question: Immigrant and Ethnic Minorities in Multicultural Europe.* Amsterdam: Amsterdam University Press.

Grillo, Ralph, and Valentina Mazzucato, eds. 2008. "Africa < > Europe: A Double Engagement." Special issue, *Journal of Ethnic and Migration Studies* 3 (2).

Grillo, Ralph, and Bruno Riccio. 2004. "Translocal Development: Italy-Senegal." *Population, Space and Place* 10 (2): 99–111.

Groes-Green, Christian. 2009. "Hegemonic and Subordinated Masculinities: Class, Violence and Sexual Performance among Young Mozambican Men." *Nordic Journal of African Studies* 18 (4): 286–304.

———. 2010. "Orgies of the Moment: Bataille's Anthropology of Transgression and the Defiance of Danger in Post-Socialist Mozambique." *Anthropological Theory* 10 (4): 385–407.

———. 2011. "The Bling Scandal: Transforming Young Femininities in Mozambique." *Young* 19 (3): 291–312.

———. 2012. "Philogynous Masculinities: Contextualizing Alternative Manhood in Mozambique." *Men and Masculinities* 15 (2): 91–111.

———. 2013. "'To Put Men in a Bottle': Eroticism, Kinship, Female Power, and Transactional Sex in Maputo, Mozambique." *American Ethnologist* 40 (1): 102–17.

———. 2014. "Journeys of Patronage: Moral Economies of Transactional Sex, Kinship and Female Migration from Mozambique to Europe." *Journal of the Royal Anthropological Institute* 20 (2): 237–55.

GTZ (Gesellschaft für Technische, Federal Ministry for Economic Cooperation and Development, Division for Economic Development and Employment, Sector Project Migration and Development). 2007. *The Cameroonian Diaspora in Germany: Its Contribution to Development in Cameroon*. Eschborn: Deutsche Gesellschaft für Technische Zusammenarbeit (GTZ).

Guyer, Jane. 1981. "Household and Community in African Studies." *African Studies Review* 24 (2/3): 87–137.

———. 1993. "Wealth in People and Self-Realization in Equatorial Africa." *Man*, n.s., 28 (2): 243–65.

Hage, Ghassan. 2002. "The Differential Intensities of Social Reality: Migration, Participation, and Guilt." In *Arab-Australians Today: Citizenship and Belonging*, edited by Ghassan Hage, 192–205. Melbourne, Victoria: Melbourne University.

Hahn, Hans Peter, and Georg Klute, eds. 2007. *Cultures of Migration: African Perspectives*. Berlin: LIT.

Hamilton, Kimberly, Patrick Simon, and Clara Veniard. 2004. "The Challenge of French Diversity." Migration Information Source, November 1. http://www.migrationpolicy.org/article/challenge-french-diversity.

Hanlon, Joseph, and Teresa Smart. 2010. *Do Bicycles Equal Development in Mozambique?* Woodbridge, UK: James Currey.

Hannaford, Dinah. 2015. "Technologies of the Spouse: Intimate Surveillance in Senegalese Transnational Marriages." *Global Networks* 15 (1): 43–59.

Hansen, Karen. 2005. "Getting Stuck in the Compound: Some Odds against Social Adulthood in Lusaka, Zambia." *Africa Today* 51 (4): 3–16.

Hanson, Stephanie. 2007. "In West Africa, Threat of Narco-States." Council on

Foreign Relations, July 10. http://www.cfr.org/world/west-africa-threat-narco
-states/p13750.

Hargreaves, Alec. 1995. *Immigration, "Race" and Ethnicity in Contemporary France.* London: Routledge.

Hawkins, Kate, Nick Price, and Fatima Mussa. 2009. "Milking the Cow: Young Women's Constructions of Identity and Risk in Age-Disparate Transactional Sexual Relationships in Maputo, Mozambique." *Global Public Health* 4 (2): 169–82.

Heil, Tilmann. 2013. *Cohabitation and Convivencia: Comparing Conviviality in Casamance and Catalonia.* PhD diss., University of Oxford.

Hervik, Peter. 2004. "Anthropological Perspectives on the New Racism in Europe." *Ethnos* 69 (2): 149–55.

———. 2012. "Ending Tolerance as a Solution to Incompatibility: The Danish 'Crisis of Multiculturalism.'" *European Journal of Cultural Studies* 15 (2): 211–25.

Herzfeld, Michael. 1997. *Cultural Intimacy: Social Poetics in the Nation-State.* New York: Routledge.

Herzog, John D. 1971. "Fertility and Cultural Values: Kikuyu Naming Customs and the Preference for Four or More Children." *Rural Africana* 14: 89–96.

Hill, Polly. 1963. *The Migrant Cocoa-Farmers of Southern Ghana: A Study in Rural Capitalism.* Cambridge: Cambridge University Press.

Hilton, Anne. 1985. *The Kingdom of the Kongo.* Oxford: Clarendon Press.

Hirsch, Jennifer S. 2003. *A Courtship after Marriage: Sexuality and Love in Mexican Transnational Families.* Berkeley: University of California Press.

Hirsch, Jennifer S., and Holly Wardlow, eds. 2006. *Modern Loves: The Anthropology of Courtship and Companionate Marriage.* Ann Arbor: University of Michigan Press.

Hirsch, Marianne.1997. *Family Frames: Photography, Narrative, and Postmemory.* Cambridge, MA: Harvard University Press.

Hochschild, Arlie Russell. (1983) 2003. *The Managed Heart: Commercialization of Human Feeling.* 2nd ed. Berkeley: University of California Press.

———. 2000. "Global Care Chains and Emotional Surplus Value." In *On the Edge: Globalization and the New Millennium,* edited by Tony Giddens and Will Hutton, 130–46. London: Sage.

———. 2003. "Love and Gold." In *Global Women: Nannies, Maids, and Sex Workers in the New Economy,* edited by Barbara Ehrenreich and Arlie Russell Hochschild, 15–30. New York: Holt.

Hoffman, Danny. 2006. Disagreement: Dissent Politics and the War in Sierra Leone. *Africa Today* 52 (3): 3–22.

———. 2011. *The War Machine: Young Men and Violence in Sierra Leone and Liberia.* Durham, NC: Duke University Press.

Holten, Lianne. 2013. *Mothers, Medicine and Morality in Rural Mali: An Ethnographic Study of Therapy Management of Pregnancy and Children's Illness Episodes.* Berlin: LIT.

Home Office. 2012. Statement of Intent: Family Migration. https://www.gov.uk

/government/uploads/system/uploads/attachment_data/file/257359/soi-fam
-mig.pdf.

Hondagneu-Sotelo, Pierrette, and Ernestine Avila. 1997. "'I'm Here, but I'm There':
The Meanings of Latina Transnational Motherhood." *Gender and Society* 11
(5): 548–71.

Honwana, Alcinda Manuel. 2012. *The Time of Youth: Work, Social Change, and Politics in Africa.* Sterling, VA: Kumarian.

Horst, Heather. 2012. "New Media Technologies in Everyday Life." In *Digital
Anthropology*, edited by Heather Horst and Daniel Miller, 61–79. London:
Bloomsbury.

Horst, Heather, and Daniel Miller. 2006. *The Cell Phone: An Anthropology of Communication.* Oxford: Berg.

Horta, Loro. 2007. "Guinea-Bissau: Africa's First Narco State." African Studies
Center, University of Pennsylvania, October. http://www.africa.upenn.edu
/Articles_Gen/guinbisauhorta.html.

Houseman, Michael. 2009. "Les épouses de mon père: À propos de la polygamie
en pays beti." *Ateliers du Laboratoire d'Anthropologie et de Sociologie Comparative*
33. http://ateliers.revues.org/8211.

Howell, Signe. 2004. "The Backpackers That Come to Stay: New Challenges in
Norwegian Transnational Adoptive Families." In *Cross-Cultural Approaches to
Adoption*, edited by Fiona Bowie, 227–41. New York: Routledge.

Hultin, Niklas. 2010. "Repositioning the Front Lines? Reflections on the Ethnography of African Securityscapes." *African Security* 3 (2): 104–25.

Hunter, Mark. 2002. "The Materiality of Everyday Sex: Thinking Beyond 'Prostitution.'" *African Studies* 61 (1): 99–120.

———. 2009. "Providing Love: Sex and Exchange in Twentieth-Century South
Africa." In *Love in Africa*, edited by Jennifer Cole and Lynn M. Thomas, 135–
56. Chicago: University of Chicago Press.

———. 2010. *Love in the Time of Aids: Inequality, Gender, and Rights in South Africa.*
Bloomington: Indiana University Press.

Huschke, Susann. 2013. *Kranksein in der Illegalität: Undokumentierte
Lateinamerikaner/-innen in Berlin: Eine medizinethnologische Studie.* Bielefeld:
Transcript.

———. 2014. "Performing Deservingness: Humanitarian Health Care Provision for Migrants in Germany. *Social Science and Medicine* 120: 352–59.
doi:10.1016/j.socscimed.2014.04.046.

Husserl, Edmund. (1913) 2012. *Ideas: General Introduction to Pure Phenomenology.*
London: Routledge.

Hydén, Göran. 1980. *Beyond Ujamaa in Tanzania: Underdevelopment and an Uncap-
tured Peasantry.* Berkeley: University of California Press.

———. 1983. *No Shortcuts to Progress.* London: Heinemann Educational.

International Organization for Migration. 2009. "Migration in Ghana: A Country
Profile, 2009." https://publications.iom.int/books/migration-ghana-country
-profile-2009-0.

Italy Magazine. 2008. "Inter's Balotelli Gets Italian Citizenship." *Italy Magazine,* August 15. http://www.italymagazine.com/italy/brescia/inters-balotelli-gets -italian-citizenship.

Jackson, Michael. 2002. *The Politics of Storytelling: Violence, Transgression, and Intersubjectivity.* Copenhagen: Museum Tusculanum Press.

———. 2012. *Lifeworlds: Essays in Existential Anthropology.* Chicago: University of Chicago Press.

Jackson, Michael, and Ivan Karp, eds. 1990. *Personhood and Agency: The Experience of Self and Other in African Cultures.* Washington, DC: Smithsonian Institution Press.

Jansen, Jan. 1996. "The Younger Brother and the Stranger: In Search of a Status Discourse for Mande." *Cahiers d'Études Africaines* 36 (144): 659–88.

Janzen, John M. 1978. *The Quest for Therapy in Lower Zaire.* Berkeley: University of California Press.

———. 1987. "Therapy Management: Concept, Reality, Process." *Medical Anthropology Quarterly,* n.s., 1 (1): 68–84.

Jean-Baptiste, Rachel. 2014. *Conjugal Rights: Marriage, Sexuality, and Urban Life in Colonial Libreville, Gabon.* Athens: Ohio University Press.

Jeffrey, Craig. 2010. "Timepass: Youth, Class, and Time among Unemployed Young Men in India." *American Ethnologist* 37 (3): 465–81.

Jensen, Steffen. 2008. *Gangs, Politics, and Dignity in Cape Town.* Chicago: University of Chicago Press.

Johnson-Hanks, Jennifer. 2006. *Uncertain Honor: Modern Motherhood in an African Crisis.* Chicago: University of Chicago Press.

———. 2007. "Women on the Market: Marriage, Consumption, and the Internet in Urban Cameroon." *American Ethnologist* 34 (4): 642–58.

Jones, Hilary. 2013. *The Metis of Senegal: Urban Life and Politics in French West Africa.* Bloomington: Indiana University Press.

Jónsson, Gunvor. 2012. "Migration, Identity and Immobility in a Malian Soninke Village." In *The Global Horizon: Migratory Expectations in Africa and the Middle East,* edited by Knut Graw and Samuli Schielke, 106–20. Leuven: Leuven University Press.

Jua, Nantang. 2003. "Differential Responses to Disappearing Transitional Pathways: Redefining Possibility among Cameroonian Youths." *African Studies Review* 46 (2): 13–36.

Kago Lele, Jacques. 1995. *Tribalisme et exclusions au Cameroun: Le cas des Bamiléké.* Yaoundé: Club de recherche et d'action culturelle.

Kane, Abdoulaye. 2010. "Charity and Self-Help: Migrants' Social Networks and Health Care in the Homeland." *Anthropology Today* 26 (4): 1–5.

Kane, Abdoulaye, and Todd H. Leedy, eds. 2013. *African Migrations: Patterns and Perspectives.* Bloomington: Indiana University Press.

Kane, Cheik Hamidou. 1961. *L'aventure ambiguë.* Paris: Julliard.

Katz, Cindy. 2001. "Capitalism and the Necessity of Social Reproduction." *Antipode* 33 (4): 709–28.

Kea, Pamela. 2004. "Maintaining Difference and Managing Change: Female Agrarian Clientelist Relations in a Gambian Community." *Africa* 74 (3): 361–82.

———. 2010. *Land, Labour and Entrustment: West African Female Farmers and the Politics of Difference*. African Social Studies Series. Leiden: Brill.

———. 2013. "The Complexity of an Enduring Relationship: Gender, Generation and the Moral Economy of the Gambian Mandinka Household." *Journal of the Royal Anthropological Institute* 19 (1): 102–19.

Kebbeh, C. Omar. 2013. "The Gambia: Migration in Africa's 'Smiling Coast.'" Migration Policy Institute, August 15. http://www.migrationpolicy.org /article/gambia-migration-africas-smiling-coast.

Keller, Heidi, Susanne Voelker, and Relindis D. Yovsi. 2005. "Conceptions of Parenting in Different Cultural Communities: The Case of West African Nso and Northern German Women." *Social Development* 14 (1): 158–80.

Kershaw, Greet. 1973. "The Kikuyu of Central Kenya." In *Beliefs and Practices*, vol. 3 of *Cultural Source Materials for Population Planning in East Africa*, edited by Angela Molnos, 47–59. Nairobi: East African Publishing House.

Keyes, Corey L. M., Dov Shmotkin, and Carol D. Ryff. 2002. "Optimizing Well-Being: The Empirical Encounter of Two Traditions." *Journal of Personality and Social Psychology* 8 (6): 1007–22.

Kilomba, Grada. 2008. *Plantation Memories: Episodes of Everyday Racism*. Münster: Unrast.

Kleinman, Julie. 2014. "Adventures in Infrastructure: Making an African Hub in Paris." *City and Society* 26 (3): 286–307.

Koenig, Dolores. 2005. "Multilocality and Social Stratification in Kita, Mali." In *Migration and Economy: Global and Local Dynamics*, edited by Lillian Trager, 77–102. Walnut Creek, CA: AltaMira.

Kofman, Eleonore. 2012. Rethinking Care Through Social Reproduction: Articulating Circuits of Migration. *Social Politics* 19 (1): 142–62.

Kofman, Eleonore, and Parvati Raghuram. 2015. *Gendered Migrations and Global Social Reproduction*. New York: Palgrave Macmillan.

Kohlhagen, Dominik. 2006. "'Illegale' Migration und Rechtskultur: Beobachtungen aus einer Feldforschung in Kamerun und Deutschland." *Zeitschrift für Rechtssoziologie* 27 (2): 239–50.

Kopytoff, Igor, ed. 1987. *The African Frontier: The Reproduction of Traditional Societies*. Bloomington: Indiana University Press.

Kopytoff, Igor, and Suzanne Miers. 1977. "African Slavery as an Institution of Marginality." In *Slavery in Africa*, edited by Suzanne Miers and Igor Kopytoff, 3–84. Madison: University of Wisconsin Press.

Koser, Khalid. 2003. New African Diasporas: An Introduction. In *New African Diasporas*, edited by Khalid Koser, 1–16. Oxford: Routledge.

Kotobi, Laurence, Zahia Kessar, Henri Courau, and Mohamed Fazani. 2012. "Le traitement de la différence ethnique dans le champ sanitaire et humanitaire." In *Du point de vue de l'ethnicité*, edited by Chantal Crenn and Laurence Kotobi, 179–276. Paris: Colin.

Kouame, Koia Jean-Martial. 2012. "La langue française dans tous les contours de la société ivoirienne." Collection Note de Recherche de l'ODSEF. Quebec: Observatoire démographique et statistique de l'espace francophone/Université Laval.

Krause, Kristine. 2008. Transnational Therapy Networks among Ghanaians in London. *Journal of Ethnic and Migration Studies* 34 (2): 235–51.

———. 2011. "Cosmopolitan Charismatics? Transnational Ways of Belonging and Cosmopolitan Moments in the Religious Practice of New Mission Churches." *Ethnic and Racial Studies* 34 (3): 419–35.

Krause, Kristine, and Katharina Schramm. 2011. "Thinking through Political Subjectivity." *African Diaspora* 4 (2): 115–34.

Kuczynski, Liliane. 2002. *Les marabouts africains à Paris*. Paris: Centre national de la recherche scientifique.

Kulish, Nicholas. 2014. "Africans Open Fuller Wallets to the Future." *New York Times*, July 20.

La Documentation française. 2006. *Politique de l'immigration*. Regards sur l'actualité, no. 326. Paris: La Documentation française.

Lambek, Michael, and Andrew Strathern, eds. 1998. *Bodies and Persons: Comparative Perspectives from Africa and Melanesia*. Cambridge: Cambridge University Press

Larkin, Brian. 2008. *Signal and Noise: Media, Infrastructure, and Urban Culture in Nigeria*. Durham, NC: Duke University Press.

Lauro, Amandine. 2005. *Coloniaux, ménagères et prostituées au Congo Belge 1885–1930*. Brussels: Labour.

Lavanchy, Anne. 2014. "Regulating the Nation in Registry Offices: Love, Marriage and Racialization in Switzerland." Presented at Of Love and Family, States and Borders: Comparative Perspectives on Afro-European Couples and Families, Paris, December 13.

Lecarme, Mireille. 1992. "Territoires du féminin, territoires du masculin: Des frontières bien gardées? Un exemple Dakarois." In *Relations de genre et développement*, edited by Jeanne Bisilliat, 295–326. Paris: ORSTOM (IRD).

Leclerc-Madlala, Suzanne. 2003. "Transactional Sex and the Pursuit of Modernity." *Social Dynamics: A Journal of African Studies* 29 (2): 213–33.

Lee, Felicia. 2014. "New Wave of Writers with an Internationalist Bent." *New York Times*, June 29. http://www.nytimes.com/2014/06/30/arts/new-wave-of-african-writers-with-an-internationalist-bent.html?_r=0.

Leinaweaver, Jessaca B. 2008. *The Circulation of Children: Adoption, Kinship, and Morality in Andean Peru*. Durham, NC: Duke University Press.

———. 2009. "Raising the Roof in the Transnational Andes: Building Houses, Forging Kinship." *Journal of the Royal Anthropological Institute* 15 (4): 777–96.

———. 2013. *Adoptive Migration: Raising Latinos in Spain*. Durham, NC: Duke University Press.

Le Monde. 2009. "Eric Besson denonce les marriages gris." *Le Monde*, November 18.

http://www.lemonde.fr/societe/article/2009/11/18/eric-besson-denonce-les
-mariages-gris_1268870_3224.html.

Les Amoureux au ban public. 2008. *Peu de meilleure et trop de pire: Soupçonné, humilies, réprimés: Des couples mixtes témoignes*. Paris: La Cimade.

Le Vine, Victor T. 2004. *Politics in Francophone Africa*. Boulder, CO: Lynne Rienner.

Lindhardt, Martin. 2010. "'If You Are Saved You Cannot Forget Your Parents': Agency, Power, and Social Repositioning in Tanzanian Born-Again Christianity. *Journal of Religion in Africa* 40 (3): 240–72.

Lindsey, Lisa, and Stephen Meischer, eds. 2003. *Men and Masculinities in Modern Africa*. Portsmouth, NH: Heinmann.

Little, Peter D., and Catherine Dolan. 2000. "What It Means to be Restructured: 'Non-traditional' Commodities and Structural Adjustment in sub-Saharan Africa." In *Commodities and Globalization: Anthropological Perspectives*, edited by Angelique Haugerud, Priscilla M. Stone, and Peter D. Little, 59–78. Lanham, MD: Rowman and Littlefield.

Lonsdale, John. 1992. "The Moral Economy of Mau Mau: Wealth, Poverty and Civic Virtue in Kikuyu Political Thought." In *Violence and Ethnicity*, bk. 2 of *Unhappy Valley: Conflict in Kenya and Africa*, edited by Bruce Berman and John Lonsdale, 315–504. Oxford: Currey.

———. 1996. "'Listen While I Read': The Orality of Christian Literacy in the Young Kenyatta's Making of the Kikuyu." In *Ethnicity in Africa: Roots, Meanings and Implications*, edited by Louise de la Gorgendiere, Kenneth King, and Sarah Vaughan, 17–53. Edinburgh: Centre for African Studies.

———. 2003. "Authority, Gender, and Violence: The War within Mau Mau's Fight for Land and Freedom." In *Mau Mau and Nationhood: Arms, Authority and Narration*, edited by E. S. A. Odhiambo and John Lonsdale, 46–75. Oxford: James Currey.

Lubkemann, Stephen C. 2005. "The Moral Economy of Nonreturn among Socially Diverted Labor Migrants from Portugal and Mozambique." In *Migration and Economy: Global and Local Dynamics*, edited by Lillian Trager, 257–87. Walnut Creek, CA: AltaMira.

———. 2008. "Involuntary Immobility: On a Theoretical Invisibility in Forced Migration Studies." *Journal of Refugee Studies* 21 (4): 454–75.

Lucassen, Leo. 2005. *The Immigrant Threat: The Integration of Old and New Migrants in Western Europe since 1850*. Urbana: University of Illinois Press.

Lucht, Hans. 2011. *Darkness before Daybreak: African Migrants Living on the Margins in Southern Italy Today*. Berkeley: University of California Press.

MacGaffey, Janet, and Rémy Bazenguissa-Ganga. 2000. *Congo-Paris: Transnational Traders on the Margins of the Law*. Bloomington: Indiana University Press.

MacGaffey, Wyatt. 1986. *Religion and Society in Central Africa*. Chicago: University of Chicago Press.

Madianou, Mirca, and Daniel Miller. 2012. *Migration and New Media: Transnational Families and Polymedia*. London: Routledge.

Maier, Katrin Dorothee. 2012. "Redeeming London: Gender, Self and Mobility among Nigerian Pentecostals." PhD thesis, University of Sussex.

Mains, Daniel. 2007. "Neoliberal Times: Progress, Boredom, and Shame among Young Men in Ethiopia." *American Ethnologist* 34 (4): 659–73.

———. 2012. *Hope Is Cut: Youth, Unemployment, and the Future in Urban Ethiopia.* Philadelphia: Temple University Press.

———. 2013. "Friends and Money: Balancing Affection and Reciprocity in Urban Ethiopia." *American Ethnologist* 40 (2): 335–46.

Makhulu, Anne Marie, Beth Buggenhagen, and Stephen Jackson. 2010. *Hard Work, Hard Times: Global Volatility and African Subjectivity.* Berkeley: University of California Press.

Makouezi, Elvis Gueri. 2013. *Dictionnaire de la Sape.* Paris: Publibook.

Manchuelle, François. 1997. *Willing Migrants: Soninke Labour Diasporas, 1848–1960.* Athens: Ohio University Press.

Mann, Kristin, and Richard Roberts. 1991. *Law in Colonial Africa.* Portsmouth, NH: Heinemann.

Mantot, Pierre. 2007. *Matsoua et le mouvement d'éveil de la conscience noire.* Paris: L'Harmattan.

Manuh, Takyiwaa. 2006. *An 11th Region of Ghana? Ghanaians Abroad.* Accra: Ghana Academy of Arts and Sciences.

Margold, Jane. 2004. "Filipina Depictions of Migrant Life for Their Kin at Home." In *Coming Home? Refugees, Migrants and Those Who Stayed Behind,* edited by Lynellyn Long and Ellen Oxfeld, 49–62. Philadelphia: University of Pennsylvania Press.

Marshall, Ruth. 1991. "Power in the Name of Jesus." *Review of African Political Economy* 18 (52): 21–37.

———. 2009. *Political Spiritualities: The Pentecostal Revolution in Nigeria.* Chicago: University of Chicago Press.

Martin, Phyllis M. 1994. "Contesting Clothes in Colonial Brazzaville." *Journal of African History* 35 (3): 401–26.

Maskens, Maïté. 2013. "L'amour et ses frontières: Régulations étatique et migrations de mariage (Belgique, France, Suisse et Italie)." *Migrations Société* 25 (150): 43–60.

Masquelier, Adeline. 2005. "The Scorpion's Sting: Youth, Marriage and the Struggle for Social Maturity in Niger." *Journal of the Royal Anthropological Institute* 11 (1): 59–83.

———. 2013. "Teatime: Boredom and the Temporalities of Young Men in Niger." *Africa* 83 (3): 470–91.

Massumi, Brian. 2002. *Parables of the Virtual: Movement, Affect, Sensation.* Durham, NC: Duke University Press.

Masvawure, Tsitsi. 2010. "'I Just Need to Be Flashy on Campus': Female Students and Transactional Sex at a University in Zimbabwe." *Culture, Health and Sexuality* 12 (8): 857–70.

Mate, Rekopantswe. 2002. "Wombs as God's Laboratories: Pentecostal Discourses of Femininity in Zimbabwe." *Africa* 72 (4): 549–68.

Mauss, Marcel. (1950) 2000. *The Gift: The Form and Reason for Exchange in Archaic Societies.* New York: Norton.

Maxwell, David. 1998. "'Delivered from the Spirit of Poverty?': Pentecostalism, Prosperity and Modernity in Zimbabwe." *Journal of Religion in Africa* 28 (3): 350–73.

Mayer, Philip. 1962. "Migrancy and the Study of Africans in Towns." *American Anthropologist* 64 (3): 576–92.

Mazzarella, William. 2010. "Affect: What Is It Good For?" In *Enchantments of Modernity: Empire, Nation, Globalization,* edited by Saurabh Dube, 291–309. London: Routledge.

Mazzucato, Valentina. 2008. "The Double Engagement: Transnationalism and Integration. Ghanaian Migrants' Lives between Ghana and The Netherlands." *Journal of Ethnic and Migration Studies* 34 (2): 199–216.

McDowell, Linda, Adina Batnitzky, and Sarah Dyer. 2007. "Division, Segmentation, and Interpellation: The Embodied Labors of Migrant Workers in a Greater London Hotel." *Economic Geography* 83 (1): 1–25.

McGregor, Joann. 2007. "Joining the BBC (British Bottom Cleaners): Zimbabwean Migrants and the UK Care Industry." *Journal of Ethnic and Migration Studies* 33 (5): 801–24.

Meiu, George P. 2009. "'Mombasa Morans': Embodiment, Sexual Morality, and Samburu Men in Kenya." *Canadian Journal of African Studies* 43 (1): 105–21.

———. 2015. "'Beach-Boy Elders' and 'Young Big-Men': Subverting the Temporalities of Ageing in Kenya's Ethno-Erotic Economies." *Ethnos* 80 (4): 472–96.

Meurs, Dominique, Ariane Pailhé, and Patrick Simon. 2005. *Mobilité intergénérationnelle et persistance des inégalités: L'accès à l'emploi des immigrés et de leurs descendants en France.* Documents de travail, 130. Paris: Institut national d'études démographiques.

Meyer, Birgit. 1998. "'Make a Complete Break with the Past.' Memory and Post-Colonial Modernity in Ghanaian Pentecostalist Discourse." *Journal of Religion in Africa* 28 (3): 316–49.

———. 1999. *Translating the Devil: Religion and Modernity among the Ewe in Ghana.* Edinburgh: Edinburgh University Press.

———. 2004. "Christianity in Africa: From African Independent to Pentecostal-Charismatic Churches." *Annual Review of Anthropology* 33: 447–74.

Miers, Suzanne, and Igor Kopytoff. 1977. *Slavery in Africa: Historical and Anthropological Perspectives.* Madison: University of Wisconsin Press.

Miller, Daniel, and Don Slater. 2000. *The Internet: An Ethnographic Approach.* Oxford: Berg.

Millot, Lorraine. 2005. "Beaucoup de ces Africains sont polygames . . ." *Libération,* November 15. http://www.liberation.fr/evenement/2005/11/15/beaucoup-de-ces-africains-sont-polygames_539018.

Modern Ghana Web. 2008. "Balotelli Attacks Ghanaian Parents." Modern Ghana Web, November 7. http://www.modernghana.com/news/189826/2/balotelli -attacks-ghanaian-parents.html.

Mondain, Nathalie, Thomas Legrand, and Valérie Delaunay. 2004. "L'évolution de la polygamie en milieu rural sénégalais: Institution en crise ou en mutation?" *Cahiers Québécois de Démographie* 33 (2): 273–308.

Monteil, Charles. 1931. "La divination chez les noirs de l'Afrique occidentale française." *Bulletin du Comite d'Études Historiques et Scientifiques de l'Afrique Occidentale Française* 5 (1/2): 27–36.

Moore, Erin. N.d. "Translating Girls' Empowerment: Gender, Adolescence, and Transnational NGOs in Urban Uganda." PhD diss. in preparation, University of Chicago.

Munn, Nancy. 1986. *The Fame of Gawa: A Symbolic Study of Value Transformation in a Massim (Papua New Guinea) Society.* Durham, NC: Duke University Press.

Musso, Sandrine. 2005. "Regard sur . . . la santé et l' 'immigration.'" *Bulletin Amades.* http://amades.revues.org/269.

Nakano Glenn, Evelyn. 1992. "From Servitude to Service Work: Historical Continuities in the Racial Division of Paid Reproductive Labor." *Signs* 18 (1): 1–43.

Ndiaye, Salif, Papa Demba Diouf, and Mohamed Ayad. 1994. *Enquête démographique et de santé au Sénégal (EDS-II) 1992/93.* Dakar: Direction de la prévision et de la statistique.

Nelson, Nici. 1992. "The Women Who Have Left and Those Who Have Stayed Behind: Rural-Urban Migration in Central and Western Kenya." In *Gender and Migration in Developing Countries*, edited by Sylvia Chant, 109–38. London: Belhaven.

Neveu Kringelbach, Hélène. 2013a. *Dance Circles: Movement, Morality and Self-Fashioning in Urban Senegal.* Oxford: Berghahn.

———. 2013b. "'Mixed Marriage,' Citizenship, and the Policing of Intimacy in Contemporary France." Working Paper 77, International Migration Institute. Oxford: IMI, University of Oxford. http://www.imi.ox.ac.uk/publications/wp -77-13.

———. 2015. "Gendered Educational Trajectories and Transnational Marriage among West African Students in France (Online)." *Identities: Global Studies in Culture and Power* 22 (3): 288–302.

Newell, Sasha. 2005. "Migratory Modernity and the Cosmology of Consumption in Côte d'Ivoire." In *Migration and Economy: Global and Local Dynamics*, edited by Lillian Trager, 163–92. Walnut Creek, CA: AltaMira.

———. 2009. "Godrap Girls, Draou Boys, and the Ivoirian Sexual Economy of the Bluff." *Ethnos* 74 (3): 379–402.

———. 2012. *The Modernity Bluff: Crime, Consumption, and Citizenship in Côte d'Ivoire.* Chicago: University of Chicago Press.

Notermans, Catrien. 2004. "Fosterage and the Politics of Marriage and Kinship in East Cameroon." In *Cross-Cultural Approaches to Adoption*, edited by Fiona Bowie, 48–63. London: Routledge.

Nyamnjoh, Francis B. 2002. "'A Child Is One Person's Only in the Womb': Domestication, Agency, and Subjectivity in the Cameroonian Grassfields." In *Postcolonial Subjectivities in Africa*, edited by Richard Werbner, 111–38. London: Zed.

———. 2011. "Cameroonian Bushfalling: Negotiation of Identity and Belonging in Fiction and Ethnography." *American Ethnologist* 38 (4): 701–13.

Nyamnjoh, Henrietta, and Michael Rowlands. 2013. "Do You Eat Achu Here? Nurturing as a Way of Life in a Cameroon Diaspora." *Critical African Studies* 5 (3): 140–52.

O'Brien, Donald B. C. 1996. "A Lost Generation? Youth, Identity and State Decay in West Africa." In *Postcolonial Identities in Africa*, edited by Richard Werbner and Terence Ranger, 55–74. London: Zed.

Olwig, Karen Fog. 2007. *Caribbean Journeys: An Ethnography of Migration and Home in Three Family Networks*. Durham, NC: Duke University Press.

———. 2012. "The Care Chain, Children's Mobility and the Caribbean Migration Tradition." *Journal of Ethnic and Migration Studies* 38 (6): 933–52.

———. 2014. "The Duplicity of Diversity: Caribbean Immigrants in Denmark." *Ethnic and Racial Studies* 38 (7): 1104–19.

Oruka, Henry Odera. 1990. *Sage Philosophy: Indigenous Thinkers and Modern Debate on African Philosophy*. Leiden: Brill.

———. 1992. *Oginga Odinga: His Philosophy and Beliefs*. Nairobi: Initiatives.

Oso Casas, Laura. 2010. "Money, Sex, Love and the Family: Economic and Affective Strategies of Latin American Sex Workers in Spain." *Journal of Ethnic and Migration Studies* 36 (1): 47–65.

Ouellette, Françoise-Romaine. 2009. "The Social Temporalities of Adoption and the Limits of Plenary Adoption." In *International Adoption: Global Inequalities and the Circulation of Children*, edited by Diana Marre and Laura Briggs, 69–86. New York: New York University Press.

Oyewùmí, Oyèrónké. 2011. "Decolonizing the Intellectual and the Quotidian: Yorùbá Scholars(hip) and Male Dominance." In *Gender Epistemologies in Africa*, edited by Oyèrónké Oyewùmí, 9–34. New York: Palgrave Macmillan.

Palriwala, Rajni, and Patricia Uberoi, eds. 2008. *Marriage, Migration and Gender*. New Delhi: Sage.

Parkin, David. 1975. "Migration, Settlement, and the Politics of Unemployment: A Nairobi Case Study." In *Town and Country in Central and Eastern Africa*, edited by David Parkin, 145–55. London: Oxford University Press for International African Institute.

———. 1978. *The Cultural Definition of Political Response*. London: Academic Press.

Parreñas, Rhacel Salazar. 2001. *Servants of Globalization: Women, Migration, and Domestic Work*. Stanford, CA: Stanford University Press.

———. 2005a. *Children of Global Migration: Transnational Families and Gendered Woes*. Stanford, CA: Stanford University Press.

———. 2005b. "Long Distance Intimacy: Class, Gender and Intergenerational Relations between Mothers and Children in Filipino Transnational Families." *Global Networks: A Journal of Transnational Affairs* 5 (4): 317–36.

———. 2011. *Illicit Flirtations: Labor, Migration, and Sex Trafficking in Tokyo.* Stanford, CA: Stanford University Press.

———. 2012. "The Reproductive Labour of Migrant Workers." *Global Networks* 12 (2): 269–75.

Parry, Jonathan, and Maurice Bloch. 1989. "Introduction: Money and the Morality of Exchange." In *Money and the Morality of Exchange,* edited by Jonathan Parry and Maurice Bloch, 165–86. Cambridge: Cambridge University Press.

Parsitau, Damaris S., and Philomena N. Mwaura. 2010. "Gospel without Borders: Gender Dynamics of Transnational Religious Movements in Kenya and the Kenyan Diaspora." In *Religions Crossing Boundaries: Transnational Religious Dynamics in Africa and the New African Diaspora,* edited by Afe Adogame and James Spickard, 185–210. Leiden: Brill.

Pasura, Dominic. 2008. "Gendering the Diaspora: Zimbabwean Migrants in Britain." *African Diaspora* 1 (1): 86–109.

Pauli, Julia. 2008. "A House of One's Own: Gender, Migration, and Residence in Rural Mexico." *American Ethnologist* 35 (1): 171–87.

Péchu, Cécile. 1999. "Black African Immigrants in France and Claims for Housing." *Journal of Ethnic and Migration Studies* 25 (4): 727–44.

Peletz, Michael. 2001. "Ambivalence in Kinship since the 1940s." In *Relative Values: Reconfiguring Kinship Studies,* edited by Sarah Franklin and Susan McKinnon, 413–44. Durham, NC: Duke University Press.

Peters, Krijn, and Paul Richards. 1998. "Why We Fight: Voices of Youth Combatants in Sierra Leone." *Africa: Journal of the International African Institute* 68 (2): 183–210.

Pink, Sarah. 2001. "Sunglasses, Suitcases, and Other Symbols: Creativity and Indirect Communication in Festive and Everyday Performance." In *An Anthropology of Indirect Communication,* edited by J. Hendry and C. W. Watson, 101–14. London: Routledge.

Piot, Charles. 1999. *Remotely Global: Village Modernity in West Africa.* Chicago: University of Chicago Press.

———. 2010. *Nostalgia for the Future: West Africa after the Cold War.* Chicago: University of Chicago Press.

Piper, Nicola, and Mina Roces. 2003. *Wife or Worker? Asian Women and Migration.* Lanham, MD: Rowman and Littlefield.

Plambech, Sine. 2010. "From Thailand with Love: Transnational Marriage Migration in the Global Care Economy." In *Sex Trafficking, Human Rights, and Social Justice,* edited by Tiantian Zheng, 47–61. New York: Routledge.

———. 2014. "Points of Departure: Migration Control and Anti-Trafficking in the Lives of Nigerian Sex Worker Migrants after Deportation from Europe." PhD thesis, University of Copenhagen.

Pordié, Laurent, and Emmanuelle Simon. 2013. *Les nouveaux guérisseurs: Biographies de thérapeutes au temps de la globalisation.* Paris: École des hautes études en sciences sociales.

Povinelli, Elizabeth A. 2006. *The Empire of Love: Toward a Theory of Intimacy, Gene-alogy, and Carnality.* Durham, NC: Duke University Press.

Price, Neil. 1996. "The Changing Value of Children among the Kikuyu of Central Province, Kenya." *Africa* 66 (3): 411–36.

Pype, Katrien. 2011. "Confession cum Deliverance: In/dividuality of the Subject among Kinshasa's Born-Again Christians." *Journal of Religion in Africa* 41 (3): 280–310.

Quiminal, Catherine. 1991. *Gens d'ici, gens d'ailleurs: Migrations Soninké et transformations villageoises.* Paris: Bourgois.

Quiminal, Catherine, and Mahamet Timera. 2002. "1974–2002, les mutations de l'immigration ouest-africaine." *Hommes et Migrations* 1239: 19–32.

Rae-Espinoza, Heather. 2011. "The Children of Émigrés in Ecuador: Narratives of Cultural Reproduction and Emotion in Transnational Social Fields." In *Everyday Ruptures: Children, Youth, and Migration in Global Perspective*, edited by Cati Coe, Rachel R. Reynolds, Deborah A. Boehm, Julia Meredith Hess, and Heather Rae-Espinoza, 115–38. Nashville, TN: Vanderbilt University Press.

Raison-Jourde, Françoise. 1991. *Bible et pouvoir à Madagascar au XIXe siecle: Invention d'une identité chrétienne et construction de l'état, 1780–1880.* Paris: Karthala.

Raissiguier, Catherine. 2010. *Reinventing the Republic: Gender, Migration, and Citizenship.* Stanford, CA: Stanford University Press.

Razy, Elodie. 2007. "Les sens contraires de la migration." *Journal des Africanistes* 77 (2): 19–43.

Reddy, William M. 2001. *The Navigation of Feeling: A Framework for the History of Emotions.* Cambridge: Cambridge University Press.

Reed-Danahay, Deborah. 2008. "Belonging among Vietnamese Americans: Citizenship, Political Engagement, and Belonging." In *Immigrants in Europe and the United States*, edited by Deborah Reed-Danahay and Caroline B. Brettell, 78–99. New Brunswick, NJ: Rutgers University Press.

Reynolds, Rachel. 2006. "Professional Nigerian Women, Household Economy, and Immigration Decisions." *International Migration* 44 (5): 167–88.

Riccio, Bruno. 2001. "From 'Ethnic Group' to 'Transnational Community'? Senegalese Migrants, Ambivalent Experiences, and Multiple Trajectories." *Journal of Ethnic and Migration Studies* 27 (4): 583–99.

———. 2008. "West African Transnationalisms Compared: Ghanaians and Senegalese in Italy." *Journal of Ethnic and Migration Studies* 34 (2): 217–34.

Richards, Paul. 1995. "Rebellion in Liberia and Sierra Leone: A Crisis of Youth?" In *Conflict in Africa*, edited by Oliver Furley, 134–70. London: Tauris Academic.

———. 1996. *Fighting for the Rain Forest: War, Youth and Resources in Sierra Leone.* Portsmouth, NH: Heinemann.

Robertson, A. F. 1987. *The Dynamics of Productive Relationships: African Share Contracts in Comparative Perspective.* Cambridge: Cambridge University Press.

Robertson, Claire C., and Iris Berger. 1986. "Introduction: Analyzing Class and

Gender: African Perspectives." In *Women and Class in Africa*, edited by Claire C. Robertson and Iris Berger, 3–24. New York: Africana.

Robledo, Manuela Salcedo. 2011."Bleu, blanc, gris . . . la couleur des mariages." *L'Espace Politique* 13. http://dx.doi.org/10.4000/espacepolitique.1869.

Rodier, Claire. 2007. "The Migreurop Network and Europe's Foreign Camps." In *Nongovernmental Politics*, edited by Michel Feher, 446–67. New York: Zone.

Rodriquez, Anne-Line. 2015. "Three Stories about Living without Migration in Dakar: Coming to Terms with the Contradictions of the Moral Economy." *Africa* 85 (2): 333–55.

Rose, Gillian. 2010. *Doing Family Photography: The Domestic, the Public and the Politics of Sentiment*. Farnham: Ashgate.

Roseneil, Sasha, and Shelley Budgeon. 2004. "Cultures of Intimacy and Care beyond 'the Family': Personal Life and Social Change in the Early 21st Century." *Current Sociology* 52 (2): 135–59.

Rowlands, Michael. 1996. "The Consumption of an African Modernity." In *African Material Culture*, edited by Mary Jo Arnoldi, Christraud M. Geary, and Kris I. Hardin, 188–213. Bloomington: Indiana University Press.

Rytter, Mikkel. 2011. "Semi-Legal Family Life: Pakistani Couples in the Borderlands of Denmark and Sweden." *Global Networks* 12 (1): 91–108.

———. 2013. *Family Upheaval: Generation, Mobility and Relatedness among Pakistani Migrants in Denmark*. Oxford: Berghahn.

Sahlins, Marshall. 2013. *What Kinship Is—And Is Not*. Chicago: University of Chicago Press.

Salomon, Christine. 2009. "Vers le nord." *Autrepart* 49: 223–40.

Sanket, Mihapatra, and Dilip Ratha, eds. 2011. *Remittance Markets in Africa*. Washington, DC: World Bank.

Saraiva, Clara. 2008. "Transnational Migrant and Transnational Spirits: An African Religion in Lisbon." *Journal of Ethnic and Migration Studies* 34 (2): 253–69.

Sargent, Carolyn. 1982. *The Cultural Context of Therapeutic Choice: Obstetrical Care Decisions among the Bariba of Benin*. Boston: Kluwer.

———. 2006. "Reproductive Strategies and Islamic Discourse: Malian Migrants Negotiate Everyday Life in Paris, France." *Medical Anthropology Quarterly* 20 (1): 31–50.

Sargent, Carolyn, and Stéphanie Larchanché. 2007. "The Muslim Body and the Politics of Immigration in France: Popular and Biomedical Representations of Malian Migrant Women." *Body and Society* 13 (3): 79–102.

———. 2011. "Transnational Migration and Global Health: The Production and Management of Risk, Illness, and Access to Care. *Annual Review of Anthropology* 40: 345–61.

Sargent, Carolyn, Stéphanie Larchanché, and Samba Yatera. 2005. "The Evolution of Telecommunications in the Context of Transnational Migration." *Hommes et Migrations* 1256: 131–140.

Sayad, Abdelmalek. 1999. *La double absence: Des illusions aux souffrances de l' immigré.* Paris: Seuil.

Schachter, Judith. 2009. "International Adoption: Lessons from Hawai'i." In *International Adoption: Global Inequalities and the Circulation of Children*, edited by Diana Marre and Laura Briggs, 52–68. New York: New York University Press.

Schain, Martin A. 2008. *The Politics of Immigration in France, Britain, and the United States.* New York: Palgrave Macmillan.

Schildkrout, Enid. 1973. "The Fostering of Children in Urban Ghana." *Urban Anthropology* 2 (1): 48–73.

Schmid, Susanne, and Kevin Borchers. 2010. *Vor den Toren Europas? Das Potenzial der Migration aus Afrika.* Bundesamt für Migration und Flüchtlinge, Forschungsbericht 7. Nuremberg: Bundesamt für Migration und Flüchtlinge.

Schmidt, Garbi. 2011a. "Law and Identity: Transnational Arranged Marriages and the Boundary of Danishness." *Journal of Ethnic and Migration Studies* 37 (2): 257–75.

———. 2011b. "Migration and Marriage: Examples of Border Artistry and Cultures of Migration?" *Nordic Journal of Migration Research* 1 (2): 80–87.

Schneider, David Murray. 1968. *American Kinship: A Cultural Account.* Englewood Cliffs, NJ: Prentice-Hall.

Schuerkens, Ulrike. 2007. "France." In *European Immigration*, edited by Anna Triandafyllidou and Ruby Gropas, 113–26. Aldershot, UK: Ashgate.

Schulz, Dorothea. 2002. "The World Is Made by Talk." *Cahiers d'Études Africaines* 42 (4): 797–829.

Searing, James F. 1993. *West African Slavery and Atlantic Commerce: The Senegal River Valley, 1700–1860.* Cambridge: Cambridge University Press.

Seelow, Soren, and Sébastien Hervieu. 2013. "À Madagascar, la folle rumeur qui a mené trois hommes sur le bûcher." *Le Monde.* http://www.lemonde.fr/societe/visuel/2013/11/12/a-madagascar-la-folle-rumeur-qui-a-mene-trois-hommes-sur-le-bucher_3512306_3224.html.

Shandy, Dianna J. 2008. "Irish Babies, African Mothers: Rites of Passage and Rights in Citizenship in Post-Millennial Ireland." *Anthropological Quarterly* 81 (4): 803–31.

Shaw, Alison. 1988. *A Pakistani Community in Britain.* Oxford: Blackwell.

———. 2000. *Kinship and Continuity: Pakistani Families in Britain.* Amsterdam: Harwood Academic.

———. 2001. "Kinship, Cultural Preference and Immigration: Consanguineous Marriage among British Pakistanis." *Journal of the Royal Anthropological Institute* 7 (2): 315–34.

Shaw, Mark. 2015. "Drug Trafficking in Guinea-Bissau, 1998–2014: The Evolution of an Elite Protection Network." *Journal of Modern African Studies* 53 (3): 339–64.

Shepherd, Andrew, Lucy Scott, Chiara Mariotti, Flora Kessy, Raghav Gaiha, Lucia da Corta, Katharina Hanifnia, et al. 2014. *The Chronic Poverty Report*

2014–2015: The Road to Zero Extreme Poverty. London: Overseas Development Institute.

Silberschmidt, Margrethe. 2005. "Poverty, Male Disempowerment, and Male Sexuality: Rethinking Men and Masculinities in Rural and Urban East Africa." In *African Masculinities*, edited by Lahouzine Ouzgane and Robert Morrell, 189–205. New York: Palgrave Macmillan.

Silverstone, Roger, and Eric Hirsch. 1992. *Consuming Technologies.* London: Routledge.

Simone, AbdouMaliq. 2011. "The Urbanity of Movement: Dynamic Frontiers in Contemporary Africa." *Journal of Planning Education and Research* 31 (4): 379–91.

Simone, AbdouMaliq, and Abdelghani Abouhani. 2005. "Introduction: Urban Processes and Change." In *Urban Africa: Changing Contours of Survival in the City*, edited by AbdouMaliq Simone and Abdelghani Abouhani, 1–26. New York: Zed.

Slobin, Kathleen. 1998. "Repairing Broken Rules: Care-Seeking Narratives for Menstrual Problems in Rural Mali." *Medical Anthropology Quarterly* 12 (3): 363–83.

Smart, Carole, and Bren Neale. 1999. *Family Fragments.* Cambridge: Polity.

Smith, David. 2012. "Portuguese Escape Austerity and Find a New El Dorado in Angola." *Guardian*, September 15. Accessed October 7, 2014. http://www.theguardian.com/world/ 2012/sep/16/portuguese-exodus-angola-el-dorado.

Solsten, Eric. 1995. "Social Welfare, Health Care, and Education." In *Germany: A Country Study*, edited by Eric Solsten. Washington, DC: Government Printing Office for the Library of Congress. http://countrystudies.us/germany/111.htm.

Sontag, Susan. 1999. "The Image World." In *Visual Culture: The Reader*, edited by Jessica Evans and Stuart Hall, 80–94. London: Sage. Originally published in Susan Sontag, *On Photography* (Harmondsworth: Penguin, 1977).

Sow, Noah. 2008. *Deutschland Schwarz Weiss: Der alltägliche Rassismus.* Munich: Bertelsmann.

Spiegel Online. 2013. "Africa's Cocaine Hub: Guinea-Bissau a 'Drug Trafficker's Dream.'" *Spiegel* Online International. http://www.spiegel.de/international /world/violence-plagues-african-hub-of-cocaine-trafficking-a-887306.html.

Spire, Alexis. 2008. *Accueillir ou reconduire: Enquête sur les guichets de l'imigration.* Paris: Raisons d'agir.

Stack, Carol B., and Linda M. Burton. 1994. "Kinscripts: Reflections on Family, Generation, and Culture." In *Mothering: Ideology, Experience, and Agency*, edited by Evelyn Nakano Glenn, Grace Chang, and Linda Renney Forcey, 33–44. New York: Routledge.

Statistisches Bundesamt. 2013. *Bevölkerung und Erwerbstätigkeit.* Wiesbaden: Statistisches Bundesamt.

Stichter, Sharon. 1987. "Women and Family: The Impact of Capitalist Development in Kenya." In *The Political Economy of Kenya*, edited by Michael G. Schatzberg, 137–60. New York: Praeger.

———. 1988. "The Middle-Class Family in Kenya: Changes in Gender Relations." In *Patriarchy and Class: African Women in the Home and the Workforce*, edited by Sharon Stichter and Jane Parpart, 177–204. Boulder, CO: Westview.

Stoler, Ann. 2002. *Carnal Knowledge and Imperial Power: Race and the Intimate in Colonial Rule*. Berkeley: University of California Press.

Stoller, Paul. 2002. *Money Has No Smell: The Africanization of New York City*. Chicago: University of Chicago Press.

———. 2014. *Yaya's Story: The Quest for Well-Being in the World*. Chicago: University of Chicago Press.

Streiff-Fénart, Jocelyne, and Aurelia Segatti, eds. 2014. *The Challenge of the Threshold: Border Closures and Migration Movements in Africa*. Lanham, MD: Lexington.

Stryker, Rachel. 2011. "The War at Home: Affective Economies and Transnationally Adoptive Families in the United States." *International Migration* 49 (6): 25–55.

Súarez-Orozco, Carola, Irina L. G. Todorova, and Josephine Louie. 2002. "Making Up for Lost Time: The Experience of Separation and Reunification among Immigrant Families." *Family Process* 41 (4): 625–43.

Surkis, Judith. 2006. *Sexing the Citizen: Masculinity and Morality in France, 1870–1920*. Ithaca, NY: Cornell University Press.

Tall, E. K. 1985. "Guerir a Cubabel: Interpretation de la maladie et pratiques therapeutiques chez les Haalpulaaren dans la vallee du fleuve Senegal." These de 3ᵉ cycle en ethnologie, École des hautes études en sciences sociales, Paris.

Tall, Serigne M. 2004. "Senegalese Émigrés: New Information and Communication Technologies." *Review of African Political Economy* 31 (99): 31–48.

Tamagni, Daniele. 2009. *Gentlemen of Bacongo*. London: Trolley.

Tamale, Sylvia. 2006. "Eroticism, Sensuality and 'Women's Secrets' among the Baganda: A Critical Analysis." *Feminist Africa* 5: 9–36.

Taylor, Edward J. 1999. "The New Economics of Labor Migration and the Role of Remittances in the Migration Process." *International Migration* 37 (1): 63–88.

Taylor, Peter J., Michael J. Watts, and R. J. Johnston. 2002. "Geography/Globalization." In *Geographies of Global Change: Remapping the World*, 2nd ed., edited by R. J. Johnston, Peter J. Taylor, and Michael J. Watts, 1–17. Malden, MA: Blackwell.

Teixeira, Maria. 2008. "Sorcellerie et contre-sorcellerie: Un réajustement permanent au monde." *Cahiers d'Études Africaines* 189/190: 59–79. http://etudesafricaines.revues.org/9762.

Terretta, Meredith. 2007. "A Miscarriage of Nation: Cameroonian Women and Revolution, 1949–1971." *Stichproben: Vienna Journal of African Studies* 12: 61–90.

Thelen, Tatjana, Cati Coe, and Erdmute Alber. 2013. "The Anthropology of Sibling Relations: Shared Parentage, Experience, and Exchange." In *The Anthropology of Sibling Relations*, edited by Erdmute Alber, Cati Coe, and Tatjana Thelen, 1–28. New York: Palgrave.

Thomas, Dominic. 2003. "Fashion Matters: 'La Sape' and Vestimentary Codes in

Transnational Contexts and Urban Diasporas." *Modern Language Notes* 118 (4): 947–73.

Thomas, Lynn. 2003. *The Politics of the Womb: Women, Reproduction, and the State in Kenya.* Berkeley: University of California Press.

Thomas, Lynn, and Jennifer Cole. 2009. "Thinking Through Love in Africa." In *Love in Africa,* edited by Jennifer Cole and Lynn Thomas, 1–30. Chicago: University of Chicago Press.

Thomas, Philip. 1998. "Conspicuous Construction: Houses, Consumption and 'Relocalization' in Manambondro, Southeast Madagascar." *Journal of the Royal Anthropological Institute* 4 (3): 425–46.

Thornton, John. 1988. "The Kingdom of the Kongo, Circa. 1390–1678." *Cahiers d'Études Africaines* 22 (3/4): 325–42.

Ticktin, Miriam. 2011. *Casualties of Care: Immigration and the Politics of Humanitarianism in France.* Berkeley: University of California Press.

Timera, Mahamet. 1996. *Les Soninké en France: D'une histoire à l'autre.* Paris: Karthala.

Tisseau, Violaine. 2014. "Madagascar: Une île métisse sans métis? La catégorie 'metis' et son contournement dans les hautes terres centrales de Madagascar pendant la période colonial (1896–1960)." *Anthropologie et Sociétés* 32 (2): 27–44.

Trapido, Joseph. 2011. "The Political Economy of Migration and Reputation in Kinshasa." *Africa: The Journal of the International African Institute* 81 (2): 204–25.

Tribalat, Michèle, Patrick Simon, and Benoît Riandey. 1996. *De l'immigration à l'assimilation: Enquête sur les populations d'origine etrangère en France.* Paris: La Découverte.

Tsing, Anna. 2005. *Friction: An Ethnography of Global Connection.* Princeton, NJ: Princeton University Press.

Turner, Victor. 1968. *Drums of Affliction.* Manchester: Manchester University Press.
———. 1969. *The Ritual Process: Structure and Anti-Structure.* New Brunswick, NJ: Transaction.

Udlændingestyrelsen. 2014. "Lovligt ophold i mindst fem år." Ny i Danmark. https://www.nyidanmark.dk/da-dk/Ophold/permanent-ophold/lovligt-oph-mindst-5-aar.htm.

United Kingdom Nursing and Midwifery Council. 2004. *Statistical Analysis of the Register, April 1, 2003 to March 31, 2004.* London: Nursing and Midwifery Council.

UNODC (United Nations Office on Drugs and Crime). 2007. UNODC Executive Director Antonio Maria Costa speaking at the Security Council on 12 December. http://www.unodc.org/unodc/en/frontpage/assisting-guinea-bissau.html.

U.S. Department of State. 2013. "Who Can Be Adopted." http://adoption.state.gov/adoption_process/how_to_adopt/childeligibility.php.

Utas, Mats. 2003. "Sweet Battlefields: Youth and the Liberian Civil War." PhD diss., Uppsala University.

van der Geest, Sjaak. 1998. *"Yebisa Wo Fie:* Growing Old and Building a House in the Akan Culture of Ghana." *Journal of Cross-Cultural Gerontology* 13 (4): 333–59.

van Dijk, Rijk A. 1998. "Pentecostalism, Cultural Memory and the State: Contested Representations of Time in Postcolonial Malawi." In *Memory and the Postcolony: African Anthropology and the Critique of Power,* edited by Richard Werbner, 155–81. London: Zed.

———. 2002a. "Religion, Reciprocity, and Restructuring Family Responsibility in the Ghanaian Pentecostal Diaspora." In *The Transnational Family: New European Frontiers and Global Networks,* edited by Deborah Bryceson and Ulla Vuorela, 173–96. Oxford: Berg.

———. 2002b. "The Soul is the Stranger: Ghanaian Pentecostalism and the Diasporic Contestation of 'Flow' and 'Individuality.'" *Culture and Religion* 3 (1): 49–65.

van Gennep, Arnold. 1960. *The Rites of Passage.* Chicago: University of Chicago Press.

Venables, Emilie. 2008. "Senegalese Women and the Cyber Café: Online Dating and Aspirations of Transnational Migration in Ziguinchor." *African and Asian Studies* 7 (4): 471–90.

Vertovec, Steven, ed. 2011. *Anthropology of Migration and Multiculturalism.* New York: Routledge.

Vie-Publique. 2013. "Qui est citoyen en France?" Vie-Publique. http://www.vie -publique.fr/decouverte-institutions/citoyen/citoyennete/citoyen-france /comment-devient-on-citoyen-francais.html.

Viet, Vincent. 1998. *La France immigrée: Construction d'une politique, 1914–1997.* Paris: Fayard.

Vigh, Henrik. 2006a. *Navigating Terrains of War: Youth and Soldiering in Guinea-Bissau.* Oxford: Berghahn.

———. 2006b. "Social Death and Violent Life Chances." In *Navigating Youth, Generating Adulthood: Social Becoming in an African Context,* edited by Catrine Christiansen, Mats Utas, and Henrik Vigh, 31–60. Uppsala: Nordiska Afrikainstitutet.

———. 2008. "Crisis and Chronicity: Anthropological Perspectives on Continuous Conflict and Decline." *Ethnos* 73 (1): 5–24.

———. 2009. "Conflictual Motion and Political Inertia: On Rebellions and Revolutions in Bissau and Beyond." *African Studies Review* 52 (2): 143–64.

———. 2012. "Critical States and Cocaine Connections." In *African Conflicts and Informal Power: Big Men and Networks,* edited by Mats Utas, 137–57. London: Zed.

———. 2014. "La marge au centre: Sur les réseaux, la cocaïne et le crime transnational à Bissau." *Socio: La nouvelle revue des sciences sociales* 3: 289–313.

———. 2015. "Mobile Misfortune." *Culture Unbound* 7 (2): 233–53.

Vincent, Elise. 2013. "Qui sont les Maliens de France." *Le Monde.* http://www .lemonde.fr/societe/article/2013/01/18/qui-sont-les-maliens-de-france _1818961_3224.html.

Viveiros de Castro, Eduardo. 2009. "The Gift and the Given: Three Nano-Essays on Kinship and Magic." In *Kinship and Beyond: The Genealogical Model Reconsidered*, edited by Sandra Bamford and James Leach, 237–68. New York: Berghahn.

von Braun, Joachim, and Patrick J. R. Webb. 1989. "The Impact of New Crop Technology on the Agricultural Division of Labor in a West African Setting." *Economic Development and Cultural Change* 37 (3): 513–34.

Vu, Hong Tien, and Tien-Tsung Lee. 2013. "Soap Operas as a Matchmaker: A Cultivation Analysis of the Effects of South Korean TV Dramas on Vietnamese Women's Marital Intentions." *Journalism and Mass Media Communication Quarterly* 90 (2): 308–30.

Vulliamy, Ed. 2008. "How a Tiny West African Country Became the World's First Narco State." *Guardian*, Africa, Guinea-Bissau, Observer, March 9. http://www.theguardian.com/world/2008/mar/09/drugstrade.

Waast, Roland. 1980. "Les concubins de Soalala." In *Changements sociaux dans l'Ouest Malgache*, edited by R. Waast, E. Fauroux, B. Schlemmer, F. Le Bourdic, J. P. Raison, and G. Dandoy, 153–86. Paris: ORSTOM.

Wanitzek, Ulrike. 2013. "Child Adoption and Foster Care in the Context of Legal Pluralism: Case Studies from Ghana." In *Child Fostering in West Africa: New Perspectives on Theory and Practice*, edited by Erdmute Alber, Jeannett Martin, and Catrien Notermans, 221–45. Leiden: Brill.

Wardlow, Holly, and Jennifer Hirsch. 2006. "Introduction." In *Modern Loves: The Anthropology of Romantic Courtship and Companionate Marriage*, edited by Jennifer Hirsch and Holly Wardlow, 1–31. Ann Arbor: University of Michigan Press.

Ware, Leland. 2015. "Color-Blind Racism in France: Bias against Ethnic Minority Immigrants." *Washington University Journal of Law and Policy* 46. Accessed August 10, 2015. http://openscholarship.wustl.edu/law_journal_law_policy/vol46/iss1/11.

Watts, Michael. 1993. "Idioms of Land and Labour: Producing Politics and Rice in Senegambia." In *Land in African Agrarian Systems*, edited by Thomas J. Bassett and Donald E. Crummey, 194–221. Berkeley: University of California Press.

Weil, Patrick. 2005. *La France et ses étrangers: L'aventure d'une poltique de l'immigration de 1938 à nos jours*. Paris: Gallimard.

Weiner, Annette. 1980. "Reproduction, A Replacement for Reciprocity." *American Ethnologist* 7(1): 1–85.

———. 1988. *Trobrianders of Papua New Guinea*. New York: Holt, Rinehart and Winston.

Weiss, Brad. 2004. *Producing African Futures: Ritual and Reproduction in a Neoliberal Age*. Leiden: Brill.

———. 2009. *Street Dreams and Hip Hop Barbershops: Global Fantasy in Urban Tanzania*. Bloomington: Indiana University Press.

West African Commission on Drugs. 2014. *Not Just in Transit: Drugs, the State, and Society in West Africa*. http://www.wacommissionondrugs.org/report/.

Weston, Kath. 1997. *Families We Choose: Lesbians, Gays, Kinship.* New York: Columbia University Press.

White, Luise. 2000. *Speaking with Vampires: Rumor and History in Colonial Africa.* Berkeley: University of California Press.

White, Owen. 1999. *Children of the French Empire: Miscegenation and Colonial Society in French West Africa, 1895–1960.* Oxford: Oxford University Press.

Whitehouse, Bruce. 2009. "Transnational Childrearing and the Preservation of Transnational Identity in Brazzaville, Congo." *Global Networks* 9 (1): 82–99.

———. 2012. *Migrants and Strangers in an African City: Exile, Dignity, and Belonging.* Bloomington: Indiana University Press.

———. 2013. "Overcoming the Economistic Fallacy: Social Determinants of Voluntary Migration from the Sahel to the Congo Basin." In *African Migrations: Patterns and Perspectives*, edited by Abdoulaye Kane and Todd H. Leedy, 19–34. Bloomington: Indiana University Press.

Whithol Wenden, Catherine, and Margo Corona DeLey. 1986. "French Immigration Policy Reform and the Female Migrant." In *International Immigration and the Female Experience*, edited by Rita James Simon and Caroline B. Brettell, 197–212. Totowa, NJ: Rowman and Littlefield.

Wieviorka, Michel. 2002. "Race, Culture, and Society: The French Experience with Muslims." In *Muslim Europe or Euro-Islam: Politics, Culture, and Citizenship in the Age of Globalization*, edited by N. AlSayyad and M. Castells, 131–45. Lanham, MD: Lexington.

Wilding, Raelene. 2006. "Virtual Intimacies? Families Communicating across Transnational Contexts." *Global Networks* 6 (2): 125–42.

Williams, Lucy. 2012. "Transnational Marriage Migration and Marriage Migration: An Overview." In *Transnational Marriage: New Perspectives from Europe and Beyond*, edited by Katherine Charsley, 23–37. New York: Routledge.

Williams, Phil. 2002. "Transnational Organized Crime and the State." In *The Emergence of Private Authority in Global Governance*, edited by Rodney Bruce Hall and Thomas J. Biersteker, 161–82. Cambridge: Cambridge University Press.

Williamson, Laura, and Nick Pisa. 2010. "Mario Balotelli's Double Life: The Bitter Family Feud That Haunts the £29m Manchester City Target." *Daily Mail*, August 5. http://www.dailymail.co.uk/sport/football/article-1300427/Mario -Balotellis-double-life-The-bitter-family-feud-haunts-29m-Manchester-City -target.html#ixzz2g0aPtVP7.

Wills, Jane, Kavita Datta, Yara Evans, Joanna Herbert, Jon May, and Cathy McIlwaine. 2010. *Global Cities at Work: New Migrant Divisions of Labour.* London: Pluto.

Wimmer, Andreas, and Nina Glick Schiller. 2002. "Methodological Nationalism and Beyond: Nation-State Building, Migration and the Social Sciences." *Global Networks* 2 (4): 301–34.

Wooten, Stephen. 2009. *The Art of Livelihood: Creating Expressive Agri-Culture in Rural Mali.* Durham, NC: Carolina Academic Press.

World Bank. 2011. *Migration and Remittances Fact Book 2011*. 2nd ed. Washington, DC: World Bank. http://siteresources.worldbank.org/INTLAC/Resources /Factbook2011-Ebook.pdf.

———. 2014. "Africa's Growth Set to Reach 5.2 Percent in 2014 with Strong Investment Growth and Household Spending." World Bank, April 7. http://www .worldbank.org/en/news/press-release/2014/04/07/africas-growth-set-to -reach-52-percent-in-2014-with-strong-investment-growth-and-household -spending.

Wray, Helena. 2011. *Regulating Marriage Migration into the UK: A Stranger in the Home*. Farnham, UK: Ashgate.

Yeates, Nicola. 2012. "Global Care Chains: A State-of-the-Art Review and Future Directions in Care Transnationalization Research." *Global Networks* 12 (2): 135–54.

Yngvesson, Barbara. 2004. "National Bodies and the Body of the Child: 'Completing' Families through International Adoption." In *Cross-Cultural Approaches to Adoption*, edited by Fiona Bowie, 211–26. New York: Routledge.

———. 2009. "Refiguring Kinship in the Space of Adoption." In *International Adoption: Global Inequalities and the Circulation of Children*, edited by Diana Marre and Laura Briggs, 103–18. New York: New York University Press.

Yuval-Davis, Nira. 2006. "Belonging and the Politics of Belonging." *Patterns of Prejudice* 40 (3): 197–214.

Zeitzen, M. K. 2008. *Polygamy: A Cross-Cultural Analysis*. Oxford: Berg.

Zelizer, Viviana. 2007. *The Purchase of Intimacy*. Princeton, NJ: Princeton University Press.

———. 2011. *Economic Lives: How Culture Shapes the Economy*. Princeton, NJ: Princeton University Press.

Contributors

Cati Coe is Professor of Anthropology in the Department of Sociology, Anthropology, and Criminal Justice at Rutgers University. She is the author of *Dilemmas of Culture in African Schools: Youth, Nationalism, and Transformations of Culture* (2005) and *The Scattered Family: Parenting, African Migrants, and Global Inequality* (2013).

Jennifer Cole is a cultural anthropologist and professor in the Department of Comparative Human Development at the University of Chicago. She is the author of *Forget Colonialism? Sacrifice and the Art of Memory in Madagascar* (2001) and *Sex and Salvation: Imagining the Future in Madagascar* (2010) and is coeditor with Lynn Thomas of *Love in Africa* (2009).

Pamela Feldman-Savelsberg is Broom Professor of Social Demography and Anthropology in the Department of Sociology and Anthropology and Director of the African and African American Studies Program at Carleton College. She is the author of *Plundered Kitchens, Empty Wombs: Threatened Reproduction and Identity in the Cameroon Grassfields* (1999) and *Mothers on the Move: Reproducing Belonging between Africa and Europe* (forthcoming).

Leslie Fesenmyer is an anthropologist and Economic and Social Research Council (ESRC) Future Research Leaders Fellow at the Centre on Migration, Policy and Society (COMPAS) in the School of Anthropology at the University of Oxford. She has published articles on migration, home, kinship, place making, and Pentecostalism in the Kenyan diaspora. She is currently completing a book that examines the interplay of physical and social distance between kin living in Kenya and the United Kingdom.

Christian Groes is Associate Professor in the Department of Communication and Arts at Roskilde University. He is coeditor of *Studying Intimate Matters* (2011) and has published numerous articles on gender, sexuality, class, marginalization, culture, migration, kinship, and exchange cycles.

Pamela Kea is Senior Lecturer in the Department of Anthropology at the University of Sussex. She is the author of *Land, Labour and Entrustment: West African Female Farmers and the Politics of Difference* (2010) and many journal articles.

Julie Kleinman is Assistant Professor of African Studies and French and Francophone Studies at Pennsylvania State University. She has published articles on Malian migration to France in *City and Society* and *Transition*. She is currently completing a manuscript entitled *Borders in the Capital: The Politics of Public Space and the Making of an African Hub in Paris*.

Stéphanie Larchanché is Coordinator of Research and Teaching at Centre Françoise Minkowska in Paris, France. She conducts applied research in the field of immigrant and refugee health.

Hélène Neveu Kringelbach is an anthropologist and Lecturer in African Studies at University College London. She is the author of *Dance Circles: Movement, Morality and Self-Fashioning in Urban Senegal* (2013), which won the Amaury Talbot Prize from the Royal Anthropological Institute, and coeditor of *Dancing Cultures: Globalization, Tourism and Identity in the Anthropology of Dance* (2012).

Sasha Newell is Associate Professor of Anthropology in the Department of Sociology and Anthropology at North Carolina State University. He is author of *The Modernity Bluff: Crime, Consumption, and Citizenship in Côte d'Ivoire* (2012), winner of the Amaury Talbot Prize from the Royal Anthropological Institute.

Carolyn Sargent is Professor of Anthropology at Washington University in St. Louis. She is the author of *Maternity, Medicine, and Power* (1989) and coeditor of *Reproduction, Globalization, and the State* (2012).

Henrik Vigh is Professor of Anthropology at the University of Copenhagen. His publications include *Navigating Terrains of War: Youth and Soldiering in Guinea-Bissau* (2006) and many journal articles.

Index

Page numbers in *italics* indicate illustrations.